1977

INTRODUCTION TO GERMAN LITERATURE

GENERAL EDITOR: AUGUST CLOSS

VOLUME IV

TWENTIETH CENTURY
GERMAN LITERATURE

TWENTIETH CENTURY GERMAN LITERATURE

Edited by

AUGUST CLOSS

Emeritus Professor of German
in the University of Bristol

Chapters on Poetry and Drama
by the Editor,
Novels by Professor H. M. Waidson, Swansea,
Music by Professor Ivor Keys, Nottingham

BARNES & NOBLE, Inc.
NEW YORK
PUBLISHERS & BOOKSELLERS SINCE 1873

Printed in Great Britain by
Butler & Tanner Ltd, Frome and London

CONTENTS

vii

THE GENERAL EDITOR'S PREFACE

Literature must be seen in relationship to life in general. Any attempt to give a comprehensive account of literature must include at least some discussion and evaluation of such subjects as architecture, painting, sculpture and music as well as economics, history, sociology, science and philosophy. It is imperative to see not only the past but also the present in its proper perspective. These are the considerations that underlie the conception of *Introductions to German Literature*.

The history of the past and its literature can be of essential value if (as is particularly the case in German) it reveals characteristic trends of expression, e.g. in his *History of Modern Germany* (London, 1965) Hajo Holborn points to the 'lasting effects' of the High Middle Ages on Germany: (*a*) the creation of a national consciousness, and (*b*) the establishment of the dependence of the princes on the estates (of prelates and nobility) and the rising power of the cities, finally (*c*) the creation of a secular culture. Medieval roots or references can still be traced in literary images of our age.

In his cycle of finely woven poems, *Die Bücher der Hirten- und Preisgedichte, Der Sagen und Sänge und Der Hängenden Gärten* (1895), Stefan George endeavours to recapture the spirit of Greek serenity and the spirit of the Middle Ages: e.g. themes like the vigil, Parzival mood, the young knight, the dawn-song. Yet in moulding his historical and cultural heritage into timeless utterances Stefan George projected into the Middle Ages some meanings which are not to be found there. His poem *Die Gräber in Speier* (*Der Siebente Ring*, 1907) recalls the contests between Pope and Emperor and conjures up amongst the illustrious names of German rulers the memory of 'the greatest of the Fredericks': Emperor Frederick II, the Stupor Mundi.

Zum Karlen- und Ottonen-plan im blick
Des Morgenlandes ungeheuren traum.
Weisheit der Kabbala und Römerwürde
Feste von Agrigent und Selinunt.

. . . His gaze unites the plans of Ottos, Karls,
With his own boundless dreams of the Levant,
Wisdom of Cabalists and Rome's decorum,
Banquets of Akragas and Selinus.
[tr. by Olga Marx and Ernst Morwitz, 1949,
Univ. of North Carolina Studies]

Another incisive effect on the history, thought and poetry of modern Europe, and particularly Germany, was created by the Crusades. In the eleventh century Pope Gregory VII (Hildebrand) had summoned Christendom to fight the paynim, thereby enabling his successors to weld all the chivalric ideals and ambitions of the West into *one* formidable weapon and place it into the hands of the church where it was soon found useful for purposes other than that of subduing Islam. Ruthless greed for the earthly 'golden' Jerusalem besmirched the Crusaders' cause. The capture and desecration of Constantinople (1204), the Byzantine capital of Christian civilization for centuries and the guardian of priceless ancient Greek art treasures, proved an outward victory which brought dishonour to the spirit of European Christianity. According to Sir Steven Runciman (*The History of the Crusades*, 3 vols.; 1954/5, Penguin 1965) the Venetians seem to have been the 'most rapacious ones', but the French and the Flemings, too, destroyed much. 'There was never a greater crime against humanity than the Fourth Crusade.' Although the Crusades in the end led to a vast fiasco from which the Moslem power emerged triumphant, they had brought about the creation of three military orders: the Templars, the Hospitallers of St John and the Teutonic Knights. In 1235 these Deutschordensritter were directed by Emperor Frederick II to the Baltic regions where they conquered and christianized the pagan Pruzzen (Prussians), but this domination of the

Northern Slavs began to weaken in the fifteenth century and has, in our time, been completely reversed by the events of the two World Wars.

The above examples, quite apart from the impact of the age of Reformation and Humanism, will amply demonstrate how past and present are inextricably interlinked in our contemporary scene. An interpretation of the totality of German literature cannot ignore the changing milieu and the interrelationship between philosophy and economics, etc., of a special period, the religious, intellectual and social events at work in Germany and indeed in Western civilization as a whole: e.g. the effect of the Thirty Years War on German literature, thought and society; nor can it ignore mysticism, Leibniz's monadology, the influence of Baroque art and music, the French Revolution and the Wars of Liberation, Hegel's concept of the State as the embodiment of national spirit which is subject to the laws of absolute universal history, Ludwig Feuerbach's and Karl Marx's materialistic philosophy, National Socialism, Communism, and the many other physical and intellectual forces which are reflected in the mirror of present-day Germany, Austria and German-speaking Switzerland. Not least of these is the influence of World-Literature (a term coined by Goethe in *Art and Antiquity*, 6.1.1827), from the Bible, Homer, Dante, Shakespeare, Cervantes and Racine to Sanscrit, Russian, Chinese and other literatures. From earliest times German literature has been heavily influenced by foreign literatures, indeed, some of the earliest Old High German works were glosses. We trust that all these interrelationships will be highlighted by the extensive bibliographies as well as the discussion.

The arrangement of material in these four volumes has been modelled on that in the *Introductions to English Literature*, edited by Professor Bonamy Dobrée. Apart from vol. I, where more space is allowed to the general introductory section covering seven centuries of early German literature, about one-third of each book is taken up by the Introduction dealing with the literature of the period in all its genres and forms, connecting it with the other arts and with religious, social, philosophical and political movements of the time. The remaining two-thirds of each book provide a 'Student's Guide': a general reading list of recommended books dealing with the period as a whole, and also a critically selected bibliography referring to the various categories of works under discussion: poetry, fiction, drama, chonicles, literary periods, etc., and individual authors and their texts. Historical data, references to leading journals, biography and recent scholarly criticism are also included. In view of the vast amount of research published in Europe and America, only the most important relevant studies can be listed in the bibliographies. Naturally, British research is stressed. Wherever possible, modern translations of German literature into English are mentioned, too. The final choice in the selection of the whole material is left to the discretion and considered judgment of each contributor.

The presentation of the *Introductions to German Literature* in four volumes (instead of five) necessitated a drastic restriction of space allotted to the literary works, genres and movements under discussion: vol. I roughly covers the period 800–1500: Old High German, Middle High German Minnesang, Epics and Romances, the Mystics and movements leading up to the Reformation; vol. II the period 1500–1700: Reformation, Renaissance, Baroque, and Aufklärung trends; vol. III is dedicated to the two centuries mainly under Goethe's influence: Enlightenment, Storm and Stress, Classicism, Romanticism, Jungdeutschland, Poetischer Realismus, up to Nietzsche; vol. IV deals with German literature from Nietzsche to our day, i.e. fiction from Thomas Mann, Hermann Hesse, F. Kafka, R. Musil, A. Döblin, etc., up to H. Böll and G. Grass; drama from Gerhart Hauptmann, F. Wedekind, F. Bruckner, G. Kaiser, etc., up to B. Brecht, C. Zuckmayer, M. Frisch, F. Dürrenmatt, R. Hochhuth, P. Weiss and contemporary Hörspiel authors; poetry from Arno Holz, R. Dehmel, Chr. Morgenstern, R. M. Rilke,

Stefan George, H. von Hofmannsthal, G. Trakl, to G. Benn, R. Hagelstange, G. Eich, H. M. Enzensberger, J. Bobrowski and P. Celan, etc. We felt justified in devoting a whole volume to the artistic achievements in German literature of our age.

A work of art, such as *Tristan, Parzival, Faust,* states UNIVERSAL TRUTHS, as does scientific research. But there is a fundamental difference between aesthetic and scientific TRUTHS. If on 4 October 1957 the first Sputnik had not been launched into space, sooner or later it would have been done by the force of technological progress. The same argument would make nonsense in creative art. Without Beethoven we would never have had the *Ninth Symphony* (whatever the human and scientific progress), without Shakespeare no *Hamlet* or *Lear,* without Mozart no *Don Giovanni.* These creations are no Homunculus-productions but aesthetic truths and human self-revelations which vindicate Hölderlin's proud word at the end of his *Empedokles*-tragedy where Empedokles says to Pausanias: 'What are the gods and their spirit if I do not proclaim them?' a phrase which reminds one of the mystic expression by Angelus Silesius (Johann Scheffler): 'God does not live without me: I know that without me God cannot live an instant.'

It is through language that the poet proclaims. Language is the key to literature. Through language we reach the reservoir of man's inmost resources; language preserves the imperishable treasures of the human mind and the human heart; language guarantees the continuity of man's spiritual existence. Ludwig Wittgenstein in his *Tractatus Logico-Philosophicus* remarks: 'The barriers of my language are the barriers of my world.'

In fact, every literary creation is translation, i.e. translation of experience into language. In his *Fragmente* the German Romantic Novalis pointed to the importance of translation. He differentiates between three kinds of translation: grammatical (i.e. literal renderings from one medium into another), interpretative (creative), mythical and symbolical in the highest sense. Novalis saw the whole universe as a symbol: 'Die Welt ist ein Universaltropus des Geistes' (The world is a universal trope of the spirit). To Novalis, Greek mythology is a 'translation' of a national religion into art. In a similar way the modern cult of the Madonna (mother, virgin, and goddess) is seen as the translation of a myth into a symbol.

Much has in the past years been written about the so-called 'willing suspension of disbelief'. In our view, it is not at all necessary to apply this strictly as a condition to art-appreciation. It is quite possible (cf. Bernard G. Heyl in *New Bearings in Esthetics and Art Criticism. A Study in Semantics and Evaluation*, Yale University Press, 1943, 1957 fourth printing) for an atheist to appreciate Rembrandt's *Christ's Supper* (Christus in Emmaus) intuitively. Moreover, we are not asked, as T. S. Eliot has rightly pointed out, to share Dante's theological creed in order to grasp the poetic greatness of the *Divina Commedia*. One could argue similarly about the revolutionary epic *The Twelve* (1918) by the Russian poet Alexander Blok: the twelve soldiers of the Red Army are not heroes; they are bestial, yet guided by a higher destiny. Christ Himself marches with them, Even Nature is symbolical: 'The wind strolls, the snow dances, / A party of twelve men advances.' Likewise, W. B. Yeats's *Sailing to Byzantium* (1927) reveals a vision of a spiritual empire to the reader without necessarily a 'willing suspension of disbelief': 'That is no country for old men . . . caught in that sensual music all neglect / monuments of unageing intellect . . . gather me / into the artifice of eternity'.

H. von Hofmannsthal mocks at the seekers of profundity, whom he contrasts with Goethe: 'The important Germans seem to swim continuously under water; only Goethe, like a lonely dolphin, moves along the shining surface' (*Tagebuch-Aufzeichnungen*). Goethe is, of course, not the only exception. Where surface and depth, the outward and inward worlds merge into an artistic unity, perfection is achieved, e.g. in

Goethe's *Mailied*, Mörikes' *Mein Fluß*, Rilke's *Die Flamingos*, George's *Teppich des Lebens*, or Heinrich von Morungen's:

> Ich hôrt ûf der heide
> lûte stimme und süezen sanc.
> Dà von wart ich beide
> fröiden rîch und trûrens kranc . . .
>
> I heard in the field
> a clear voice, a sweet song,
> whence my sorrow grew light,
> and my joy waxed strong.
> [tr. by Margaret F. Richey in *Medieval German Lyrics*, 1958]

to mention at random just a few examples, which express poetic truths.

W. B. Yeats is right when he states: 'We can create truths, but we cannot scientifically "know" them'; and Saint-Exupéry says: 'We do not discover truth, we create it.'

The poets, however, who are over-anxious to capture the *Zeitgeist* by using up-to-date scientific nomenclature at any price, are far away from poetic truth. The ineffectiveness of mere actuality is obvious. Neon-lights instead of oil-lamps do not make the poem more original! There is no shortage of topical events: the opening of the first railroad from Nürnberg to Fürth in December 1835 and the first railway journey from Leipzig to Dresden a few years later caused sensation and aroused heated controversies about the 'iron beast'. To Jungdeutschland the locomotive became the symbol of a new era which supplanted Romanticism. Heine's attitude to the 'iron beast' (das eiserne Vieh) is expressed in his *Pferd und Esel*: the horse and the donkey look with melancholy at the new monster. The noble horse is obviously the loser, but the poor ass will survive.

A glance at later versifications of technical achievements (mostly by the time of Impressionism and Expressionism) will prove the outdatedness of such literary effusions. Here are some German examples (apart from many other ones

such as W. Whitman's poem on a locomotive in the winter):
D. v. Liliencron: *Die neue Eisenbahn*, G. Falke: *Im Schnell-zug*, Gerrit Engelke: *Lokomotive* and *Auf der Straßenbahn*,
H. Lersch: *Die Lokomotive*, Otto zur Linde: *Bau der Untergrund-bahn*, R. Dehmel: *Drohende Aussicht*, H. Carossa: *Der Eisen-wagen*, Günter Eich: *D-Zug München-Frankfurt*, A. Petzold:
Der Werkbahnhof and *Bergfahrt*, G. Kölwel: *Bahnfahrt durch den Vorfrühling*, A. Wolfenstein: *Fahrt*, Rene Schickele: *Ballade von unserer Lieben Frau im Coupé*, E. Stadler: *Fahrt über die Kölner Rheinbrücke bei Nacht*, G. Benn: *D-Zug*, Th. Fontane:
Die Brücke am Tay. With a few exceptions, e.g. Fontane's and Benn's poems, almost all the above poems are either forgotten now or live on as specimens of outdatedness. Landscape is still a dominant factor in many of those poems. In our epoch of scientific laboratories and engineering triumphs, the natural order and humanistic scale of Nature have disap-peared from ultra-modern works in favour of an intellectual pattern which claims to be impersonal but also anti-historical and anti-ptolemaic.

It would be misleading to assess twentieth century litera-ture by measuring it solely with the standards of Goethe's concept of organic form and universality of outlook. Instead of totality we now have fragmentation, accompanied by signs of a temporary retreat from language, cf. *The Retreat from the Word* (G. Steiner, *Listener*, 1960). The indisputable fact remains that the 'universal' image is shattered. In his *Second Coming* W. B. Yeats, surely the most inspired European poet of our age, expresses the present dilemma:

> The falcon does not hear the falconer,
> things fall apart; the centre cannot hold . . .

Instead of the 'total' view of poetic vision we are offered pieces of images, like pictures in a kaleidoscope, by rotation of the metal tube. The self-sufficient artist's ego is dethroned or absorbed into the web of bewildering patterns of events, ambitions and manifestations.

Basically, the shattering of the Goethean 'universal' images signifies not only the loss of a once generally accepted world-order, but it also triumphantly declares the supremacy of linguistic artistry over an apparently chaotic fragmentation of the universe. Yet, we should remember that in the creative literature of a nation the resources for renewal are inexhaustible. It is therefore unrealistic to speak of a complete 'tabula rasa', however strongly such a mood must have been felt under the stress of Germany's apocalyptic downfall in and after the last War. But we heartily welcome bold experiments which emerged on the German literary scene since 1945.

To *this* present our thoughts and efforts are directed. In *this* present lie the seeds of our future. Allowing for some variation of the theme, Gottfried's words (which actually refer to the community of the noble hearts, the 'edele herzen') in his 'Prologue' to *Tristan und Isolt* may lend expression to what is our deepest concern:

> . . . dem lebene sî mîn leben ergeben,
> der werlt will ich gewerldet wesen,
> mit ir verderben oder genesen . . .

> . . . To this life my life be dedicated,
> To this world let me belong,
> With it to perish or be saved . . .

A. Closs

PREFACE TO VOLUME IV

The third and fourth volumes are divided into three sections: Poetry—Drama—Fiction. The classification of literature into the magic triad of specific genres: lyrical—dramatic—epic, has tempted many scholars and critics to overlook the intra-connexions within the trichotomy. This division is basically justified, as is proved by our non-literary experience: there is the 'lyrical' emotion arising in our hearts when looking at the sun which sets over the horizon of a vast sea-scape; there is the drama of the clashing of collective and individual interests; there is the 'narrative' chain of retold events. Yet far more important than the above neat division into literary genres seem to be their interrelationships and the fate of creative modern writing which, to a great degree, seeks the sources of poetic creation in the intuitive mind, i.e. in thought as opposed to human emotion and to merely commensurable intellectual understanding, cf. e.g. Rilke's *Duino Elegies*, Benn's brilliant craftsmanship, or Celan's compelling visions. It would be grossly misleading to interpret such works of imagination as nothing more than 'cerebrations' of dazzling virtuosity.

A sense of adventure pervades contemporary German literature. No doubt, love of sensation plays its part in some recent enterprises, as was evident in the summer gatherings, organized by *Poetry International*, of poets, novelists and playwrights in the Royal Albert Hall, 1965, and the South Bank Festival, 1967. Extreme language-experiments act as demolition charges which are intended to smash hitherto accepted expressions; apparently unconnected words are forced into a bizarre wedlock; linguistic artifices are a prominent feature of contemporary verse; leading post-war poets such as Günter Grass and H. M. Enzensberger boldly attack the old order of society; finally there are those who like J. Bobrowski and

P. Celan seek to penetrate the mystery of the 'Unsayable' and the secret of poetic creation itself.

The crisis between logos and myth is, however, not only a contemporary event; it does not set in with H. v. Hofmannsthal's *Brief des Lord Chandos* (1902) or Rilke's *Die Aufzeichnungen des Malte Laurids Brigge* (1910) or Kafka or Benn—its unmistakable symptoms can be discovered already over a century and a half ago, in the Romantic manifestations of the *Athenäum*. Here lie the roots of the 'progressive cerebration' in art and life and of the present break-up of the power of myth. The contemporary tendency to blend art and wit and nature in literary artifices reminds one of Friedrich Schlegel's demand to intermingle the most heterogeneous elements into an artistic unity. The meeting of the 'Group 47' can therefore hardly be hailed as the 'starting point' of contemporary writing, quite apart from the heritage of Benn, Brecht, Kafka, K. Kraus and others.

Walter Jens's book *Deutsche Literatur der Gegenwart*, which reads like a poetic pamphlet and which vividly reflects the ambiguity of the contemporary scene, is in itself proof of the present-day blending of diverse forms and subject-matters. The zones of time and space are penetrated vertically as well as horizontally. Classic myths and technological progress are seen in a new amalgam. Its language, in which the logic of the image pairs up with the immediacy of the ironical, unites the 'poetry of science with the intellectualism of lyricism'.

In the contemporary European drama the revue-like presentation of scenes seems particularly suited to plays of a Utopian or eschatological character. Another feature of the twentieth century drama is the endeavour to mask a faceless existence by macabre clownery. Not only the actors of the stage assume masks, but the characters themselves wear them. The literary roots of such a dramatic interpretation lie with Strindberg, Pirandello, Wedekind, etc. The so-called 'antiplays' (Beckett, Genet, etc.) with intentionally undramatic scenes are artistic extravaganzas about the emptiness of human existence.

After the deaths of E. Toller (1939), F. Werfel (1945), G. Kaiser (1945), G. Hauptmann (1946), W. Borchert (1947), F. Bruckner (1958) it was maintained that there were no modern German speaking playwrights of distinction, yet the works of B. Brecht (+1956), H. H. Jahnn (+1959) and C. Zuckmayer contradicted such prejudices. Now, through the performances of plays by F. Dürrenmatt, M. Frisch, R. Hochhuth, M. Walser and P. Weiss, etc., new impulses are flowing on to the German stage which once again can reckon on international response.

Professor H. M. Waidson is the author of the article on German fiction. In dealing with some decisive forces (twelve prose-writers: Th. Mann, H. Mann, H. Hesse, F. Kafka, A. Döblin, H. Broch, R. Musil, W. Bergengruen, H. v. Doderer, M. Frisch, H. Böll and G. Grass) he selected twelve important works which are linked together by introductory observations about the German novel and Novelle. Professor Ivor Keys wrote the essay in the Appendix on German Music.

The *Student's Guide* is meant to widen and deepen the understanding of German writing: see the bibliographic details about Stefan Andres, Lion Feuchtwanger, Hermann Hesse, Ernst Jünger, Heinrich Mann, R. M. Rilke, Martin Walser, Ernst Wiechert, Franz Werfel, etc., and also the references to the experiments in Eugen Gomringer's or Peter Rühmkorf's texts. Behind the variety of length in the notes there lies a carefully planned distribution of important items in question. As to translations of important works it was obviously impossible to list all texts in question. Influential English versions, however, were not omitted: cf. H. v. Hofmannsthal, R. M. Rilke, Stefan George, Franz Kafka, Günter Grass, etc., or cases where the titles of translated works are difficult to recognize: cf. Hermann Sudermann, Carl Sternheim, Fritz Hochwälder and others.

Several scholars have helped me in collecting and selecting the extensive bibliography. Their names are gratefully recorded at the foot of their respective entry. All unsigned entries are my own.

The documentation, which of necessity must be selective, covers our present age: 1900–1967/8. Traditional forces still surviving in present-day German writing are not neglected. Moreover, some extreme examples of the so-called 'Trivial-Literatur' are also referred to. In spite of the editor's conscientious endeavour to offer a detached scholarly and critical appreciation of the contemporary scene this fourth volume of the *Introductions* would be faceless if in problems of assessment and evaluation his personal commitment were not reflected. The stress lies on predominant features and tendencies including ultra-modern ventures in the field of linguistic artistry and on all key-issues which allow the Twentieth Century German Literature to stand out in full relief.

A. CLOSS

POETRY

Friedrich Nietzsche's Influence on German Impressionist, Neo-Romantic and Neo-Classic Writers

Friedrich Nietzsche lived in the nineteenth century (1844–1900), but there is hardly an important literary movement in contemporary Germany upon which he has not exercised a decisive influence. The Darwinian theory of evolution provided the author of *Also sprach Zarathustra* with the basic idea of man's power over suffering. German Naturalism drew inspiration from his criticism of the decadent era and its social as well as moral equivocalness. German Impressionism and Neo-Romanticism and Neo-Classicism also fell under the spell of his aesthetic conception of life and the magic of his language, cf. the poem *Venedig*. Amongst his admirers, apart from G. Benn and other early Expressionists, were writers such as Richard Dehmel, Christian Morgenstern and Stefan George who in his cycle *Der Siebente Ring* published the poem *Nietzsche*:

> Was wäre stich der qualle: schnitt dem kraut!
> . . . sie hätte singen
> Nicht reden sollen diese neue seele!
>
> A stab
> Is nothing to medusae, shears to weeds!
> . . . It should have chanted,
> The first new soul, it never should have spoken.
> [tr. by Olga Marx and Ernst Morwitz,
> Chapel Hill, 1949]

Nietzsche's contempt of complacent catchwords, of the mass-instincts and the 'enervating' cult of history, above all, his apotheosis of the 'superman' led to fatal misunderstandings and gross misinterpretations—not only amongst National Socialists but also representatives of the post-war generation in Germany and abroad. By the 'will to power' (Wille zur Macht) Nietzsche essentially meant the will to self-sacrifice. Yet it must be admitted that Nietzsche is, no doubt, to some extent himself responsible for some misconception of his interpretation of our human existence, as there remains the unreconciled antithesis between his fatalistic view of the cycle of existence, the 'external recurrence of the same', and his dream of superhuman heroism—a dream which responds to the acceptance of the demand to live in such a manner that one desires to live again. His *Dionysos-Dithyramben* (1884–8) re-echo the conflict between virtue and instinct: the eagle in a rhythmically symbolic downward swoop, kills the lambs (cf. *Nur Narr! Nur Dichter*).

Both aspects: the monotony of life and the longing for the superman, are difficult to harmonize in Nietzsche's work. His song of the Übermensch in *Also sprach Zarathustra* (1883–5), put to music by Frederick Delius, contains a profound affirmation of joy:

> O Mensch! Gib acht!
> Was spricht die tiefe Mitternacht! . . .
> . . . Lust—tiefer noch als Herzeleid.
> [*Das trunkne Lied*].

Christian Morgenstern in his poem *Gebet* ('Melancholie') seems to refer directly to Nietzsche whose praise of human life he turns into that of human suffering—man's best friend: 'Dich ruf ich Schmerz; mit aller deiner Macht triff dieses Herz . . .'

Already in his first great work, *Die Geburt der Tragödie aus dem Geiste der Musik* (1871–2), Nietzsche reveals the essence of man's tragic existence. Through suffering the Greeks came to know joy: 'How must this people have suffered in order to attain to such a realization of beauty . . .' Thus Greek tragedy is interpreted as being rooted in the polarity between serene sublimity and man's death-wish. Man's instincts which, according to Nietzsche, have been weakened by Socratic and Christian morality, are reaffirmed in the Gesamtkunstwerk by Richard Wagner, in whose 'music-drama' the Dionysiac and Apollonian forces again merge into grandiose artistic unity. In Nietzsche's view the healing power for man lies not in knowledge or a rational optimism but in art through a rebirth of myth (as in the 'Feuerzauber') and in the obliteration of the frontiers between life and death (as in 'Isoldes Liebestod').

Soon, however, art itself became a dubious value to the author of *Menschliches, Allzumenschliches* (1878-9). To him Wagner's craving for effect and above all the idea of grace and redemption in *Parsifal* seemed incompatible with a recognition of our tragic existence.

Nietzsche's brilliant interpretation of the *Birth of Tragedy* with its polarity of Apollonian serenity and Dionysiac out-burst of passionate self-destruction is in some measure already foreshadowed by H. v. Kleist's thoughts in his essay *Über das Marionettenheater*, and it is now in the twentieth century re-echoed in Federico Garcia Lorca's concept of the *Duende*; cf. E. W. Palm's essay *Kunst jenseits der Kunst* ('Akzente', 1966, H.3). All three artists seek artistic expression beyond the accepted boundaries of life and art. The lifeless puppet becomes the medium of a most vivid human drama; similarly in the creative work the artist's individuality must be sacrificed, i.e. reduced to the state of a medium in order to be able to reveal the powerful 'Other': 'Er versetzte, daß es dem Menschen schlechthin unmöglich wäre, den Gliedermann darin auch nur zu erreichen. Nur ein Gott könne sich auf diesem Felde mit der Materie messen, und hier sei der Punkt, wo die beiden Enden der ringförmigen Welt in einander griffen' (Kleist: *Über das Marionettentheater*). Garcia Lorca, in his *Teoria y juego del duende* (*Theory and Presentation of the Duende*), speaks of the duende: i.e. goblin or magician or artistic demon who breaks the barriers of our existence and leads the artist through elemental chaos into an existence beyond the artistic mastery of technique and perfection. Thus the created work is rooted in the experience of primordial frenzy, in which archaic forces demanding blood and death are reinstated.

Arno Holz, Richard Dehmel

In the year of the completion of Nietzsche's *Also sprach Zarathustra* and one year after *Moderne Dichter-Charaktere* ed. by Arent, Conradi, Henckell and Hart, Arno Holz (1863–1929) published his *Buch der Zeit* (1885). These 'poems of a modern man' introduced a new Storm and Stress movement in German literature. They are directed against stylistic artificiality, pretence and anaemic refinement of language. The *Buch der Zeit* is pithy, coarse, modern from top to toe and 'saugrob wie Luther' (*Initiale*), because: 'modern sei der Poet / modern vom Scheitel bis zur Sohle' (*Programm*).

But although Holz's literary idols are Zola (died 1902), Ibsen (died 1906), Tolstoy (died 1910), his cycle of thirteen poems *Phantasus* betrays a Romantic vein. Later, in 1898, two small, attractive collections of verses appeared under the same title *Phantasus*. Holz's 'Mittelachsenverse' were arranged round an invisible central axis, e.g.

> Draußen die Düne,
> Einsam das Haus,
> Eintönig,
> ans Fenster
> der Regen. . . .

By 1916 those two booklets had been expanded into an elephantasus, a folio-sized colossus, in which syntactical labyrinths of a Rabelaisian imagination contain islands of precious jewels such as *Schönes, grünes, weiches Gras, Über die Welt hin ziehen die Wolken . . .* and *Rote Rosen*. But in this lyrical word-painting the master of Impressionistic registration (Kunst des Treffens) proves his skill in creating a Neo-

Romantic mood: he joins pictures of his inner vision which might have been inspired by Albrecht Dürer's *Ritter, Tod und Teufel* and Andrea Verrochio's equestrian statue of *Colleoni* in Venice, to a mosaic with most decorative and suggestive effect. Holz displayed a unique deftness in imitating other styles, cf. his literary satire *Blechschmiede* (1902) and the vivacious lyrical portrait in *Dafnis* (1903) in the style of Baroque poetry. But in theory and practice he first advocated the art of 'konsequenter Naturalismus'. Going beyond Zola's definition: 'une œuvre d'art est un coin de la nature vu à travers un tempérament', Holz stubbornly and foolishly maintained that art, according to the medium used, tended to be nature! —thus denying art an absolute will to abstraction: 'Die Kunst hat die Tendenz wieder die Natur zu sein.' The word is the medium of expression and representation. The distinction between the lyrical, narrative, dramatic genres is, according to Holz, irrelevant.

In collaboration with Johannes Schlaf (1862–1941) he composed sketches *Papa Hamlet* etc., which, next to J. Schlaf's *Frühling* and *In Dingsda*, can be called models of Impressionistic technique of description.

Papa Hamlet appeared in 1889, the year when Gerhart Hauptmann (1862–1946) brought his naturalistic Milieudrama *Vor Sonnenaufgang* on to the Freie Bühne in Berlin. Naturalism, in contrast to Impressionism, is essentially political and based on Marxism dialectics, though there are many points of contact, mainly stylistically, e.g. the minute treatment of detail, the use of dialect, the photographic and phonographic registration of milieu and events. Both literary movements had of course their literary ancestors and models, e.g. the Impressionistic treatment of atmosphere by D. v. Liliencron (1844–1909) in his poems *Heidebilder, Viererzug, Nach dem Ball, Die Musik kommt,* etc., although he has by no means 'eyes without intellect'.

Richard Dehmel (1863–1920), like his friend Liliencron, considered himself a child of his age and disdained *l'art pour l'art* as an expression of decadent pessimism. But Dehmel, whose poetry occasionally re-echoes Heine's Romantic mood, yearned for a reconciliation of the world of the senses with that of the spirit, and for a new union of the individual with the community. Under the influence of Nietzsche's *Zarathustra* he affirmed life to which he ecstatically abandoned himself, cf. his poems *Mein Trinklied, Venus Regina*: '. . . leben heißt lachen mit blutenden Wunden / Jahre sind Stunden . . .' Dehmel is also the author of the *Arbeitsmann*, of delightful children songs (together with Paula Dehmel) such as *Fitzebutze* and *Die Reise*, and of the sombre vision: *Anno Domini 1912*. Another equally important poem by Dehmel is *Die Harfe*, in which the tree is symbol of the poet's existence. Like the mighty fir he is lonely yet connected with all life. Thus ego and universe are seen in unity. The Harfe ends with the words: 'Gib mir die Kraft, einsam zu bleiben, Welt!—'

Bruno Markwardt, in his *Geschichte der deutschen Poetik* (vol. V) judiciously assesses the creative work of Richard Dehmel whom he considers: 'Ohne Nietzsche kaum denkbar', particularly with reference to Dehmel's poetry, his *Zwei Menschen* (Roman in Romanzen) and aesthetic theories.

Rainer Maria Rilke, Hugo von Hofmannsthal, Georg Trakl

Rainer Maria Rilke (1875–1926) is a formidable poet who does not fit into any literary category. But a number of contemporary critics and poets are lukewarm in their evaluation of his importance to us nowadays. Has he really turned into a crashing bore? W. H. Auden in his Inaugural Lecture, *Making, Knowing and Judging* (Oxford, 1956), paid homage to him but with the following reservation: 'I still think Rilke a great poet though I cannot read him any more . . .' This personal experience, however, does not allow any generalization. Many present-day readers once they have become acquainted with Rilke's poetic language and vision, his philosophical landscapes, his symbols: Orpheus, the Angel, the rose, the game of ball, the mirror of appearance and reality, etc., still respond most vividly to the *Duino Elegies* etc.

Rilke's first lyrical attempts were rather feeble, but his travels to Russia, his stays in Worpswede, in Florence, and particularly Paris, his extensive friendships and his contacts with creative forces of his age: Tolstoy, Valéry, Rodin, Hofmannsthal, etc., deepened his poetic vision. In his novel *Die Aufzeichnungen des Malte Laurids Brigge* (1910) (with the theme of a modern, burnt-out Werther) he suggests that in order to be able to write poetry one must visit cities, must get to know men and things, must 'observe gestures . . .', and in his *Briefe an einen jungen Dichter* he declares that the poet must mature slowly, like a tree, withstanding the storms of spring, without fear that the summer may not follow . . .

Rilke's first great literary success was the *Stunden-Buch* (1899–1903). The poet's seeking for God—'Du Nachbar Gott'—is often misinterpreted as mysticism, but Rilke's love of form is stronger than anything else. In the three parts of this *Stunden-Buch* death is a key-theme: 'O Herr, gib jedem seinen eignen Tod . . . Denn wir sind nur die Schale und das Blatt. Der große Tod, den jeder in sich hat, das ist die Frucht, um die sich alles dreht . . .' Rilke, like the Danish author Jens Peter Jacobsen, whose *Frú Marie Grubbe* (1876) he admired as a masterpiece of Impressionism, saw life and death as a unity. His Paris stay proved decisive. Paul Valéry taught him to reconcile reason and ecstasy: 'enchaîner une analyse à une ecstase'. Moreover, under the influence of Rodin who, unfortunately, had no German, Rilke's poetic presentation of things matured. He endeavoured to create objective, plastic images, though often charged with symbolic meaning. Accordingly, art was considered by Rilke as 'humblest service' and inner intensity—through the power of condensing. By the time of his stay in Paris—1902–6—his *Buch der Bilder* (1902) was published. The *Neue Gedichte* and *Der Neuen Gedichte Anderer Teil* (1907–8) reveal Rodin's influence on the poet: cf. the poems: *Der Panther, L'Ange du Méridien,*

Das Einhorn, Die Fensterrose, Die Gazelle or *Die Flamingos*. In poems such as these, Rilke is able to give permanence to the fleeting moments in nature. In the *Flamingos* there is no moral, no purpose—only his poetic vision of these animals. Each of the four verses offers significant features:

(1) Their colours, white and red, are as voluptuous as those of a Fragonard: 'In Spiegelbildern wie von Fragonard . . .'

(2) they are more seductive than Phryne: 'verführen sie verführender als Phryne . . .'

(3) they are shy and lovable: 'in der eignen Weiche . . . Schwarz und Fruchtrot sich versteckt . . .'

(4) they are proud and haughty: 'und schreiten einzeln ins Imaginäre'.

Similarly, in *Die Gazelle* the essence of this animal is suggested by key-words in the four verses which are pregnant with symbolic meaning:

(1) The musical curves of the horns: 'Verzauberte . . . Aus deiner Stirne steigen Laub und Leier . . .'

(2) 'Worte weich wie Rosenblätter . . .'

(3) the ambiguous term: 'Lauf' (leg; gun-barrel); 'jeder Lauf geladen . . .'

(4) the comparison with the half-averted, startled face of the bathing girl: 'Die Badende . . . den Waldsee im gewendeten Gesicht'.

Thus the mysterious entity of the 'Gazelle' has been intensely and symbolically recaptured by the poet's compelling capacity for empathy. Rilke is indeed a poet of symbolic lyrics rather than the author of 'Dinggedichte' in the strictest sense of the term. Even *Der Panther* or *Die Flamingos* are charged with lyric symbolism.

One of the main impulses in his poetry is his Christian and mystic tendency (cf. his *Stunden-Buch* or his *Duineser Elegien*), though he is, as can be proved also by his Tagebücher and letters, not a true mystic; his main concern is his unique artistic achievement.

Rilke's call for patient acceptance of our existence and for 'inwardness' are basic for the understanding of his later poetry. In the *Requiem* for Wolf, Graf von Kalckreuth, 1909, his message is: 'überstehn ist alles': 'to endure is all', until in the end lament transforms itself into a permanent image:

> Wie sich der Steinmetz einer Kathedrale
> verbissen umsetzt in des Steines Gleichmut . . .

J. B. Leishman's creative Rilke-translations and thoughtful introductions, notes and commentaries: cf. *Requiem, Duino Elegies* (in collaboration with Stephen Spender), *Sonnets to Orpheus, Later Poems, Poems 1906 to 1926, New Poems*, etc., had a decisive influence on Rilke-scholarship in this country. Leishman had the rare gift to identify himself closely with Rilke's language and thought.

One of the fundamental themes in Rilke's work is change (Umschlag) which is brought about by the acceptance of fate. Rilke's faith in the power of transmutation reminds one of Virgil, V. *Aeneis*:

> —quidquid erit, superanda omnis fortuna ferendo est.
> —whatever it will be, fortune is to be mastered by accepting it.

In an essay in *Austrian Literature* (Oct. 1965), Rudolf Kassner speaks of Rilke, his friend and fellow-countryman, as living in a world within, and he significantly quotes the line from Rilke's last sonnet to Orpheus: 'Ist dir Trinken bitter, werde Wein'.

The 'overcoming' has been achieved in the *Duino Elegies* (1912–22) and *Späte Gedichte*. Rilke himself considered the *Duino Elegies* his greatest achievement, whereas an earlier and much lighter work, *Die Weise von Liebe und Tod des Cornets Christopher Rilke* (1906, but composed in 1899), is perhaps his most popular.

The *Duino Elegies* reveal the oneness of death and life and the affirmation of our human existence. In a letter (Nov. 1925) to his Polish translator Hulewicz, Rilke states the poet's task: '. . . The earth has no other refuge except to become invisible: in us . . .' Man's existence remains limited; he will never reach the Angel's higher reality; he must learn the art of patient endurance. Only the unrequited lover (cf. IInd Elegy) is the real giver, i.e. the pure lover; also in the Vth Elegy which is to a great extent inspired by Picasso's *Les Saltimbanques* the question of pure and superficial love-relationship is the main theme: the acrobats symbolize the lovers, their futile attempts, their exhibitionism, and their rare moments of perfection, of serene balance. In spite of all our shortcomings 'Hiersein ist herrlich' (VIIth Elegy): 'Chartres war groß—und Musik . . . überstieg uns'. Thus lament and happiness are *one*. Yet, the spring of joy has its origin in sorrow (Xth Elegy).

Rilke, as mentioned already, is not a mystic; his poetic genius sacrificed everything in the service of art. Rather he can be called the existential poet of our age. Rilke's world, in contrast to some contemporary artifices or the extreme manifestations of Social-Realism, is still a dialogue between the human heart and the inexplicable depth of our existence. The metaphor which Rilke uses to express man's sensory organ for the 'pure tension' (reine Spannung) of life in the universe, is the technical image of antenna: 'Die Antennen fühlen die Antennen' (Son. XII, 1).

We are the receivers: 'Earth gives . . .' Man is powerless without those limitless fountains of creation which readily respond to an 'open' heart. Our existence is rooted in a play of mysterious forces: cf. Son. X, 2nd part:

> . . . Ein Spielen von reinen
> Kräften, die keiner berührt, der nicht kniet und bewundert.

Hugo von Hofmannsthal (1874–1929) is rooted in the cosmopolitan, aristocratic heritage of European and particularly Austrian culture. He was a prodigy child. As a schoolboy he already wrote verse of classical perfection. In his lyrical drama *Der Tor und der Tod*, written at the age of nineteen, he describes a youth who never really possessed life but only watched it. Mother, beloved, and friend pass by like shadows when called up by the tunes of death's violin. Claudio poignantly realizes his guilt, his withdrawal from human relationship. He is filled, not with cloyed dislike of life but with hunger for it; yet no second life is granted to him. The poem *Und Kinder wachsen auf mit tiefen Augen*, which was written a few years after *Der Tor und der Tod*, reflects the emptiness of human existence. The theme is suggestively expressed by sound and rhythm and by a subtle use of consonants and the repeated *und* which acts as a link in the endless chain of irrelevant happenings. The poet has yet no answer to all his questionings. In the same year (1896) another poem of rare artistic beauty, *Die Beiden*, was written. But this aestheticism was soon renounced and transformed into the ethical demand for sacrifice and action. This is indicated in the remarkable poem *Vor Tag*. The oppressive mood after a thunderstorm at early dawn symbolizes the poet's deep anxiety. The Christian image of the Passion of Christ who, carrying his Cross, meets in silent dialogue his mother Mary, merges with the concept of the Romantic union between heaven and earth. Earth's burdened, old body is getting ready for the new day. The feeling of guilt and sorrow is stressed by the mention of the sleepless patient and by the lover who secretly returning from a woman's bed sees himself in the mirror like a ghostlike stranger. The stable-door opens. The new day has started.

Through the image of the deep well Hofmannsthal refers to the silent knowledge of our pre-rational existence:

> Der tiefe Brunnen weiß es wohl,
> Einst waren alle tief und stumm
> und alle wußten drum.
> [in the poem *Weltgeheimnis*]

Now that 'the world has lost its innocence' it is, in the

poet's view, impossible to create or even enjoy a work of art, unless he can recapture the world of magic and myth. 'Naturalism' presents a distortion of nature's mystery which he endeavoured to depict in his musical poems: e.g. *Vorfrühling* and his lyrical dramas charged with meditation and wistful wisdom.

In his famous 'confession'—the fictitious *Brief des Lord Chandos an Francis Bacon* (1902)—the author speaks of the crisis which he experienced at that time and also later on. The two main questions were: whether or not to withdraw into one's artistic self-sufficiency and ignore the demands of our human conscience, and whether the very means of one's creative power—language—was not in danger of disintegrating through misuse by empty generalizations:

> . . . Gradually, however, these attacks of anguish spread like a corroding rust . . . For me everything disintegrated into parts, those parts again into parts; no longer would anything let itself be encompassed by one idea. Single words floated round me; they congealed into eyes which stared at me and into which I was forced to stare back . . .

The harmony was shattered . . . that 'immense sympathy, a flowing over into these creatures, or a feeling that an aura of life and death, of dream and wakefulness, had flowed for a moment into them . . .' (*H. v. Hofmannsthal. Selected Prose*, tr. by Mary Hottinger and Tania and James Stern, London, 1952).

His *Buch der Freunde* contains the following significant passage about reality: 'Situations are symbolic; it is the weakness of our time that we treat them analytically and in so doing dissolve the magic.' In a letter to Anton Wildgans, Hofmannsthal refers to the crisis (which is not confined to the *Chandos-letter*). It is the eternal antinomy between knowledge and life, speech and action and particularly between the isolated, creative individual and the world of social conventions, a conflict which later on was mirrored in the subtle and effective Lustspiel: *Der Schwierige* (1921): the fastidious count refuses to be committed to the indecency of words and the general as well as personal misunderstandings.

Georg Trakl (1887–1914), a native of Salzburg, was by profession a dispensing chemist who, like his favourite sister Grete, early in his career fell a victim to alcohol and drugs.

At the beginning of World War I, in the autumn of 1914, he was an Austrian Red Cross Officer in Galicia where, after the battle near Grodek, he had to attend many wounded soldiers. He was overwhelmed by the sight of suffering and by his own helplessness. Sick in body and in spirit he was sent to the Military Hospital at Cracow where early in November 1914 he died from an overdose of cocaine.

Was he merely decadent, a schizophrenic drug addict, haunted by the awareness of utter loneliness and a sense of despairing pity for mankind? Was he under the shadow of a guilt complex? One might be tempted to interpret the poet's references to his sister Grete as incest, but there is no convincing evidence of Trakl's alleged sexual relationship with his sister, though the brother–sister theme does assert itself in his poetry: cf. e.g. *Unterwegs*:

> Im Nebenzimmer spielt die Schwester eine
> Sonate von Schubert . . .

and for the last time in *Grodek*:

> Es schwankt der Schwester Schatten durch den
> schweigenden Hain.

Throughout this poem, which (apart from Stefan George's *auf stiller stadt lag fern ein blutiger streif*) is one of the few great war poems in modern German poetry, Trakl seems to be morbidly obsessed by tender melancholy and a vision of universal decay. The *fin-de-siècle* atmosphere is here mercilessly stated. This poem is, at the same time, a masterful counterpart to sombre visions in Symbolist and Expressionist poetry such as *Une Charogne* (Baudelaire), *Der tote Hund* (Dehmel), *Jesus und der Äserweg* (Werfel), *Mann und Frau gehen durch die Krebsbaracke* (Benn) or *Ophelia* (Heym).

Trakl's poem *Der Herbst des Einsamen,* and above all *Unterwegs,* may be singled out as an illustration of his artistic technique, his love of autumnal scenery and of musical colour effect: cf. hyazinthen, rot, bläulich, dunkel, schwarz, golden, purpurn; and leise, einsam, in der Stille . . .

The intimate picture of the first part in *Unterwegs* (the dead 'stranger', the sister who plays a sonata of Schubert, the grandmother kindling the golden candles . . .) changes in the second part into a description of autumn (a November night); an old park, tall trees, a song accompanied by a guitar, an open window . . . In the concluding four lines (the third part) the lonely playing turns silent. The singer's head heavy with wine sinks into the gutter.

It is misleading to try to explain Trakl's poetry away as a drug addict's wallowing in impressions of decomposition. His images of disintegration and destruction arise from a well deeper than that of a psychopathic character. In spite of obvious literary echoes from Nietzsche, Dostoevsky, Baudelaire's *Les Fleurs du mal,* Rimbaud's *Bateau ivre,* Verlaine, Lenau, Hölderlin and Novalis, he is a poet of originality, with an intense love of his own dream-world and a rare power of suggestiveness, as for instance, in his musical and sensuous descriptions of ripeness and death.

Stefan George

Stefan George was born in Büdesheim near Bingen in 1868 and died in Minusio near Locarno in 1933. George is 'Der seltsame, große Mensch', as Hofmannsthal calls him in a letter to Karl Wolfskehl only a few days before his own death (1929). In the same letter Hofmannsthal speaks of the true reality which to a poet lies in the life of the language: 'aber dort ist Wirklichkeit, wo auch Sie sie suchen, im Leben der Sprache'. The cool crystallizations of George's spiritual landscapes provide a rare fascination to the modern mind. We seem to move in a sphere of frozen brilliance. To George, Nature contains chaotic, hostile forces which must be exorcized, whilst Rilke sought in Nature the totality of human existence. As a poet, Rilke surrendered to life by recreating it inwardly. George's approach to Nature is an essentially un-Romantic one. He exorcizes her powers. This very necessity of subduing them forbids the poet's felicitous abandonment and his communion with the Universe. There is no outpouring of emotion, as for instance in Eichendorff's *Mondnacht* or in Goethe's monologue in *Faust*: 'O sähst du, voller Mondenschein . . .' Sharply differentiated from the 'Other' in the intangible forces of Nature are the park-landscapes in George's nature descriptions which are states of mind. Nature is broken up into mosaic patterns of finely woven material.

The *Maximin* myth (in *Der Siebente Ring*) is based on the poet's vision of a union of spiritual and physical beauty, the divine norm, an ideal balance of exaltation and lucidity—'Rausch und Helle'. George's own anthology of Goethe poems is truly significant, as he left out poems such as *Wandrers Sturmlied*, *An Schwager Kronos*, *Harzreise im Winter*, etc. He was obviously anxious to choose only those Goethe poems which contain the golden mean: the deepest glow of life in the finest control, rule and radiance, 'Herrschaft und Helle'.

Moreover, his *Goethe-Tag* (*Der Siebente Ring*) and *Goethe's Lezte Nacht in Italien* (*Das neue Reich*) are not only a key to his interpretation of Goethe but also to George himself, just as Enzensberger's recent arbitrary selection of Schiller's poems characterizes the editor himself. In the poem *Der Schleier* (*Der Teppich des Lebens*) George through three images symbolizes the poet's power who, by throwing the veil, conjures up an Eastern city with cupola, tent and battlement, an Ossianic landscape, and an Arcadian scenery; the fourth verse stresses the magic spell of the veil:

'So wie mein schleier spielt
wird euer sehnen'.

In the first stages of his work (which is almost entirely dedicated to poetry) there are many echoes of Freudian symbolism, though his language is harshly disciplined. The language in *Hymnen, Pilgerfahrten, Algabal* (1890–2) moves in an atmosphere of hyper-intellectual, cult-like and subtle artificiality. Algabal, the priest-emperor, is symbol of man's inexorable will in a disintegrating society. The poem *Ein Angelico* which is based on Fra Giovanni da Fiesole's *Coronamento della Vergine*, is a masterpiece of exquisitely selective art.

In the volume *Die Bücher der Hirten und Preisgedichte, der Sagen und Sänge und der hängenden Gärten* (1895), George endeavours to recapture the spirit of Greece, the Middle Ages and the Orient in timeless images: cf. Jahrestag, Sporenwache, Die Tat, Tagelied, etc., though undeniably there is a lack of primordial expression, yet George here succeeded in creating poems of most precious inlay work and magic incantation. His poems *Jahr der Seele* (1897) reveal his distancing attitude to Nature which remains self-sufficient: e.g. 'Komm in den totgesagten park und schau', 'Wir schreiten auf und ab im reichen flitter', 'Der hügel wo wir wandeln liegt im schatten'.

In these verses George is hardly (if at all) emotionally involved. What a striking contrast to such 'nature-poems' is for instance offered in Keats's *Ode to a Nightingale*.

The volume *Der Teppich des Lebens* (1900) stresses the polarity of Greece—Golgotha, and Classic—Romantic. In the volume *Der Siebente Ring* (1907) George speaks of the heritage (*Ursprünge*) and the forces of the spirit that have shaped or influenced his poetic genius in his native Rhineland. This volume contains some of his very best, later poems: e.g. *Nietzsche, Böcklin, Porta Nigra* and *Die Gräber in Speier*. In the last two volumes, *Der Stern des Bundes* (1914) and the much-misinterpreted *Das Neue Reich* (1928), the prophetic tone prevails; George raises his voice against contemporary civilization and degeneration.

George mastered several European languages. His translations of Shakespeare's *Sonnets* follow the original closely and fairly accurately; at the same time these renderings give us a valuable insight into the difference between the character of the English language (*un*inflected and rich in masculine rhymes) and of the German language (inflected and rich in feminine rhymes).

George's achievement as a creative force must not be mixed up with the so-called rather specious 'Georgeanism'. Once this is fully accepted or at least understood, present-day sophisticated minds will readily respond to George's highly intellectual and disciplined verse; cf. D. J. Enright's pungent criticism of Georgeanism, in *Stefan George, Friedrich Gundolf and the Maximin Myth* (Alexandria, 1948, extract from Farouk Univ. Bulletin).

Whereas *Jahr der Seele, Der Teppich des Lebens, Der Siebente Ring*, etc., deserve and will most probably experience a revival, much German poetry of the first half of the twentieth century has already been discarded on to the cemetery of withered literary glories. Hofmannsthal, in the above correspondence with Wolfskehl, condemns the literature of his age as being ghostlike: '. . . unser ganzes Literaturwesen . . . gespenstisch'.

Fritz Mauthner, Christian Morgenstern; Dada

Fritz Mauthner (1849–1923), the author of studies in parody: *Nach berühmten Mustern,* and of the *Beiträge zu einer Kritik der Sprache,* used stronger words. He once compared the history of literature with a huge hollowness, filled to bursting-point with foolishness and stared at by toadies and lick-spittles. Fate often dallies ironically with great names and works, both in ancient and in modern times. Gross misconceptions still linger on in the judgment of many a critic.

Christian Morgenstern (1871–1914) has won popularity on the grounds of a misunderstanding. He wrote humorous as well as serious verse, but to many readers he is still only the author of the *Galgenlieder* (1905) or *Palmström* (1910), *or Palma Kunkel* (1916), or *Der Gingganz* (1919) and the poet of super-real reality, of thoughtful thoughtlessness in which, for

example, the Moon must adapt itself to the German language
and form an 'A' (Abnehmen) when waning, and a 'Z'
(Zunehmen) when waxing; or in which the Knee of the
fabulous beast Nasobem leads a life of its own. The hopeless
isolation of our life through over-specialization could not
have been more happily depicted. It is possible that Sterne's
Tristram Shandy was an indirect source of inspiration here;
German authors such as Heine, Busch, Nietzsche, apart from
Mauthner, even Stefan George, Arno Holz: *Blechschmiede*,
etc., have influenced or provoked Morgenstern, whilst he
himself inspired J. Weinheber's writing. Language, to
Morgenstern, is a poetic escape from himself and a freeing
of himself from the snobbishness of bourgeois gravity. It
suffices to give something a name for it then to exist: cf.
Nasobem or *Das Perlhuhn* which counts its pearls. And con-
versely, nothing can exist for which there is no word or name
or aim, as, for example, the poor *Werwolf* which has no
plural; or the *Unterhose* 'the pants' which flutter gaily on the
washing line, free from all duty, whilst *Die Nähe* 'nearness'
attains personality with an individual fate of its own (Nähe!
Näher! Näherin!). *Der Würfel* has a life of his own and be-
moans the fact that the earth has shyly covered the bottom,
the 'sixth side'—his proud body. The *Lattenzaun*, the fence
of wooden laths, is also a being in his own right; its 'spaces'
have been removed by the creator—a blow to the attacks of
Rationalism. The poem *Das ästhetische Wiesel* evidently plays
with the art and practice of contemporary rhyming. *Fisches
Nachtgesang*—an abstract poem in perfection—graphically
pictures the dumb snapping movements of the fish!

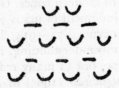

With these *Galgenlieder* and his other 'nonsense'-poems,
which take up the fight against superlatives as well as mental

atrophy, Morgenstern, without malice or lasciviousness, achieved popularity. F. Schlegel's concept of irony and praise of transcendental buffoonery, e.g. in *Über die Unverständlichkeit* (1800), Novalis's idea of 'Natur-Anarchie' as the origin of creation, and Tieck's *Verkehrte Welt* are literary forerunners of such linguistic playfulness, which in the parodies, satires, aleatory elements and language tricks of the Dada movement and Surrealism, however, go far beyond Morgenstern who, ultimately, was concerned with reconciliation of our shattered existence and with the wholeness of human knowledge and will. Behind his nonsense-verse there is a deep sense of responsibility which finds a kindred expression in G. K. Chesterton's remark that it is 'better to speak wisdom foolishly, like the Saints, rather than to speak folly wisely, like the Dons'. At the basis of Morgenstern's 'gallows-humour' lies the conviction that man's life is absurd and that God alone can comprehend it. Hans Arp's *Dada* (which means 'nothing') or Kurt Schwitters's *papiers-collés* and particularly *An Anna Blume* remain on the surface of pure and often delightful nonsense.

The Dadaists favoured an eccentric shock-art, a 'fight against the fat' (Huelsenbeck), but like the chanson-poets Brecht, Mehring and others, were not the first to recognize the literary potentialities of parody. One can easily draw up an impressive list of German satirists from Walther von der Vogelweide to Goethe, Heine, W. Busch and up to our time: A. Holz, J. Ringelnatz, H. v. Gumpenberg, E. Kästner, K. Tucholsky, B. Brecht, F. Mon, H. M. Enzensberger, P. Rühmkorf, G. Grass and Wolf Biermann.

So far the contemporary sublimation of parodistic verse into a high literary quality (Brecht called it 'Gegenentwurf' and Schleiermacher spoke of 'Goldene Parodie') has not yet been fulfilled, cf. the formal excesses in Rühmkorf's variation of Matthias Claudius's *Abendlied* or the macabre travesty of Thomas a Celano's *Dies Irae* in Mehring's *Graduale*.

Parody can certainly rise from the banal caricature of an original to a product of real artistry, when interpreting old conventions as a set-off to our own situation. The contemporary predilection for parodistic treatment of verse, quite apart from the rejection of the so-called 'Erlebnislyrik', lies rooted in our vogue for formal virtuosity and language experiments. These reached their culmination in publications such as '*MOVENS. Dokumente und Analysen zur Dichtung, bildenden Kunst, Musik, Architektur*', 1960, ed. by F. Mon with Walter Höllerer and Manfred de la Motte. In its concluding chapter: 'Summary', F. Mon's '*Articulations*' are elucidated:

> The language of instantaneous composition is achieved through purely physiological articulation, in contrast to the language of communication that is made an efficient instrument by the repetition necessary to it. In the former, it is possible to reduce the meaning-values to such an extent that the articulatory process itself becomes a sign of intrinsic gesticulatory value, whereas the articulatory process disappears in communication. In instantaneous composition, the next step follows spontaneously from the constellation immediately preceding. The organs of articulation move of themselves from one position to the next . . .

Bazon Brock (born 1936 in the Baltics) speaks of the heuristic use of language as the essence of poetry:

> The language of modern poetry is like a Chinese sky that covers all things in the same manner. The result is the homogenesis of all plurals, absence of dimensions, a simple juxtaposition of the elements of consciousness without regard to their sequence, the transposition of horizontal tensions (plot and character development, motivation) into vertical shocks (gregueria, cartridges, photographic screens, sprachgitter) . . . the word is not reproduction, and language is taken only as a point of departure. . . .

Expressionism: 1. Influences and Manifestations

Expressionism, like Naturalism, is a 'Bürgerschreck', a rebellion against the art and culture of the Wilhelmenian era; for anthologies, periodicals and theories see Paul Raabe and

Fritz Schlawe, op. cit., also Richard Samuel and R. Hinton Thomas: *Expressionism in German Life, Literature and the Theatre 1910–24* (1939). German Expressionism began in 1910, shortly before the First World War. Ecstatic language, grotesque presentation of things and human beings, and satirical hints at cosmic deterioration and man's disillusion are the characteristic features of many Expressionist works on the threshold of the twentieth century, particularly in the anthology *Menschheitsdämmerung*, which includes almost all leading Expressionist poets, e.g. Benn, Däubler, Heym, Lasker-Schüler, Stramm, Werfel.

Kurt Wolff and Ernst Rowohlt were amongst the influential publishers of Expressionist literature. The following are the leading organizers and figures of early Expressionism (see *Der Expressionismus* in H. Kunisch's *Hdb.*, l.c.):

(*a*) Kurt Hiller (born 1885) in Berlin, the creator of a *Neopathisches Cabaret* (in 1910), which under the influence of Nietzsche's philosophy aimed at the unity of intellectualism and life, of 'zerebrale Ulkigkeiten und panisches Lachen', a cerebral buffoonery, an anti-historic and anti-traditional vitality, not Schiller's or George's pathos but a new 'Gehirnlyrik'. Amongst Hiller's Cabaret group, Georg Heym and Jakob van Hoddis were the most distinguished members. Heym's *Der Krieg* (1910) is not only a poetic expression of the life-killing evil but also of Erlebnisintensität, a vehement intensification of our existence. It is clear that such a vision is already far removed from Hiller's 'black humour'. Hiller's *Zeit- u. Streitschrift* 2 volumes (1913) is one of the pioneering feats of the movement. He eventually drew his logical conclusions by condemning art altogether. Instead of poetry he advocated life: 'Wozu Gedichte machen? Lieber Geschichte machen.'

(*b*) Herwarth Walden (Ps. for Georg Levin), too, came from Berlin, where he was born in 1878. Else Lasker-Schüler was, from 1901 to 1911, his wife. For his weekly lecture-programme in the *Verein für Kunst* he won a circle of illustrious musicians, painters, poets, playwrights, novelists and critics: R. Strauß, Lovis Corinth, Rilke, Dehmel, Holz, Thomas Mann, Wedekind, Karl Kraus, etc. In 1910 Herwarth Walden founded the provocative *Sturm*. He defended and furthered also Expressionist artists: Marc, Klee, Kandinsky, Kokoschka, Feininger, and above all the new 'Wortkunst' and Stramm's experiments. Language was to be purified to its sensuous quality and liberated from the rules of traditional grammar, from the chains of reasoning.

(c) Barely one year after *Sturm* the magazine *Aktion* (1911) was edited by Franz Pfemfert (born 1879 in East Prussia, grew up in Berlin; died 1954 in Mexico). Pfemfert's political radicalism (as Spartacist in 1918 and later as Trotskyist, as defender of Karl Liebknecht and Rosa Luxemburg) and above all, his militant pacifism, were directed against militarism and nationalism in general. He created the term 'Aktionslyrik' and edited revolutionary 'action poetry'.

In the utterances and propaganda programmes of the above Berlin representatives, the main tendencies of Expressionism as revealed later on in *Menschheitsdämmerung* (1919–20, new ed. 1959), are clearly recognizable.

Although the young generation of today readily responds to many aspects of Expressionist art and literature, there is a fundamental difference between the youth of 1910–20 and the youth of today, cf. also A. D. Klarmann's *Expressionism in German Literature. A retrospect of a half century*, MLQ, March 1965. Our young generation is less hopeful about future developments. The collapse of the humanistic world-conception and the threat of total extinction of the human race by nuclear warfare, have swept away the optimistic dream of a millennium of prosperity and peace. The dominant expression now lies in the presentation of agonizing ugliness and tortured visions, a world of distortions, disproportions and caricatures. There is a marked eagerness amongst the contemporary poets to record their disquiet.

It is no coincidence that an Expressionist forerunner, Frank

Wedekind (born in Hanover, 1864) also Büchner (born 1813) and Baroque authors are rediscovered or reassessed now. The Expressionists had already recognized an affinity to the subjectivity and tendency of spiritualizing reality in old masters such as Matthias Grünewald; in art-criticism Wilhelm Worringer in *Abstraktion und Einfühlung* (1908) confirmed the Expressionists' intuitive approach to existence.

Georg Trakl, though connected with Expressionism by his apocalyptic vision of human fate (cf. Heym, Toller, Kaiser, etc.), stands somewhat outside, particularly on account of his insistence on the aesthetic effect, on the musical perfection of his sombre world-picture (see p. 14). Similarly, it would be misleading to interpret a brilliant craftsman such as Benn as a pure Expressionist.

Expressionism was, on the whole, a left-wing revolutionary manifestation, but amongst the Expressionists there were also writers such as K. Heynicke, Hanns Johst and Benn who, like Bronnen, went over to National Socialism, at least for a limited period. Amongst the various interpreters of Expressionism there are two outstanding voices: Georg Lukács and Herwarth Walden. Lukács criticizes Expressionism as being 'kleinbürgerlich' and Bohemian rather than a proletarian-revolutionary movement; he maintains that fascist literature has important features in common with Expressionism: particularly empty rhetoric and abstraction (Abstraktionspazifismus). Walden saw in Expressionism an essentially revolutionary attitude towards life and art.

Expressionism: 2. Expressionist Poetry

a. *Georg Heym, Ernst Stadler, Franz Werfel, Theodor Däubler*

In his introduction to *Lyrik des expressionistischen Jahrzehnts* (1955), Benn speaks of Whitman's influence on Expressionism and singles out certain characteristics of expression. These are: the anti-historical attitude (a racing car can be more beautiful than the NIKE of Samothrace), and the rejection of the individual in favour of mankind and world-brotherhood. Instead of depicting man's heritage, race, dialect and family, the Expressionists stress the totality of things. Their ecstatic vision of life lays emphasis on horror and ugliness. Their explosive, abstract style is by no means limited to the literary and social revolt before the First World War. According to Wilhelm Worringer in *Abstraktion und Einfühlung* the urge to abstraction is 'the outcome of a great inner unrest in man by the phenomena of the outside world . . .' There is, unfortunately, no space here to survey the development of German Expressionist art which was violently broken off in 1937, the year of the purge of modern art (the alleged 'Degenerate Art') under Hitler. Expressionism is and will remain one of the essential features of German art and literature since the Middle Ages (Wolfram von Eschenbach sings of the 'claws' of the rising sun) and since the German fifteenth and sixteenth centuries, particularly Grünewald. Modern Expressionist artists want to shock and disturb by distortion or brutalization of forms, by the emphasis on the irrational, by the use of highly emotive expression and of symbolic colour as in paintings of the *Brücke* and *Der blaue Reiter* artists. The above-mentioned 'inner tension' is also reflected in Goethe's dynamic language in poems such as *Ganymed, Mahomets Gesang, Wandrers Sturmlied, An Schwager Kronos, Herbstgefühl, Auf dem See,* cf. the compounds (Sternenblick, Flammengipfel), the combination of prepositions or adverbs and verbs (grüne herauf, wolkig himmelan, anglühen, eratmen), the use of intransitive verbs as transitive ones (euch umsäuselt, euch betauen), simple instead of compound (be-decken, aus-brütet), etc. In Goethe's *Schwager Kronos* the bold images occur . . . 'toothless jaws chatter and the shambling legs'—(Entzahnte Kiefer schnattern und das schlotternde Gebein). The list of Expressionist metaphors could easily be enlarged, e.g. Lenau in *Winternacht* writes: 'Es klirrt mein Bart.' In many respects Lenau is closely akin to Trakl, his compatriot, whose poetry reveals features of Symbolist and Expressionist art.

Georg Heym (1887–1912), who died in a skating accident at the age of twenty-four, is one of the most original German Expressionist poets. In his *Tod des Pierrots* Heym is under the spell of Rimbaud's *Le dormeur du val*:

> . . . Il dort dans le soleil,
> la main sur sa poitrine,
> tranquille. Il a deux trous
> rouges au côté droit.—

Heym does not, like Rimbaud, offer a communication of realistic scenes but rather a suggestion, an inner state of experience. Heym uses symbolic colours: blue—red—golden —white—black. Thus Impressionism and Expressionism merge into his poetic vision of autumn—loneliness—death. Yet death is the great lover: 'Da küßt ihn Schlaf'—and the swan-song is a praise of the autumnal Nature which is symbolized by its colours and sounds. The white Pierrot who has neither name nor sex nor age nor home, sinks back into the landscape: 'so zittert fort in seiner weißen Flöte der Wind, die seiner Hand entsank'.

The mood in Heym's *Ophelia*, though morbidly lingering on decomposition and decay, is magically transformed by the colour effects.

Heym's presentation of *Der Krieg*:

> . . . den Mond zerdrückt er in der schwarzen Hand—
> auf den Bergen hebt er schon zu tanzen an
> das schwarze Haupt er schwenkt
> drum von tausend Schädeln laute Kette hängt . . .

is clearly more expressionistic in its images than in its grammar. So is on the whole also the personification of *Der Gott der Stadt*, though intransitive verbs are turned into transitive ones: cf. verirren, sträubt.

In both famous poems there is a gradual intensification of scenery into horror, cf. the use of verbs and particularly of *er* in *Der Krieg*. Krieg is never mentioned by name in the poem itself, but usually referred to as *er*; only in one special case it is changed into the equally uncanny *es*.

The Expressionist's language is reflected in the madly distorted nature images, cf. Alfred Lichtenstein's poem: *In den Abend* where blind hills 'glide' . . . ragged trees 'tramp' into the distance, drunken meadows turn themselves in a circle—or in Albert Ehrenstein's rather playful artistry: *Der ewige Schlaf*, which echoes Whitman's catalogues:

> Ich? Wer bin ich?
> Ich bin ein Zeitblock . . .

and ends in a *memento mori*. In contrast to this poem, Kasimir Edschmid's Expressionist prose *Rasendes Leben* is ecstatic in vision and language. One of the sketches, *Der tödliche Mai*, describes a man (his occupation and rank—Maler und Offizier—are significantly put as something quite irrelevant into brackets) in agony: Death 'tore his entrails'; '. . . the crying bent itself' into a silence slowly, and suddenly jubilating sounds turned into yodelling.

Kasimir Edschmid's call for frenzy, intoxication and adventure:

> Man soll keine Erinnerungen haben . . . Man soll Dinge
> von sich werfen . . . Tosendes . . . rasendes Leben . . .

is the antithesis to Rilke's or Proust's love of recollection and call for artistic patience.

The name of the Alsatian Ernst Stadler (1883–1914) is often coupled with that of Heym. Both are 'Frühexpressionisten'. Whilst his *Präludien* (1905), with its love of colours, jewels and word-artistry, is still under Neo-Romantic influence, in the volume *Der Aufbruch* (1914), however, he becomes a pioneer of Expressionism. In the poem *Worte* the crisis in the poet is unmistakingly stated:

> Wochen liefen kahl und spurlos,
> und nichts wollte sich melden, unsre Leere fortzutragen,
> Und langsam begannen die bunten Worte zu entblättern.

Though the Romantic longing is not completely renounced:

> . . . Aber an manchen Abenden geschah es,
> daß wir heimlich und sehnsüchtig
> ihrer verhallenden Musik nachweinten

yet the change of expression is undeniable, cf. his poem *Kleine Stadt* in which the landscape is put into motion; mountains sway and the pine-forest pushes itself forward:

> . . . schwankt Gebirge . . . Kiefernwald: der stößt . . . an
> die Fröhlichkeit der Sandsteinkirche.

Stadler's *Fahrt über die Kölner Rheinbrücke bei Nacht* shows an affinity to Whitman's rhetorical enumeration and accumulation of nouns or fragments of sentence, which are welded together to a free-rhythmic vision of the thundering express-journey across the Rhine.

Franz Werfel (1890–1945) is considered one of the outstanding metaphysicians amongst the Expressionists. His poem *Vater und Sohn* (in *Wir sind*, 1913) has been called (by Professor A. D. Klarmann) 'one of the finest poems of the era': father and son, old age and heir, once tied by the bonds of blood and love ('einst im grenzenlosen Lieben'), are separated in iron hostility; but there are evenings when the unrest is silenced:

> Und die leichte Hand zuckt nach der greisen
> Und in einer wunderbaren, leisen
> Rührung stürzt der Raum.

Here we have an abandonment to emotion which is totally foreign to many intellectual exercises of the present-day avant-garde; though the latter, in common with Expressionism, rebels against man's materialistic existence, yet there is no all-loving Creator above us and no faith in redemption as in Werfel's and other similar metaphysical poems.

In Theodor Däubler's (1876–1934) cosmological lyrical epic *Nordlicht* (1910) the sun is the creator of all life; Perseus, Roland, Parzival, etc., are stages in our quest for perfection. According to Däubler the existence of plants, animals and mankind points to a return to the sun.

There were, of course, also Expressionists, for instance Kurt Hiller, Franz Pfemfert, etc., who were radicals and as such politically committed, but, as indicated above, it is wrong to call all Expressionists Communists or Marxists. They were inspired by a visionary hope for a new world. Some were genuine pacifists, whilst others, for instance the 'Activists', advocated violence.

(b) Gottfried Benn

Although some of the poems by Gottfried Benn (1886–1956) appeared in *Menschheitsdämmerung*: e.g. *D-Zug, Mann und Frau gehn durch die Krebsbaracke, Synthese*, and later in the volume *Trunkene Flut* (Ausgewählte Gedichte, up to 1935), his poetry is fundamentally opposed to the Expressionist pathos of world-brotherhood. There are roughly three stages of his artistic development: the Expressionist beginning, Nihilism about 1930, his artistic maturity. When in March 1933 Hitler came into power, the essentially non-political poet Benn, to his friends' shock, approved of ideas and aims expounded in *Mein Kampf*. He saw in National Socialism a challenge to the evils of our civilization and sterile intellectualism and the hope for new biological and artistic resources of energy: see his broadcast *Antwort an die literarischen Emigranten* and his no less ill-conceived *Der neue Staat und die*

Intellektuellen and *Kunst und Macht* (1934). But already by 1934 he came to realize that he was wrong. Much has been written about Benn's politics. His essays and aphorisms in *Ausdruckswelt* (1949) throw some light on his enigmatic and controversial attitude to the 'Third Reich': Germany had helped to build up the greatness of Europe, and those who did stay in Germany in 1933 and after, were, in Benn's view, able to look deeper than those who had emigrated, because those writers (apart from Thomas Mann) mainly interpreted the German problem in the light of a conflict between spirit and power.

Scholars blamed him for lack of foresight. In his uncompromising *Abrechnung (Settling Accounts)*, W. Muschg saw in Benn's work pretentiously metaphysical nonsense, a horrid hangover and many grotesque effusions (cf. 'Verlorenes Ich, zersprengt von Stratosphären'), to which he preferred Morgenstern's and Arp's nonsense-verse.

According to Benn, modern man is centripetal [*Der Ptolemäer* 1947]; there is no past for him, nor any future. Only the artist can decide things. Life is a spittoon in which everything spat: 'Das Leben,—dies Speibecken, in das alles spuckte.' There is only suffering: cf. *Statische Gedichte* (written between 1937 and 1947): 'Leben—niederer Wahn . . . Form nur ist Glaube und Tat.' This is a negation of Goethe's message of and belief in Death and Rebirth.

In *Probleme der Lyrik* (1951), Benn tells us that it took him twenty years to create the 'absolute poem' in two verses: *Welle der Nacht* (1948):

> Welle der Nacht—, Meerwidder und Delphine
> mit Hyakinthos leichtbewegter Last,
> die Lorbeerrosen und die Travertine
> weh'n um den leeren istrischen Palast,
>
> Welle der Nacht—, zwei Muscheln miterkoren,
> die Fluten strömen sie, die Felsen her,
> dann Diadem und Purpur mitverloren,
> die weiße Perle rollt zurück ins Meer.

It is fascinating to follow the process by which this poem was formed. With certain words he evokes special associations. Thus the tragic fate of Emperor Maximilian in Mexico and his palace Miramar on the Adriatic Sea are subtly suggested by the mention of shells—diadem—pearls. In such a word-artifice composition becomes more important than inspiration. By advocating the timeless 'absolute poem', Benn at the same time decries the four symptoms of outdated expression: (a) the Romantic address (Andichten) to Nature; (b) the use of similes with *as* or *like*; (c) an outworn colour-effect; (d) the beautiful, mellifluous diction. But certain words are charged with a special meaning. These so called *chiffres*, particularly the word 'blau', must work magic. Benn calls *blau* Südwort, Wallungswert, Exponent des ligurischen Komplexes, with which he conjures his dream-world. Ultimately, however, the 'absolute poem' is a monstrosity, because it can never achieve what music can do. Yet in his most successful poems, as in the above example, Benn is able to charge his *chiffres* with a depth of meaning which gives reality to his images. His preoccupation with history and prehistory (the Urschleim) is balanced by his vision of the future of mankind.

The eight verses of Benn's *Verlorenes Ich* in *Statische Gedichte* (see p. 49) are representative of a world which has become nihilistic, devoid of myth: '. . . Die Mythe log . . .' Time and space are illusory; all questioning about our origin and goal remains unanswerable. Man has lost his Self. Only a fragmentary ego is left, 'blown up by stratospheres', victim of electrically charged molecules (Ions) and radioactive rays (Gamma-Strahlen). Not only the individual but mankind itself has lost its centre; cf. also *Reality and Creative Vision in German Lyrical Poetry. Symposium*, l.c.

At the end of the poem and indeed already in its first verse the references clearly suggest Christian imagery: Lamm, Notre-Dame, Kelch, Blut . . . 'alle rannen aus der einen Wunde, brachen das Brot . . .'

Here a lost system of belief is almost nostalgically recalled from which modern man has been estranged. Thus the two extremes: our transitory existence (Welt als Flucht) and the hour of Christian fulfilment (erfüllte Stunde), man's earthly lust (ein Spiel von Bestien) and his Romantic vision (als . . . die Denker nur den Gott gedacht) are by the poet held in a precarious juxtaposition.

How easily Benn's 'absolute poem' (as advocated in his *Probleme der Lyrik*) which is arrived at by a process of distillation and purification of poetry of its content, lyrical mood and profundity, can lead into a blind alley, is evident in the semantic exploration of language by avant-garde 'word-mechanics' and 'laboratory workers' whose senseless addition —reduction—and simplification methods produce bare word skeletons. Peter Rühmkorf (*Zeit* 1962, April) condemns H. Heissenbüttel's *Kombinationen* and E. Gomringer's *Konstellationen*, as both under the influence of Max Bense ('Chefideologe des Rezesses') manufactured 'texts' rather than poems. A few years before this attack H. Heissenbüttel (in Dec. 1959, N.D.H. = Neue Deutsche Hefte) had harshly criticized P. Rühmkorf's *Irdisches Vergnügen in G.* as representing a fashion rather than a work of art.

Bertolt Brecht

In the poem *Schlechte Zeit für Lyrik* Bertolt Brecht speaks of the conflict in him between enthusiasm about the blossoming apple-tree and the horror of 'the house-painter's' (i.e. Hitler's) speeches; but only the latter forces him to the writing-table as under the circumstances to write rhymed poetry seemed to him almost wantonness. Brecht can, of course, make use of rhyme most effectively, whenever needed. Many critics consider Brecht greater as a poet than as a playwright, though this is a controversial matter. In his early verse up to the *Hauspostille* (1927) he uses rhymes almost throughout, but these rhymes are intentionally simple and frequently even trite. Postille means prayer-book: Middle-Latin *postilla*, from *post illa verba sacrae scripturae*. This first collection of Brecht's poetry has because of its materialistic and nihilistic attitude been called the devil's prayer-book. It certainly offers reviling and blaspheming verse such as *Legende vom toten Soldaten* and *Großer Dankchoral* which is a parody ('Kontrafaktur') of the seventeenth century religious hymn by J. Neander: *Lobe den Herren, den mächtigen König der Ehren.* But the *Hauspostille* contains a few priceless gems such as the *Erinnerung an die Marie.* There is a gentle touch in the poem which does not allow even a slight irony to assert itself for long; see also p. 53. Since the tender hours of love under the young plum-tree many months have gone, many plum-trees have been cut down; the poet has even forgotten the face of the beloved, and he would have hardly remembered the kiss —had it not been for that white cloud 'weiß und ungeheuer'. There is also the poem *Vom ertrunkenen Mädchen* which takes up the Ophelia-theme so popular in Symbolist and Expressionist poetry since Rimbaud's *Ophélie.*

The general key-note of the *Hauspostille* is decay and the process of deterioration in human existence. Images from nature are presented unsentimentally: 'der bleiche Haifischhimmel ... bös und gefrässig' (in *Vom Schwimmen in Seen und Flüssen*). This poem characteristically emphasizes the inert mood in man's drifting towards nothingness: 'und sich treiben lassen ...' Compared with Mörike's lyrical masterpiece *Mein Fluß* it pales into insignificance. With Mörike, too, the experiences of swimming and living merge into one; however, in Mörike's poem the merging of the images of the bold swimmer and ecstatic lover ('kühlt mit Liebesschauerlust') creates mystery and lyrical depth. In contrast to Brecht's poem there is a mood of utter abandonment to the elements: 'Mit Grausen übergieße mich! / Mein Leben um das deine!' Yet, the swimmer must renounce the Liebestod, and waves take him back to the river-bank: 'So trage denn allein dein Glück.' The river which reflects sun and moon, and which returns to the eternal source of all existence, has become symbol of life itself.

Already in Brecht's early verse, Nature was suppressed, as were to some degree also human emotions. There are poems

of general human significance but very often instead of
Nature Brecht offers us the Marxist conception of history, i.e.
the class-struggle between the bourgeois and the workers, and
a determination to change the tyranny of bureaucracy in a
class-prejudiced community. Brecht felt that he could do
this not only in his songs but particularly also in a non-
Aristotelean drama-form by breaking down distances: i.e.
the distances between actor and audience in the theatre, and
by didactic comments in the trial-scenes of his 'Lehrstücke'.
The plot became unimportant. Its place was taken by debat-
ing events and by cabaret-like revues in which the songs
had an alienating function, e.g. in *Aufstieg und Fall der Stadt
Mahagonny* and the *Three-Penny Opera* which is based on Gay's
Beggar's Opera (see p. 52). Throughout his work, Brecht in-
sists on applying man's knowledge to the changes which he
wants to bring into society. In the *Legende von der Entstehung
des Buches Taoteking auf dem Wege des Laotse in die Emigration*
(*Gedichte IV*) Brecht refers to Laotse's dictum that there is
nothing on earth that is softer and weaker than water, but
that which is weak defeats that which is strong. Moreover,
'It's not enough to praise this action / by a sage ... / For the
wise man's wisdom also needs extraction' (tr. by John Willett).

Brecht's late verse takes to laconic briefness, e.g. *Rudern*,
Gespräche and Brecht's favourite use of parallels: 'zwei Falt-
boote, zwei nackte junge Männer. Nebeneinander rudernd
...'; or the poem *Der Hund*: the dog who has been trained
to be a friend of men, is no good watch-dog any more. The
short poem abruptly closes with the gardener's question:
'Wofür bekommt er sein Fressen?'

Here again we encounter a characteristically Brechtian
form of expression: he likes to leave the question open, thus
inviting various possibilities of answering it.

Literature under National Socialism

Rolf Geissler (in H. Kunisch's *Handbuch*, op. cit.) maintains
that—apart from a few lyric panegyrists—National Socialism

did not produce any great writers. In fact, several authors favoured by National Socialism, had (with the exception of Josef Weinheber) already established their literary reputation before 1933, i.e. in the first three decades of the twentieth century. The following dates are illuminating:

1901:	Gustav Frenssen: *Jörn Uhl*.
1916:	Hanns Johst's expressionist, ecstatic drama: *Der junge Mensch*.
1917–25:	Erwin Guido Kolbenheyer's trilogy *Paracelsus*:
	1917: *Die Kindheit des Paracelsus*
	1921: *Das Gestirn des Paracelsus*
	1925: *Das dritte Reich*.
1917:	Heinrich Lersch: *Deutschland*.
1918:	Hermann Stehr: *Der Heiligenhof*, 2 vols.
1922:	Wilhelm Schäfer: *Die dreizehn Bücher der deutschen Seele*.
1924:	Robert Hohlbaum: *Die deutsche Passion*.
1924:	Hans Friedrich Blunck: *Das werdende Volk*, and 1925 ff.: *Urvätersaga*.
1926:	Hans Grimm: *Volk ohne Raum*.
1927:	Otto Gmelin: *Das Angesicht des Kaisers* (about the Hohenstaufen Emperor Frederick II), and 1930: *Das neue Reich*.
1927:	Friedrich Griese: *Winter*.
1928:	Richard Billinger: *Perchtenspiel* produced by Max Reinhardt.
1931–33:	Bruno Brehm: (Romantrilogie) *Apis und Este*, *Das war das Ende*, *Weder Kaiser noch König* (novels about the decline of the Austrian Monarchy).

Apart from Josef Weinheber, authors such as Richard Euringer, L. F. Barthel, Heinrich Zerkaulen and E. E. Dwinger, who had just published the trilogy about the First World War *Die deutsche Passion* (1929–32): 'Die Armee hinter Stacheldraht', 'Zwischen Weiß und Rot', 'Wir rufen Deutschland', came into prominence only in the Third

Reich. Zerkaulen's political play *Jugend von Langemarck* (1933) about the academic volunteers who, singing *Deutschland, Deutschland über alles*, perished in an attack in Flanders, must, next to Hanns Johst's *Schlageter*, have had a violent effect on the emotions of young National Socialists at the time.

The official National Socialist literature mainly stressed regional and conservative tendencies, an idealized rural seclusion, patriotic sentiments, Germanic myths and racial ideologies. In the lyrical medium National Socialist authors found their most favourite expression, cf. the marching songs, hymns of friendship and political dedications, choral works in the shape of short oratorios, and homages to Party and Führer by Gerhard Schumann, Baldur von Schirach and others.

The poet, playwright and novelist Richard Billinger (born 1893 in St Marienkirchen, Upper Austria, died 1965 in Linz; son of a peasant) has not infrequently and all too summarily been dismissed as a mere 'blood and soil' author. The reason for this is not difficult to find: his dramas depict the antagonism between peasants and townsmen. Some of his favourite themes are the 'bewitched' farmhand and the demonic power of nature over man, the uprooted peasant-girl in a city, the contrast between inward religion and the established system of the Church, e.g. cf. his poems: *Über die Äcker* (1923), *Sichel am Himmel* (1931), and his dramas: *Rosse* (1931), *Rauhnacht (Yule Night)* (1931). Both dramas were first performed by Max Reinhardt. Later, when R. Billinger, who is deeply rooted in nature, seemed to have left the themes of his native soil, he became powerless like Antaios when off the ground.

General Bibliography

Joseph Wulf: *Literatur und Dichtung im Dritten Reich. Eine Dokumentation*, 1963.

Rolf Geissler: *Dekadenz und Heroismus, Zeitroman und völkisch-nationalsozialistische Literaturkritik*, 1964.

Dietrich Strothmann: *Nationalsozialistische Literaturpolitik*, 1963, 2nd ed.

Soergel-Hohoff: *Dichtung und Dichter der Zeit*, 2 vols, 1961-3.

Ernst Loewy: *Literatur unterm Hakenkreuz—Das dritte Reich und seine Dichtung*, Preface by H. J. Gamm, 1967.

German Literature in Exile and Inner Emigration

In Germany and Austria—and indeed in Central Europe in general—the political upheavals overtook many authors who had first thought that the coming of National Socialism into power was a passing phase, and not, as the surviving emigrants later realized, a period of twelve to fifteen years of exile. The main events developed with uncanny speed and precision:

On 30 January 1933, Adolf Hitler became German Reichskanzler. In February 1933 the Reichstagsgebäude was destroyed by fire. In the night from 10 to 11 May 1933, Göbbels had the literary works of leading 'degenerate' or Jewish authors publicly denounced as 'intellectual filth' and burnt in an auto-da-fé. The Reichskulturkammer Gesetz of 22 September 1933 regulated and controlled under his Presidency the whole cultural life of Germany. Moreover, in 1933 the Prussian Dichter-Academy was reorganized: 'undesirable elements' were rejected, such as Alfred Döblin, Leonhard Frank, Georg Kaiser, Thomas Mann, René Schickele, Fritz von Unruh, Jakob Wassermann and Franz Werfel. Ricarda Huch voluntarily left the Academy, whilst others were called into the Academy, e.g. H. F. Blunck (who also became Chairman, then Altpräsident of the 'Reichsschrifttum-Kammer'), Paul Ernst, Friedrich Griese, Hans Grimm, Hanns Johst, E. G. Kolbenheyer, Börries von Münchhausen, Wilhelm Schäfer, Emil Strauß and Will Vesper; Ernst Jünger and Hans Carossa did not accept nomination, but in 1941 Carossa became President of the 'Europäischer Schriftstellerverband' in Germany.

Those who fled to Vienna became fugitives again when

Hitler marched into Austria in 1938. For a few years, Amsterdam, Prague, Paris, Moscow, Zürich, Stockholm, etc. had become centres of resistance and manifestos for German émigré-literature. The threatening danger of the outbreak of World War II struck terror into the fugitives who tried to leave Europe for Palestine, Mexico, Chile and the U.S.A. where the 'American Guild for German Cultural Freedom' was founded. Particularly Princeton became a harbour of displaced writers and scholars, and Hollywood for foreign artists and actors.

About this time the German literary scene outside and inside Germany presents a complex situation. It is important not to blur the picture by over-simplification of facts. There were roughly five fundamentally different literary groups, although the boundaries occasionally became fluid:

1. There was the group of outward emigration: e.g. Bert Brecht, Alfred Döblin, Heinrich and Thomas Mann, Ernst Toller, Jakob Wassermann, Franz Werfel, Arnold Zweig, Stefan Zweig;
2. the National Socialist group;
3. some traditional, nationalistic authors who (e.g. Hans Grimm) later formed an inner opposition to National Socialism;
4. there were also those who did not emigrate but whose work resists generalizing assessments such as the so-called 'innere Emigration': e.g. Stefan Andres, Werner Bergengruen, Hans Carossa, Gerhart Hauptmann, Ricarda Huch, Ernst Jünger, Wilhelm Lehmann, R. A. Schröder and Walter von Molo.
5. resistance fighters inside Germany, such as Rudolf Pechel, director of the *Deutsche Rundschau*, until it was prohibited in 1942; Albrecht Haushofer, author of the *Moabiter Sonette*, who was shot in the Berlin Moabit prison in April 1945; cf. C. W. Hoffmann: *Opposition Poetry in Nazi Germany* (1962).

The two journals of the so-called 'innere Emigration' were

Corona, founded by Martin Bodmer and Herbert Steiner in 1930, and, to a certain degree, also *Das innere Reich*, ed. by Paul Alverdes and Karl Benno von Mechow, since 1934. Ernst Jünger's novel *Auf den Marmorklippen* is considered by many critics the chief work of the inner German resistance-literature.

The term *innere Emigration* was probably coined by Frank Thiess, 1949. It describes 'those writers who had remained in Germany in 1933 but had dissociated themselves from the Nazi régime'. The term *innere Emigration* is certainly not a very suitable one, as it is obviously not always possible to draw exact lines between committed writers and *innere Emigration*, e.g. Benn, Jünger, Thiess, Wiechert, von Molo, Kolbenheyer, Carossa, Weinheber. Outsiders are Barlach and Loerke and Langgässer, who were not able to get their works published.

The six opposition poets: Bergengruen, le Fort, Wiechert, Schröder, Schneider and Klepper, are rooted in Christian faith. They have a Christian and humanitarian standpoint but they also shared 'certain conservative interests and ideas with the National Socialists'. An 'ageless' prose-style is characteristic of several of these authors; cf. '*Die innere Emigration: a disputed issue in twentieth century German Literature*' (by H. R. Klieneberger, 'Monatshefte', May 1965), D. Strothmann, *Nationalsozialistische Literaturpolitik*, l.c., and H. Böschenstein *The German Novel 1939–44*, 1949.

As to *German literature in Exile*, cf. W. M. K. Pfeiler's comprehensive monograph, University of Nebraska Studies, new series, 1957; moreover: Hildegard Brenner: *Deutsche Literatur im Exil 1933–1947* (pp. 677 ff.), and Herbert Wiesner: *Innere Emigration* (pp. 695 ff.), in H. Kunisch's *Handbuch der deutschen Gegenwartsliteratur*; Alfred Kantorowicz: *Deutsche Schicksale*, 2 vols, 1949: and *An den Wind geschrieben. Lyrik der Freiheit, 1933–1945*, ed. by Manfred Schlösser and H. R. Ropertz, 1961, 2nd ed. in Schriftreihe 'AGORA', Darmstadt; it contains a documentary section with brief biographical notes and lists of bibliographies, e.g. about Hermann Adler (born

1911, 1945 liberated from the K.Z. in Bergen-Belson, now in Basel) who wrote *Das Lied vom letzten Juden* in Yiddish, which later appeared under the above title (1951) in a German paraphrase by J. Katzenelson (died 1944 in Auschwitz); *Deutsche Exil-Literatur 1933-1945*, 'eine Bio-Bibliographie', by W. Sternfeld and Eva Tiedemann, with a Preface by H. W. Eppelsheimer, 1962; *Exil-Literatur 1933-1945*, ed. by K. Köster, 1967[2].

Rudolf Alexander Schröder, Josef Weinheber, and Ballad Writers

R. A. Schröder (1878-1962) was one of the most celebrated authors (poet and translator) of his generation. This was recognized abroad when he became President of the German Society of the Romain Rolland Friends and of the German Shakespeare Society. He, like R. G. Binding and Hofmannsthal, was one of the last strongholds of the Classic spirit in German letters and of Humanism in the twentieth century. Among his models were Sophocles, Dante, Michelangelo, Shakespeare, Herder, Hamann, Goethe, Schiller, Winckelmann, Novalis, Hölderlin. His *Geistliche und weltliche Gedichte* are based on our Classical and Christian heritage. They bear testimony to the continuity and unity of European literature. But, at the same time Schröder kept in touch with contemporary movements. He founded the reputable journal *Die Insel*; later on, with Hofmannsthal and Rudolf Borchardt he started the *Bremer Presse* for bibliophiles. When he fell into disfavour with the National Socialist régime before the last War, he had to confine his public lectures or readings to religious gatherings. He supported an Una Sancta movement which reflected his cosmopolitan attitude to life. In England R. A. Schröder became known as a translator of Shakespeare and of T. S. Eliot's *Murder in the Cathedral* (*Mord im Dom*).

Other representatives of the traditional forces are the ballad writers Börries Freiherr von Münchhausen, Lulu von Strauss und Torney, and, above all, Agnes Miegel (1879-

1964), Germany's greatest contemporary ballad poet; but in comparison with the prototype of its genre, the Scottish ballad *Edward*, Agnes Miegel's ballads are essentially modern: impressionistic Stimmungsbilder.

The ballad is not a dying genre, as some scholars seem to think. On the contrary, it had its modern revival; cf. K. Riha: *Moritat—Song—Bänkelsang* (1967). By the side of the traditional form of ballad there is the satirical ballad, the chanson of the cabaret, and the contemporary grotesque: e.g. F. Wedekind's Gassenhauer, H. C. Artmann's bizarreries, Alfred Lichtenstein's Expressionist satires, Bert Brecht's *Hauspostille*, Walter Mehring's *Ketzerbrevier*, or songs by G. Grass, Christa Reinig, etc., cf. also Erwin Rotermund: *Gegengesänge. Lyrische Parodien vom Mittelalter bis zur Gegenwart* (1964) and *Dada*: p. 19.

The Austrian poet Josef Weinheber (1892–1945) was in the Third Reich one of the few truly original artists and a master of rare virtuosity. He was able to use Classic versemetres with ease and elegance; cf. e.g. his variations of Hölderlin's ode *An die Parzen*. Josef Weinheber was by no means a mere time-server, though he was committed to the régime. His poetry is free from crude propaganda. In 1945 when Austria and Germany collapsed he took his own life. His chief work *Adel und Untergang* (1934) contains some of the most perceptive poems written after Rilke and George. His *Wien wörtlich* (1935) conjures up the imperial beauty of Vienna and its surroundings: Belvedere, Schönbrunn, Fiaker, Wurstelprater, Beim Heurigen, Grinzing, Wiener Wald, etc.; its past glory is recorded by Weinheber in broad Viennese dialect.

Zero Hour—Der Grüne Gott: Wilhelm Lehmann, Elisabeth Langgässer, Karl Krolow, Heinz Piontek

During the Second World War and the years soon afterwards, tradition, literary *heritage* and *new experiments* stand side by side, as the following brief lists of important novels and stories can easily illustrate: 1942/3: *Glasperlenspiel* (Hermann Hesse) and *Wir sind Utopia* (Stefan Andres); 1945: *Der Tod des Vergil* (Hermann Broch) and *Stalingrad* (Theodor Plivier); 1946: *Das unauslöschliche Siegel* (Elisabeth Langgässer); 1947: *Die Stadt hinter dem Strom* (H. Kasack) and *Doktor Faustus* (Thomas Mann); 1949–59: *Sintflut = Tier aus der Tiefe, Die Arche, Der graue Regenbogen* (Stefan Andres); 1951: *Sie fielen aus Gottes Hand* (Hans Werner Richter).

In lyrical poetry, too, the living springs of German writing have not been smothered, though the questions of private and collective guilt and the physical as well as the spiritual chaos after total defeat made the generation of these authors who were born just before or in the First World War, long for a complete break with the past in order to be able to start with a clean sheet, cf. e.g. H. E. Holthusen's moving poem *Tabula Rasa* in *Hier in der Zeit*, 1949: 'Ein Ende machen. Einen Anfang setzen, / Den unerhörten, der uns schreckt und schwächt . . .' An absolute tabula rasa is, of course, an illusion, as neither the lyrical word-artistries of the post-war nor the preoccupation with literary fragmentation and linguistic conceits reminiscent of Baroque and Surrealism, nor theoretical attitudes, manifestos or abstractions ultimately live in a vacuum.

The new artistic experiments find their counterweight inside the inexhaustible heritage of the poet's language and in the poet's communion with nature, as for instance in the poetry by Wilhelm Lehmann, Elisabeth Langgässer, Karl Krolow and Heinz Piontek—a group of authors who are usually and all-too conveniently called *nature-poets*, although one cannot speak of a 'school'. Yet there does exist a close affinity between these writers. Oskar Loerke, whom his intimate friend Lehmann called 'die große Natur', is spiritually closely related to them. But these so-called 'nature-poets' are no mere descendants of the Romantics: Clemens Brentano, Tieck, or of Droste, etc. Although the magic enchantment of e.g. Lehmann's rhymed verse is essentially rooted in ecstatic nature-observation it also springs from an ultra-modern artistic consciousness which, in extreme cases, is nearer to Benn than to Brentano and actually produces the very opposite of that which we usually call 'nature', i.e. the perfect work of art.

For Benn, myth is an illusion; he seeks the hermetically self-sufficient artistic product. In Lehmann's and Langgässer's poetry, however, age-old myth (mainly Classical and Germanic) and modern science live together, cf. the significant pronouncement about 'Gedankenlyrik' by Elisabeth Langgässer:

> 'Reflective Lyric'? God forbid! but a thinking lyric poet with all necessary premisses: Heisenberg's coefficient of uncertainty, the outline of atomic science, the mathesis universalis of Leibniz and the philosophy of 'Being and Time', Üxkuell's dialectical thinking and theory of environment, the Holy Sacrament teaching of modern Pastoral Theology, and Max Scheler's sociology—this is the man whom we must bring to the fore unless the cosmic realm of lyric poetry is to narrow down to a pasture for pious sheep, to a gentle isle in deep-blue seas, and to a space-rocket heading for the void. . . .

There are also outward literary influences, for instance Karl Krolow's poetry came under the influence of Surrealism. In his introduction to his translations from Apollinaire, Aragon, Cocteau, Eluard, O. V. de L. Milosz, Reverdy, etc., Krolow, who is a master of the art of suggestion, pinpoints their characteristic features of expression which, to a considerable degree, can also be ascribed to him: suggestiveness, hermetically framed illogicality, the cold brilliance of magic mirrors and mannerism (cf. *Die Barke. Phantasie*, 1957). The blending of what in Schiller's term might be called 'sentimentalisch' and 'naiv', is one of the most striking aesthetic effects in those poems. The highly gifted poet Heinz Piontek is very conscious of this dialogue between naïvety and sophistication in modern poetry which is unable to penetrate the totality of human existence. After

the great movement of Expressionism German poetry found
no successor of equally decisive impact on European letters.
Yet the experiments which replaced it bear testimony to the
struggle to overcome a sense of frustration and historical
fatalism. Indeed, the experimental poetry is to be welcomed
as a way towards a new artistic expression. Every poem is, of
course, an experiment, a new venture, but the many new
linguistic artistries of present-day German poetry are symptomatic of the above situation.

In his *Ateliergespräch* which is evidently modelled on the discussions by the nineteenth century German Romantics (see
Zeitwende. Die neue Furche, Jan. 1966) Piontek introduces two
poets, Clemens and Albrecht, who examine the function
of language, ambiguity and the experimental character of
poetry in 1966. Piontek's speakers do not reject experimental
verse; referring to Schiller's fundamental essay on *Naive und
sentimentalische Dichtung* they seek a true dialogue of expressions: there is the cerebral enterprise, a craving for novelty,
a deliberate emancipation from nature and personality, obscure suggestiveness of private *chiffres*; there is the so-called
'unwanted poem' (das unerwünschte Gedicht) which does
not aim at an impersonal artifice or topical pronouncement
but at a 'symbol of our soul' (Kommerell). Such symbolic
language does speak to us through some of the most remarkable creative achievements in post-war poetry by writers
such as Bobrowski, Celan and Hagelstange.

Rudolf Hagelstange

In the year of Germany's defeat the poet Rudolf Hagelstange
(born 1912) became widely known through the publication
of his *Venezianisches Credo* (1945). These sonnets are a condemnation of war-guilt and violence, and an eloquent plea
for the freedom and dignity of man: 'Nur Freien bleibt ein
freies Vaterland'. Apart from poetry he also wrote *Spielball
der Götter* (*Aufzeichnungen eines trojanischen Prinzen*) (1959), a
delightful ironical story which can be called a literary

successor to Friedrich Schlegel's *Lucinde*. But Hagelstange's *Ballade vom verschütteten Leben* (1952) (English translation by Herman Salinger, *Ballad of the buried life*, Univ. of North Carolina, 1962) is, in our opinion, next to Celan's *Todesfuge* one of the most important literary achievements in present-day German lyrical poetry. It is not only a document of our time, but also a poetic symbol of the transitoriness of man on earth. The theme is based on a report in the Associated Press (June 1951) which later on turned out to be a hoax. According to that report, Polish workmen whilst clearing away a huge supply shelter discovered the last two survivors of six German soldiers who were trapped there in an explosion shortly before the collapse of Germany in 1945. During the six years of captivity their golden cage turned into a grave for four of them. Monotony and frost had butchered their souls and bodies. Hagelstange created out of this story the modern saga of dust and despair. The number SIX becomes significant: six years of war, six years of imprisonment in the 'Schlaraffenfalle' of the bunker with the fairy-provisions, six soldiers. These are subtly varied: there is the dreamer Benjamin who later commits suicide, then the sergeant with the symbolic name Wenig—a penitent sinner who shoots himself, the third is the Schreiber—a clerk who perishes 'sans grace', and finally Christof who dies as a steadfast Christian; the two survivors are a carpenter and THE OTHER: 'Bist der andere'—'You are the other'. Thus the key-motif, 'memento mori', is effectively rounded off.

East German Literature: Wolf Biermann

The division of Germany in 1945 into East (Deutsche Demokratische Republik = DDR) and West (Bundesrepublik Deutschland = BRD) added to the complexity of the literary scene. Martin Walser in *Erfahrungen und Leseerfahrungen* speaks of the German Mosaic ('Ein deutsches Mosaik') which cannot be called a German nation. 'Das deutsche Volk ist eine Bevölkerung geblieben, eine Versammlung von Stämmen, die gerade noch eine gemeinsame Sprache als Krone erträgt.' In DDR literature, publishers and press came under the political control of SED—Sozialistische Einheitspartei Deutschlands. Its working-class poets have notable German literary predecessors: e.g. Bröger, Lersch, Barthel, whose poetry is, however, either forgotten or neglected and discarded because of their direct or indirect association with the National Socialist régime. According to the doctrines of the SED, literature has a political and social function to perform; it is not an autonomous but a so-called *Agitationpropaganda* (*Agit prop*) literature, i.e. a weapon in the hands of official East German ideologists, e.g. Hans Marchwitza (born 1890 in Upper Silesia), who in DDR is considered 'one of the most important prose-writers of the German working class' (cf. *Deutsches Schriftstellerlexikon von den Anfängen bis zur Gegenwart*, ed. by K. Böttcher and P. G. Krohn, 1961,[2] 1963[4]).

The main aim of East German literature is an anti-bourgeois 'sozialistischer Realismus' which is hostile to aesthetic formalism and Western thought in art and literature, to Benn and Kafka, etc. Political ideology overrules formal values. Some recent events are symptomatic of the doctrinarian influence in cultural matters: The 'Academy of Arts' became a 'Socialist Academy' (in 1957). In 1963 the Chefredakteur of *Sinn und Form*, Peter Huchel, was replaced by Bodo Uhse (died 1963) and W. Girnus. Thus the constantly reorganized planning by the Z.K. (Central Committee) of the SED must have had effects on those writers who returned from abroad to East Germany after the War.

The dilemma in which these writers saw themselves was intensified by the violently uprooted past in a new classless society. Even Brecht several times got into conflict with the political régime. However, noted pacifists and Marxists have evidently found their anchor in the DDR: Ludwig Renn (Ps. for Arnold Friedrich Vieth von Golßenau) left Mexico for East Berlin; Anna Seghers (Ps. for Netty Radvanyi), highly honoured by several prizes, returned from Mexico to

the DDR as Chairman of the East German Schriftstellerverband; Arnold Zweig went from Palestine to East Berlin,
where he was honoured by the DDR Nationalpreis and the
Leninpreis.

Other emigrant writers went to the BRD of West Germany. Alfred Döblin, who became a Frenchman and fled (in
1940) to San Francisco, returned in 1946 to West Germany,
where he died in 1957. Hans Henny Jahnn, who had settled
in Denmark in 1934, returned to Hamburg after the War.
Albrecht Schaeffer (as he himself told me when I visited him
in New York soon after the War) had in fact not 'emigrated'
to the U.S.A.; he simply did not wish his children to be
educated in Germany under the National Socialist régime.
He went of his own free will to the U.S.A. and was soon
caught by circumstances. The outbreak of hostilities prevented him from returning to Germany. However, he felt
frustrated as a writer whilst in New York. He went back to
Germany in 1950, and died in Munich in the same year.
Fritz von Unruh, who emigrated to France and the U.S.A.,
seems to divide his sojourn between West Germany and
America.

A number of distinguished writers never returned, neither
to East nor to West Germany: Hermann Broch died in New
Haven; Lion Feuchtwanger, though much appreciated and
honoured in DDR and almost unknown in BRD, died in
California; R. Friedenthal went to London; Thomas Mann
settled in California but returned to Europe (Zürich-
Kilchberg) in 1952, where he died three years afterwards.
His brother, Heinrich Mann, died in Beverley Hills in 1950.
Erich Maria Remarque also went to the U.S.A. but is now
at Ascona/Tessin. Nelly Sachs lives in Sweden. Ernst Toller
committed suicide in a New York hotel in 1939. Franz
Werfel died in Beverley Hills in 1945. Karl Wolfskehl ended
in Auckland, New Zealand, 1948. Carl Zuckmayer, returned
from the U.S.A. but settled in Switzerland. Stefan Zweig
went to England and to the U.S.A. and finally to Brazil,
where in 1942 he took his life. Moreover, Martin Buber

emigrated to Israel, Albert Einstein to the U.S.A., Sigmund Freud to London.

About East German literature see H. G. A. Winter, in *Essays on Contemporary German Literature*, vol. IV of German Men of Letters, ed. by B. Keith-Smith (1966); see also Hildegard Brenner (ed.): *Nachrichten aus Deutschland. Lyrik, Prosa, Dramatik. Eine Anthologie der neueren DDR-Literatur* (1967).

Wolf Biermann, born in Hamburg, 1936 (now living in East Berlin), is one of the most original young poets in East Germany. His political songs appeared with some scores for the guitar under the title *Die Drahtharfe* (1965). He ridicules enemy and friend. His mood is aggressive. In the *Tischrede des Dichters* he declares his opposition to the bourgeoisie: 'Der Dichter ist kein Zuckersack!' Biermann's attacks are directed against sloth and faint-heartedness, but he fights against pusillanimity as well as against political intimidation. Patience is a 'whore' of cowardice. Although he loves his Communist comrades he finds himself at odds with the collective spirit; see the poem *Rücksichtslose Schimpferei*:

> . . . Ich bin der Einzelne
> das Kollektiv hat sich von mir
> i s o l i e r t . . .
> . . . ich liebe euch heiß
> aber jetzt laßt mich bitte allein sein . . .

The language of our collective age is also reflected in the satirized abbreviations: LPG = Landesproduktionsgenossenschaft, HO = Handelsorganization, etc.

The most important poem in the above collection is the *Ballade auf den Dichter François Villon*, his 'großer Bruder'. It is at the same time symptomatic of Biermann's clash with and criticism of the DDR régime whose loyal son he had been acclaimed:

> Sie sind uns wohl bekannt,
> Als treuer Sohn der DDR . . .

The poet rebels, as did Villon his guest, against servility and vanity and 'die Herren von der Polizei' who searched his room at 3 a.m. This is obviously a reference to a rencounter of the author with the East Berlin State Security. But it is in the East where his loyalties ultimately lie, and particularly in Berlin:

> . . . Im Westen steht die Mauer
> Im Osten meine Freunde stehn, . . .
> . . . Berlin, du blonde blonde Frau
> Ich bin dein kühler Freier
> dein Himmel ist so hunde-blau
> darin hängt meine Leier.

The Supremacy of Linguistic Artistry in
German Avant-garde Poetry: Paul Celan, Peter Huchel,
Günter Grass, Ingeborg Bachmann, H. M. Enzensberger,
Günter Eich, Georg Britting, Johannes Bobrowski . . .

In contrast to Biermann and other East German poets, a number of contemporary West Germans, as mentioned already, are too much in love with linguistic artistry and thus run away from nature and emotion altogether. Language which has a double rôle to play will always be the key-problem in creative writing. Whilst in the world of logic, according to Ludwig Wittgenstein's *Tractatus Logico-Philosophicus*, values are non-existent or irrelevant, the world of poetry is concerned with values, pronouncements, visions and artistic suggestiveness. This kind of ambiguity inherent in the use of language is often sharply reflected in the avant-garde poetry of our time. When in *Faust* (part II) Helen, meeting Faust, wonders what it is that can give 'such sweetness' to the voice, he replies: the language of love ('es muß von Herzen kommen'). Nowadays the opposite might be said about language: one is tempted to ask modern poets about the 'strangeness' of their voice, and their answer reveals an intense love of language. The loss of the sweet 'language of love' nowadays is counteracted by the supremacy of linguistic artistry. The reasons for this new attitude need not be listed here. The sparrows on the roofs are whistling out the obvious truth, that with the onslaught of the nuclear age we are experiencing a neurosis, a psychological derangement on account of the changes in art, society and politics and of the disorders brought about by such upheavals. In the horrors of reality, art is considered as something less than life yet greater.

Gottfried Benn epitomized the situation in his poem: *Verlorenes Ich*, see above, p. 30. Its eight verses from *Statische Gedichte* are not merely an arrogantly smart montage of particles, abstractions and imaginative visions but a manifestation of the lost system of beliefs from which modern man has been estranged and which are nostalgically recalled: 'Ach, als sich alle einer Mitte neigten . . .' This centre is shattered now. Yeats's *The second coming* ('the falcon cannot hear the falconer . . .') comes into one's mind. Benn calls myth an illusion; space and time too are deceptions; and all questions about origin and goal remain unanswerable.

Yet the poet's task is to interpret an existence whose order he doubts, and to make us aware of ourselves in an age of Einstein, Jung, Freud, Kafka, Sartre, and Hitler and Stalin. The following criteria seem characteristic features of contemporary (not only German) poetry: Craftsmanship is stressed at the cost of the content, cf. Benn's *Marburger Rede* of 1951. Inspiration, according to Valéry, is not an artist's state of mind. The modern poet's tone is often antihuman, depersonalized, sophisticated; his refined, controlled language wants to shock and surprise. *Dada* is revived, its roots go back to F. Schlegel, Tieck, E. T. A. Hoffmann, etc. There is a love of Otherness: the uncommon, the absurd, and a withdrawal from personal and social involvement. This tendency is, however, counteracted by contemporary 'littérature engagée'. Superficially mere language-artifices stand against openly committed poetry, but in a deeper sense all art responds to the spiritual and physical climate in which it is created: some poets react negatively (e.g. Benn) through escape into a linguistic universe, others positively (e.g. Grass and Enzensberger) through full commitment, and others (Celan in particular) by transforming, through their power of the creative medium, the suffering and evil done to man into a promise of a new existence, thus manifesting that poetry is not only a mirror of our modern physical and mental disturbances but that it is much more than just a slice of life. The old saying 'quod scripsi vixi' is only a half-truth. Art creates permanent symbols, it reveals our deeper self; it is not only a criticism but also a discovery of life; it manifests the poet's power to give permanence to our human experience and very existence.

If Theodor Adorno considers it 'barbaric' to go on writing lyrical poetry after Auschwitz, every human heart will be moved by the sentiment of such a statement, but surely he is proved wrong by the creative work of poets of our time: Paul Celan's *Todesfuge* is [by the side of unique literary post-war achievements such as Brecht's *Mutter Courage* or P. Huchel's *Chausseen, Chausseen* or R. Hagelstange's *Ballade vom verschütteten Leben*—see p. 44] one of the greatest and lasting poetic manifestations of the suffering, despair and horrors of our time. Its theme is a dance of death, a *memento mori*, presented in lyrical language with a unique modern technique and with the background of the gas-chambers. Then there is Peter Huchel's poem *Chausseen, Chausseen* which invokes the inferno of Stalingrad. The Christmas message of the birth of the Saviour and of peace on earth is violated by man's brutality: Mary is slain, the stable in Bethlehem destroyed; instead of the Magi three masked *militia*-men pass by; they bring not incense—gold—myrrh but oil and soot, they don't see the star, they don't hear the cry of the child. The road before Stalingrad leads into the snow and death:

> Wie Wintergewitter ein rollender Hall.
> Zerschossen die Lehmwand von Bethlehems Stall.
>
> Es liegt Maria erschlagen vorm Tor,
> Ihr blutig Haar an die Steine fror.

Drei Landser ziehen vermummt vorbei.
Nicht brennt ihr Ohr von des Kindes Schrei. . . .

Moreover, even where nihilism or playful absurdity seems to prevail, the negation is made bearable when counter-balanced by artistic technique, as in G. Grass's poem *Saturn* (in the collection of poems *Gleisdreieck*) where the consciously 'anti-poetic' Grass, always avoiding any suggestion of ponde-rousness, ends the poem with a grotesquely serious image. Grass does not reject natural objects of observation, however abhorrent, and he takes a delight in seeing them from an un-expected corner and treating them with bold malice and, at times, with withering directness, e.g. in *Normandie*: '. . . Wind, Sand, Papier and Urin: / Immer ist Invasion'. But to a great extent Grass's poetry is punning, playful 'black humour', cf. his poems: *Im Ei, Die Seeschlacht*:

Die Seeschlacht
Ein amerikanischer Flugzeugträger
und eine gotische Kathedrale
versenkten sich
mitten im Stillen Ozean
gegenseitig.
Bis zum Schluß
spielte der junge Vikar auf der Orgel.—
Nun hängen Flugzeuge und Engel in der Luft
und können nicht landen.

His seriously presented nonsense-verse and his cool view of absurd situations make him particularly welcome to English critics, who see him in the tradition of Busch, Morgenstern and Arp: e.g. Grass's *Gesang der Brote im Backofen* ('the loaves sing in the oven') or *Freitag* ('the herrings get startled in the frying pan').

A few brief examples from Goethe's poetry will, by way of contrast, allow the contemporary scene, particularly as re-gards nature- and love-poetry by Brecht, Enzensberger, Celan, Eich, Krolow, Bachmann, Britting, Bobrowski, etc., to stand out in sharp relief. In his *Mailied* (1771, May): 'Wie herrlich leuchtet mir die Natur ...' Goethe sings of a dithyrambic union of love and nature. He breaks into raptures. The untranslatable and yet so simple and evocative adjective 'volle' (Welt) calls up the oneness and richness of our whole existence. In the poem *Auf dem See* (15 June 1775) Goethe expresses his soul's affliction and ultimate victory through serene landscape images which are rooted in complete union with nature: 'wie ist Natur so hold und gut ...' —a view which is violently rejected by G. Eich and other avant-garde poets of our day. In *Warum gabst du uns die tiefen Blicke* (April 1776, to Frau von Stein) Goethe speaks of the mysterious force of Fate which predestines the relationship between man and woman. It is characteristic of Goethe that also in the *Trilogie der Leidenschaft* (1823–4) he seeks comfort and salvation in nature. Love ennobles him, as Eros awakens a platonic endeavour to human perfection and a desire for a higher existence. The language is not inflated, not besotted, and it has nothing to do with extravagancies which can be found e.g. in Adalbert von Chamisso's *Frauen-Liebe und Leben* (1830) ('... Er, der Herrlichste von allen ...'). Such outbursts of emotion are unbearable to us now. Chamisso's poem only survived through Schumann's musical composition.

Today the answer to such mentally and emotionally stupefied language is cynicism or irony. The lyrical artist's aims do here not essentially differ from those of modern playwrights who, such as Dürrenmatt, deliberately seek the grotesque and absurd from which to extract the world of tragedy. Brecht, for instance, shows us how cynicism can provide the soil out of which a moving though not great love-poem can emerge; e.g. his poem: *Die Liebenden* (in the drama and opera *Aufstieg und Fall der Stadt Mahagonny*, 1929). Here, in the flight of two longing cranes, the master of Verfremdung has formed a compelling image: 'Sieh jene Kraniche in großem Bogen ... so ... fliegen sie hin, einander ganz verfallen.' The poem reminds one of C. F. Meyer's *Zwei Segel*, but the words (in the form of a duet in Brecht's drama) are spoken by a man and woman in a brothel. In another poem, *Erinnerung an die Marie A,* Brecht remembers a lovable dream: 'Da hielt ich sie . . . wie einen holden Traum . . . Ich küßte sie dereinst.' Even the true Brechtian remark about her having by now perhaps the seventh child ('hat jetzt vielleicht das siebte Kind') cannot break the spell or blot out the memory of that first kiss.

Krolow's cycle of four *Liebesgedichte* and three *Gedichte von der Liebe in unserer Zeit* when contrasted with Brecht's cynical directness, betray mannerisms, e.g. the trite and forced metaphor: 'Morgenrot . . . das wie ein Stückchen Speiseeis zerschmilzt . . .' What a difference between this and Eduard Mörike's inspired image: '. . . die Purpurlippe, die geschlossen lag, haucht, halbgeöffnet, süße Atemzüge' in *O flaumenleichte Zeit der dunkeln Frühe.* Krolow's is a cerebral artifice; see his startling images for the beloved's mouth, the turning of night into a rosy dawn which melts like ice-cream. Leslie Meier (Ps. for P. Rühmkorf) has probably such extravagant affectations in mind when he (not entirely without reason) calls K. Krolow an 'Oberparfumeur' (*Studenten-Kurier*, Dec. 1956).

Ingeborg Bachmann's love-poem *Erkläre mir Liebe* is a sophisticated glorification of the power of Eros in nature. Her own feeling remains rather concealed. She enumerates examples of the force of love: the preening peacock, the cooing dove, with its erected ruff around its neck, the shrieking drake, the fish plunging into the coral-bed, the dancing scorpion, the beetle scenting the beloved from afar. Yet, the poet's own fate is nothing but suffering the pangs of an unanswered love and loneliness. Even a stone can soften another stone: '. . . Ein Stein weiß einen andern zu erweichen! . . .' Why, then, must just she do without love? The author herself answers her own question: she sees the salamander who can endure fire and live in it without pain: 'Erkläre mir nichts. Ich seh den Salamander durch jedes Feuer gehen. Kein Schauer jagt ihn, and er schmerzt ihn nicht.' Ingeborg Bachmann's symbolic vocabulary reminds one of Paul

Celan's poetic language. This is particularly evident in her use of the image of the 'stone' (Celan's favourite *chiffre*) and in the treatment of themes such as forgetting, remembering, spring-time and sorrow.

Paul Celan in the love-poem *Corona* in *Mohn und Gedächtnis* says: 'Wir sagen uns Dunkles.' To the lovers dream and existence, forgetfulness and memory are inseparable. Sleep is like wine in the shells, like the ocean in the blood-red rays of the moon. But the dream-world merges barely with a sparingly revealed reality. It is Sunday; the lovers embrace each other in the window; people from the street look at them; the autumnal scene of nature suggests the relentlessness of time— time, the insoluble mystery.

Here Celan uses his favourite image, the 'stone': stone is to turn into life. It is time that the stone breaks into blossom:

... Es ist Zeit, daß der Stein sich zu blühen bequemt ...
Es ist Zeit, daß es Zeit wird ...

The poem is addressed to Nothingness, the stony Emptiness which is called upon to 'condescend' (sich bequemen) to be transformed into blossoming. We are in this connexion much reminded of Robert Creeley's lines:

The poem supreme, addressed to
Emptiness—this is the courage
Necessity ...

It is a new Promethean defiance, yet not to the Gods but to Nothingness. An absolute surrender would annihilate the poet's self. By the power of his vision and language, as we have seen in Paul Celan's case, the poet can turn existence overshadowed with suffering and senselessness into lasting, lyrical expressions and thus, in and through creative art, redeem his spiritual freedom.

Some of Celan's love-lyrics, e.g. in *Von Schwelle zu Schwelle* (1955, 2nd ed. 1964), reach the very threshold of silence, e.g. the poem: *Wo Eis ist* ('Wo Eis ist, ist Kühle für zwei ...')

or *Fernen*, which is even less communicative than the preceding love-poem: the two lovers are together and at the same time separated by the veil which hides them from each other. The poem *Das Nelkenfeld* by H. M. Enzensberger, in *Landessprache* (1960), calls up a field of pinks, but the true significance of this metaphor emerges by way of concealed references to the face and fragrance of the eyelashes. Transitoriness is the key-note of this poem. Almost a hundred and fifty years ago Goethe wrote a poem, also about transitoriness and love, yet its first part sounds uncannily modern. His words are 'written into dust' and blown over by the wind:

Nicht mehr auf Seidenblatt / schreib' ich symmetrische Reime ...
dem Staub, dem beweglichen, eingezeichnet
überweht sie der Wind ...   [Nachlaß, *West–östlicher Divan*]

But in the second part of Goethe's poem the thought of transitoriness is counterbalanced by the knowledge that the lovers are not alone; they are seen as a link in the chain of immortal prototypes ('Musterbilder'); in their songs the lover and poet recognizes himself: 'Aber, die Kraft besteht ... vor mir liebte der Liebende. / War es Medschnun der zarte? / Ferhard der kräftige? / Dschemil der dauernde? ...' In Goethe's poem the unity of the earthly and eternal is manifested. Such a vision of the cosmic harmony and of the divine force of love is, however, unacceptable for contemporary avant-garde poets.

In present-day love-poetry there is frequent emphasis on violence and suffering. The positive approach to violence and ugliness is of course not a feature mainly characteristic of Expressionism, cf. the dream-visions of Grünewald, of the apocalyptic phantasies of Hieronymus Bosch and Peter Brueghel, or the presentation of suffering and violence in Greek tragedy and in Shakespeare, or in the recent past the fascination of the macabre in Baudelaire's *Une Charogne:* battalions of larvae take possession of the 'superb' carcass which is compared with a budding flower. Moreover, who is not moved by the expression of shameful bewilderment in Rodin's *La vieille*

Héaulmière which drew inspiration from François Villon's *Les regrets de la belle Héaulmière*? This ugliness can become a medium of artistic values. Benn depicts, much more drastically than Baudelaire, with dissecting cynicism the repulsive sight of human flesh (the eating and copulating body), and its degrading transitoriness. Ugliness, particularly in his early poetry, has to fulfil a special aesthetic function. Ultimately, for Benn reality lies in his hermetic stronghold, i.e. his intellectual artifice. Robert Neumann in the poem *Lenz* parodies Benn's *l'art pour l'art*: 'zwischen Leda und Lues scheidet doch nur der Aspekt . . .' Venus turns out to be harlot ('a nymphomanische Nutte'). How dangerously near to the notorious condemnation of 'degenerate art' an ex-cathedra pronouncement can get became evident in Emil Staiger's statement about literature and the public (Dec. 1966, Zürich) and the cloaca of contemporary writing. Max Frisch aptly rejected such a 'court-martial'.

We have deliberately selected extreme examples in order to bring into focus some characteristics of contemporary love-poetry. In this connexion two authors (one West German, the other East German) whose love-poems bear testimony to the inexhaustible resources in a living language, deserve special mention: Georg Britting (1891–1964), who began as a poet under the influence of Expressionism, depicts in his poem: *Was hat, Achill* the mercilessness of all earthly existence and the ruthless conflict of the sexes in their love-hatred passion. This poem which won enthusiastic praise from Benn, is unexampled amongst contemporary West German love-poetry as regards its call for awareness, readiness and brave acceptance of man's fate. Achilles and Penthesilea confront each other like two tempests:

> . . . Die nackte Brust der Reiterin.
> Ihr glühend Aug.
> Die Tigerhunde . . .
> . . . Der Mann der Männer.
> Die Tonnenbrust.
> Auf starkem Hals das apfelkleine Haupt . . .

Like a falcon, Penthesilea swoops down to drench herself in
the blood of the victim:

> . . . Er sieht die Reiterin.
> Und sie sieht ihn.
> So stehn sich zwei Gewitter still
> Am Morgen- und Abendhimmel gegenüber. . . .
> . . . Der Falke schwankt betrunken auf der Beute.
> Was hat, Achill,
> Dein Herz?
> Was auch sein Schlag bedeute:
> Heb auf den Schild aus Erz.

The *Liebesgedicht* in *Sarmatische Zeit* (1961) by the East
German Johannes Bobrowski (1917–65) is also remarkable.
It expresses direct sensuous desire, but, at the same time, it is
deeply rooted in the mystery of nature and the unity of all
being:

> . . . an die Wolke
> streift der Lichtschein, der tönt
> von deiner Stimme.

This synaesthesia invokes a Neo-Romantic mood. Another
poem (in the same collection) *Am Strom*, sings of the strength
the lover draws from nature:

> Mädchen,
> dein Blick aus dem Röhricht.
> Ich rief dich den langen Tag.
> Füll mir die Hände mit Sand,
> die Feuchte will ich, die Schwere.
> Nun atmen wir tiefer die Finsternis.
> [tr. by R. and M. Mead in *German Writing*,
>   ed. by Chr. Middleton, 1967]

Love and nature are the preserving forces for Bobrowski.
He compares the Sarmatian landscape to a gigantic sleep, an
immense space. Heaven and earth are ONE. The vast heaven
is like a 'bell-archway' with larks high in the air. The

Sarmatian plain opens the way for wandering nations. Patrick Bridgwater in a sensitive study (see p. 218) calls his poetry 'beautifully lyrical and yet often—at least ostensibly—impersonal, oracular in the manner of Hölderlin. His perceptions are enacted in language that is stark, dynamic ... Outstanding features of this language are its nervous strength and its total precision ...' Although Bobrowski's versification tends towards the free movement and treatment of word and syntax in Klopstock's and Hölderlin's verse his nature-poetry is very near to Goethe's conception of nature and to Dehmel's; cf. Dehmel's *Die Harfe* (p. 6).

Goethe's attitude to Nature is mirrored in the line 'Wie ist Natur so hold und gut' (*Auf dem See*). He believes in man's kinship with Nature: 'Erhabner Geist, du gabst mir, gabst mir alles / warum ich bat ... Lehrst mich, mein Brüder / im stillen Busch, in Luft und Wasser kennen' (*Faust I*, 'Forest and Cavern'). To a modern poet such as Günter Eich nature is hostile, negative: cf. Eich's poem: *Bericht aus einem Kurort* '... Natur ist eine Form der Negation' (*Zu den Akten*).

A number of Eich's images, like so many in contemporary poetry, are obscure. Ingeborg Bachmann, too, makes demands upon the reader, e.g. in the poem *Das erstgeborene Land* (from *Anrufung des Großen Bären*) she reverses the order of nature: 'Land' is used figuratively as the poet's child, her own ego. On her journey south she is attacked by a viper. This encounter with evil is interpreted as an act of self-sacrifice; by drinking her own self, life is renewed: 'Da fiel mir Leben zu ...' This remarkable vision of rebirth seems, however, to live on borrowings from literary sources, mainly from Nietzsche and Celan; cf. *Also sprach Zarathustra* III ('Vom Gesicht und Rätsel'), where a young shepherd is saved and transformed after biting off the head of the black, big snake which had crept into his throat. Moreover, there is Celan's poem *Zwiegestalt* (in *Von Schwelle zu Schwelle*) with the image of the candle's wick which is lit by the glance of the eye; it can hardly be an accident that this image is also used by Bachmann almost literally.

Celan: Laß dein Aug . . . sein eine Kerze,
         den Blick einen Docht
         ihn zu entzünden.

Bachmann: Der Docht schnellt auf,
           wenn ihn
           ein Blick entzündet.

Paul Celan has in modern German poetry undisputably
no equal as the author who gave lyrical expression to the
human suffering of our time. The approach to his work is not
an easy one. He uses nature for certain key-words in a closely
knit system of conceits with compelling inner consistency,
e.g. Stein, Auge, Baum, schwarze Rose, etc. Without the
knowledge of the artistic function of such key-words Celan's
poetry will remain but puzzling enigmas to readers. 'Stone'
is Celan's favourite *chiffre* signifying guilt, negation, violence,
tears, but even the stone can and must be transformed, i.e.
the cruel experience is to be turned into a creative act. This
is the meaning of the transformation of the stone into a growing plant: '. . . das Haupthaar des Steins aus der Tiefe' (*Der
Stein aus dem Meer* in *Mohn und Gedächtnis*). Thus the evil done
to human beings becomes the soil in which new healing
forces are awakened. We have already referred to his *Todesfuge*; cf. also the poem *Welchen der Steine du hebst* (*Von
Schwelle zu Schwelle*). 'Stone' and 'black' are *chiffres* consistently
used by Celan. Out of suffering the promise of a new existence
is to arise; i.e. the 'black rose'.

Celan's withdrawal into his special poetic vocabulary
leads him ultimately away from nature and love. The mystery
of his creative activity of language becomes his real home and
last anchor. Celan loves to dwell on the theme of the act of
poetic creation—a theme which has already occupied twentieth century authors: Paul Valéry in *La Pythie* ('mes deux
natures vont s'unir'), Stefan George in *Der Schleier* (*Teppich
des Lebens*), and above all, Rilke, who praises the poet's
power to transform the visible world without into an invisible
world within; it is a transformation into imperishable

achievements: 'Chartres war groß—und Musik / reichte noch weiter hinaus und überstieg uns' (7th Elegy). Ingeborg Bachmann in *Mein Vogel* names the owl as the symbol of inspiration, the watchful nocturnal bird.

Celan's preoccupation with language and the act of creation is the logical development of his genius; he has withdrawn into his own self, and has become prisoner of his own artifice. This process began in *Von Schwelle zu Schwelle* and becomes an obsession in the collection of poems: *Niemandsrose* (1963) with its over-sophistication, obscurity, its plays-upon-words and madly repetitive conjugations: 'sie gruben und gruben ... ich grabe, du gräbst ... waren wir, sind wir, werden wir ... ich weiß und du weißt, wir wußten. . . .' His last volume *Atemwende* (1967), however, is not marred by such mannerisms.

In *Atemwende* Celan succeeds in coining not only playful words but also expressive neologisms which are rooted in the poet's despair about the mystery of nothingness and creation, non-existence and existence: e.g. Genicht—Gedicht, ver-nichten—ichten. Such brilliant new coinages, in some measure, remind one of earlier experiments (see Morgenstern's obsession with words) though Celan's mysterious word-formations flow from the specific religious unrest of one of Germany's most creative poets after 1945.

In contrast to the lyrical experiments of many contemporary West German writers, Bobrowski's wiry language (like Huchel's) is not given to abstractions or dialectic disputations and linguistic artifices, nor does he conventionally keep to a metrical and rhyming scheme. Old Prussian and Baltic Slav folklore play an important part in Bobrowski's poetry which deals with an archaic, elemental world; see also p. 57. His architectonic lines are frequently achieved by symmetrical or repetitive arrangements or isolated words, through which content, meaning and sound effect are weighed against each other.

The most promising young East German poet of chansons in the Brechtian manner is Wolf Biermann; cf. p. 47. But in West Germany, too, the present linguistic devices are counterbalanced by robust satire and politically committed poetry such as that by Günter Grass and H. M. Enzensberger. As editor of the *Kursbuch* (1965 ff.), Enzensberger forcefully states his aims: to create connexions but not to give directions: 'Was schon da ist, muß erst aufgeklärt, und das heißt revidiert werden.' His *Anweisung an Sisyphos* is not to relish impuissance, but to increase the wrath of the world:

> es herrscht ein mangel an männern,
> das aussichtslose stumm tuend,
> ausraufend wie gras die hoffnung,
> ihr gelächter, die zukunft, rollend,
> rollend ihren zorn auf die berge.
> [see Gertrude Clorius Schwebell in
> *Contemporary German Poetry*,
> introduction by V. Lange]

Celan, however, has withdrawn into the *hortus conclusus* of his linguistic adventures. He who was Orpheus, has turned into Narcissus. According to Rilke's *Narziss* (*Späte Gedichte*) Narcissus symbolizes the cost at which the poet's task is performed:

> . . . Narziß verging. Von seiner Schönheit hob
> sich unaufhörlich seines Wesens Nähe . . .

Thus Narcissus perishes, as he 'gazes' (tr. by H. B. Leishman); he, like the poet, sacrifices his own identity.

Yet the same Celan has given lyrical expression to death and unspeakable suffering and demonstrated a contemporary writer's power of creating permanent symbols. By giving expression to the poetic experience he can recapture meaningfulness in life and thus conquer our deadening isolation.

II

DRAMA

Is Tragedy still Possible on the Twentieth century Stage?

Modern European tragedy is planted in the individual; it depicts an inner fatality, e.g. in H. Ibsen's *Ghosts* from which there is no escape until the accounts are squared, until the revenge is done, or (to borrow a Greek term) until the 'dike' (justice?) has been accomplished. Uncompromising characters such as Antigone—Electra—Orestes are favoured by contemporary authors. We need only refer to Anouilh, Giraudoux or Sartre. In *Antigone* (1944) (tr. by Lewis Galantière, 1951) the chorus leaves us in no doubt as to Anouilh's conception of tragedy: 'Death, in a melodrama, is really horrible because it is never inevitable . . . But in tragedy, where there is no temptation to try to escape, argument is gratuitous: it's kingly.'

Antigone, who wants everything or nothing, forgoes cheap happiness; she rejects reconciliation. But is tragedy, as we know it, still possible and acceptable on the twentieth century European stage?

In Germany the *Atriden-Tetralogie* (1941 ff.): *Iphigenie in Aulis, Agamemnons Tod, Elektra, Iphigenie in Delphi* by Gerhart Hauptmann (then already over eighty years of age) reveals through the Greek myth the inescapable cycle of crime and retribution. But the world is not an absolute void; the dark destiny of human existence is brightened up by Iphigenie's expiatory death; she dies three deaths: when her father Agamemnon sacrifices her to the goddess Artemis; when as priestess of Artemis she renounces life; finally when she dies at her own hands in order to take away the curse from the House of Atreus. It is not without significance that this tetralogy was written during the Second World War; perhaps apart from plays by Camus, Anouilh, O'Neill, Brecht (*Mutter Courage*) cf. p. 84, etc., and some relatively lesser examples (e.g. Ferdinand Bruckner's *Kampf mit dem Engel*, or Luigi Pirandello's inroad into the realm of the subconscious in *Enrico IV*) it may be called a gigantic attempt in re-creating 'high tragedy' in the twentieth century.

Bertolt Brecht's artistic, intellectual and political intentions have often been misread or misinterpreted. His commitment to Communism and his creative activity are not always happily linked together, as Martin Esslin in *Brecht: A Choice of Evils* has indicated. Brecht creates an 'epic theatre' through the so-called V-effect = Verfremdungseffekt (alienation, distantiation or estrangement). Instead of giving us the illusion of reality on the stage he constantly reminds us that we merely get a report of past occurrences, even in his powerful drama *Mutter Courage und ihre Kinder*. Brecht intentionally made Mother Courage a harsh, unsentimental and unloving creature, as there seems to be no possibility of an individual being or becoming good in a society which is bad. But the mother with her grotesquely tattered cart is a moving symbol of suffering mankind under the stress of war.

In O'Neill's American trilogy *Mourning becomes Electra* (1929 and 1931) we have universal themes in a modern play which is very near to the Greek tragedy, particularly to Aeschylus's *Oresteia*. Great are the passions, bold the decisions and crimes in these characters who are caught in their passions and pitiless fate. The dead are too strong—they revenge themselves on the living. Alas, that modern tragedy lacks one essential feature: the imaginative poetic language, and can therefore not be placed with that of Shakespeare, Schiller or H. v. Kleist. Modern drama does, of course, not completely lack imaginative poetic language, cf. the lyrical as well as satirical ballad effects in Brecht's *Die heilige Johanna der Schlachthöfe*, or *Leben des Galilei*, e.g. scene 1, following the recantation. But surprise and grotesque incongruity play an important part on the modern stage.

In his book *After the Lost Generation* (1959) J. W. Aldridge maintains that the only hope for a successful dramatic effect lies today in the depiction of the grotesque and abnormal; 'for it is there and there only that the tragic situation of modern life exists'. But is the life of the normal family-man in itself mediocre and is his domestic situation never capable of tragedy and therefore unrepresentable in tragic terms? It is true that the grotesque, chance and the morbid and abnormal have (apart from several occurrences in Shakespeare) been deliberately used by playwrights such as Georg Büchner (*Woyzeck*), Christian Dietrich Grabbe (*Scherz, Satire, Ironie und tiefere Bedeutung*), and in our time by Frank Wedekind (*Erdgeist*), Gerhart Hauptmann (*Vor Sonnenaufgang*), Ernst Toller (*Hinkemann*), Bert Brecht (*Dreigroschenoper*), Samuel Beckett (*Waiting for Godot*) and many others. Ernst Barlach, in particular, succeeded in blending the grotesque with the tragic: see for instance the bizarre scene VI in *Der arme Vetter* with the man disguised as Venus: 'Am Tisch rechts ein feister, jovialer Herr in primitiver Maskerade als Frau Venus mit Damenhut, Handspiegel . . .' or the tavern scene in *Der blaue Boll* with the devilish Elias: 'Hier, Tante Unk, tu einen Schritt retour, hier sind Leute und verstehn sich auf Flötentöne. Hier heißt es zur gemütlichen Teufelsküche, hier kannst hocken, da setz dich und laß dich vom Stuhl auf deinen frommen Steiß küssen', and the Doppelgänger-theme in Boll's life.

Both tragedy and comedy, however, are rooted in the Dionysiac festivities: cf. $\tau\rho\acute{a}\gamma o\varsigma$ = he-goat; goat-song: tragedy; $\kappa\tilde{\omega}\mu o\varsigma$ = the Dionysiac procession; $\kappa\tilde{\omega}\mu o\varsigma$ $\check{\omega}\delta\eta$ = revel-song: comedy. It is an over-simplification to state that tragedy deals with an elevated theme in an elevated diction and that comedy ridicules gods, myths, authority, and human frailty. Both tragedy and comedy aim at cathartic effects on the spectator: tragedy through the enactment of the deadly conflict between freedom and necessity; comedy through the theatrical travesty of our human situation or of 'the world beyond' which is debunked and dragged down into our own ordinary life and language. In comedy the unexpected, chance, topical events and polemics spotlight everyday familiar scenes.

Both tragedy and comedy wield the destructive weapon of the human intellect, but on different levels: Friedrich Schlegel in *Athenäum* and *Lyzeumsfragmente* speaks of the crushing power of wit: 'Witz ist eine Explosion von gebundenem Geist' . . . 'Witz ist die Erscheinung, der äußere Blitz der Phantasie. Daher seine Göttlichkeit und das Witzähnliche der Mystik' (*Ideen*); but again on a lower level, wit is logical sociability, a surprise-meeting: 'Manche witzige Einfälle sind wie das überraschende Wiedersehen zwei befreundeter Gedanken nach einer langen Trennung . . . Nichts ist verächtlicher als trauriger Witz . . . Witz als Werkzeug der Rache ist so schändlich wie Kunst als Mittel des Sinnenkitzels.'

The drama of mixed elements, i.e. tragi-comedy, has proved a welcome and suitable vehicle for the modern world where the individual does not seem to be any longer capable of influencing social and intellectual events; cf. F. Dürrenmatt's *Theaterprobleme* and also Martin Walser's essay on contemporary drama in *Leseerfahrungen*.

In his study *Theater der Gegenwart* (Frankfurt, 1956) Siegfried Melchinger uncovers some basic faults in a number of modern plays: the disappearance of the suspense in a play which has no central heroic figure, the leaning towards abstraction, and blindness to colour, the inclination towards theory and social preaching, and lastly the style in scenery and in characterization simplified to stultification, which, evidently under the influence of the film and the mass-wish for a dream-picture, has created the so-called 'hard-skinned and at the same time soft-hearted' hero. If we endeavour to find our way back to a theatre which frees us from the abstract and the convulsive style of modern drama and leads us back to real tragedy, this can only be through a play in which the general and individual destiny merge and integrate to form a super-naturalistic play, a super-reality which presents an overpowering spiritual, if not religiously inspired experience, in which authors, actors, and audience take part. Such an attitude is to many a prerequisite of all the art of tragedy, as much today as at the time of the Greeks and in Shakespeare's days. Moreover, there remains an element of dignity and humanity, even in the lowest victim. He or she, in suffering or active decision, will be judged by that human (not social) nobility of mind. The hero need not be free in his actions and he need not be socially significant (he can be a salesman), but his suffering must move us much as that of Prometheus Bound when he cries out: 'You see how unjustly I suffer', or as that of Richard II, a weak-willed but intellectually and artistically exceptional character. This is not a world of rational explanation. Blind necessity rules. Much depends on the height of the fall (Fallhöhe), not on society or outward rank and distinction.

The revival of old rites, of biblical and generally religious themes (e.g. in H. v. Hofmannsthal's dramas) is a remarkable fact, which, with other factors mentioned already, may point to some rehabilitation of tragedy in our time. When the mythology of birth and death is re-created, it is by no means just fire blown into cold ashes.

The substance of tragedy is, as has been indicated above, contained in Aeschylus's *Prometheus Bound*. It is restated in our time, in Ferdinand Bruckner's (Theodor Tagger's) *Der Kampf mit dem Engel* (1957), where old themes: conflict between brother and brother (Cain–Abel), mother and son (Klytamnestra–Orest), raise a contemporary scene (bankruptcy of criminal money-speculations) to the reassertion of man's inner nobility. The son's (Klaus's) last words to his mother are significant: 'Was bliebe von uns übrig, wenn wir uns um die angeborne Würde bringen ließen': 'What would be left to us if we allowed ourselves to surrender our inborn dignity.' Here the demands usually made in regard to tragedy are restated: moral responsibility and personal decision, self-determination and human greatness, a claim to the nobility of the human soul and a communal feeling of being involved and of sharing this experience with the characters of the play.

In many a nineteenth and twentieth century drama, in contrast to the Shakespearean and Greek tragedies, however, the question of good and evil, or of moral responsibility, does not even arise; it is then merely a problem of human suffering. The human individual appears completely submerged in the process of human fatality. Already in Christian Dietrich Grabbe's nihilistic tragedies (i.e. over 100 years before Bertolt Brecht) life is depicted as futile and guiltless. The tragedian Grabbe (1801–1836) is the surgeon or satyr who plays with chaos. Georg Büchner (1813–1837) is the most uncompromising author of the nineteenth century. To him, the only certainty lies in the fact that existence is suffering. Nihilism seems to take all moral decision away from the individual. In his *Dantons Tod* (1835) the world too is godless but not without a mystic concept of life: (Danton) 'Ich bin ein Atheist. Der verfluchte Satz: etwas kann nicht zu nichts werden! Und ich bin etwas, das ist der Jammer!— Die Schöpfung hat sich so breitgemacht, da ist nichts leer, alles voll Gewimmels . . .'

We see that with Büchner (as with Grabbe) the themes are: death and suffering. The redeeming features are sacrifice and comradeship. His nihilism becomes still more pronounced in *Woyzeck*. Büchner found his successors in Tolstoy, Gorky, Synge and Brecht, but great art, already long before Büchner, challenged the sacred, traditional definitions; e.g. Rembrandt treats all men on the same terms. So does Büchner. His tragedy does, in contrast to Samuel Beckett's plays, not yet advocate the total negation of all values, including our last and undeniable value: human existence.

Now, in our twentieth century when the heliocentric view of our world has been replaced by that of the atomic age and when the individual is threatened to be submerged by the demands of mass-movements, our already tragic situation is sharpened by the apparent inevitability of unprecedented technological expansion, which may have in store for us either untold happiness (eternal peace and prosperity) or total extinction.

The question is whether twentieth century tragedy is still possible at all. Neither Paul Ernst in *Der Weg zur Form*, nor Albrecht Schaeffer in *Dichter und Dichtung*, could foresee the present situation. Bruno Markwardt in the fifth volume of his monumental *Geschichte der deutschen Poetik* (1967) very aptly draws attention to the two different terms: 'tragisch'—'traurig', the first being anchored in the belief in a mysterious fate and character, the second in determinism. In the Naturalist drama of G. Hauptmann, Max Halbe or in the novels of Max Kretzer, the 'German Zola', the biological and sociological influences are the iron necessities to which the human victim who knows: 'ich bin wie ich bin . . .' must surrender helplessly.

Under our very eyes the pattern of tragedy has changed. Our present-day scene reveals an unmistakable turn from tragedy to satire, parody and grotesques. This development is not confined to Germany but affects the whole European and American theatre. Historical parallels are not always helpful and, indeed, they often prove dubious, but it is tempting to recall the situation at the time when Greek high tragedy was replaced by comedy and Athens, under Pericles's successor (Kleon), had lost its lustre. The parallel between the two otherwise unlike cultures lies in the speed with which developments took place.

The following data will reflect the dramatically swift transformation in Greece at the period of the Peloponnesian wars: Aeschylus, at the age of sixty-nine died in 456; six years later Aristophanes was born (450). Sophocles, at the time of Aristophanes' birth, was forty-five years old, and Euripides was just thirty-one years old. Aristophanes' literary satire *Frogs* appeared in 405, probably the year when the ninety-years-old Sophocles died. Euripides had died just a year before (406). The rhythm of historical and intellectual events moved with breathtaking rapidity.

With similar speed though in a very different way the

German scene underwent a fundamental change within recent years; cf. Gerhart Hauptmann, 1862–1946; Bertolt Brecht, 1898–1956. Brecht, thirty-six years younger than Hauptmann, died only ten years after him. Between the births of Hebbel (1813–1863) and Brecht lie eighty-five years. Essential reorientations have in the meantime taken place: cf. the Expressionist drama; Brecht's *Leben des Galilei* (written 1938–9), a play epically constructed in fifteen tableaux; above all the theatre of the Absurd and the Drama Documentary.

Gerhart Hauptmann, Hermann Sudermann

With the exception of Gerhart Hauptmann all important German playwrights emigrated before the Second World War: Brecht, Bruckner (Theodor Tagger), Kaiser, Zuckmayer. Hauptmann's early dramas which mirror the effect of heredity, milieu, social inequality, poverty, etc., on the individual, are under the influence of the Naturalist mimicking of speaking and acting. He borrowed it from Arno Holz, the leader of the so-called 'konsequenter Naturalismus'. Language here assumes the rôle of a gesture. This technique and the stress on the sociological and biological conditions are evident in Hauptmann's *Vor Sonnenaufgang* (1889), and *Die Weber* (1892), which is based on the history of the rebellion of the Silesian weavers in 1844.

Every theatre, and particularly the Naturalist theatre, responds to its contemporary audience whose supreme concern is their own private existence. In his substantial essay about 'Imitation oder Realismus' (see *Erfahrungen und Leseerfahrungen*) Martin Walser contrasts the characters of a play with the social condition under which they act, and which soon gets outdated. According to him, old plays —even, to a certain extent, Brecht's plays—have only a historical rôle to play; we should not try and reinterpret them in our time, which after all is totally different from that of a play written under other conditions. But Brecht like

G. Hauptmann transcended his time. Hauptmann's un-rivalled greatness lies in his creation of characters which have survived as artistic masterpieces all literary movements, cf. particularly the unsurpassed characterizations of the thievish washerwoman Wolff in the *Biberpelz* (1893), the compelling figure of the *Fuhrmann Henschel* (1898), the scheming wife of the shoe-maker Fielitz in the tragi-comedy *Der rote Hahn* (Conflagration) (1901), and the tragic *Rose Bernd* (1903). All these character studies are presented in Naturalist technique, but they have deeper roots than those of a milieu-drama.

In the play *Hanneles Himmelfahrt* (1893) a new phase in G. Hauptmann's concept of drama is introduced. Dream phantasies and squalid depravity intermingle: the duality is represented in Hannele's beloved teacher (in the shape of the Saviour) and the drunken father. In the *Versunkene Glocke* (1896) the two worlds: realism (the bell-founder's home and family) and fairy element (the Undine-like Rautendelein), are, however, not fused very happily. In the 'Glashütten-drama' *Und Pippa tanzt* (1906), we are drawn into symbolic happenings; four men struggle for the possession of beauty: the personified force of nature, the enlightened industrialist, the German Michel—the dreamer, finally the resigned old age.

Throughout his long life, Hauptmann's creative activity swings between the two extremes of realism and fantasy. It is a span of over forty years from the social reformer Loth in *Vor Sonnenaufgang* to Matthew Clausen in *Vor Sonnenunter-gang* (1932), in which the author's art almost reaches the height of great tragedy, but this 'modern Lear-Drama' can hardly claim a serious comparison with Shakespeare. Instead of poetry, Hauptmann offers us psychoanalytic ruminations, but there are moments of great theatrical effect, as when the lonely man's own children refuse to sit down to lunch with his young bride Inken Peters, and above all, when he, in wild despair on hearing that his family will declare him in-sane, tears up the picture of his beloved wife and is struck down by sudden death.

In the plays *Die goldene Harfe* (1933) and *Die Tochter der Kathedrale* (1939) the author is influenced by Heraclitian philosophy, the Gnostic and Cathar heresies, and also by translations of medieval romances as well as O. Rahn's reflections on the problem of the Grail. Hauptmann once, in his *Griechischer Frühling* (1908), called human sacrifice the 'bloody root' of tragedy. Three years later, in his *Ratten* (1911) he inserted a debate about the possibilities of tragedy. The question whether a charwoman can be the object of a great tragedy is answered in the affirmative, but as already indicated above, it was not until his old age that Hauptmann created his tetralogy, one of the few contemporary great tragedies. It is rooted in his Classical heritage, but is at the same time modern: 1941 *Iphigenie in Delphi*, 1944 *Iphigenie in Aulis*, 1948 *Agamemnons Tod* and *Elektra* (published two years after his death). On the occasion of the Hauptmann centenary (1962) in the Theater am Kurfürstendamm Erwin Piscator produced a shortened version of the whole Atriden-Tetralogie on one evening. Symbolic references to the recent apocalyptic downfall of Germany lifted this tragedy of sin and retribution high above the level of a merely modernized ancient theme. The play conveyed to the audience the message of the power of healing through sacrifice.

Hermann Sudermann's *Die Ehre* (1889), which appeared a few weeks after Hauptmann's first drama, was a bigger theatrical success, though Sudermann (1857–1928) could hardly ever reach the depth and irrationality in Hauptmann's best work. His dramatic works have, however, withstood the passage of time much longer than for instance those of K. Bleibreu (1859–1928), whose Byronic interpretation of historical heroes, Napoleon, Cesare Borgia, etc., and whose literary treatise *Revolution der Literatur* had once given decisive impulses to the Naturalist movement.

Arthur Schnitzler, Ferdinand Bruckner,
Hugo von Hofmannsthal

Arthur Schnitzler, who was born in the same year as Hauptmann, is particularly skilful in the art of interior monologue and psychological narrative. 'Both in the cyclical play and in the story of interior monologue he created new forms' (H. B. Garland: *German Men of Letters*, II, ed. A. Natan). The *Reigen*, a cycle of dialogues of one-act plays, is a famous example of Schnitzler's Impressionist technique of variations and repetitions. Hofmannsthal once compared the Impressionist with 'a bottle from which not a drop is flowing'. The characters are without development, and they are essentially interchangeable. Introspection and scepticism, wistful yearning and witty disenchantment are already key-notes in Schnitzler's *Anatol* (1893), dialogues between Max, the detached, critical observer, and Anatol, the melancholy and lighthearted charmer of the Wiener süße Mädel. Anatol's affections only play with love. He never really seeks the human personality in his girl. He remains lonely. Of Schnitzler's numerous one-act dramas, *Der grüne Kakadu* (1899) is the most striking. The scene is laid in a Parisian tavern, where before an aristocratic audience a masked play is performed; this is changed into deadly earnest by the storming of the Bastille. In *Professor Bernhardi* the author dramatized a conflict between the Jewish doctor of a hospital and the Church. The doctor refuses to admit the priest, as the patient, a young girl, does not realize that she is dying. The human conflicts: death and youth, beauty and fatal illness, are a favourite subject-matter, especially in his novel *Sterben*. In *Professor Bernhardi* political considerations enter the conflict which, however, is not developed into a tragedy but into arguments illumined by wit and irony about ministerial bureaucracy, bigotry and prejudice.

Ferdinand Bruckner's dramatic theories are remarkable as

regards contents and time. He attacks Brecht's epic drama and emphasis on Marxism, social problems and situations; he also attacks the avant-garde theatre of the absurd (Beckett, Ionesco, etc.). In his *Symbole des Tragischen* (*Wort in der Zeit*, II, 1957) Bruckner sees the essence of tragedy in the inevitable clash between man as an individual and as a member of the society. A total victory of technology would mean the abdication of man, as the machine would rob man of his sense of existence, and paralyse or depersonalize him through fear and anxiety. The bigger the power of the machine the greater man's terror of the (nuclear) monster. There is only one way open to man—the way to inwardness. Tragedy depicts the inescapable conflict as we know it since Aeschylus' *Prometheus Bound*.

In his treatise *Vom Wesen des Tragischen* Bruckner attributes our present-day devaluation or the abolition of tragedy to two causes: an outward reason and an inward one—(*a*) the replacement of a theatre representing psychological situations by the didactic 'Theater der Vernunft' which is to educate men to a scientific way of life, (*b*) the inward cause is advocated mainly by Paris avant-garde writers who interpret human tragedy as that of the utter meaninglessness and hopelessness of our existence; our life, according to *Waiting for Godot*, is nothing but waiting. But Bruckner ends his sombre deliberations on a hopeful note: if through avant-garde tendencies we have 'poisoned' or even 'destroyed' tragic form it is our duty to discover and re-create it again; cf. his appeal to man's dignity in *Der Kampf mit dem Engel*, p. 66.

This concept of man's inherent resources was already evident in Bruckner's pre-war drama *Elisabeth von England* (1930). It is one of his best-known plays: Queen Elizabeth loves the mediocre Essex and hates the Spanish King Philip; but her human predicament (her solitude and age) is conquered by the sense of duty to her country. It was this work which established Bruckner's reputation as a leading modern dramatist, and it incidentally also revealed his true identity, but the author continued to call himself Bruckner, not Tagger.

Hugo von Hofmannsthal (see p. 12) went through an artistic crisis which he described in his famous 'Lord Chandos' letter. Having given up lyrical verse he now turned to an intense occupation with the theatre dealing with the problem of truth and mask, the reality of wonder and the wonder of reality, and the antithesis of artist and society. To him the frontiers between dream and reality, as Michael Hamburger points out in his lucid *Zwei Studien*, were fluid. Life was for the poet not so real as he once had thought, and the stage not so dreamlike as it seemed to him. The art of the playwright seemed to him to be akin to that of the musician. In Hofmannsthal's imaginary conversation between Balzac and the Orientalist Hammer-Purgstall: *Über Charaktere im Roman und im Drama*, Balzac says:

> Let me tell you that characters in the theatre are nothing but contrapuntal necessities. The stage character is a contraction of the real one. What enchants me in the real one is precisely its breadth. Its breadth, which is the basis of its destiny . . . One must not confound destiny with catastrophe. Catastrophe as a symphonic composition, that's the business of the dramatist who is so closely related to the musician . . . [*H. v. Hofmannsthal. Selected Prose*, tr. by Mary Hottinger and Tania and James Stern, 1952, London.]

It was not until four years after his drama *Der Schwierige* (1920–1) and four years before his death in 1929, that Hofmannsthal created in his *Turm* the dramatic image of some of his most absorbing thoughts about man's future.

The 'Kinderkönig' in this late tragedy *Der Turm* (1925), which is based on Calderon's *La vida es sueño*, expresses the author's hope of a new World-Order. The 'Tower' is a symbol of conflicting powers and suffering, but at the end of the drama the 'Kinderkönig' brings hope to the dying King Sigismund: 'Wir haben neue Gesetze gegeben, denn die Gesetze müssen immer von den Jungen kommen' (1st version). There are three printed versions of this drama. The second version is, on the whole, a shortened first version. In the third version, however, the last two acts have been considerably altered: King Sigismund, who in the first version endeavours to reconcile the old order and the new generation, encounters quite a different fate in the soldier (Oliver) whose ruthless power dominates the final events. Instead of the promise of a new era: 'renovabis faciem terrae' (1st version), a murder closes the last act. The King is treacherously shot by his enemy.

Hofmannsthal's personal and literary contacts were influential. Carl J. Burckhardt once described his nearly twenty years older friend as highly sensitive and receptive, and 'attentive to every fine reaction of his searching and anxious mind'. Hofmannsthal was in touch with many creative writers and critics of his age: e.g. with Schnitzler, Kassner, Burckhardt, Schröder, Wassermann, Eberhard von Bodenhausen, Max Reinhardt—whose production of *Jedermann* outside the Salzburg Cathedral became world-famous— Stefan George (though an estrangement between the two essentially incompatible characters was inevitable) and above all Richard Strauss. But even this creative collaboration (since 1908) was again and again hampered by differences of artistic mood and imagination, as for instance is shown in the composition *Ariadne auf Naxos*; here the fusion of the *buffo* of the *commedia dell' arte* with the heroic-mythological figures has not succeeded so well as the blending of the humorous with the serious, and the theatrical with the supersensitive in the *Rosenkavalier*. The collaboration suffered from Hofmannsthal's tendency to project symbolical and psychological meanings into his main characters, for instance Ariadne's and Zerbinetta's different concepts of love.

Frank Wedekind; German Expressionism: Georg Kaiser

Frank Wedekind (1864–1918) is a link between Sturm und Drang, not Naturalism, and Expressionism; moreover, there is an affinity with Surrealism, and also with Kleist, Büchner (*Woyzeck*), Grabbe (*Scherz, Satire, Ironie und tiefere Bedeutung*), Sternheim, Brecht, Jahnn (whom he foreshadows) and above all with Nietzsche, who had a marked influence on him. But Wedekind's Übermensch is oversexed like Lulu the serpent.

In his songs, ballads and Moritaten, too, he is connected with the nineteenth century (especially Heine) and, at the same time, he anticipates the immediate future, i.e. Bertolt Brecht, see e.g. his *Schriftstellerhymne* with the refrain:

> Schöner grüner Lorbeerzweig, der dich neckt
> Und die Stirn bedeckt, wenn der Lump verreckt,
> Mit ausgefransten Hosen.

Wedekind, who liked to act some main rôles in his dramas himself, criticized the theatre of his time as being too literary and lacking in the theatrical. To him, the theatre is more important than the play. He combines drama with circus and cabaret; marionettes and grotesque (the ghoulish caricatures of the teachers in *Frühlings Erwachen*) play an essential part in his work. Sex is the point from which almost all life proceeds. Wedekind is particularly effective because he mixes extreme vitality with extravagant intellectualism, so producing intense contrasts and tragi-comic affects as in his *Hidalla oder Hetman der Zwergriese* and *Marquis von Keith*.

In the *Prologue* of the *Erdgeist* (1895) (and later in *Lulu*) the Ringmaster, i.e. the author himself, introduces his circus characters as animals to the audience.

With this *Prologue*, a kind of inverted Schiller-oration, Wedekind declared war against the contemporary drama which he considered tame and anaemic:

> Schlecht sind die Zeiten! . . .
> Was seht ihr in den Lust- und Trauerspielen?—
> *Haustiere*, die so wohlgesittet fühlen,
> An blasser Pflanzenkost ihr Mütchen kühlen . . .

There is also an unmistakable gibe at Hauptmann's *Vor*

Sonnenaufgang '. . . Der eine Held kann keinen Schnaps ver-
tragen . . .' Instead of domesticated animals Wedekind offers
an unrestrained show of savagery. The stage is purposefully
used by the disillusioned moralist, not as a 'moralische
Anstalt' but as an institution of a-morality.

Many of Wedekind's dramatic figures are autobiographical portraits which justify their treatment as 'Schlüssel-
Literatur': e.g. the author is father (Dr Schön) and son
(Alwa) in *Lulu*; he is also depicted in the mis-shapen Hetman
in *Hidalla*; the beautiful young Fanny is modelled on Tilly,
his wife; the impostor *Marquis von Keith* is modelled on his
adventurous Danish friend Willi Gretor, an art-dealer whose
secretary Wedekind had once been; above all, *König Nicolo*,
who has been degraded by a brutal society and is turned into
a court-jester, reveals features of the author himself.

Some distinctive features of Expressionism have already
been discussed in the section about Expressionist poetry; see
p. 23. A characteristic form is the so-called 'Stationen-
drama', a play with a loose sequence of episodes, such as
Strindberg's *Road to Damascus* or Kaiser's *Von Morgens bis
Mitternachts*. Its prototype is the Passion Play of the Middle
Ages with a succession of scenes representing the Stations of
the Cross.

One of the most important exponents of Expressionist
technique and ethos during its high tide (1910–about 1924)
is Georg Kaiser (1878–1945). To him we shall therefore
devote special space here, whilst further details about the
other German playwrights wholly or partly connected with
Expressionism such as Barlach, Sternheim, Kraus, Unruh,
Csokor, Kokoschka, Johst, Sorge, E. Toller, Borchert, etc.,
are given in the bibliographies. The transformation and
purification of character are the main themes in their
dramas. It is no coincidence that Sternheim's devastating
comedy *Die Hose* (1909–10) (see also p. 378) about the
philistine bourgeois has been successfully revived since the

Second World War; its 'hero', a time-serving civil servant, undergoes a fundamental change of character. Barlach's *Der blaue Boll* (1926) in a much more searching and deeper sense depicts man's readiness to accept responsibility in our human society; the country-squire Boll thus becomes a spiritually transmuted being.

In his discerning monograph on Kaiser, B. J. Kenworthy (see p. 296) speaks of 'the division of Kaiser against himself', a dichotomy which penetrates Kaiser's dramas. There are the plays about the rebirth of the Man, the 'New Man', and the plays with the theme of escape from our existence. The dialectical energy which swings between two opposing extremes has led the author to the creation of paradoxically varied comedies and tragedies, ranging from ecstatic visions, 'Stationendramen' about man's moral evolution to critical disputations and 'Hirnspiele', satires and parodies. This contradiction between the two poles is dissolved (as is demonstrated in Kenworthy's monograph) in Kaiser's last important plays: the verse-dramas or the so-called *Griechische Dramen: Amphitryon, Pygmalion, Bellerophon*, which he wrote whilst in exile near the Lago Maggiore in 1943-4. They are by no means mere modern versions of old themes. In *Bellerophon* he created a symbol of himself as the artist and of man's power of regeneration. Moreover, in those late plays a change in the physical relationship between man and woman is advocated by the sublimation of the sexual bond into a spiritual union. The problem in many earlier plays of his is the conflict between body and mind, physical weakness or impotence and intellectual strength (e.g. *Rektor Kleist*), or the urge of the flesh (e.g. *Jüdische Witwe*) and senility.

In *König Hahnrei* (composed 1910, publ. 1913) Marke is represented as an impotent cuckold who lecherously watches Tristan and Isolde; the adulterers are of no use to him once their love has died, and therefore he destroys them; cf. *Introductions*, vol. I, p. 84. In Kaiser's play *Der gerettete Alkibiades* (1917–19, publ. 1920), Socrates personifies the triumph of mind over the body, not without a touch of humour: a cactus spine in the sole of the foot causes him to strike about with his sword in agonizing pain, and thus he saves the life of Alkibiades.

Kaiser's regeneration-dramas are presented as 'Stationendramen' in a revue-like technique: a row of scenes is held together by one central character: e.g. *Von Morgens bis Mitternachts, Hölle Weg Erde, Gilles und Jeanne*. Redemption of man through humble sacrifice is the theme in *Die Bürger von Calais* (1913, publ. 1914), perhaps Kaiser's best-known play. The historical incident of 1347 is related in Froissart's Chronicle. It inspired Rodin to his famous group of sculptures and Kaiser to the Christ-like figure of Eustache, the 'New Man' who sacrifices himself, so that the deed may remain unsullied and the other six comrades will not think of saving their lives at the last moment. But Eustache's death turns out to be unnecessary: King Edward III pardons them, as a son has been born to him the night before.

In the trilogy *Die Koralle* (1917), *Gas I* (1918), *Gas II* (1919), a coral is a symbol of our lost paradise. It is the only comfort of a lonely millionaire on his way to death. His son, too, fails to lead the workmen back to a natural existence; they themselves demand the production of gas. His grandson has become an ordinary worker in the state-owned factory. He wants to build up a new world but is frustrated by the chief engineer, and in an act of self-annihilation the Milliardärarbeiter breaks the vessel of poison-gas over himself.

Die Spieldose (1942) is a good example of how Kaiser skilfully was able to apply his Expressionist technique to contemporary scenes. The time is World War II; the place a village in Brittany; the theme: the tinkling sound of a musical box brings back to Paul, a young French farmer's son, his memory. He was betrothed to Noelle who in the meantime has become his father's second wife. Paul kills his father by throwing him over the cliff. But Noelle shrinks from the murderer who wants to marry her, and when for the death of a German soldier hostages from the occupied village are demanded, Paul steps forward and offers himself as a sacrifice in atonement for the crime against his own father. Noelle's child is to become the 'New Man' who will bring a happier future to mankind.

Wolfgang Borchert's Beckmann in *Draußen vor der Tür* is also a doomed Heimkehrer, unwanted by his wife, unwanted by the society, and unwanted even by death. In this drama or rather chain of individual scenes and meditations by the outsider Beckmann, the final fate remains undecided. God is powerless and cannot alter things; the 'new God' is death as the undertaker whom nobody can escape. The play is obviously indebted to the Expressionist drama; see P. B. Salmon, p. 221; Borchert's drama, written in the year of his early death, 1947, appeared in an English translation by D. Porter in 1952.

Karl Kraus composed his huge 'tragedy of mankind', *Die letzten Tage der Menschheit*, five acts with Vorspiel and Epilogue, in 1922. Although Kraus does not refrain from reproducing details of historical events and word-for-word conversation he succeeds in avoiding a merely photographic likeness of facts by merging quotations and events into a gigantic world-drama. In the Theater an der Wien performance it was condensed into twenty-four scenes. The vast span of this disjointed play ranges from historical data, newsreels and social satire to apocalyptic visions. On a bizarre canvas there is the caricature of the fat Teutons, Siegfriedchen, and the no less massive Elschen. At the time when Kraus (mainly during the First World War) wrote this tragedy for a 'Martian' stage the atom-bomb was still unknown, yet in these stark satires and in the symbolic figure of death he intuitively foreshadowed our present world-situation at the hour of technological triumphs.

In spite of the enthusiastic response of students in Vienna to Kraus's recitals, aphorisms and poems, it is a sad fact that Kraus's work is too little known nowadays, although his *Fackel* was once a much-feared and much-admired journal, dedicated to the German language—'the most profound of

languages' . . . 'the most shallow of speeches'. From words
K. Kraus drew inspiration; out of words he forged deadly
weapons.

Bertolt Brecht

Bertolt Brecht (1898–1956): The 'estrangement-effect' or the
so-called 'alienation' on the stage is, as we have already
mentioned, a characteristic feature of Brecht's art. He wanted
his actors to stand *outside* their rôle but at the same time they
were expected to make the audience familiar with the
essence of the characters and events of the play.

Brecht is said to have admired Brueghel's *Fall of Icarus*
(Vienna), in which the disastrous fall of the youthful flier is
presented with detachment in an idyllic landscape: a farmer
ploughs his field, a shepherd looks after his flock of sheep. In
this serene arcadia nobody notices the catastrophe which
happens far away over water.

Similarly Brecht also aimed at detachment in his art but
in a special sense: he wanted to make his audience think
rather than become emotionally involved. He was anxious to
open their minds. Therefore he did not shrink from an aggressive, dialectic and persuasive socialist disputation on the subject concerned. But Brecht did not formulate a Marxist
theory of aesthetics. He was not always lucky in his choice of
form for his dramatic work. It is, for instance, a pity that
his 'Historische Gängsterschau' *Der aufhaltsame Aufstieg des
Arturo Ui* (1941) is presented in the style of a classical play,
i.e. 'im großen Stil' which, according to Brecht, is to create
a 'Doppelverfremdung' (gangster group and echoes in blank-
verse from great tragedies). But this tension between subject-
matter and technical devices leads all argument finally ad
absurdum: the Austrian Chancellor Dollfuß appears in a
scene modelled on that between Gretchen and Faust
(Spaziergang), then there are reminiscences from Shakespeare's *Richard III* (bridal quest), Schiller's *Wallenstein* ('Dem
Gängster flicht die Nachwelt keine Kränze'), and again

Faust I: 'Herr Ui, wie halten Sie's mit der Religion.' Names are skilfully 'verfremdet': Giri = Göring, Givola = Göbbels, Ui = Hitler, Dullfeet = Dollfuß, Dogsborough = Hindenburg (cf. colloquial plural: Hünde = Hinde), Ernesto Roma = Ernst Röhm, cf. also R. Grimm: *Bertolt Brecht. Die Struktur seines Werkes* (1965[4]).

The dramatic struggle between uncontrollable instinct and disciplining 'ratio' is a key-problem in Brecht's interpretation of excess. Violence can act as a negative as well as a positive stimulus: e.g. in *Mann ist Mann* (1927) it causes ruthless changes in the human body and society; the sergeant castrates himself in order to be able to control the terrible urge of his sensuality. There is also self-castration in Brecht's version of Lenz's *Hofmeister* (*The Tutor*). Brecht had a liking for new adaptations and interpretations of literary themes: e.g. his *Antigone* (based on Sophocles' drama), *Coriolan* (from Shakespeare), *Don Juan* (from Molière), *Pauken and Trompeten* (Farquhar's *The Recruiting Officer*), and *Eduard II* (from Marlowe) in collaboration with Feuchtwanger.

The parable of Brecht's *Ballad of Mazeppa* is obvious: the Cossack, tied to a wild horse, is dragged to death; the control lies for Brecht in his commitment to scientific Marxism and Communism, particularly in the group of plays of 1929 to 1933–4 in which his Marxist views are stressed more than in his later or earlier dramas which are less doctrinaire: e.g. his *Baal* (1920, publ. 1922), *Trommeln in der Nacht* (1922), *Dreigroschenoper* (1928) based on J. Gay's *Beggar's Opera* (1728): here violence acts as a negative force in the hands of drunkards, rakes and profiteers. Violence is, however, advocated as a positive value by the Communist agitators in *Die Maßnahme* (*The Disciplinary Measure*) (1930–1), as otherwise the Party Order would be jeopardized: the theme is Communism and World-Revolution; the method of representation is that of questioning and argumentation and decision. The young comrade, by his spontaneous sympathy for the oppressed, upsets the political plan of his own party-men who in the end kill him. He is not the blind tool of agitators but a human being. His conflict is an inescapable, a tragic one. He believes in *both* values: compulsion and freedom; he cannot win the one without offending the other and becoming guilty.

Brecht's didactic play, *Die Mutter* (1932), based on Gorki's novel, is nearest to orthodox Communism, a propaganda piece. In the drama about the round—and pointed—heads, *Die Rundköpfe und Spitzköpfe* (1932 ff), the National Socialist race-doctrine is ridiculed with consummate clownery, but like the drama on Arturo Ui, this play is amazingly light-weight and weak propaganda, considering the sombre background and the tragedy which has overtaken not only Germany but also the whole Western world. Brecht himself was obviously a Schweykian character in his art.

In his poem *Vom armen B.B.* he makes the confession that he cannot be relied upon: '. . . In mir habt ihr einen, auf den könnt ihr nicht bauen . . .' Yet behind the harsh roughness there was his power of understanding and sharing other people's suffering. It is essentially one of the qualities through which Brecht's genius won sincere admirers in the West, even when he openly made artistic concessions to the East, such as the alterations made in *Trial of Lucullus* with a view to the ideological temper of the East Berlin audience. It is an irony that (as H. Politzer put it in MLQ, 1962: *How epic is Bertolt Brecht's Epic Theatre?*) 'Brecht's survival may depend on the survival of the West which he, by all ordinary standards, had tried so hard to prevent.'

But notwithstanding all Brechtian cynicism there is in his work a glowing, almost missionary-like will to change the world. Brecht, the most important German Communist writer of his time, had a great influence on the Western intellectuals. But he was also indebted to the past: Villon, Verlaine, Rimbaud, and later Kipling; moreover the Japanese and Chinese theatre became strong influences on him. Above all, he stands in the German tradition; it is particularly Brecht's use of the colloquial language in his dramas which connects him, to some extent, with German Naturalism, though (apart from Wedekind, Kaiser,

Sternheim) the Cabaret and the medieval Morality Plays and German Baroque literature (Grimmelshausen) had a much more direct impact on Brecht's so-called *epic theatre* of the thirties. He then turned to the *dialectic theatre*.

The chief aim behind his 'Verfremdungstechnik' (V-effect) is to bring about a radical change in the human conditions and attitudes of our society. Compared with Sartre's *No Exit*, Brecht's *Der gute Mensch von Sezuan* (*The Good Woman of Setzuan*, cf. MLQ, 1961, Ernst Loeb) seems to offer a solution for creating goodness in this world—but at a loss of freedom of choice. Yet who would prefer 'future goodness' achieved by rather doubtful means to one's personal freedom of finding meaning in life?

Brecht's surviving dramatic work was created to some degree in spite of his political doctrine and elaborate V-technik. According to his views in *Kleines Organon für das Theater* (1948–9) the aim of the theatre is entertainment, but all depends on what kind of low or high entertainment is to be provided; moreover, the prevailing political, social and scientific movements are to be mirrored on the stage. In our age which is an essentially scientific one a sound knowledge of dialectics is expected from the playwright who must avoid one-sided emotional commitment: 'Die echten V-Effekte haben kämpferischen Charakter.' Music and song provide alienating commentary. Brecht reminds us of the use of masks on the Greek and medieval stage, and of pantomime and musical effects in the Asiatic theatre. But his drama is rooted in the modern scene and therefore demands a different technique of presentation.

Brecht's greatest achievements are much more than just dramatized scenes of social forces and discussions, particularly in his *Mutter Courage*, the story of which was inspired by Grimmelshausen's story *Landstörzerin Courasche*. Kattrin's death is tragic self-sacrifice, an act of moral decision which would have thrilled Schiller. Here the audience cannot sit back and declare 'it's all a fake'. Here surely is a scene in which the human being transcends the narrow ego. Here,

Brecht, like Schiller, wanted to shake the audience into an awareness of human cruelty and into compassion for innocent victims, and the alienation effect in his 'epic' presentation of the play clearly breaks down.

In *Die heilige Johanna der Schlachthöfe* (*St Joan of the Stockyards*) (written 1930, performed 1959), which is directed against Schiller's moral idealism, Brecht's endeavour was to dissociate his theatre from Schiller's concept of tragedy; however, even here he does not quite succeed. The dying Johanna speaks for all workers when she declares that it is only violence which can help us out of violence: 'Es hilft nur Gewalt, wo Gewalt herrscht.' It is not enough to be good, we must make the world a better place to live in. But stylistically the use of parody proves an effective means of alienation.

Brecht's outstanding dramatic successes: *Mutter Courage und ihre Kinder* (written 1939; 1941), *Der gute Mensch von Sezuan* (1942), *Der kaukasische Kreidekreis* (1948), *Leben des Galilei* (written 1938–9, 2nd version 1957), reflect a significant change in his artistic development. His earlier uncompromising principle of Marxism and Communism mellowed in the process of artistic maturity and human disillusionment. In *Der kaukasische Kreidekreis* it is the cunning and lascivious Azaak who gives a just judgment. In *Mutter Courage* mother-love conquers the sutler's greed for money and comfort when in the farewell talk to the cook she refuses to leave her daughter. Mutter Courage gets a lot out of War, but she has to pay a price for it; in the end she loses her family, her possessions, yet not her wagon and her determination to survive. Instead of a dramatic construction and unity of scenes, Brecht shows by narrative means the effect of war on material and human beings. The cart becomes a symbol of the devastations through war, Mutter Courage the embodiment of life-force (though not the embodiment of all mothers in war). This play is perhaps one of the most notable, if not the greatest of all modern German plays on the modern stage, restating man's tragic condition in Brecht's 'Verfremdungstechnik', his epic style of drama.

In *Leben des Galilei* Brecht depicts an epicurean character who is afraid of physical pain and therefore recants, thus paralysing the heroic gesture of tragedy in the old sense of the term. The intellectual rebel loves his body (the introductory scene on the stage shows his delight in washing and touching his body). The hedonistic aspect of Galileo's temperament causes his downfall. Such lack of social responsibility led ultimately to the manufacture of the atom-bomb. Brecht realized that science and mankind will be irrevocably split. There is Galileo's long speech on optimism, scene 1: 'die alte Zeit ist herum, und es ist eine neue Zeit'. The hero goes on living but disillusioned; cf. also scene 14 with Andrea.

The V-effect is not at all a new technique. It must be well known to anyone acquainted with classical tragedy, Shakespeare (*Richard III*), Ibsen, Strindberg and Wedekind. If the court-scene can be considered the centre of all 'epic' and 'dialectic' theatre, then Kleist's *Der zerbrochene Krug* is one of its most important German forerunners. Brecht carried this technique to its extreme conclusion by means of contrasts, puns (e.g. 'verordnete Unordnung'), irony, ambiguity of language and presentation, quotations, and surprise statement: 'Friede ist ausgebrochen' (an event is turned into something sensational, as if a kind of threat was implied). The so-called 'gestus' of the *non*-verbal expression of the speaker and of the speech itself plays a vital part in Brecht's drama. The inserted songs are a chief factor in the alienation effect. Their main function is not to awaken emotions but to offer calculated gesture and devices by which to explain and illustrate the proceedings from a detached view. Flat singing, the use of didactic prologues, etc., and the rejection of the traditional structure of three- or five-act dramas in favour of a number of tableaux (e.g. in *Leben des Galilei* or in the comedy *Schweyk in the Second World War*) suit the epic and didactic presentation. But when Brecht speaks for the underdog, his stage turns into a moral institution which before him had found an ingenious advocate in Schiller. According to *Commentary* (TLS 29.II.68) it was

Sergei Tretiakov who probably suggested the term 'Verfremdung' to Brecht.

Carl Zuckmayer, Max Frisch, Friedrich Dürrenmatt

Carl Zuckmayer (1896–) is, after Brecht and Hauptmann,
the most celebrated German playwright of the older generation. He combines stark realism with Romantic imagination. His most successful comedy is *Der Hauptmann von
Koepenick* (1931). In spite of its subtitle, *A German Fairy Tale*,
it is a rumbustious satire of bureaucracy and militarism,
with unmistakable hints at National Socialism which came
into power two years afterwards. The theme of the play, as
in Nicolai Gogol's *The Government Inspector*, is the imper-
sonation of a VIP (a captain) by a lowly cobbler and ex-
convict who cannot find roots in a society which had rejected
him. But when the shoe-maker Wilhelm Voigt gets hold of an
old uniform his identity is assured, and soon events change
drastically. He makes his way to the town hall where he
arrests the mayor and the treasurer. The deception, however,
is discovered, and Voigt is imprisoned.

Des Teufels General (1946) is Zuckmayer's most ambitious
dramatic achievement. The suicidal end of the General of the
Luftwaffe is based on that of the flying ace Ernst Udet.
The place of the drama is Berlin, the time: winter 1941,
shortly before America entered the War. Harras is a
General and expert technician in aircraft production. His
great passion is flying: 'Mein Lebensinhalt—das war immer
die Fliegerei . . . und nu kann ich's nicht mehr bleiben
lassen', he says. Being a devoted pilot he 'goes along with
things' which he really hates. By his suicide General Harras
achieves moral redemption. Recently, the whole third act
was rewritten by Zuckmayer, in the light of historical developments and with particular emphasis on the resistance
fighter Oderbruch, who is an engineer in the Air Ministry,
and whose one aim is the downfall of Hitler's Germany and the
establishment of 'Eternal Justice' which is to bring freedom

again to mankind. Oderbruch is a saboteur, out of idealism. General Harras, who himself is suspected of sabotage
because of a considerable number of crashes, does not betray
him. The opposite character and mouthpiece of National
Socialism is the Kulturleiter Dr Schmidt-Lausitz. The play,
though perhaps Zuckmayer's best drama, is not without
faults: the women (except Frau Eilers) are unconvincing.
The audacious General Harras, who has nothing but contempt for 'the devil', and who is attracted by the thrill of
flying, is finally redeemed by his death, which, however,
does not solve anything in the end. But the potentially tragic
character of the excellent milieu-drama cannot be denied,
cf. the words of the General himself to his young officer
Hartmann (3rd act): 'Ich habe seine (Gottes) Hand nicht
ergriffen. Ich habe—die andere gewählt . . .'

The *Gesang im Feuerofen* (1949, performed 1950) also deals
with a War-theme. French maquis fighters are betrayed and
caught in a burning castle. The German wireless operator
tries to warn the enemy and dies with them. The blending of
two different styles: the language of the soldiers and the
words of Vater Wind, Mutter Frost, Bruder Nebel, proves
incongruous and mars the artistic effect of the whole play.

The hero in *Das kalte Licht* (1955, a play, to some extent,
based on Dr Klaus Fuch's espionage case) has a certain
affinity to the *Teufels General*. Both make a pact with the evil
forces and both regain their better self in the end. Here the
central figure is a nuclear physicist who becomes a spy.

Although Zuckmayer's plays usually draw a large, enthusiastic audience he has not always fared well in recent
critical appraisals. The main reason for this seems to lie in his
unwillingness to adapt himself to the anti-realistic techniques
of a stage which now stands under the influence of experimental writers such as Eugène Ionesco and Samuel Beckett.

Max Frisch: architect, playwright and novelist, was born
in Zürich in 1911.

One of his first successes on the stage was the Heimkehrer-

Drama *Als der Krieg zu Ende war* (1949). As a Zeitstück it deals with a topical theme: the scene is laid in a partially bombed house: a room occupied by Russians, and a cellar occupied by the returning soldier (Heimkehrer), who is a war criminal, and his wife, in Berlin in 1945. The Russian Colonel loves Agnes, but when her husband Anders is discovered, the Russian believes that she had made love to him merely in order to protect her husband, and he leaves her. Anders forgives her; he equates her love for the Russian and his own war crimes against the Jews as necessities arising out of war conditions; in despair Agnes commits suicide. The full possibilities of tragedy cannot develop. The character of the husband lacks true compassion; he merely considers his wife's love for the Colonel to be a kind of retribution for his own deeds committed at Warsaw.

The farce *Die chinesische Mauer* (1946, new version 1955) seems to indulge in a Strindbergian irrational atmosphere, but in fact it deals with current events. The world is in the sense of Shakespeare and Hofmannsthal presented as a stage. The historical and fictitious guests at the Chinese Emperor's Garden Party (Cleopatra, Napoleon, Don Juan, etc.), listen to the vainglorious talk about the Great Wall, a symbol of deception. The human beings wear masks, with the exception of only one character, the author. He alone sees through the illusion: 'Die Zeit läßt sich nicht aufhalten . . .' and becomes a rebel. The events end in a failure, as the hero becomes dictator. At the end of the play Princess Mee Lan says to him (Der Heutige): 'Das ist die Wirklichkeit: Du, der Ohnmächtige, und ich, die Geschändete, so stehen wir in dieser Zeit, und die Welt geht über uns hin. Das ist unsere Geschichte . . .' Human freedom and the forces of history are shown to be essentially hostile to one another, cf. also Dürrenmatt's *Die Ehe des Herrn Mississippi* or Kaiser's *Von Morgens bis Mitternachts*.

Reinterpretation of history is also the theme in *Graf Öderland* (*Eine Moritat*) (1951, new version 1961). A public prosecutor being bored with his bourgeois existence as public prosecutor (Staatsanwalt) and with the routine of a writing desk, abandons his family and career and becomes the hero of revolutionary forces. The symbol of rebellion is his axe. The Graf Öderland kills everybody who is his opponent. Yet even as Prime Minister he is not free. He, too, is tied to his writing desk. He must govern. He cannot alter his fate— but he can end it by suicide. Thus the play is much more than just the exposure of the murderous impulses which lie dormant beneath one's honourable exterior and which can break loose through a single man's anarchic action. This essentially didactic play is well calculated, but its characters lack the fullness of life necessary to be convincing.

The same criticism applies to the 'Lehrstück ohne Lehre': *Biedermann und die Brandstifter* (radio-play or Hörspiel 1956, stage-play 1958). The reader or spectator of this black comedy, *The Fire-Raisers*, which is an unmistakable invective against political weakness, will, no doubt, think of the Munich appeasement. Biedermann, a man of bourgeois honesty, and uprightness is most successfully hoodwinked when he is told the truth. The peace-loving person simply does not believe it—but this self-righteous, hard-working Biedermann is hardly worth saving, as he himself invited the questionable fire-raisers hospitably to his house, and even handed the villains the matches to light the petrol drums. He thinks that what may happen to others cannot happen to him. Thus he deserves to be fooled; the catastrophe over-takes him, and he fails to arouse our sympathy. The satirical parable is too much on the level of mere cabaret entertain-ment. The 'final' version has an epilogue: Biedermann and his wife descend into hell though they feel themselves inno-cent victims. The devils are the fire-raisers. On earth those who wear uniforms can kill and are saved! Therefore the devils must again visit our earth and start new conflagrations.

Another of Frisch's favourite themes is the problem of man's identity and man's acceptance of differentness. Already in his first play *Santa Cruz* (composed in 1944) the central theme is the problem of man's authentic personality and the influence of the opinions or dreams of society and friends on one's identity. In his comedy *Don Juan oder die Liebe zur Geometrie* (1953) a scholar adopts as a defence the rôle of the seducer. In his rather thin novel *Mein Name sei Gantenbein* (1964) the theme is that of the blind man who is really not blind. The harrowing play *Andorra* (1962), his greatest so far, deals with 'a collective scapegoat', an alleged Jew who in fact is not Jewish. But *Andorra*, too, is deprived of the possibilities of a great tragedy, as it suffers from serious flaws: it piles up horrors and improbabilities; the characters turn into a series of marionette-like figures on the strings of an adroit engineer behind stark stage-events: mother and youth are murdered, the bride becomes a soldiers' whore, the teacher hangs himself. Frisch, in an interview with D. E. Zimmer (Dec. 1967, *Zeit*), called *Biedermann* and *Andorra* parables. They show *quod erat demonstrandum*.

Friedrich Dürrenmatt (born 1921, the son of a pastor at Konolfingen, Canton Berne) and his compatriot Max Frisch are, like Rilke and George, often rather thoughtlessly bracketed together. There are, however, outstanding points of contact and similarity between both Swiss authors: they are known for their love of revising and rewriting their works; both are fond of a cabaret-like treatment of drama; both tend to express a message or moral commitment, though not always directly; both occasionally choose kindred subjects, e.g. Frisch's *Graf Öderland* (1951) and Dürrenmatt's *Die Ehe des Herrn Mississippi* (1952, new version 1957): in both plays the key-character is that of a public official (public prosecutor) who in a mood of madness breaks away from his orderly bourgeois existence and by the very success of his criminal ambition loses his inner freedom. He who becomes the 'Henker' of his enemy is himself guilty. This is a favourite theme of Dürrenmatt, cf. the story *Der Richter und sein Henker*.

At the end of Dürrenmatt's early drama *Es steht geschrieben* (1947) in which the anabaptists are brought to destruction, the moral truth is pronounced by the bishop: 'It is well for him who rediscovers God on the wheel.' Such a statement contains the germs of tragedy, but Dürrenmatt, to whom the human situation is essentially absurd, likes to mix tragedy with grotesqueness, loquacity and satire. In the unhistorical historical comedy *Romulus der Große* (1949) those elements have been successfully blended. The last Roman emperor, tired of keeping up the pretence of sovereign authority and being more dedicated to his chicken-farm than to politics, surrenders his crown to the foreign assailant.

Der Besuch der alten Dame (1956) (*The Visit*) is considered the author's masterpiece. He significantly calls it 'eine tragische Komödie'. In this play the fusion of both worlds (tragedy and comedy) apparently almost works. The 'old lady' appears as the bizarre personification of revenge. Klara had a love-affair with a man who, when she became pregnant, denied his fatherhood. Misery and shame transformed her character. She has, after many years, become wealthy and returns, transformed also outwardly: she has had aircraft and car accidents and wears artificial limbs instead of arms and legs. The millionairess brings along the coffin for her victim, her former lover and seducer. Money serves her macabre end. She contrives to win over a corrupt society, and 'justice' or better 'retribution' is carried out according to her murderous intentions.

The satire on the venality of human beings is transparent. But there is also the tragic aspect of the victim's fate: there is an inner change in the soul of the village shopkeeper who acknowledges his guilt and attains nobility of character in the hour of death. He is the only really tragic being in the play.

Dürrenmatt's predilection for the fantastic is revealed in his play *Ein Engel kommt nach Babylon* (1953, second version 1957). The lovable girl Kurrubi is sent out of God's hand by an angel on to the earth and given the poorest human creature, i.e. to Nebuchadnezzar (the King of Babylon), who is disguised as a beggar. He then surrenders her to the real beggar Akki, but Kurrubi loves the king and recognizes him later in his royal robes. Yet only as a beggar is he 'real' ('Nur als Bettler bist du wirklich') to her. With Akki she ultimately flees into the desert.

In *Die Physiker* (1962) grotesque and tragic elements merge uncomfortably. Three nuclear physicists suffering from paranoia endeavour to keep their research secret behind the rubber cells of a lunatic asylum, but ironically the Head of the asylum, a psychiatrist, directs a world-trust for the industrial benefit of which she can make, by means of photostat copies and hidden microphones, good use of those scientific discoveries.

One of Dürrenmatt's latest theatrical successes is *Der Meteor* (1965-6), a comedy about a Nobel Prize winner and literary critic who wishes to die. In Ionesco's *Le roi se meurt* (*Exit the King*) (1963), the theme of dying has a different aspect: the king is a kind of Everyman who is frightened of the hour of death, but who must die. However, in the *Meteor* the hero cannot die; moreover, the characters are too eccentric to create a convincing Lazarus drama, particularly the main scene between the death-longing intellectual star and his fourth wife's mother who, once a strumpet, is now assigned to the lavatory staff as toilet-woman and bawd in a large hotel.

Dada; the Theatre of the Absurd

Post-war German writing, in its extreme modern expression, has *one* main purpose: it wants to *disturb* the reader. It throws its searchlight on a close-up, on a mere fragment in its naked nearness, and, at the same time, it removes the object from its conventional or obvious surrounding, e.g. impersonal poems mirror the poet's preoccupation with language and its structure, with the word itself and its potentialities of surprise, modification, modulation, deviation and innovation, parallelism and disharmony which is reflected in the fragmentation of reality ('Zersplitterung der Realität'), full of paradoxes and verbal clownings. Unreason has the function of demolishing complacency, set ideas and established habits, and of regaining spontaneity for man.

Although the Absurd or the Macabre is a characteristic feature of contemporary satire on the stage as well as in prose and poetry (e.g. the grotesque elements in Eugène Ionesco's *Les Rhinocéros*, S. Beckett's *En Attendant Godot*, B. Brecht's *Baal*, F. Dürrenmatt's *Der Besuch der alten Dame*, Jean Genet's *Le Balcon*, E. Jardiel Poncela's *Cuatro corazones con freno*, K. Capek's *RUR*, etc.) it is by no means new. In his penetrating study *The Theatre of the Absurd* (1961), Martin Esslin traces the theatre of the absurd back to the Roman mimes and the Italian harlequinades in the 'Commedia dell' arte', etc.

Grotesques such as Schnitzler's *Der grüne Kakadu* (1899), or particularly Wedekind's cemetery scene in his *Frühlings Erwachen* (1891), Alfred Jarry's *Ubu Roi* (1896) and A. Strindberg's *Advent* (1899) may be considered immediate forerunners of contemporary theatre of the absurd which finds its justification as a welcome stimulant to the curiosity of our modern audience. Sacred taboos have lost their mysterious spell or have been deliberately stripped of their witchcraft. Fernando Arrabal's recent play about *The Emperor of Assyria and the Architect* betrays a predilection for faecal words. They are no less blasphemous than Baal's language. Brecht's *Baal* reminds one of Jarry's *Ubu*. To the depraved and lascivious Baal the world is a huge strumpet. In his talk to his friend Ekart whom he later kills in a fit of jealousy, Baal calls the world the dung discharged from God's bowels ('sie ist das Exkrement des lieben Gottes'), and Ekart cynically adds: from the beloved God who has distinguished Himself by combining man's genitals with man's urethra.

The Dadaists try to establish a rationalistic basis of their fantastic grotesques, i.e. a certain sense in nonsense. Much depends on the audience and on the artistic interpretation of works; cf. the English and the German performances of plays, e.g. by Ionesco, S. Beckett, or Dürrenmatt and P. Weiss.

In the so-called Living Theatre the barrier between art and reality disappears. The audience is drawn into the play in order to participate in the presented events. The aesthetic screen between spectator and actor has been swept aside. In extreme cases, instead of art, we are offered naked unimaginative reality, matter raw and untransformed, or intellectual experiments. This is also evident in the modern music-drama, e.g. the 'electronic opera' by Boris Blacher: *Incidents during Emergency Landing*, in two phases and fourteen situations, world-première in Hamburg, 1966.

As in Surrealism the beautiful blends with the ugly, they are not contrasts any more. The realm of the rational experience mixes with that of unmotivated nonsense. By disrupting our social, conventional reality and accepting a world of senselessness the author of the absurd seeks to approach man's ultimate realities. Thus, in Dostoevsky's sense, unreason is not evil but an assertion that men are free human beings, not lackeys or the keyboards of pianos. Modern artists and writers *want* to offend. They need the effect of surprise. The object, when deprived of its usual function and placed into a new milieu, exhibits its 'pure' form; see p. 262.

In all truly creative work, however, it is the author, playwright or poet rather than the experiment or theory who has a chance of survival.

The product of a word-montage by automation (such as *Love Letters* manufactured by a computer) is but a mechanical combination of interchangeable words and lines, without personal vision, experience or emotion—sensational oddities which, with the improvement of the robot machine, can be split into untold, playful variations. The graphic arrangements of texts so audaciously exploited by Dadaists, such as Hans Arp, Kurt Schwitters, Raoul Hausmann and their imitators, need not be taken for more than an enterprising 'lettrist' venture. In a number of cases, however, the isolation of consonants or vowels is no less amusing or impish than, for instance, an ingenious advertisement of uncrowded beaches. The theme of such playful texts is no object, no man or landscape, but it is the function and 'movens' of the word-material itself, it is a play with its letters: cf. *Movens: Dokumente und Analysen zur Dichtung, bildenden Kunst, Musik, Architektur*, ed. by Franz Mon with Walter Höllerer and Manfred de la Motte, 1960; see p. 20.

The Radio-Play, Hörspiel

The Hörspiel or Radio-Play is another literary genre which came into being under the influence of a most powerful agent of our contemporary technological mass-media. By its very nature it requires short, rapidly moving scenes, a regular change of tension and relaxation. It avoids description or long philosophical ruminations; it is usually based on one clear action which, however, can be effectively blended with another action by way of contrast or parallel, e.g. G. Eich's *Die Mädchen aus Viterbo*. Music often plays the essential part of a curtain-raiser or of an interpreter, e.g. the music accompanying the ride into the forest or the outburst of fire in the radio-play of Goethe's *Novelle*.

The Hörspiel is not just a dramatized version of a story (e.g. *Wuthering Heights*), but it is guided by its own laws of aesthetics. Above all, it is not a drama in the traditional sense with the formal Aristotelean pattern: exposition—peripetia—catastrophe, with its Classical unity of time—space—action and the so-called peepshow ('Guckkasten') arrangement; it is also not a play in a play, but rather an anti-drama, a succession of lyric-epic scenes ('Stationen'), a pattern familiar to the Expressionists and long before them to the Morality Plays; see p. 77. Although there is no unity in the traditional sense the components of a Hörspiel are subtly blended into the events, as for instance in Günter Eich's *Die Mädchen aus Viterbo*, where two parallel actions run simultaneously, the one illustrating or uncannily hinting at the development of the other one.

The Hörspiel has its limitations as well as its amazing possibilities. Its restrictions are inherent in its art: it is not

visibly enacted ('augenlos'), only spoken; it brings the words
without presenting the person who speaks them, and as soon
as the voice is silent the person disappears from our horizon;
it is the voices which act, not the human beings.

But the loss of the spectaculum is outweighed by great
advantages: space and time are unlimited and can be used
by the author with sovereign intention. The end can be put
into the start of the play and the beginning right into the end.
Thus it can favour the analytical method of elucidation of
facts. Some German critics like to differentiate between the
radio-play (Hörspiel) and the radio-tales (Funkerzählung),
but the alleged differences are perhaps not so important as
to establish two literary categories of the same genre. The
radio-play can slow down; it can speed up events; future,
past and present can be presented in parallel sequences. One
of its potentialities lies in the use of satirical scenes. Eich's
Man bittet zu läuten (in his collection of *Vier Hörspiele: In
anderen Sprachen*) presents the grotesquely bloated figure of a
porter of a deaf-and-dumb home, chairman of the Pilz-
freunde. The author's play with words and his negation of
time and space reach with artistic intention dimensions of
caricature.

In the Hörspiel by W. Weyrauch, *Die japanischen Fischer*,
the whispering voices are most suggestive. The noise of a
hatchet in E. Reinacher's *Der Narr mit der Hacke* hints at the
gradual conquest of the mountain of guilt. The disembodi-
ment and anonymity of the voice in the radio-play can
create an atmosphere of intimacy similar to that when a person is shown undressing on the screen. The very intimacy of
the presentation can, by use of direct and indirect speech, by
intensification or penetration of the various dimensions of the
voice, reach the dream regions of the human mind and heart.

According to the *RLL* the first German Hörspiele were
written in 1923–4, and the first to be broadcast in 1925 was
R. Gunold's *Spuk* (*Gespenstersonate nach Motiven von E. T. A.
Hoffmann*); cf. *RLL* and H. Schwitzke: *Standortbestimmung des
Hörspiels* (in *Literatur und Kritik*, June 1966); see also *Drei*

Hörspiele: Das Schiff Esperanza by Fred von Hoerschelmann, *Das Unternehmen der Wega* by Friedrich Dürrenmatt, *Sabeth* by Günter Eich, ed. by L. McGlashan and I. R. Campbell (London, 1966).

The Drama-Documentary and the Theatre of Demonstration; Rolf Hochhuth, Peter Weiss, Heinar Kipphardt, Günter Grass

The drama-documentary, particularly through the bold productions of the modern moralist of the theatre, Erwin Piscator (1893–1966), has become an influential attempt to deal with war and post-war problems, the conflict between the generations seen against current events (see also M. Walser, p. 389), personal and collective guilt, the responsibility of the scientists towards the community, the establishment of post-war communism (see P. Hacks, p. 265) and, above all, the challenge of the mass-age to the individual. The author almost disappears behind the reportage of court-trials and historical documents. But in the face of heinous crimes against humanity such as the extermination of the Jews in gas-chambers, the mere enumeration of horrible atrocities, however strikingly selected, becomes in the end stultifying, whilst the reports in reliable dailies can indeed be dramatically much more effective.

In 1963 Rolf Hochhuth (born 1931) became famous for his controversial play *Der Stellvertreter* (*The Representative*). The author accuses Pius XII for not publicly protesting against Hitler's persecutions and massacre of the Jews. Hochhuth's Pope lacks tragic stature, but Pius XII seems to have been an essentially tragic character, being the political Head of the Catholic Church as well as the Representative and Follower of Christ. In 1937 his Encyclical *Mit brennender Sorge* was directed against racial persecution, and there is also his letter of 1943, 30 April, to Bishop Preysing of Berlin; yet being evidently anxious to prevent worse happenings he refrained from further drastic action, i.e. the excommunication of the enemies of the Church.

In *Neue Deutsche Hefte* (IX/X, 1964) Hannah Arendt courageously asks the question as to what any public protest by the Pope would have resulted in. She also refers to Hitler's Concordat with the Vatican (summer 1933), an agreement that created a political situation between Rome and Germany which prevented direct interference in a number of important matters. Heinz Beckmann, a most judicious critic, calls *The Representative* a pamphlet rather than a drama. A playwright should love his characters, even the criminal, but in the play the Pope, already at the start, seems to be more interested in church finances than in representing God: 'filled, as we are, with burning concern for our factories. Power stations, railway stations, dams, *every undertaking* demands supervision and protection' (*Il Gran Rifiuto*, Act IV, tr. by R. D. MacDonald). Instead of a drama we are mainly given lectures. However, the scene between the Jesuit Riccardo Fontana, the Pope's antagonist who volunteers to join the Jews in a train-load to Auschwitz, and the Ordens-general, and above all the last scene between Riccardo and the satanic camp-doctor, have Shakespearean greatness. The author calls the handsome Selector of Auschwitz the man behind the scenes, with the stamp of absolute evil; cf. Scene Two (Act V) in which the Doctor denies the existence of God:

Has he shown any sign of recognition? . . . God in person turns Mankind on the spit of history. . . . History: dust, altars, suffering, rape where every reputation mocks its victims. Creator, creation, creature, all these three Auschwitz negates. The *Idea* of life is dead . . . accursed be he who creates life. I dispose of life, that is today's humanity—the sole salvation from the future. I am quite serious about it, even in private, out of pity I even buried my own children right from the start —in contraceptives. . . . [l.c.]

Most other figures are puppets, and with the exception of the character of the old Fontana, Riccardo's father, who first demands moderation and later himself takes his son's side against the Pope, there is no fully convincing human figure in the play.

Hochhuth's much-discussed and long play *Soldaten* was performed on the Freie Volksbühne, Berlin, in October 1967. It is an attempt, inspired by the moral indignation of a spiritual disciple of Schiller, to denounce from the stage the inhumanity of modern warfare in general, and in particular, the bombing of the German civilians, and the flagrant disregard of the 1864 Geneva Convention which protects unarmed non-combatants of both sexes and of every age at sea and land. (At that time there was no clause to protect them from aerial attacks.)

There is a play within the play: at Coventry Cathedral the Geneva Convention is to be commemorated; moreover there is a conflict between father (Dorland) and son, an unrepentant bomber pilot—a conflict in some way reminiscent of the father-and-son clash of opposing principles in the *Stellvertreter*. The play *Soldaten* itself has three main acts, with Sir Winston Churchill as the dominating force of events: (*a*) the afterdeck of H.M.S. *Duke of York* (in 1943) on the way to Scapa Flow; (*b*) Churchill's bedroom; (*c*) the park of Chequers with Churchill and the Bishop of Chichester arguing about the bombing of German civilians.

Churchill is in no way described as a cynic but rather a passionate yet ruthless patriot and a man of contradictions. According to Hochhuth's interpretation, Churchill, largely urged by the sinister advice given by people such as Lord Cherwell and others, condoned the murder of General Sikorski in order to prevent Stalin from making a separate peace treaty with Hitler. Whether the assassination of General Sikorski was done with Churchill's connivance or at his direct command, will not be known until the full facts are established, but Hochhuth, notwithstanding a creative author's right of poetic licence, claims to be true to history.

The main flaw in the play seems to be a lack of convincing

cohesion between the various plots and sub-plots. The profusion of its rhetorical and argumentative material needs pruning.

Whilst Hochhuth's literary ancestors are to be sought amongst the German Classic writers, particularly Schiller, those of Peter Weiss (born 1916) are Grabbe, Büchner and Wedekind, without whom *Marat* is almost unthinkable. Weiss is a master of theatrical orchestrations and macabre stage-effects: dumb-shows, harlequinades, play-acting lunatics, miming and singing, ceremonies, debates about revolution and justice, flagellation, etc. Weiss's *Die Verfolgung und Ermordung Jean Paul Marats dargestellt durch die Schauspielgruppe des Hospizes zu Charenton unter der Anleitung des Herrn de Sade*, was first performed in 1964. This gruesome display of mental derangement has as its background a highly topical theme: individualism (de Sade) against collectivism (Marat), *or* West versus East, the decadence of extreme egoism against the fanatical puritanism of the revolutionary. Parallels between the 1810s and the 1960s, Napoleon's régime and West German 'Restauration' are evident. The lack of dramatic action is made up by discussion of ideas between de Sade and Marat.

Peter Weiss's *Ermittlung* (*The Investigation*) (1965) stirred the emotions of all who saw or listened to it. A reading, given by the Royal Shakespeare Company, was prepared by Peter Brook and David Jones and recorded at the Aldwych Theatre in October 1965. This documentary presentation of a series of carefully selected extracts from the Auschwitz trial, 1965, is called 'an oratorio in eleven cantos'. There are eighteen accused persons and nine anonymous witnesses, one judge, one defending counsel and one prosecutor. The above-mentioned characteristic features of the drama-documentary are poignantly revealed in Weiss's *Ermittlung* and also in *Gesang vom lusitanischen Popanz* (1967) (a parallel to events in Vietnam). His *Vietnam Discourse* (1968) covers the vast period from 500 B.C. to A.D. 1964; it is, in spite of some effective scenes, rather an historical panorama than a theatrical success.

In der Sache J. Robert Oppenheimer (1964) (*The Case of J. Robert Oppenheimer*) by Heinar Kipphardt is a documentary reconstruction of the Oppenheimer trial in the days of McCarthyism in 1954; he, the 'father of the atom-bomb', was then considered a security risk and had to defend himself before the Security Committee of the United States Atomic Energy Commission against the charge of sabotaging the production of the hydrogen bomb. Here, as in other cases, the drama-documentary lends itself better to a television production than a stage performance. H. Kipphardt also wrote the documentary reportage *The Joel Brand Story* (1965), in which Brand, a Hungarian Jew, tries at Eichmann's suggestion to barter away the lives of a million Jews for ten thousand brand-new lorries. Joel Brand's mission fails, as Lord Moyne refuses to negotiate with mass-murderers, and as there is no room for the million of Jewish refugees. Brand finally says: If there is no room on this planet there is nothing left for us except to go into the gas-chambers.

Dokumentarstücke are also Tankred Dorst's *Große Schmährede an der Stadtmauer*, 1961, a play clearly influenced by B. Brecht, and Hans Günter Michelsen's *Helm*, 1965, a one-act drama about war-guilt: five old soldiers are guests in Helm's forest; Michelsen leaves the question open whether Helm takes his revenge on those for whom he once had to cook and who had done harm to him.

Günter Grass's international fame rests on his prose and poetry (see p. 51) but he also, though less successfully so far, turned to the documentary stage. His drama *Die Plebeier proben den Aufstand* (*The Plebeians Rehearse the Revolt*) (1966), on the workers' uprising and on Bertolt Brecht, who at the time of the revolt (17 June 1953) was working in East Berlin, was received with boos and applause. Grass, who does not accuse an author of plagiarism, if this (as in Shakes-

peare's case) is done with originality, and who declares that
'it is not easy to steal, and it is even more difficult to adapt',
criticizes Brecht's *Coriolan*. The very theme of Grass's
drama with the sub-title: 'a German tragedy', is directed
against Brecht, the revolutionary artist, who uses the workers
as objects for his artistic presentation of the *Coriolanus* adaptation, and who fails in his attitude to the workers' revolution.
We are not shown the scenes of their uprising, but the
assistants to 'Der Chef': Litthenner and Podulla, appear (in
Act IV, 2 ff.) with material from their observation of the
street-fighting. Podulla has taken an active part against the
Russian tanks. The Director ('Der Chef') interrupts himself
as he is about to express sympathy for the defeated workers,
and decides not to go on with *Coriolan*; he foresees the
future: 17 June will become a public holiday when people
go to the countryside: 'Satt ins Grüne ziehen seh ich im
Westen ein Volk.' But the Chef adds to this: 'Was übrig
bleibt: leer-gefeierte Flaschen, Butterbrotpapier, Bierleichen
und richtige Leichen; denn an Feiertagen fordert der
Verkehr ein Übersoll an Opfern.—Hier jedoch werden die
Zuchthäuser nach elf, zwölf Jahren die Wrackteile dieses
Aufstandes ausspeien. Die Anklage wird umhergehen. . . .'

III

PROSE FICTION. SOME
OUTSTANDING GERMAN NOVELS

The novel is a form of imaginative communication from an individual author to unknown readers who absorb the world he creates each in their own isolation; it is a vehicle of individualism, coming into effective existence with the Renaissance and the invention of printing and replacing the epic. Arno Schirokauer[1] has traced the development of the genre from this starting-point until he sees it attaining a peak of vitality and originality with the individualism of the nineteenth century, and from thence moving into the age of mass-civilization and technology, where psychology and sociology may have implications not directly realized by novelists of an earlier generation. With James Joyce and Thomas Mann the critic sees the serious novel moving from the individual to the typical-mythical, returning to the primitive epic but in a veiled, self-conscious form. At the same time the previously dominating rôle of the printing-press is yielding to the new media of screen and microphone. Thus the rise and fall of the novel might be envisaged as a phase of civilization now approaching its end. The assumption of 'late periods' will, however, be based on the acceptance of a cyclic view of civilizations which as Werner Betz has said[2] 'has up to now never really been proved inductively, it has only been inferred deductively here and there'. Whether there has been,

[1] Arno Schirokauer, 'Bedeutungswandel des Romans'. In: *Zur Poetik des Romans*, ed. Volker Klotz. Wissenschaftliche Buchgesellschaft, Darmstadt, 1965.
[2] Werner Betz, ' "Spätzeiten" in der Geschichte der deutschen Sprache'. In: *Spätzeiten und Spätzeitlichkeit*, ed. Werner Kohlschmidt, Francke Verlag, Berne and Munich, 1962, p. 147.

or is, in the twentieth century a crisis of the novel, clearly some novelists have been affected as if there were such a crisis; others nevertheless may have been less preoccupied by this current of thought, or may have absorbed something of it into a more traditional approach.

The modern novel offers a 'bright and confusing picture', and it will be well to avoid normative generalizations and not to expect to arrive at a conception of an 'ideal' novel, as Horst Oppel[1] indicates. Some points that he makes in this context are that modern man resigns himself to living without real contact with the world at large; that language is not in the service of communication, but has become a means to fragmentary self-knowledge. Where purpose has given way to chance, novels may have abrupt beginnings or open endings; specific episodes may be illuminated, while much else is left in obscurity. If modern literature resigns itself not to giving an interpretation of life, is it worth while spending time reading it? It may be that some modern German novelists feel themselves to be more involved in a crisis of their genre than do their English counterparts; Horst Oppel quotes John Wain here: 'I, and most of my contemporaries, simply took it for granted that any writer just beginning his life's work was free to choose whether to use the already matured "experimental" forms, or go back to the traditional.'

For some critics of the novel, the relationship of the narrator to his material is of considerable importance, and a shift of emphasis has been noted in the course of the present century. In place of the omniscient narrator who intervenes as he pleases and acts as present mediator between the story that is being told in the past tense and the reader, there may be a preference for first-person narrative or for a consistent use of 'points of view', third person narrative where the reader identifies himself with the perspective of one or more of the protagonists, or for narrative presentation aiming at an

[1] *Der moderne englische Roman*, ed. Horst Oppel. Erich Schmidt Verlag, Berlin, 1965, pp. 7–14.

objectivity comparable to that of drama. Franz K. Stanzel[1] has stated that 'expressed in the most general terms, the aim of the tendency of the more recent novel which has become ever more strongly marked since James, Proust and Joyce is the striving towards an illusion of a comprehensive autonomy of the depicted world, towards the fiction of its independence of the author or of the narrator whom he might insert'. The less the reader is aware of the presence of an author or narrator directing and commenting on the fictional characters, the more he will be convinced of the independent stature of these figures. Other critics have championed the right of the narrator to intervene as he pleases and have asserted vigorously that to reject or to restrict the narrator's function as a matter of principle would deprive the novel of its most significant aspect.[2]

The twentieth century novel has also been characterized with regard to its conception of realism. Traditionally the realistic novel takes place within a specific and measurable period of time and aims at being a 'true reflection' of reality. Modern German authors tend to move away from the direct portrayal of outward realism from a social-moral point of view in favour of an inward, subjective approach which is more tentative and more differentiating. As Roy Pascal puts it:

> The modern author knows that the film can outdo him in visual objectivity, the psychological and sociological sciences in thoroughness, and the documentary in exactitude. Thus this more recent realism is distinguished by selection and laconism, the metaphors repeatedly, if inconspicuously refer to the subjective, to the inner meaning. It is not so much the outer world that is discovered and conquered, as with Balzac, as rather the inner.[3]

---

[1] Franz K. Stanzel, 'Thomas Hardy: *Tess of the D'Urbervilles*'. In: Horst Oppel, op. cit., p. 34. See also Franz K. Stanzel, 'Die Erzählsituation und das epische Präteritum' and 'Episches Präteritum, erlebte Rede, historisches Präsens'. In: Volker Klotz, op. cit.

[2] Käthe Friedemann, 'Die Rolle des Erzählers in der Epik' and Wolfgang Kayser, 'Wer erzählt den Roman?' In: Volker Klotz, op. cit.

[3] Roy Pascal, 'Fortklang und Nachklang des Realismus im Roman'. In: Werner Kohlschmidt, op. cit.

The relationships between things and people, places and times in the outer world can no longer be taken for granted. The subjective and reflective factors interpose themselves, and there is much greater uncertainty as to the sense and coherence of what is outwardly apprehended.

With *Buddenbrooks* Thomas Mann created a work that to a great extent belonged to the nineteenth century tradition in its realism and narrative methods. *Doktor Faustus* too has its origins in a similar background, and the narrator's vision ranges over a half-century of German history. From immediate realism, however, the reader's attention is directed towards the mythical and typical; whereas the Buddenbrooks family are the Buddenbrooks family, Adrian Leverkühn is not only himself but also Faust, apart from other figures and themes into which he is merged. While he was working on *Doktor Faustus* Thomas Mann had occasion to glance back on his earlier work. In a letter of 19 April 1945 he notes that it sometimes almost seems as if *Tonio Kröger* were the work of his own which he himself liked best. He describes (16 Jan. 1944) how Franz Werfel, while recently ill, had re-read *Buddenbrooks* and referred to it as an 'indestructible masterpiece'; he wonders whether, after the successful creation of felicitous youthful works, it may not be a question of living the rest of one's life 'in a tolerably worthy way', although one may remain 'the man of that first work'. His thoughts look forward to the theme of a 'Künstler-Novelle' (in a letter of 21 Feb. 1942), 'which will perhaps become my most daring and uncanny work'. A little more than a year later he is reminded that the Faust theme had occurred to him in 1901 as one that might be suitable for his pen. It was to become a major preoccupation until its completion could be announced on 29 January 1947, and its unique importance for the author is revealed in the subsequent publication of a commentary on its genesis, *Die Entstehung des Doktor Faustus*, 'the novel of a novel'. The work is one which he takes most seriously and which has made greater emotional demands on its author than any earlier one: 'It is a life-story of almost culpable relentlessness, a peculiar kind of transferred auto-biography, a work which has cost me much and has preyed upon me more than any earlier one . . .' (12 Dec. 1947).

The events in the life of the composer Adrian Leverkühn are narrated by his friend and 'famulus' Serenus Zeitblom. As he traces the musician's biography from his birth in 1885 to his collapse in 1930 and death ten years later, the narrator incidentally recounts the main events in his own life and his reactions to major happenings in German history. Adrian's life has given Serenus Zeitblom's own life its essential content, as he comments while briefly describing the funeral. For Zeitblom the composition of his account is essentially to be seen in the context of the time taken by it, from 1943 to 1945, and his impressions of events affecting Germany during that period are intercalated with his interpretation of Adrian Leverkühn's life and lifetime.

Zeitblom introduces himself as someone who likes to be considered as a successor to the German humanists, and who finds no difficulty in reconciling this outlook with his Catholic origins. He sees his classical training as eminently suitable in his vocation as an educationalist, though he distrusts the daemonic element in Greek civilization as in other spheres. He has retired early from school teaching in order to dissociate himself from the policies of the state, but it is possible that after the end of the war, and of his work on his friend's biography, he may return to pedagogic activity. He loved Adrian Leverkühn, who was two years his junior, all through his life, hardly expecting this affection to be re-turned. Leverkühn's moods of humour are shared by Rüdiger Schildknapp, but Zeitblom describes himself as no great friend of laughter, as being made unsuited to it by a certain dryness and stiffness in his temperament, and as being always too serious and tense in his care for his friend to be able to share these relaxed moods. As a student Zeitblom reacts against theological tendencies at Halle; he would accept a free, subjective religiosity, while having little patience with dogmatic systematization. He is sceptical about the cult of nature which is welcomed by many of his fellow-students. He is glad to have been uninvolved in his friend's decision to give up theology for music; he prefers not to have had direct responsibility for so momentous a decision, just as the two friends never talk about sex, except in a literary, impersonal context. Conversation, he tells the reader, is not his strong point, though he is not a bad speaker and teacher. He has a ready and warm sympathy for anyone who deviates from conventional normality; Rudi Schwerdtfeger is surprised to hear Zeitblom defend Ludwig II of Bavaria with sensitive insight as a maligned and misunderstood ruler. Zeitblom's married life has been happy and unproblematic, though he is grieved that his sons do not share his dislike of National Socialism. In 1914 the humanist shares for a while in German patriotic aspirations, until the end of the war convinces him that an age has now finally passed, that of 'middle-class humanism'. Zeitblom inclines towards revolutionary Russia in 1919, and then becomes a supporter of the new republic and of democracy, especially in view of the dangerous potentialities which he sees in the opinions of the Kridwiß circle. The reader sees events mostly from Zeitblom's point of view, and the circumlocutions and didactic interpolations are expressive of his personality. He comments sometimes on his own narrative method, that he is not writing a novel, nor claiming a novelist's traditional omniscience, and that he need feel constrained by no narrative conventions (as for instance when speaking of the 'invisible' Fran von Tolna, Adrian's patroness whom neither he nor Zeitblom ever meets). Clearly, very much of the atmosphere of *Doktor Faustus* depends on the person of the narrator, who is both a serious representation of the author's attitude, or one important aspect of it, and a figure devised to introduce an element of contrast, of serenity and playfulness. These two aspects of Serenus Zeitblom's rôle are mentioned by Mann in a letter of 18/21 June 1943 (the account is given 'through the medium of a narrator of completely rational-humanist attitude') and on 8 June 1945 the narrator is referred to as a 'pure, loving, humane soul'. Zeitblom's political outlook corresponds 'fairly closely to the stations of my own "development" ' (24 Dec. 1947).

Adrian Leverkühn is introduced by his friend as indifferent, lonely and cold in his personal relations. His approach to the study of theology is motivated by pride, and is linked with the Lutheran background of his parents' farm and of Kaisersaschern. Grotesque, superstitious remnants of the latter Middle Ages in this town are a prelude to the teaching which Adrian has in Halle from Kumpf, with his sixteenth century mannerisms and preoccupation with the devil, and from Schleppfuß' co-ordinations of evil, magic and woman. Adrian's life is, however, from early stages to be directed towards music. His mother's latent musical talent and the singing of canons with the maid Hanne anticipate the full revelation of music which he experiences when his uncle in Kaisersaschern provides him with tuition from Wendell Kretzschmar. The latter's lecture on Beethoven's piano sonata opus 111 is the first detailed musical analysis which the novel presents, and although Adrian is shown in his reactions to much from the corpus of musical tradition, the analogy with Beethoven is pursued most closely. 'Harmonic subjectivity, polyphonic objectivity' are brought into a new relationship in Beethoven's later works; opus 111 is the farewell to the sonata form. In his last year at school too, Adrian is introduced to Shakespeare by Kretschmar:

> Shakespeare and Beethoven together formed an all-illuminating dual star in his intellectual firmament, and he greatly loved to point out to his pupil strange relationships and correspondences in the creative principles and methods of the two giants . . .

For Adrian at this period the overture 'Leonora No. 3' is 'almost the definition of God'. When he subsequently gives up theology in order to study music at Leipzig, Adrian feels

a 'secret terror' that he may be betraying the divine. Kretschmar has been the decisive influence here, and Zeitblom
is aware of the tension between Adrian's mother and his
music-teacher. Elsbeth Leverkühn loses her son to music,
only to regain him after the collapse of his personality in
1930. Kretschmar has no misgivings about persuading Adrian
to make the all-important decision, though subsequently he
has little part to play in the novel, and his links with his pupil
quickly become more tenuous. From the fateful encounter
with the prostitute Hetaera Esmeralda on the day of his
arrival in Leipzig, the development of Adrian's own musical
style will render the teaching of Kretschmar superfluous.
When Leverkühn and Zeitblom meet again in Leipzig, they
go together to hear a performance of Beethoven's quartet
opus 132. The relationship of words to music, of Shakespeare
to Beethoven, preoccupies Adrian for much of his creative
life. The pact-scene in Italy makes him feel the venereal
infection as a diabolical condition, a promise of heightened
ecstasy and intensified depression; disease opens the way to
irony, and Adrian will not return to the ways of salvation
because of his pride and fear of the mediocre, nor is he to
know a love that warms. If his music is to be genuinely
creative, it must penetrate beyond the present-day crisis of
the art; the diminished seventh is right, at the beginning of
opus 111, but it is impossible for Leverkühn. The nineteen
further years of the composer's creative life are spent at the
Schweigestill farm south of Munich, a domestic setting that is
close to that of his childhood. Adrian lives increasingly in
retirement from the world, but the landscape of the novel
widens through the added social background and the
characterization of the Munich circles shortly before 1914
and during the years immediately after 1918, with which
Leverkühn and Zeitblom are connected. The two major
episodes of Adrian's efforts to enter into a closer human
relationship—his wooing of Marie Godeau and his affection
for his five-year-old nephew Nepomuk Schneidewein—are
shown in their tragic consequences with Thomas Mann's

finest narrative skill. The death of Nepomuk is expressed by
Adrian in moving terms. The good and the noble are not to
be; he wishes to 'take back' Beethoven's ninth symphony.
The next day he says goodbye to Zeitblom, quoting Pros-
pero's leave-taking from Ariel:

> Then to the elements
> Be free, and fare thou well!

Zeitblom finds this parting less discouraging than the greet-
ing he had received the day before. Adrian's final composition, the choral and orchestral 'D. Fausti Weheklag', is
designed as the lament which is to take back the 'Ode to
Joy'. But just as in the pact-scene Adrian had indicated that
complete despair might be close to salvation, his friend finds
hope in the ending of the cantata:

> No this sombre musical work admits to the end of no consola-
> tion, reconciliation or transfiguration. But what if there cor-
> responded to the artistic paradox that the expression—the
> expression of lament—is born from the structure of the whole,
> the religious paradox that from the depths of wickedness, even
> if only as the gentlest question, hope would arise? It would be
> hope beyond hopelessness, the transcendence of despair—not
> the betrayal of it, but the miracle that goes beyond faith.

Adrian evokes pity and sympathy; if he has something cold
and inhuman about him, Mann writes (12 Dec. 1947), he
also has much quality of self-sacrifice. Zeitblom is surprised
to hear his friend asserting that art must find its way to the
people, and in his comment disagrees with his friend's words:

> —The whole mood of art will change, believe me, and in fact
> into what is more cheerful and modest—it is unavoidable, and
> it is fortunate. It will lose much melancholy ambition and
> gain a new innocence, indeed harmlessness. The future will see
> art, and art will see itself, as servant of a community which will
> embrace much more than educational development and will
> not so much possess culture as be culture.

If Zeitblom is surprised to hear these opinions from his friend, and in his own reflections on the independence of art from society seems to be commenting for his author, Mann uses the identical words, speaking for himself, in a letter of 28 January 1946. And so the author can identify himself, if he chooses, both with the composer and with his friend. In *Die Entstehung des Doktor Faustus* he writes of his being as much in love with Adrian as was Serenus, and more so than with any other character whom he had created. He recognizes that the minor characters in the novel might well be rounded and individualized, but that the two principals could not be presented in palpable form—they would otherwise give away the secret of their identity one with another. Adrian and Serenus have to be lifted out of the realistic setting, where most of the other characters are at home, in order to be shown in the multiple, general rôles the author expects of them.

Thomas Mann's elder brother Heinrich satirized aspects of German social life in imperial Germany with *Im Schlaraffenland* (1900), *Professor Unrat* (1905) and *Der Untertan* (1918). It was in his exile in France during the nineteen-thirties that he completed a historical novel which reflects his humane aspirations in a warm evaluation of a French monarch and which combines narrative vigour with mellow maturity. In a letter of 10 September, 1938, Heinrich Mann says of his *Henri Quatre*: 'My first intention to write it goes back ten years. I brought the preliminary studies and first pages here from Berlin. This was the content of my whole time of emigration until now.' The two volumes of this work show Henri both as a private and a representative figure, closely linked with the people of his time. Apart from a few excursions outside, to the court of Queen Elizabeth of England for instance, the novel is set within the borders of France. Here there are two environments, the menacing complexity of court and city life in Paris, and the easier and more open atmosphere of the rest of the country where Henri can feel more truly free. It is in Paris that he loses the last carefree mood of childhood and youth. His mother's death there ominously foreshadows the trapped, humiliated period of his captivity there; his reception at the Louvre, his marriage with Margot of Valois and the shock of the massacre of Saint Bartholomew form a first major crisis in the narrative. After the distress and frustration that follow, Henri's escape and journey south herald the long period of the gradual establishment of his authority and power, and although it has its difficulties, this time of numerous episodes and skirmishes builds up hopefully to Henri's becoming king, shortly after the defeat of the Spanish Armada and the death of Catherine de Medici. The assumption of monarchy brings Paris back as the central background of the second volume, and renews Henri's awareness that he is exposed to enemies. In this later section of the work the culminating period is one of happiness and fulfilment, after the Edict of Toleration and before the death of Gabriele d'Estrées. The final years after the fateful reunion with the Medici family through Henri's marriage to Marie see his court returning to the atmosphere of violence and intrigue that had darkened it during his early years.

Heinrich Mann shapes his mass of material by making full use of variety and movement. Political negotiation and intrigue alternate with scenes of military action, and both are offset by accounts of the succession of love-affairs, from the youthful idyll with Fleurette to the final preoccupation with Charlotte de Montmorency. With the carefree manner of Henri's private life, as presented here, is contrasted the formality of ceremonious scenes, such as the official meeting between Henri and his future brother-in-law, Charles IX, in the garden of the Louvre, or the first homage paid to Henri as King of France by the ambassadors from the Republic of Venice, or the church drama of the attempt on his life instigated by Margot, or the court assembly to bid farewell to colonists who are leaving for the New World (with the presence of Rubens to catch the occasion in painting). Some important figures can only occupy the forefront for a limited period: Henri's mother and Admiral Coligny, Charles IX, and in the later years his mistress Gabriele d'Estrées and his minister Rosny. But the continuity of human ties is emphasized. After his mother's death, something of her rôle as personal guide and advocate of Huguenot faith passes to Henri's sister Catherine. Margot of Valois, at the time of her marriage to Henri, is a temptation and a refuge to him, inevitably associated with the revulsion caused by Saint Bartholomew's night.

But she returns to Paris at the age of fifty-three, and is allowed to take part in court life, forgiven and no longer capable of harming her former husband. Henri's repeated reliance on his attendant d'Armagnac and on the friendship of Agrippa d'Aubigné are, however, a reassurance when many companions and advisers are indifferent if not hostile to his well-being.

The novel tells its story in chronological sequence, but the author is seldom occupied only with the moment as it passes, being conscious of the need to link this with his hero's life as a whole, by drawing the reader's attention to what has gone and what is to come. The narrator shares his omniscience with the reader, who is invited to wonder too at the changes that have been affected, or are going to be affected, by time. When Henri enters Paris and makes his way through its deserted streets at the age of eighteen, we are told that he will be forty by the time he has re-entered it as king. If Henri fails to anticipate the coming massacre, the reader is granted the author's confidence here, as elsewhere, in particular in the case of Gabriele's death and that of himself. Popular omens and prophecies add to these effects. A historical novel must usually assume that the reader is aware to some extent of the events' outcome.

Henri is a man apart and an ideal figure, but portrayed with consistent warmth by the author. His sense of humour does not win him the respect of others as a child, and is to be regarded as equivocal by those around him until his death. He learns early in life to live in a society where there are divided loyalties with regard to religious faith, and he does not share the rigid approach of Coligny to these matters. His dislike of Habsburg power is partly religious in origin, partly a matter of French nationalism. Insouciance may be an instinctive reaction, it may be a mask when he has to bide his time after the night of Saint Bartholomew, or it may be a refusal to accept the possibility of evil; he would prefer to be uncertain as to whether his mother was poisoned or died naturally: 'But too much hate causes weakness.' Later, as king, his dislike of executions causes discontent among the Paris crowd. Humour can be twisted into the grotesque; Henri has to assume a clown's rôle and to tolerate the association with the dwarf Bertha at one time in his youth, only to find that his marriage with Marie is to bring him the proximity of her unlovely companion Leonora. Throughout his adult life, the justified fear of assassination haunts him, and is one motive for his change of faith as king.

On one occasion his sister says to him: 'Always only your own advantage. . . . The happiness of others is something you entirely forget, and yet you are good, people say humane. Unfortunately also forgetful.' Henri's life has its necessary continuity, with its persistent motifs, but it is one of mobility and change too, and these are illustrated in his relationships to women and to the churches. When his Protestants speak of his betrayal, he meditates on the eve of assuming Catholicism when he is king, that he is following life and being obedient to reason. He says to Parliament:

> I have always sought only my own salvation and constantly prayed to the Divine Majesty that I might be permitted to find it. The Divine Majesty led me to understand through the inhuman horrors that were perpetrated by others in Paris, though I myself had to accept responsibility for them, that my salvation would be identical with the provision of right, and this is the most complete form to me of the humane.

Henri becomes the advocate of moderation and reason as means to the attainment of human happiness and goodness;

Montaigne's intellectual guidance finds understanding response in the king's mind.

> He [Montaigne] wished to see whether a moderate, sceptically minded outlook could successfully resist the excesses of unreason which threaten it everywhere. For human nature continuously wastes itself in these, as history teaches and classical writers confirm. The human race shows itself usually in the shape of deluded men who only rage and cannot perceive. The rare mortal to whom the Lord of the Heavens has granted a healthy soul must above all conceal it with cunning from the violent sick; otherwise he will not go far.

Henri's tolerance and good will constantly encounter a type of person who reacts with violence and hatred to these qualities:

> His nature stays serene and moderate above its own abysses. But he knows there is one type of man who will not have this, and it is precisely such a type that he is to meet everywhere, until the end. They are not Protestants, Catholics, Spaniards or Frenchmen. They are a type of man; they want dark violence and earth's heaviness, they love excesses or horror and impure ecstasy. They will be his eternal opponents, but he is, once and for all, the ambassador of reason and human happiness.

His popularity with the people and his affection for his children are consistent with the warm benevolence of his nature, which is contrasted to the calculating coldness of many of his courtiers. Heinrich Mann shows him as an ideal monarch, a bringer of some light to an age that is largely uncomprehending or hostile, a model also for twentieth century rulers, and yet complex and fully human.

Like the brothers Mann, Hermann Hesse was a widely known and established novelist for the greater part of his life, from the turn of the century until the period after the Second World War. His work took on a less traditional note after

1918, *Der Steppenwolf* (1927) being his most experimental, contemporary-style novel. While sharing Heinrich Mann's opposition to the German government's approach to the War of 1914–18 and always distancing himself from nationalism, Hesse had a lyrically traditional and subjective style which distinguished him from the sharper critical and satirical tones of the Manns. He too wrote as one of his later works a substantial novel that epitomizes much that is characteristic of his outlook and writing, and that, like *Doktor Faustus*, looks back on an intellectual culture that is threatened. *Das Glasperlenspiel* (*The Game of Glass Beads*) sums up various aspects of cultural and artistic developments up to the twentieth century and puts them in the context of a future world. Some three hundred years later than his own time Hesse imagines the existence of Castalia, a community dedicated to the conservation and encouragement of intellectual and artistic aspirations, apart from but tolerated and supported by the state. The game of glass beads, 'a kind of world language of intellectuals', owes its unique position to a fruitful combination involving music and mathematics. As an educational community, Castalia lays emphasis on links with tradition. The spirit of music which the central character, Josef Knecht, regards as definitive is that of classical music between 1500 and 1800:

> The gesture of classical music means knowledge of mankind's tragedy, acceptance of human fate, courage, serenity! Whether this is the grace of a minuet by Handel or Couperin, or sensuality sublimated to a delicate gesture, as with many of the Italians or Mozart, or the quiet, resigned readiness for death as with Bach, there is always here a defiance, a bravery in the face of death, a chivalry and a sound of more than human laughter, of immortal joyfulness. This is how it is to sound too in our games of glass beads, and in our whole lives, acts and sufferings.

Whereas Thomas Mann's Adrian Leverkühn is tragically and isolatedly concerned with questioning the possibilities of music after the collapse of the classical tradition, Josef Knecht has accepted a tradition which integrates the essence of the classical tradition in music into the aesthetic-intellectual fulfilment of the Castalian order. He sees music as the inheritance of the ancient world and of Christianity, as the expression of a spirit of serene and courageous piety; the practice of contemplation has been incorporated into the community of Castalia and informs its life.

The central and most extended section of the novel is a description of what is known of the life of Josef Knecht, as seen through the eyes of a subsequent generation. At the age of twelve or thirteen Knecht's ability leads to his selection, by the old Music-master, for training at one of the élite-schools; their violin-playing together on the occasion of the interview is remembered by Knecht as a form of 'calling'. Knecht's development as a youth in the monastic modesty of the 'Pedagogic Province' (Hesse refers specifically to Goethe, and thus to the educational interests of *Wilhelm Meisters Wanderjahre*) is largely free from problems. Later he can recall the precious quality of the association of early spring with Schubert's harmony; it is his Music-master who teaches him meditation. But he has misgivings about the nature of the Castalian community that has to exclude people from itself at various initial stages; and he is concerned about the nature of history, asking whether it is to be interpreted as development and progress, or as decline and meaninglessness. His friendly arguments with Plinio Designori, a contemporary of his with a sceptical attitude to the function of Castalia within the whole of society and to the exaltation of an academic-contemplative way of life, lead to a crisis which Knecht overcomes with the help of the old Music-master. Subsequently Knecht's development goes from strength to strength. He makes a significant contribution to the relationship between Castalia and the Benedictine order at Mariafels, where Pater Jakobus influences him, in particular by his treatment of the themes of politics and history. 'To study history means yielding to chaos and yet retaining faith in order and meaning.' When he is not quite forty years old Knecht becomes 'magister ludi' and thus representative and administrative head of the Order. It seems as if the misgivings about Castalian life are to disappear in the acceptance of immediate responsibilities. If his friend Fritz Tegularius indicates in his sensitive personality some problematic aspects of the Order's position, Knecht can see his old Music-master as his principal inspiration, as a saint and example of a fulfilled life. Knecht becomes concerned that the Order is becoming atrophied through separation from the everyday world. While Tegularius dismisses history as an unenlightening sequence of conflicts, Knecht tells him that history's preoccupation with reality may give it a priority over the abstractions of the Game. Renewed contact with Designori leads to the crisis of Knecht's withdrawal from the Order, his return to the outside world as tutor to Designori's son and the abrupt termination of his life by drowning.

Already as a youth Knecht had received from the Music-master the advice that he should not seek a system of teaching that would be absolute and complete, but the perfecting of his own personality. His life in the Order was one of service to a community; here he did not find fulfilment, but hoped that his new, free life would allow him to serve, though in a form of commitment that was entirely his own. If Goethe's Wilhelm Meister becomes a member of a collective organization in the service of which he gives up his search for breadth of personality, Hesse's Josef Knecht finds himself impelled to sever connexions with a community to which he has been closely attached for most of his life in order to look for what may well be a much narrower sphere of activity, but one that is more essentially the expression of his own individuality. Josef Knecht had attained an exemplary place in an apparently ideal community, but sensing its potential sterility and decay had broken abruptly from it. His death is, however, not in vain; it will inspire Designori's son and contribute to the subsequent revitalization of Castalia's purpose.

Perhaps we may think here in terms of Hegel's dialectic. The first appendix to the central narrative, which consists of poems written by Knecht in his youth, includes the lyric 'Stufen', which he discusses with Tegularius before finally taking leave from his friend. The stages of life, in an individual and a civilization, express the necessity for change and for accepting it as a challenge to higher development.

> Der Weltgeist will nicht fesseln uns und engen,
> Es will uns Stuf' um Stufe heben, weiten.

Even death may be an introduction to renewal in fresh spheres:

> Des Lebens Ruf an uns wird niemals enden . . .
> Wohlan denn, Herz, nimm Abschied und gesunde!

As a young man Knecht wrote three fictitious autobiographies, as one of the regular exercises required of students. The narrator regards these as 'perhaps the most valuable part of our book'. They demonstrate Josef Knecht's dilemma as to his form of service in different periods of history; as 'rainmaker' in a primitive tribe, as a Christian ascetic in the desert and as ruler in an Indian kingdom, his personality has to contend with the problem of the right conduct of an individual whose way of life separates him from the majority of mankind. A further fictitious autobiography, placed in the world of eighteenth century Swabian Pietism, we are told, was planned but not written. The relationship of master to pupil is the major formative influence in these autobiographies. As a boy Knecht admires the rainmaker Turu and succeeds him in his office. For the Indian Dasa the childhood encounter with the meditating Yogin remains fundamental throughout his life; after the failure of his period as a worldly ruler, his final vision is of a return to the Yogin who at last accepts him as his pupil. The anchorite Josef feels the urge to give up the authority he has acquired as a counsellor to the unfortunate and become the servant of a fellow-priest. The educational relationship is given a directly religious connotation in all three autobiographies. In the central narrative the career of Josef Knecht in Castalia runs a course that is more protected and impersonal than the lives of the protagonists of the autobiographies. The continuity of relationship between pupil and teacher is maintained; as Knecht receives inspiration from the Music-master, so he can be of individual guidance to Designori's son. If it is accepted that the position of teacher and priest is problematic at all times because it involves an encounter between an individual and a group who are to receive, then it may seem as if the hierarchical community of Castalia may have overcome something of this difficulty; but perhaps Castalia has lost educative and mediating urgency, and Knecht therefore leaves the community in favour of a return to a simpler, more primitive form of teaching.

Hesse's central narrative proceeds at a leisurely pace and moves in a world where violence and sensual passions play little or no part. It does not trouble itself with colourful sequences of quick action, with witty repartee nor with a realism that is either sharp or homely. It is quiet and nearly always untopical, and convinced of the worthwhileness of the preservation of cultural traditions, looking as it does towards serenity and positive meaning as realizable in the individual's life.

While not offering conscious innovations in language and style, Kafka's work represents a break-away from the more usual sense of space, time and character that are associated with the nineteenth century realists, or with Thomas and Heinrich Mann and Hesse. The reader can no longer feel at home and secure in Kafka's world, as he might well have done in that of the traditional realists. Realism, based on Prague or the nearby countryside, is subordinated to a unique combination of anxiety and vision, of flight and quest, with an all-encompassing intimation of myth that is not made explicit. A tale such as *Die Verwandlung* and the novel-torsos take the reader into an imaginative world that is of dreamlike quality, though with its own sombre strength, paradoxical but full of aspiration. Kafka's work can be associated in its time and in its sympathies with the Expressionist movement, but the extent of its fascination has transcended any such bounds, and it has been widely accepted as a rare embodiment of twentieth century mood.

K., the central figure of Kafka's *Das Schloß*, tells Olga towards the end of chapter fourteen that 'My highest, in fact my only wish is to put into order my affairs with the officials.' The events of the novel are seen mainly from his point of view, while in the conversations other personages give their individual interpretations of the situations he and they have found themselves in. A comprehensive solution of the problems involved in the relations of the characters to each other and to the community around them would be difficult to work out, and the interpretation of all that may be implied from the narrative is more elusive still. In different dialogues K. expresses varying opinions about himself and other characters. It is not easy to be sure that we are intended to take sides with K. against the officials of the castle or the villagers. For the other figures come to life and lay claim to the reader's sympathies, independently of their relationship to K., while his own attitude changes in the course of the novel.

A man apparently in his thirties, K. arrives at the Brücken-hof, the village inn, after a long and difficult journey that has lasted a number of days and that has been an excessive strain to him. He refers to sacrifices that he has made in order to come here. From a distance the castle corresponds on the whole to his expectations, as he sees it on the morning after his arrival, but on coming closer he is disappointed, and compares its tower unfavourably with the church-tower of his old home-town. A little later he recalls how as a boy he once succeeded in climbing a high wall encircling the church and its graveyard at home; this achievement gave him confidence that seemed as if it might support him for a lifetime. Indeed it supports him now as he struggles in the snow.

His first need when he comes to the Brückenhof is sleep. He does not appear to know where he is: 'Into what village have I strayed? Is there then a castle here?' He maintains that he has been summoned here as a surveyor; authority at first denies knowledge of him, and then to his surprise countermands this. Later it is suggested that no problem would have arisen for K., had not the officious Schwarzer interfered with his immediate urge to rest. The first phase of K.'s stay in the village is marked by a confidence that expresses itself in aggressive and patronizing behaviour to the people he encounters. This takes surprising form in his snowball throwing, and his refusal to treat the two assistants allocated to him as separate individuals. He falls asleep for several hours in a strange house. Later the innkeeper's wife at the Brückenhof emphasizes his insignificance here and calls him defiant and childlike. K. fears that he may become absorbed into the village background and its mentality of subservience to, or reverence for the castle. The arrival of Barnabas with the letter from Klamm, a castle official, gives K.'s seeking a certain direction. He finds Barnabas sympathetic, and regards his function as messenger as being of importance to himself, though he is disappointed that he too is only a villager. Through Barnabas' sister Olga, K. visits the Herrenhof, an inn for castle officials and their servants when they have work in the village.

Chance, together with his own impulse and calculation, lead to K.'s seduction of Frieda, the waitress in the bar-room of the Herrenhof. His proposal to her puts him on another footing in his relationship with the village. He may still aim to confront Klamm personally and to speak 'freely before a man of power', but his acceptance of the unpaid work as school-servant and of one of the schoolrooms as accommodation for himself, Frieda and the two assistants indicates his willingness to become part of the community and with misgivings and rebelliousness to allow himself to be fitted into it. While

Frieda is setting up home in the new surroundings, K. pays his second visit to the Herrenhof, meets Frieda's successor in the bar-room, Pepi, and tries unsuccessfully to encounter Klamm who is known to be about to depart. His defiance of the rules of the Herrenhof makes him feel (at the end of chapter eight) that he has won a new freedom, but at the same time that nothing could be more meaningless and more despairing. His love-making with Frieda, on his first visit to the Herrenhof, had given him the sense that he was lost and in a remote country. Now K. expresses the wish to penetrate beyond Klamm 'further, into the castle'. He asserts his independence by refusing to be interrogated by Momus, Klamm's village-secretary, just as he had declined Gardena's offer of help. Consequently it is not surprising that the attempt of Frieda and K. to live together and make a home breaks down. Three times she refers to the alternative they have of emigrating and finding their own happiness, but K. is determined to remain. He has come here of his own free will, he says; he has not come here to lead a life in honour and peace; life is a struggle, he is the attacker. His striving is not reconcilable with her more domestic aims. Her suspicions of his relations with Barnabas and the latter's sisters, Olga and Amalia, are unjustified but understandable. These three represent, for K., guidance to the penetration of the castle; Frieda mistrusts them, just as she does not share K.'s quest.

The long chapter fifteen consists essentially of Olga's inset narrative of her family's story during the last three years. The more closely knit manner in which this episode is related sets it apart from the main sequence of events, and gives it a particular position in the novel as a whole, as it now stands. The Barnabas family have lost their security and place in society in consequence of Amalia's refusal to follow Sortini, a castle-official who wishes to assert his seignorial rights over her. They have been ostracized by the community, though no official action has been taken. Amalia's refusal to obey the summons is described by Olga as heroic, and her subsequent steadfastness is emphasized: 'She stood eye to eye with truth and bore this life, then as now.' The fate of their father corresponds to the position of K. in the larger framework of the novel, but the attitudes are reversed. Amalia's father has a sense of guilt about her act of defiance which undermines his whole personality, while K.'s first reactions in the new environment are of indignation and revolt. It is perhaps indicative of the modification which is taking place in K.'s attitude that the chapter concludes with an expression on his part of appreciation of Olga's rôle; she has attempted to go with her father rather than Amalia, even to the extent of consorting with the castle servants:

> ... he wanted to keep them [Barnabas' messages] and at the same time not to forget Olga, for Olga was almost even more important to him than the messages, her bravery, her discretion, her prudence, her self-sacrifice on behalf of the family. If he had to choose between Amalia and Olga, he would not need to consider it long. And again he cordially pressed her hand while he was already swinging on to the fence of the neighbouring garden.

Shortly after Olga's narrative K. receives a summons to an interview at the Herrenhof with Erlanger, one of Klamm's first secretaries. This forms a dramatic climax to the sequence of events so far, coming as it does immediately after the news that Frieda has given K. up and returned to work in the Herrenhof. His conversation with her in these surroundings finalizes their parting, and allows him to put into words the new insight that their association has given to them both:

> ... since we have known each other, both our lives have taken quite a new way, we still feel uncertain, after all it is all too new. I am not speaking of you, that is not so important, fundamentally it is I who have continuously been receiving gifts since you first turned your eyes towards me ...

The interview with Bürgel, a chance stumbling by K. upon an official in the middle of the night who is prepared to help him, might be the means by which the seeker can penetrate through the intricacies of the administration and obtain the fulfilment to his request. K. realizes that Bürgel's words may concern him closely, but he is overcome now by a 'great distaste for all things which concerned him' and succumbs to sleep. The official interview with Erlanger is brief and not significant; but the unexpected conversation with Bürgel might have led K. to the solution of his problems. An important opportunity has been missed.

Although only a few days have passed since his arrival at the village, K. has undergone experiences that have changed him very considerably. It is Pepi who takes care of him after the Bürgel–Erlanger episode, and offers him unofficial accommodation with herself and two other chambermaids. What alternative has he? '. . . it is cold, and you have neither work nor bed, come to us.' The winter is long and monotonous, but eventually spring and summer will come, even if they are short-lived. By this time, K. has told her that he realizes the shortcomings of his earlier impatient approach to his problems.

The motivation of the administrative hierarchy is difficult. The villagers have reverence for them. They cannot pardon, but only judge and make administrative settlement. The officials are extremely sensitive and overloaded with work. The two assistants were sent to K. primarily to cheer him up. There is no question of throwing him out. The village superintendent is kindly towards K., and prepared to explain in detail the early history of the discussions about appointing a surveyor. But the telephone is not used seriously, and the letters that Barnabas brings have no meaningful context. Arrangements are inconvenient and frequently sordid. The officials' sexual relations with village women, especially in the case of Amalia and Sortini, arouse K.'s indignation at the possibility of such an abuse of power. The owner of the castle, Count Westwest, is mentioned, but he is remote and apparently sinister. If K. finds fulfilment to his striving, it is by overcoming the obstacles put in his way by the administration and perhaps by being able to be reached by a force outside or beyond. According to Max Brod, Kafka intended to conclude the novel with the castle authorities' giving K. permission to live and work in the community, although the message would reach him only as he lay exhausted on his deathbed.

Are the women who play such a part in K.'s first week in the village a help or a hindrance to him in his major quest? If K.'s first approach to Frieda is a form of exploitation (of her position as Klamm's mistress), his final parting from her shows appreciation and gratitude towards her. She gives up her privileged relationship with Klamm for love of K. 'She has saved you and sacrificed herself in doing so,' Gardena tells him. Frieda tries to shield K. from the teacher, and is particularly pathetic in her attempts to set up house in the school. K. later defends Frieda against the criticism of Pepi, speaking of her calm and commonsense nature, her spirit of sacrifice, and the influence of Klamm's relationship upon her. Then Olga and Amalia both arouse K.'s admiration, the more pliant Olga rather than her sister. Finally, if Pepi appears less impressive than these three, she offers K. what shelter she can. During the course of the novel K. is concerned both with the achievement of his aim, permission to settle as a surveyor in the community, and with the working out of emotional relationships which give texture to his life at this stage. There is much that is baffling in *Das Schloß*, but it can be seen, without excluding further interpretations, as a narrative about human beings who, if involved in situations that can be ridiculous or sordid, are also capable of dignity and tenderness.

Alfred Döblin's concern for the ethical-social problems which the Expressionists took up is revealed in an exotic, Chinese setting in *Die drei Sprünge des Wang-lun* (1915). *Berlin Alexanderplatz* (1929) provides an extensive and lively panorama of the big city and gives a convincing sense of the collective, anonymous element in large-scale urban life, while at the same time bringing out the fascination and stimulus that this atmosphere can have. The author, however, avoids the fragmentation of structure that might result from too large an area of city life being viewed simultaneously; he firmly centres his narrative upon the story of one man, and in author's comments and chapter headings draws the reader's attention to his concern for this man's welfare. The novel does not present a life-story, but a fairly short span of time, from towards the end of 1927 to early in the year 1929, during which the hero undergoes severe crises which lead to an important change in his whole way of life. The aspect of Berlin life shown is deliberately restricted to the environment of a section of the underworld and their existence in close proximity to the teeming crowds around the Alexanderplatz.

The narrative opens with Franz Biberkopf's release from Tegel at the age of thirty after serving a sentence of four years' imprisonment for the manslaughter of Ida, a young woman with whom he had been living. After the protected institutional life he has to adapt himself to the at first overwhelming challenge of fitting afresh into Berlin life. A Jew who takes a compassionate interest in the bewildered and anxious stranger tells him: 'There now, what is to happen won't be so bad, after all. There is surely no question of going to the bad. Berlin is a big place. Where a thousand can live, one more will be able to live.' If these words anticipate the outcome, where Franz eventually finds a settled place as an assistant porter at a factory, they can hardly be expected to do justice to the extent of the problems and misfortunes which befall him on the way. He begins a new life, as street vendor and newspaper salesman, but has the first setback after his confidence has been betrayed by a mate. The main action of the novel unfolds when Franz begins again; after an interlude of solitary drinking, he comes into contact with the more unscrupulous and intelligent Reinhold who, on the return from an organized robbery, throws Franz out of a fast-moving car and causes him to be severely injured. A period in hospital is followed by Franz's 'third conquest of Berlin', when he begins once more in another environment, that of Herbert Wischow and Eva who now protect him again, as they had been his friends before he went to prison. A period of happiness ensues when Franz begins his association with Mieze (Emilie Parsunke), a young prostitute. The murder of Mieze (by Reinhold), when revealed to Franz as a fact in a newspaper report, leads to his arrest and protracted illness in the mental hospital of Buch, from which he emerges finally to put his whole past behind him and begin anew. Franz's life has its patterns. A tendency to unconsidered violence had led him to the manslaughter of Ida, at the thought of her leaving him. At one stage his relationship with Mieze threatens to follow a similar direction; and if her death at Reinhold's hands is not directly his doing, he knows that he bears some responsibility. Franz is attracted by the vitality of the large city, but needs to withdraw from it. The periods of disassociation are not consciously planned—the prison sentence, the bout of drinking, the stay in the Magdeburg hospital, and the 'psychic trauma' of Buch—but are essential to the rhythm of his life during the time of the novel's action. The work describes Franz's actions during a crisis period of rather more than a year. A 'new' man ultimately emerges; the pattern of his life will be completely different.

Franz Biberkopf is limited in his range of thought, confused in his relations with other people and society as a whole, involved in situations where his behaviour would be regarded by many readers as crude, but he can be doggedly persistent and he has a great reserve of good will. The author feels the need to act as intermediary between his hero and his reader, for the latter cannot be expected to take Franz's personality and adventures for granted. The reader is not to despair, for events will come about for good in the end. The narrator assumes a function of counsellor and consoler to the reader in a manner that contrasts with Kafka's presentation of his material: 'There is no need to despair. When I continue this story and take it to its hard, terrible, bitter conclusion, I shall again often use the phrase! there is no need to despair.' The author's prefatory remarks and the comments at the head of various sections and chapters not only summarize but also interpret the narrative that is to come, for the instruction of the reader. Franz is to learn, and the reader with him. Comments on his story see it sometimes in terms of fate, or alternatively as providential guidance in a biblical sense. He is compared to Orestes and Achilles, and also to Adam and Job. His suffering is to be taken seriously. 'But, ladies and gentlemen who are reading this, what is Franz Biberkopf weeping about? He is weeping because he is suffering, and he is weeping about what he is suffering, and about himself too.'

Apart from the author's comments on his narrative, the point of view of Franz and that of other characters are shown. Interspersed with these are motifs which, as a form of *montage*, link Franz with the other inhabitants of the city around him. Popular songs and hymns pass through his consciousness, as do newspaper headlines and reports, public notices and advertisements. This is one way in which the individual is merged into the mass; the common factors of topical news or tunes will relieve him from his isolation and will help identify him with the Berlin, or the world, of his time. Intercalated episodes make us realize that Franz is not alone; others suffer and struggle around him, and if he has a room in a block, we may learn about his neighbours above, around and below him. While he is lying in torpor at Buch, medical staff will disagree about their diagnosis of him. The unknowing passivity of cattle as they are led to the slaughter mirrors the fate of many humans, and specifically that of Mieze. The account of Ida's death at Franz's hands is accompanied by references to Orestes and to Newton. The rising of the sun may call forth reflections on man's smallness in the universe, and at the next moment may evoke joy with its warmth and brightness. The author notes the crowds in the Alexanderplatz, recalls that each person is an individual, and is resigned to having to pass most of them over unconsidered: 'They are men, women and children, these last mostly holding the hands of women. It is hardly possible to count them and to describe their fates, this could only succeed with a few.' After the shock of Mieze's death, Franz's state of mind becomes increasingly troubled; this is indicated through visions and symbols—the sparrows' commentary, the two angels, the wind, the mice, the struggle between life and death—and the style becomes rhapsodic and emotionally intense, furthest removed from the impersonality of the collections of data given in other contexts.

Berlin Alexanderplatz gives the story of Franz Biberkopf against the background of the environment in which he moves. The hero is an individual and also an Everyman of this milieu. The author combines the analysis of private emotions with the evocation of the impersonal quality of city life, and welds his material into unity by dominating it with his own interpretation of its texture and significance.

While Döblin came to writing after training and experience as a medical practitioner, Hermann Broch gave up a leading position as an industrialist in order to devote himself to study and writing. Broch too had a strong ethical impulse in his work. In comparison with *Berlin Alexanderplatz*, which had appeared two to three years earlier, his *Schlafwandler* is an austere work, impressive in its realism and in its intensive preoccupation with the changing moods of society over four decades, which are represented in the style and structure of the work as well as in its thought and action. The three volumes of *Die Schlafwandler* provide in their titles signposts to the direction which the work is taking. The action of each is concentrated upon a limited period during the years 1888, 1903 and 1918, a time of crisis in the lives of the principal protagonists. That these three figures, Pasenow, Esch and Huguenau, are fitted into a more general context, is indicated by their association with 'Romanticism', 'Anarchy' and 'Factuality' ('*Sachlichkeit*'). The structure of society is continually becoming less stable, and with it the patterns of belief. This process of dissolution is reflected also in the narrative method. In *Pasenow* it is direct, with a series of actions and decisions which interlock with precision and with clearly perceptible consequences. Already in *Esch* the novel moves forward in a more expansive manner and dwells largely upon the central figure's inner problems. The third section provides a culminating sequence of action where the two chief figures of the earlier parts confront each other and the third titular protagonist; but this material is interspersed with a series of episodes which run parallel to it in time and in mood without being connected by any requirement of plot, while the prose narrative form is broken up by the insertion of verse passages and of reflections on the 'collapse of values'. As the work moves on, its narrative pace is slowed down, and to this corresponds a broadening of its texture.

The first part is devoted primarily to Joachim von Pasenow's problems during a period of tension in his earlier years. He is at odds with his father, and the latter with him. The death of his brother Helmuth affects him deeply. The love-affair with Ruzena, a Czech girl living precariously in Berlin's entertainment world, is broken off so that the expected marriage can take place with Elisabeth, the fiancée whose background of Prussian land-owning gentry is close to his own. Pasenow cannot see clearly the implications of his actions, and tends to be overwhelmed by emotional confusion. He feels the need of order and support in his life, and looks for these in the military code, and in the usages of the society in which he has grown up. In this search for help from the external sources that are familiar and easy to him, Pasenow is criticized by his friend Eduard von Bertrand, the liberal-thinking businessman. Once the Church would have supplied guidance to Pasenow, Bertrand reflects, but now earthly hierarchies and uniforms have taken its place; 'it is always romanticism, when something earthly is raised to the absolute'. Bertrand holds aloof from accepting a life bounded by conventional feelings, approaches the traditional Prussian world with scepticism, and remains the solitary, the wanderer. Love, he tells Elisabeth, is something absolute, but when it is to be expressed in concrete form, it takes on an element of pathos and is 'terribly earthly'. Bertrand refuses to become personally involved in his friend's relationships with Elisabeth and Ruzena, or to allow his own feeling for Elisabeth to find direct expression; his reluctance to be committed to any form of 'romanticism' will not permit him to come closer. Pasenow is at times suspicious of his friend, for Bertrand as well as Ruzena represent forces of disorder in his life, a disturbance to the shelter of conventional factors to which he clings. But Bertrand's practical assistance is needed by Pasenow to enable him to return to the form of stability that he requires as support.

While in *Pasenow* both Bertrand and the titular hero claim attention and sympathy, Esch dominates the action of the second section almost completely. 'A man of impetuous attitudes', Esch is uncertain about his loyalties and would like to find an order in his relationship with the world about him. His sympathies for political agitation are regarded as misguided and confused by the committed Social Democrats. His venture away from his familiar work as book-keeper into the sphere of variety entertainment is a further source of disorder in his life, and in this environment he is reminded that he is a 'fellow who has been thrown about in the world, who has hardly known his mother'. His belief that Bertrand, as influential industrialist, is responsible for the imprisonment of his friend the agitator Martin Geyring, leads him to action that is useless and harmful; Esch, like Pasenow, finds himself attracted to Bertrand's personality in spite of his firm suspicions. While Pasenow had a firmly established set of conventions that he could accept as values, Esch is struggling in an environment that provides him with little support; as he says to Martin Geyring:

Besides, one no longer knows what is black and what is white. Everything is confused. You don't even know what has finished and what still exists. . . . You sacrifice yourself for the future; you have said that yourself . . . that is all that remains, to sacrifice oneself for the future, and atonement for what has happened; a decent man sacrifices himself, otherwise there can be no order.

America is a distant ideal, as is Ilona, the Hungarian woman. But the uncertainty of these months is resolved by his marriage with the widow Mutter Hentjen, the one point of security to which he can come back at this time:

> He also felt gratified that there was here someone who presented herself unequivocally and clearly, someone who knew where to find her right and her left, her good and her evil. For a moment he had the feeling that here was the longed for point which rose from the general disorder with clarity and stability, and to which one might cling. . . .

The first two volumes of the novel show separately the inner conflicts of two men during a period of their lives which has an interim quality; the confusions are brought to the end of this particular critical phase by their marriages. Pasenow and Esch reappear as older, settled men in the third volume; here they are brought together in a town in the Mosel area during the last months of the First World War, where Pasenow is town governor and Esch editor of the local newspaper. Pasenow's leading-article of 1 June 1918, with its hope of salvation of the state through religious faith, arouses Esch to a renewal of the search for values. At a time when the outward stability of civilization is becoming daily more threatened, he turns to the Bible and gathers a group of seekers around him for its interpretation. For Pasenow Esch becomes for a while the brother whom he lost thirty years earlier. The culminating point of the friendship is reached when Pasenow appears at one of Esch's Sunday gatherings, and both sense their unity of mood and belief. For all the disturbing factors of 'romanticism' and 'anarchy' the major from a wealthy Prussian background and the social democrat find a common hope in an idealism that is often obscurely expressed but looks back to a tradition that is still meaningful to them.

In the outward pattern of the novel it is Huguenau, the younger man from Colmar, who is living through a period of uncertainty that is terminated with the end of the Mosel episode, his return to his home background and later his marriage. Unlike Pasenow and Esch he is in no way a seeker of moral ideals, and with his 'partial' values from the world of commerce and his proclivity to intrigue and his sense of egoistically materialist purpose he succeeds only too well in destroying the new friendship. The temporary breakdown of normal order in November 1918 provides him with the opportunity to give full vent to his hatred of Esch and to usurp the latter's place by Pasenow's side; Esch's death has been part of his sacrifice. The decline of values has moved over a period of thirty years, rushing headlong as the old order of society collapses. The noisy emptiness of the 'victory celebrations', the distress of Lieutenant Jaretzki, the apathy of Hanna Wendling, the loneliness of the child Marguerite, the slow awakening of Gödicke to new life: these themes supplement the main narrative and fill in a wider picture of this particular Mosel community. The 'story of the Salvation Army girl in Berlin' is linked rather tenuously to the series of inserted reflections on the destruction of values.

Die Schlafwandler is a sombre, strong achievement, an interpretation of an era through the vision of a minatory but hopeful prophet. The third and longest section is rendered less convincing by the interpolation of only indirectly relevant episodes and essays; the two preceding parts can almost be taken as separate novels in their own right, and it is here that the major impact of the work's narrative force lies. The work as a whole is not always endearing, but undoubtedly monumental.

Robert Musil published two volumes of *Der Mann ohne Eigenschaften* in 1930 and 1933. A fellow-countryman of

Broch, he too had training and experience (in engineering, for example) in fields outside the range of many novelists; he conceived his novel on an even vaster scale, and his acuity of observation and comment reveals itself in the context of people rather than of place.

Ulrich, the hero and central figure of Robert Musil's *Der Mann ohne Eigenschaften*, is at the age of thirty-two uncertain of the direction his life is taking. With time 'a certain readiness to negation', to criticize what was commonly praised and to defend what was forbidden, has established itself in his attitude. He has had the desire to distinguish himself intellectually, and has considered various possibilities (pilgrim, adventurer, poet, or 'one of these disillusioned people who only believe in money and violence'), but he has a secret dislike of all that claims to stand firm in life (ideals, laws, 'the contented character'). Feeling himself largely carried along by a passive scepticism, Ulrich sometimes speculates whether he has been born 'with a gift, for which at present there was no purpose', and wonders whether he may not discover a meaning, deeper than words, that will give wholeness to the fragmentary nature of his view of life. In their boyhood at the turn of the century Ulrich and his friend Walter had been caught with enthusiasm for the aspirations to a rebirth of culture that the time had brought, but as the new century took its course disillusionment overcame them. At school Ulrich had admired Napoleon, and his first attempt to fulfil himself was in the army. After this experiment he turned to engineering, and then to mathematics, where he gains a certain reputation. But the realization that his specialized work will lead him to becoming a 'race-horse of genius' causes Ulrich, in August 1913, 'to take a year's leave from his life' in order to examine where he stands. It is Walter who refers to him in critical tones as a 'man without qualities'.

The events of the first two sections of the novel centre upon Vienna, and Ulrich's own personality reflects something of the flux and anonymity of the city as well as the intelligent but directionless functioning of the Austro-Hungarian Empire

('Kakanien') and its administration. Ulrich, a bachelor, lives in a Rococo house to which other styles have been added. As the novel opens, he acquires a new mistress, a married woman whom he calls Bonadea. His relationship with his friend Walter is complicated by the latter's wife Clarisse, who refuses to have marital relations with her husband and later hopes, in vain, that Ulrich will be her lover. The interest which Clarisse and her circle take in the reports of the psychopathic murderer Moosbrugger reflects the presence of an underworld atmosphere of criminal violence that forms an uneasy background to the lives of the intelligentsia.

Through his father's initiative Ulrich is offered the post of secretary to a newly formed body which is to promote arrangements for the celebration in 1918 of the seventieth anniversary of the emperor's reign. One of the major participants is his cousin, 'Diotima', wife of the civil servant Tuzzi. Ulrich, ironically detached, is amused at her respect and enthusiasm for the world of culture, and the affinity of the Prussian businessman and successful author Arnheim with Diotima presents Ulrich with an intellectual opponent against whom he can pit himself. Diotima and Arnheim are eloquent advocates of an ethical and cultural idealism as a basis for living and for the planned national Campaign. Ulrich finds Arnheim's ideas pretentious, and prefers the unassuming manner of General Stumm von Bordwehr and comes to admire Count Leinsdorf, the originator of the Campaign, when he is with the latter at a time of crisis, during a popular demonstration at the expense of the Campaign. This indicates a rejection of the world of modern commerce and industry, here associated with Goethean idealism, in favour of a scepticism that is quietly in support of Austrian tradition. However, the mood of this second section of the novel is primarily one of satirical humour, tempered by a tolerant affection for the pre-1914 Austrian way of life. Further groups of characters are introduced. Hans Sepp, with his racialism, is caricatured, while Ulrich's relationship with Gerda Fischel, who is close to Hans Sepp, although her father is a Jew, breaks off in abrupt disaster. Another strand of narrative is provided by the affair that develops between Rachel, Diotima's maid, and Soliman, Arnheim's young servant.

The first two sections of the novel present for the most part the amused and detached exposition of Ulrich's personal relationships with a number of women and his participation in the anniversary Campaign, an organization which from the standpoint of author and reader, after the events of 1914–1918, can only be seen as futile. Musil's narrative method is traditional. He looks at the situation through the eyes of various characters, making his own comments on them and on general issues. Reflections of the author, or of Ulrich and Arnheim for example, are interpolated; the 'essayistic' approach may present informed and subtle comment on relevant topics, and offers the analysis of possibilities, in keeping with Ulrich's non-committal irony, but evidently slows down the pace of the action, which is presented usually in normal chronological sequence.

Section Three opens a new facet of the novel. Earlier Ulrich has stood apart from the people around him, regarding them for the most part with amused detachment. The activities of the Campaign organization he hardly takes seriously, and he succeeds in remaining emotionally uninvolved in his attitude to women. But a crisis of dissatisfaction with his present way of life builds up in a series of episodes— the incident with Gerda, the offer of employment by Arnheim, the news of his father's death and the attentions of Clarisse. The setting moves from Vienna to the provincial town where his father, an academic lawyer, has lived and where the funeral takes place. The encounter with his younger sister brings about the turning-point in Ulrich's development at this stage. Childhood memories return to the surface of his mind, and he sees in Agathe a close complement to himself, the imaginative emotional partner to his intellectual seeking. The satirical mood gives way to a longing

for lyrical fulfilment as Ulrich retreats from the world of
Viennese society and the Campaign, and encounters a higher
reality in the new intimacy with his sister. It is Agathe who
makes the practical decisions here; she breaks off her links
with Hagauer, her second husband (the sudden death of her
much-loved first husband had been a deep shock to her), and
takes the initiative in the intrigue concerning her father's
will. She is prepared to put into action the opposition to
traditional morality, which Ulrich advocates theoretically.
He would reject good and evil, but look forward to a new unknown faith which would combine the implications of science
and mathematics with the possibility of a visionary reality on
another plane:

> And so I believe and yet I don't believe!
> But perhaps I believe that in time people will become on
> the one hand very intelligent, on the other hand mystics. Per-
> haps it is happening that even today our morality is separating
> out into these two component parts. I could also put it like this:
> into mathematics and mysticism. Into practical improvement
> and unknown adventure! It was years since he had been so
> openly excited.

Ulrich revisits Vienna and keeps in touch with the activities of friends there, though feeling more detached from
them than even earlier. Here Agathe arrives to live under his
roof, as his 'twin-sister'. In the ambiguity of the relationship
with her brother, Agathe thinks of taking her own life; this
leads to her forming the acquaintance with Lindner, whom
however she soon finds as unsympathetic as Hagauer. The
later part of Section Three alternately focuses on the private
idyll of the brother and sister, with their yearning for a millennium of love and contentment, and on the continuing, but
still rudderless, activity around the anniversary Campaign; a
sombre, harsh note is introduced with the visit of Clarisse,
herself showing signs of unbalance, and her friends to the
mental hospital.

At this point the novel, as published during the author's

lifetime, breaks off. The two main themes, the anniversary Campaign and the brother and sister relationship, have not been brought to a conclusion. The imminence of the First World War will evidently sweep the Campaign into limbo, while the fate of Ulrich and of his inner seeking is uncertain. If chapters of the work are taken in isolation, one can admire the virtuosity of the style, the elaborate and polished presentation of far-ranging thought and the dry, detached analysis of character; but the forward drive of the action falters, and it is difficult to imagine that the work, from what was published by 1933, was designed as a convincing, shapely whole. *Der Mann ohne Eigenschaften* remains a massive, fascinating and tantalizing fragment.

Am Himmel wie auf Erden came to the author, Werner Bergengruen, as a first impulse in 1931 and was published in 1940. It is the major work of a particularly fruitful decade in this writer's career. In his later *Schreibtischerinnerungen* Bergengruen looks back on his life in Germany in the 1930s and during the Second World War, and has a number of comments to make on his writing during this period. He is sceptical about attempts to consider the 'laws' of the novel form, and defends the historical novel as a type of fiction in no way inferior to narrative works taking place within the period of the author's lifetime. A historical narrative will make demands of craftsmanship on the author which are less likely to trouble the writer who depends primarily upon his own memories; Bergengruen speaks of the problems of being tempted to didacticism and anachronisms, to the use of affected language, to giving overt support to a particular side in his narrative, or to including too much background material. These problems are successfully solved in *Am Himmel wie auf Erden*, which can be regarded as a work of the 'inner emigration'. However, the tendency to turn to historical or mythical themes in the 1930s was not confined to those authors who were living within Germany at the time, as is seen in Heinrich Mann's *Henri Quatre* and Thomas Mann's *Joseph und seine Brüder*.

The action of this novel is concentrated within six weeks of the summer of 1524 in the state of Brandenburg, above all in Berlin. We are given a carefully filled-in picture of life in a small community during a period of crisis. A prophecy of a flood that will destroy the city is inevitably shown to be erroneous; but the complex reactions of the people of Berlin under the fear of an expected disaster give rise to some unusual tensions and tragic situations. Bergengruen can, in his use of this historical material, give a view of a complete social structure and at the same time trace the part played by the individual personality. This is a society where each single human being has a good chance of being cared about, and where he is unlikely to be forgotten as he might be in a community of a larger and more anonymous character.

The state of Brandenburg binds together groups of disparate nature. The Elector Joachim is a key-figure in his capacity as ruler and outward controller of the whole and as director of the group at court who are loyal to him. He can count on the support of the visiting Archbishop Blankenfelde, formerly his protégé, but has to reckon with the hostility of those who sympathize with Elisabeth, the wife from whom he has become estranged. Doktor Carion, astrologer and humanist, is the principal link between various strands of the action. As adviser to Joachim, he first sets in motion the expectation of a flood disaster; he can play the part of an observer, however, since he is from the Neckar area and can free himself, if he chooses, to take office outside Brandenburg, at the court of Ferrara, for example. When he decides finally to remain in the Elector's service, he is identifying himself voluntarily with the fortunes of Berlin. Joachim is limited by considerations of the subordinate position his state must take within the Empire as a whole; Wolf Hornung, the wronged husband of Joachim's mistress Katharina, is a potential danger to Brandenburg through his connexions with the state of Saxony. The court circle stands apart from the citizens of Berlin, and the lack of contact between the Elector and his people is brought about largely by Joachim's own personal attitude during these particular weeks. In the course of the fateful day when the flood is expected, Joachim effects a reconciliation with his wife, and by returning from Tempelhof when he does he can regain the affection of the Berliners. But all the German people of Brandenburg form a unity in their relationship to the subject minority of the Wends, whose alien folk-traditions and aspirations to independence are felt to be separating factors. However, Wends and Germans are brought together in the ultimate dividing factor of the community; the healthy are united in their fear of the lepers, who are outcasts from the normal laws of society and have to live in the quarters prescribed for them, and be deprived of most of the distinguishing factors of civil life. They feel that they have nothing to lose from any threat to the order of a community which puts them irrevocably aside.

It is a society with its own peculiar hierarchy and with divisions that may become a dangerous threat in time of trouble. The need for the preservation of order is in the forefront of the Elector's mind, and he is supported by Carion who sees guarantees of an orderly universe in birth and death, the seasons and the stars, and human conscience. For the Archbishop, on the other hand, the predicted Flood can be seen as a further indication of the inevitability of change, compatible with the discoveries, new learning and new religious life of the age. Joachim is an uneasy ruler, who would have preferred to devote himself more to learning. He has become embittered at the difficulties he has had to face, especially in his younger years. He feels isolated, and if he appears ruthless, as in his condemnation to death of Schwerdtke and Ellnhofen, it is through his will to establish justice and consistency. The final insight into his own fallibility allows for moods of despair and self-reproach, but a sense of duty compels him to continue in his rôle. The humility of the Wends is reflected in the Elector's coachman Juro, whose serenity almost persuades Joachim to yield to the impulse to pardon Ellnhofen; Juro is revealed after his death as the 'secret king' of the Wends. Worschula, the woman-servant of Carion, who has to be put away from normal society in her old age, is both a Wend and a leper. She becomes for a time a leader to the outcasts through the assertion of her newly found prophetic convictions. She develops a fanatical dislike of the normal ordering of the world and of its interpretation through Christianity, and looks forward to the coming of the Flood as the beginning of a new realm, when a Wendish king shall rule and when the lepers shall be cleansed by the flood waters.

The rulers, advisers and prophets all have their clearly defined rôles, which interact with each other and with the fates of those less closely associated with the direction of the community. Bergengruen shows how those who are concerned with the guidance of the state are interrelated with others, citizens and lepers, who have their own individuality. He has said that parallels with the Third Reich may be seen in this novel, for instance in the comparability between leper's hospital and concentration camp. But his portrayal of sixteenth century Berlin shows a place where the individual is seldom if ever lost in the mass.

As the motto to the novel declares, the theme of fear underlies the work. Fear is inventive, Bergengruen writes:

> Sometimes it chooses the disguise which appears to its victims as the most terrible one, because it is appropriate to the opinions of the age. At other times man's need of fear hurls itself upon war dangers, upon monetary devaluation, upon poverty and hunger; upon widespread and highly infectious diseases, upon coming revolutions and persecution in the state; finally upon a collapse of all familiar, tried and beloved forms of intellectual and social existence—a collapse which is seen as imminent in the immediate future.

And apart from its impact on the group, there are many forms in which it expresses itself within the heart of the individual. Or it may be indirect, but none the less far-reaching, in its effect on a human life; we see this in the figure of Juliane von Schwanebeck, the seventeen-year-old fiancée of Ellnhofen, and also in the fate of Katharina Hornung. The Franciscan Brother Meinhard is arrested on account of the sermon he preaches on the text 'Be not afraid'. The passing of the predicted date of disaster removes the immediate fear of the Flood from people's minds, but the emotion may reappear in other shapes. After his encounter with the leper Köckeritz, Carion realizes that he is now condemned to a new solitude:

> He now had to learn to overcome also the fear of leprosy which was much harder than that of the Flood, for it was deprived of the consolation of a fate which is general, being shared equally by countless others. The threat from the flood had finished with the coming of St Henry's Day, but the threat from sickness could not end earlier than his own death, and thus his whole future life was overshadowed by it.

Joachim and Carion live through the period of the Flood crisis and are chastened by it; it brings death to others—Ellnhofen, Juro, Worschula, Katharina and Wolf Hornung, for example. The author weaves his plot with care for the fortunes of all his characters, and allows Carion to close the work on a note of affirmation: 'For all God's works please me, in heaven as on earth.'

Although Heimito von Doderer published a number of works before 1945, it was not until the 1950s that *Die Strudlhofstiege* and, a few years later, the even more largely proportioned *Die Dämonen*, established him firmly as a novelist of stature. Centred upon Vienna, it is an impressive evocation of a whole imaginative world. It is a realistic, or naturalistic novel; visionary, speculative elements are kept severely in check. It presents an extensive number of characters, and corresponding to these incisively drawn figures are a varied series of striking episodes. The result is a finely devised whole, where the many strands of narrative are skilfully drawn together to form a complex and satisfying pattern; there is a masterly balance of shape and substance. An appreciation of the labour and care that went to the creation of *Die Dämonen* can be derived from Dietrich Weber's monograph and from the first two sections of the novelist's *Tangenten*, a writer's diary for the years 1940–50. The author sees himself as a craftsman in the first place, as did Bergengruen. In the preface to the diaries he refers to these as

> An illustration of the author's thesis that art does not play by any means such a large part as is generally believed, and that in art all that is 'higher' is always only really there for other people. But the artist works with his eyes down, looking at his hands and at the technical factors.

In *Die Dämonen*, in the context of Jan Herzka's mood after hearing the news of his unexpected inheritance, the author comments: 'To be a businessman and a writer needs a kind of sober but energetic imagination. Today there was no question of any such thing.' The figures and episodes are held together by the author's planned concern. They move towards crisis and fulfilment on 15 July 1927, and are linked with the burning of the Palace of Justice in Vienna. Here is a major culminating event, which helps to emphasize the shape of the series of simultaneous happenings and personages that have been described as from the autumn of 1926 onwards. Action itself is important to the author, and the relevance of apparently isolated incidents to the whole structure has evidently been carefully considered. Through such attention the material has been controlled and balanced against an expressed dislike of 'order' in favour of 'life', and against the novel's potentiality to be 'total' and 'universal'. *Die Dämonen* was begun in 1930–1, and the first section was completed 1936–7. Work on it was then interrupted. The diary for 1940 reveals detailed replanning at that time. Writing was resumed in 1950, and taken to completion and publication in 1956 (cf. Weber). In the entry for 30 January 1940, Doderer decided that there could be no central 'theme' in the work:

> Now here is the point at which I can perceive that a novel cannot develop at all in a 'thematic' manner; but only from a character or characters or from a basic narrative, even if purely a narrative-technical, device, by means of which the personages are given *ab ovo*. . . . A 'theme' can only be present as something imagined by individual personages, it should have no other existence, and certainly not one as a leading thought of the author, who has only to imagine people, but not ideas.

Nor would it be possible to insist in the 'total novel' on a unity of point of view or of style (2 February 1940): 'Rather must everything be constantly changed here, the narrative-technical methods just as also the linguistic rhythm.' The memory and its often apparently trivial associations, as the principal narrator of *Die Dämonen*, Geyrenhoff, notes, are further an indication of the vastness and uncontrollability of the past.

If the author imposes caution on anyone who would wish to interpret the novel's life according to a pattern, we like to discover shape there all the same, and we find an important aspect in the different characters' approach to the reality they experience. The novel centres upon Vienna. The city is presented with topographical detail and realism. It is also seen through the characters' eyes, with lyrical brightness, for instance, when Geyrenhoff describes his early morning walk on 24 May. The pure, firm colours of sunrise, the almost horizontal arrows of light and the silence broken only by the noise of birdsong (and even the birds surprise by a short pause in their singing) combine to give him the impression of a battlefield; the quiet morning is at the same time a picture of wild movement, and awakens in him an anticipation of the future:

> I look on to a battlefield. Why I felt that then is quite incomprehensible to me, for after all I was put completely out of

the position of being able to interpret later, factual material into the situation. But the silent tumult that was there awakened this impression in me: blocks of houses, thrown into the centre, slanting and oblique, church towers on the right, a gasometer behind, here and there the still bright green like flames, the sharp drop of the terrain in front of me, everything sharpened in contours by the arrows of light, shooting almost horizontally, with flat trajectory: all in all, this quiet morning picture was a wildly moving one.

The newspaper-man Holder speaks with some enthusiasm of the colourful people whom he has observed in the Vienna underworld. When Grete Siebenschein comments on his romanticism in this context, he accepts the description in a friendly manner:

> For me the word 'romanticism' is in any case not a derogatory one at all. A bit of romanticism often helps me into a livelier mood better than black coffee. A large city is in my opinion definitely romantic in its essence, a kind of artificial fairy-tale forest, even when it all seems to be so technical and factual. It is a return of the forest which used to be there previously, it is the last stage of the forest. . . .

The city is part of a tradition, and can be seen as an organic, incalculable totality. It may have its own reality, or it may acquire a heightened or distorted reality, as part of it is caught by the imagination of one or other of the characters.

The problem which besets a number of the characters is the subjective and distorted interpretation which they place upon experience. Grete Siebenschein's defence of the 'security' of modern life as compared with earlier ages is greeted with mockery by Eulenfeld, Körger and Orkay. When Kajetan von Schlaggenberg refers to his own soul or inner life as appearing like a well of unlimited depths or as a room one side of which is open and exposed to the unknown, his wife Camy is greatly surprised; she sees her nature as complete, concluded, and incapable of presenting to her anything incomprehensible. On hearing Schlaggenberg's account of this gap between himself and Camy, Geyrenhoff reflects that hers is the 'better, more sensible and indeed also the easier way to live'. Stangeler, the character whose life-story comes closest to that of the author himself, propounds his theory of a first and second reality, where the latter, imposed by the limitations and delusions of the individual personality, distorts and damages the former. He is responsible for Gürtzner-Gontard's development of the conception; political revolution falls into this category, and a totalitarian ideology forces its own false pattern on to reality:

> In a 'racially pure' society every simpleton and frustrated brutalist will at least represent an 'Aryan'; the same distinction can be seen, with an 'idealism' that has taken another direction, in being considered as a Prolet-arian.

Schlaggenberg's obsession with fat ladies is another form of escape or misinterpretation, which he comes to recognize as such and to give up. Jan Herzka overcomes his preoccupation with a fantasy-figure of Agnes Gebaur, and becomes reintegrated with the happy dispersal of fantasy by realization. It is in the context of Jan Herzka that the comment is made: 'But there is only the everyday, there is absolutely nothing else beyond it; and it is here and now that one has to prove oneself.' In a note of 29 August 1956, at the beginning of the diary entries for 1942-3, Heimito von Doderer describes his life in the German army during the Second World War as a form of second reality which he refused to regard as a 'real world'; when this particular life was over, he was conscious of the presence of a first reality.

For some of the characters in Doderer's work the pattern of life may be seen as a movement from second to first reality, where there is a moment of crisis in which an earlier form of living is seen with a new awareness, or terminated by shock or change, and the individual has to begin again and to reinterpret himself and the world in the light of his fresh perspective, which has provided him with a deeper correspondence between his inner life and the world outside. It is in such changes that the forward movement of the action centring on such figures as Mary K. and Leonhard Kakabsa may be observed, as Weber points out. Mary K. has been compelled to begin a new life as a result of the tram accident that took place on 21 September 1925; this disaster forms the main culmination of the earlier novel *Die Strudlhofstiege*, and in *Die Dämonen* Mary K. gradually overcomes her disability. Catastrophe has irrevocably thrown her from the 'narrow-gauge tracks' of her earlier life: 'But through her suffering— the relative extent of which it does not behove us to measure —she had been definitively thrown out of the narrow-gauge tracks of ready-made directions.' The coming together of Mary and Leonhard represents a new phase of life for both of them.

The second reality is to be contained and absorbed within the first. Doderer's approach to the novel gives priority to the outer world, and subjective visions and interpretations are to be subordinated to wider experience. Stangeler, realizing the changed quality of his relationship with Grete Siebenschein, decides that no amount of self-examination can present the palpable certainty offered by facts from concrete, outer life. *Facta loquuntur*. 'Only the facts speak. Profundity is outside.'

The Swiss novelist and dramatist Max Frisch has written in *Homo Faber* a taut and closely contrived work; one factor which separates it from other novels that are being discussed here is that it does not bring into focus one regional or national environment. Walter Faber, the first-person narrator, writes his main account within less than three weeks. The concentration in time offsets the complexity of the movements in space. Faber relates his journey from New York to Central America, in the course of which he departs from the timetable of his work in order to accompany a German fellow-passenger Herbert Hencke to the tobacco plantation in Guatemala where they find that Herbert's brother Joachim, a former friend of Faber, has taken his life. On his return to New York Faber meets Ivy again and finally breaks off his relationship with her as he sets sail for Europe. Then follows the central narrative of the work, Faber's encounter with Sabeth on the ship, his further meeting with her in Paris and the 'honeymoon' of their motor tour which is terminated by the girl's accident in Greece; on meeting her mother again he becomes aware that Sabeth is certainly his daughter, and soon afterwards she dies in hospital in Athens. The death of Joachim, the parting from Ivy and, after an idyllic interlude, the death of Sabeth are emotional crises which befall Faber within a few weeks. The shorter closing section of the novel, as Faber writes his notes in the Athens hospital, a few days after the main narrative has been written, recapitulates in part the travel pattern of the earlier narrative. From New York Faber goes to Central America where he finds Herbert in a state of inertia and apathy. In Cuba he encounters the eighteen-year-old Juana, confides to her the story of Sabeth and determines to change his life. From Düsseldorf, where he visits the Henckes' business office, he rushes off to Zürich, the home of his early years, and finally to Athens.

Faber presents the action through his own temperament, that of a technologist who has accustomed himself to interpreting life in terms of factuality and of mechanistic determinism. His local origins have been lost in his adult identity as a citizen of the world to whom all localities mean equally much or little, since his training and skills have the same significance wherever a modern community exists. The older cultures and values, whose disintegration was mourned by Broch, have been replaced for Faber by the assumption that the purpose of life, if there is one, is to be seen in the controlling of the chaos of nature through the application of scientific knowledge. His reluctance to see anything exciting or emotionally affecting in his normal experiences does not prevent him from describing them in sensuous and sharply realistic terms. In his relationships with women he would like to minimize the elements of emotion and personal involvement. It is indicative that while he is saying goodbye to Ivy, as he sets off for Europe, he should be taking pictures of the occasion. The camera is a means of putting distance between himself and the outside world, indeed of controlling, selecting and making it anew for himself. It provides ready-made memories; it can give a convincing picture of the past, but one that is willed and created by the individual owner. It is an instrument of technology, like the aeroplane, the ship, the car, the electric razor, the typewriter, the telephone, the hospital. These seem to make living easier; they certainly make it different.

Faber takes technology for granted, though throughout his experiences in the course of the novel it is shown as faulty. He is fully aware of this, and sees it as part of his function in life to repair deficient mechanisms. The world which the technologists are building is not yet perfect, and Faber acts and thinks on various occasions on the assumption that any repairs he can carry out are a priority. While he is waiting for Ivy to get ready to go out, he mends his electric razor;

> 'Walter,' she said, 'I'm waiting.'
> As if the likes of us had never waited!
> 'Technology!' she said—not only uncomprehendingly, as I am used to with women, but in fact mockingly, though this did not prevent me from taking the little mechanism completely to pieces; I wanted to know what was wrong.

At the tobacco-plantation in Guatemala Faber can take pictures of the dead man and can overhaul the neglected car that is kept there. If an emotional crisis occurs, he can deflect some of its impact by making use of his technical skills. While repairing the car, Faber thinks of the Maya civilization, the ruins of which are in the neighbourhood, and ascribes its doom to its lack of technology: '. . . in spite of this they did not evolve any technology out of their mathematics (and we must appreciate their achievement in mathematics) and were therefore doomed to destruction . . .' For him, particularly in the surroundings of underdeveloped tropical country, nature is there to be conquered; she is the enemy. The life of jungle plants and creatures is fecund and savage, as he is reminded for instance by the ominous activities of the vultures. If technology can keep nature at bay, it is performing its first and vital task. In the tropics the European's whole personality can be changed, leading to the decline of Joachim, and then Herbert, on the tobacco-plantation; but air-conditioning in a train can revive a European to normal energy. The vulnerability of modern man-made living is preeminently marked in air-travel. As the novel begins Faber's flight from New York is three hours late because of snowstorms, and the newspaper which the stewardess hands out shows 'First Pictures of World's Greatest Air Crash in Nevada'. The forced landing and stay of eighty-five hours in the Mexican desert make Faber acutely aware of the little that is required to threaten civilized custom with the inroads of chaos:

> What could be heard: the wind, now and again the squeaks of sand-mice which, it is true, could not be seen, the rustling of a lizard, above all a constant wind which did not stir up the sand, as has been said, but caused it to trickle, so that our footprints were continuously being obliterated; it looked continuously as if nobody had been here, no party of twenty-four passengers and five crew.

It is during this episode that Faber feels the need to justify to himself his attitude of technological realism. The rocks, the agaves and the Super-Constellation are calculable objects in a three-dimensional world; he must mistrust any imaginative urge within him to see them as prehistoric monsters, damned souls and a dead bird. 'Why should I have an experience of something that isn't there at all? . . . The end of the world, how indeed? I can't imagine nonsense merely in order to have an experience.' But a universe without myth, fantasy and personal interpretation is empty, and once technology has nature under control the routine of living has no wider purpose. That Faber is beset by these thoughts with any sense of urgency is due in part to his physical ill-health. At the intermediate stop in Texas the neon-lighting in the toilet makes his face in the mirror appear 'repulsive, like a corpse' and the attack of giddiness that follows shortly causes him to decide to let the plane go on without him and not to reply when his name is called. The stewardess conscientiously finds him after the flight has been delayed on his account, and the further course of his movements is thus determined. This first departure from normality in Faber's actions is accompanied briefly by the wish to change his identity—a theme characteristic of Frisch which can be traced through many of his works—and if Faber holds on to his earlier self in many respects, with the help of his training as a technologist, he is none the less driven into the catastrophic confusion of Sabeth as daughter and bride.

The impact of the imagination and the emotions upon the composure of the technologist is a hostile force which Faber wishes to ward off in the same way that he sees nature in the outside world as destructive of man. In these last weeks of his life, which include his fiftieth birthday, emotional crisis is accompanied by a precipitate deterioration of his physical health of which he is not fully aware. After resisting a permanent relationship with Ivy he proposes marriage to Sabeth and journeys from Paris to Greece with her on a 'honeymoon' that is lived in the present. The 'blindness' of Faber during this period is followed by the violent shock of the confrontation with Hanna and the consequent revelation of Sabeth's identity followed by the girl's death (here an error in diagnosis does not give technology its opportunity to save her life). The pattern of ancient myth looms behind the surface reality. If in the earlier parts of the closing section Faber goes back to the past, it seems for a while as if he may begin life anew. But the showing of his films in Düsseldorf brings back to him the uniqueness of his experiences and the finality of the loss of Sabeth. Yet Faber retains his will to live and to build afresh on the ruins of the past:

I hang on to this life as I never have done before, and even if there is only one miserable year, or three months, or two months (that would be September and October). I shall go on hoping, although I know that I am lost. But I am not alone. Hanna is my friend, and I am not alone.

Frisch's confrontation of the technologist with the sphere of nature and the imagination is carried out with great skill. The style, with its contemporary idiom and poetic imagery, can move from the commonplace to the grandiloquent as in the scene where Faber and Sabeth describe the night and the sunrise in Greece, or where Faber runs through his films in Düsseldorf. By means of concentration of form and direct language this novel can effectively present issues which transcend locality in their diagnosis of a modern type of man.

Whereas Max Frisch's protagonist in *Homo Faber* has looked at the contemporary world from the vantage-point of a cosmopolitan who avoids all ties of family and locality, Heinrich Böll's *Billard um Halbzehn* is a novel of family life in a specific German urban setting that is intimately bound with public issues from recent German history. Amid the flux of the world they live in, the Fähmel family represent an element of stability. The portrait of the three generations implies a sense of unity and the preservation of something permanent in face of the transience and destruction which each leading male representative confronts. Heinrich, who is celebrating his eightieth birthday on 6 September 1958, has seen the destruction of imperial Germany in the years 1914–18; his son Robert tried to remain apart from National Socialist Germany, while Robert's son Joseph has been growing up in the course of the establishment of the Federal Republic. All three have had their private lives damaged, perhaps seriously warped, by the impact of national events. Heinrich, a farmer's son, had come into the city, no doubt Cologne, and established himself as a successful architect, marrying the daughter of a lawyer. As an old man he feels that he is only a husk, a public figure, a monument to himself, and that he has more in common with Kaiser Wilhelm II than he would have imagined as a young man. He has learnt to live with the discrepancy between his personal outlook and the general trend of society, bridging the gap with irony, although he has realized that 'irony was not sufficient, and never would be sufficient'. Robert's conflict with the norm of society in the 1930s has been more overt than his father's. His protective friendship with Schrella led to a demonstration against authority which occasioned harsh retaliatory measures. After flight to Holland came the return home, a turning-point which was to numb his sense of purpose and of emotional directness permanently. He is responsible for the blowing up in 1945 of the abbey which his father had built; for his son Joseph the discovery of this fact threatens to become a major obstacle in their relationship. The abbey may perhaps represent the family's unity in the shadow of the church, in spite of all the disintegrating forces of latent personal conflicts, of German society and indeed of factors within the church. The Fähmels embody both positive and negative aspects of tradition. Heinrich and Robert, moulded by what their family and church stand for, have suffered and been eroded by the events of history. Their earlier spontaneity has yielded to compromise, but they have retained their essential integrity.

The novel contains the actions and thoughts of a group of characters during the course of about ten hours on one day, the place being restricted to the city and its neighbourhood. The preoccupation with time, already indicated in the title, is precise, as it is elsewhere in Böll's work. Past alternates with present, and the picture of the family's earlier years, from Heinrich's arrival in the city in 1907, through the First World War and on to the conclusion of the Second, is built up in the memories of the characters. We are given the perspective of their various points of view, often in the third person and past tense, and also as interior monologue in the first person and present tense. The first six of the novel's thirteen chapters, rather more than half its length, are primarily exposition, where the Fähmel family are seen predominantly in the passive stance. The action in the present effectively begins with the return of Schrella in chapter seven, and while the ensuing six chapters account for a passage of time that is roughly equivalent to the proportion of space allocated to it by the novelist, a sense of quicker movement is conveyed by the advent of Schrella, who acts as a catalyst as far as Robert is concerned, and by the drawing together of other parts of the action. Heinrich's wife Johanna, who lives in the 'enchanted castle' of a mental hospital, confuses past and present in one shapeless continuum, and it is only with a laborious struggle that she can come to a realization of the actuality of time as the normal world experiences it; her sense of returning to inclusion in time impels her to go out into the larger world (it is the occasion of her husband's eightieth birthday), though with an ill-directed impulse to violent action.

Quotations, images and gestures are used as leitmotifs throughout the work. The repetition of actions by characters helps to give an effect of pattern and continuity over the years, and to show the individual's tendency to protect himself by routine as well as to try to impose some sense of his own meaning upon the flux; thus Heinrich has taken breakfast at the Café Kroner with monotonuous regularity, while Robert has played billiards at the Prinz Heinrich Hotel with a habitualness that has become ceremony and liturgy for the porter concerned. The various leitmotifs also help to extend the substance of the narrative by indicating further horizons, as well as to bind it together by showing links in meaning that might otherwise be more elusive. The most pervasive example of this approach is seen in the contrast of lambs and buffaloes. The lambs derive from the Bible, with particular reference to John's Gospel ('Feed my lambs'), and would include all who are persecuted and who are vulnerable, while aggressive nationalism and complacent conformity are among the traits associated with the buffaloes. Schiller's *Kabale und Liebe* and Hölderlin help to denote the differences. Schrella, the stateless citizen who has not revisited Germany for twenty-two years, is the principal lamb-figure, while Nettlinger, formerly a Nazi and persecutor of Schrella when they were at school together, and now a self-satisfied, sociable and highly regarded member of the new democracy, is a buffalo that has shed his aura of terror.

During his years away from Germany Schrella has lived mainly by teaching German in England and Holland; in both countries he has been in trouble for taking an apparently pro-German attitude at an awkward time. He has remained a wanderer, without a home in Germany or any other country; he refuses Robert's invitation to stay: 'I am afraid of houses where you make yourself at home and let yourself be convinced of the banal fact that life goes on as usual and that time is a healer.' Schrella believes that it is better for him to continue teaching elementary German in a foreign country; the repetition of the principal parts of verbs becomes a leitmotif, a quick and constant reminder of the passing of time. Chapter nine contains a significant episode for Schrella, the tram-ride to the suburb of Blessenfeld and therewith the return to the scene of his childhood. It is a pilgrimage, but accompanied by the fear that old associations may arouse desolately deep feelings within him; however, he is relieved (like Robert on his return visit to the abbey) to discover that it is possible for him to remain detached and that the 'ice-flowers' of memory can be prevented from thawing out. He has been afraid of the return home because it may melt his heart, just as his mother had been exhausted by her own pity and kindness; Erika Progulske, who almost recognizes him, has hardened her heart and survived.

Billard um Halbzehn combines colloquial language, social satire and three-dimensional realism with a use of leitmotifs and a consciousness of time that builds its material into a taut structure. At the same time the intellectual framework is an appropriate vessel for the expression of the author's vision and deep emotion.

Günter Grass's *Hundejahre*, ebullient in fantasy and realism, extends its time sequence from the nineteen-twenties to the fifties. The first episode shows Walter Matern and Eddi Amsel as nine-year-old boys by the edge of the Vistula. Amsel makes scarecrows and is bullied by other boys at school until Matern becomes his protector; in partnership they thrive, Amsel's creative ability makes a considerable impression in the locality and with the help of Matern and an adult, the ferryman Kriwe, it is put to commercially successful purpose. Matern and Amsel are here already bound together in a relationship that is not simply a friendship but a form of co-operation that can be both fruitful and ill-fated. After long separation the two come together again, brought face to face by the dog Pluto at the 'Zoologischer Garten' station in Berlin. In the final episodes Amsel conducts Matern round his underground scarecrow-factory in the Harz, and the novel ends with the two men taking baths to clean themselves after the tour through the mine-works.

During the Berlin episode Amsel has said to Matern:

> Certainly one may say that out of every man a scarecrow can be made; for after all, as we should never forget, the scarecrow is created in man's image. But of all the peoples who drag out their lives as scarecrow-arsenals, it is primarily the German people that, even more than the Jews, have every likelihood of presenting to the world one day the prototype scarecrow.

Here, as frequently elsewhere in the novel, incidents and conversations are no doubt weighted with symbolism. There is a basis of detailed, graphic realism which willingly merges into exuberant fantasy. The main lines of the work are developed with firm emphasis, though with encyclopaedic minutiae as well as with ebullient playfulness, more or less independent episodes interrupt them. It is the childhood and youthful experiences in and around Danzig that come to life most strikingly, and which are to cast their shadows irrevocably on all that follows after. Amsel's and Matern's lives subsequently are a working-out of the consequences of earlier years or a return to their memory. Experiences that took place before 1939 later acquire a legendary character. The scarecrows of Eddi Amsel's childhood grew out of an imagination fed by immediate impressions and by mythology from school lessons. During the war years Amsel almost realizes his preoccupation with them in the form of a ballet, but an air-raid brings disaster. With 1945 comes an interim period as occupation official and black-market dealer, before he emerges as managing director of Brauxel & Co., and the scarecrows become the object of a large manufacturing organization. The reunion of the two men spans an arch across the thirty years, returns them to their childhood perhaps and lets them be reborn.

The major turning-point in their relationship, and a central climax in the narrative, is the violent attack on Eddi Amsel by a group of storm-troopers led by Walter Matern, in the late nineteen-thirties. In the falling snow, with crows overhead, Amsel is left as a scarecrow himself, a snowman. An unexpected thaw allows him to recover sufficiently to escape to Berlin where with a new identity and new teeth he can begin another existence; he needs to change his name from Amsel to Haseloff, and then to Brauxel (or Brauksel, or Brauchsel), though his personality retains its continuity.

The novel falls into three principal sections, each with its own narrative manner. In the first Amsel is writing; he is in charge of the 'authors' collective' as of his business in the Harz, and the chapters are entitled 'Early shifts'. He introduces the scenes from early childhood and from the Danzig Realgymnasium, concluding with the discovery of Jenny as a foundling infant and her adoption by the teacher Oswald Brunies. The second section is in the form of imagined letters from Harry Liebenau to his cousin Tulla Pokriefke; they are contemporaries of Jenny Brunies, and about ten years younger than Amsel and Matern. It is Harry Liebenau who is the observer of Amsel's beating-up and of the parallel incident of Jenny's being bullied by Tulla and left as scarecrow-snowman by the Gutenberg monument. Like Eddi Amsel, Jenny is transformed by the experience. Later the narrative ceases to be a series of letters to Tulla and becomes a 'concluding fairy-tale', with episodes introduced by 'Once upon a time . . .' The section concludes with the dog Prinz leaving the Führer's headquarters and finding a new master, Walter Matern, who is taken prisoner of war in the spring of 1945. The third section follows the adventures of Walter Matern until the final reunion with Eddi Amsel takes place. The sequence of mainly sexual episodes where Matern destructively hunts down incidents from his past is less real than the earlier parts of the novel taking place in the Danzig milieu. Matern's father, set up by Amsel in a windmill home between Düren and Krefeld, predicts the future and can anticipate West Germany's financial prosperity. Amsel's magic spectacles enable young people of 1955 to see the political past of the generation before them. It is in these post-1945 episodes that the narrative power of the novel diminishes, recovering itself for the nightmare finale in the underground factory. Here Matern comments that the impression made by this setting is one of hell, while Amsel's last spoken words are 'Orcus is above!'

Matern's reaction when he and Amsel as boys discover a skeleton in the underground passage below the town church, differs from that of his companion. While Amsel is affected by no seriousness of mood and wishes to remove the skull to use it for scarecrow-modelling, the other boy responds with a sense of awe, which is here combined with hatred and the impulse to kill, with a characteristic grinding of teeth, with a reference to Amsel's Jewishness and a few blows with his cudgel to curb his companion:

> The grinder says nothing. The grinding of teeth is intended to be clear enough. It says: Amsel is not to stretch out his small fingers. Amsel is not to take. The skull may not be taken. Don't disturb it. Don't touch it. Place of skulls. Golgotha. Giant's grave. Grinding of teeth.

Tulla Pokriefke, with whom Harry Liebenau is vainly in love, embodies qualities sharply contrasted to those of the good-natured Jenny Brunies. Her persecution of the latter begins even before the shock of the drowning of her deaf-and-dumb brother Konrad when she is seven. An example of the author's use of the grotesque in his delineation of extreme emotional distress is shown in the description of Tulla's remaining for more than seven days in the dog's kennel. Sexual irregularity later leads to her expulsion from school. It is she who is responsible for Oswald Brunies, and two Ukrainian workers, being sent to Stutthof concentration camp, and it is she who penetrates beyond the barbed wire to bring back to Matern and others of the anti-aircraft battery evidence that the distant mound consists of human bones. The crows live there, with no scarecrows to disperse them. Tulla presents a skull to Matern and he replies by striking her on the face. His reaction is an echo of his behaviour as a boy when he and Amsel discovered the skeleton beneath the church.

The novel contains a wealth of episodes and of subordinate characters; though the main tension lies between the contrasting figures of Matern and Amsel, with the subsidiary female characters of Tulla and Jenny corresponding to them, there are many other strands of motif to be traced out. If the bizarre quality seems at times forced and if the urge to shock appears to run away with artistic intention, one is repeatedly impressed by the ingenuity of the author's imagination.

The novels which have been discussed in the preceding pages are essentially a personal selection, and the dangers of arbitrariness inherent in making this choice are realized. Evidently other works by these authors could have been singled out, and other authors might very well have been represented above too. While being aware of the limitations of this approach and of the sketchiness of the present attempt to follow it, we believe that these twelve novels will reveal something of the vitality and variety of imaginative prose in the German language during the present century, and the sense of dedication and earnestness with which German authors have conceived their rôle. Perhaps it would be as well to mention too that much has had to be left out by considering only novels and omitting the shorter prose-forms. A number of these authors have made distinguished contributions to the Novelle and short story, where themes and moods of the age are also reflected. Thomas Mann's *Tonic Kröger* looks back to the nineteenth century and evokes the lyrical mood of Storm as well as the problems of the artist and Bürger at the turn of the century. Kafka's *Die Verwandlung* brings into fiercely clear perspective the mood of individual crisis conveyed in his novel-fragments. Bergengruen is among those who have cherished a traditional approach to the Novelle, while since 1945 especially the short story with a contemporary, everyday setting, has become increasingly popular among German authors, the contribution of Böll having played a considerable part here.

The first sixty years of the twentieth century may seem at times abruptly discontinuous, with a sense of a need for radically new beginnings in 1918 and 1945, and yet the literature of the age, while reflecting these changes, seems to have a sense of continuity. If it does, this is due in part to the way many authors have been able to provide links, through their own personality and writing, between one literary fashion or historical segment and another. Writing in his autobiographical essay *Meine Zeit* (1950) Thomas Mann was conscious of this, as of the sensation that the time of his youth was fundamentally different from that of his last years; to have lived in the world before 1914 implied a 'cultural advantage over those who have been born straight into contemporary disintegration'. To have spanned the two epochs meant to have experienced 'the continuity, the transitoriness of history': 'For history is fulfilled in transitions, not in fits and starts, and in every *ancien régime* the seeds of the new age are already alive and intellectually at work.'

IV

STUDENT'S GUIDE

Select Bibliographies

CONTENTS

Abbreviations

ADB:	*Allgemeine deutsche Biographie*
AUFRIß:	W. Stammler's *Deutsche Philologie im Aufriß*, 2nd enlarged ed.
CL:	*Comparative Literature*
DLL:	*Deutsches Literatur-Lexikon*, 4 vols. ed. by W. Kosch, and abbreviated ed.
ÉG:	*Études Germaniques*
EU:	*Euphorion (Dichtung und Volkstum)*
FuF:	*Forschungen und Fortschritte*
G:	*Germanistik. Internationales Referatenorgan mit bibliogr. Hinweisen*
GLL:	*German Life and Letters*
GRM:	*Germanisch-Romanische Monatsschrift*
Hdb:	*Handbuch der deutschen Gegenwartsliteratur*, ed. by H. Kunisch
KLW:	*Das Kleine Lexikon der Weltliteratur*, ed. by H. Pongs, 6th enlarged ed.
LW:	*Lexikon der Weltliteratur*, ed. by G. v. Wilpert, 2 vols.
MLN:	*Modern Language Notes*
MLQ:	*Modern Language Quarterly*
MLR:	*Modern Language Review*
PMLA:	*Publications of the Mod. Lang. Assoc. of America*
RLL:	*Reallexikon der deutschen Literaturgeschichte*, 4 vols. new ed. by W. Kohlschmidt and W. Mohr

ed.:	edited, editor, edition
Ges.:	Gesammelte(Werke)
KZ:	Konzentrationslager
l.c.:	loco citato
posth.:	posthumous(ly)
Ps.:	pseudonym
tr.:	translated, translator, translation

and some conventional abbreviations used throughout the book.

Some Significant Literary and Historical Dates

1859: Ch. Darwin: *The Origin of Species*
    Richard Wagner: *Tristan und Isolde*

1862: Gerhart Hauptmann and Arthur Schnitzler born; J. N. Nestroy died

1863: Arno Holz and Richard Dehmel born; Friedrich Hebbel died

1864: Frank Wedekind born

1868: Dostoevsky: *The Idiot*; Maxim Gorki and Stefan George born

1869: Leo Tolstoy: *War and Peace*

1871: Heinrich Mann and Christian Morgenstern born

1872: Fr. Grillparzer died

1874: H. v. Hofmannsthal born

1875: Thomas Mann and R. M. Rilke born; E. Mörike died

1877: Hermann Hesse born; Ibsen: *The Pillars of Society*

1881: Dostoevsky died; Ibsen: *Ghosts*

1883: Richard Wagner died; Nietzsche: *Also sprach Zarathustra*

1884: *Moderne Dichtercharaktere*

1885: A. Holz: *Das Buch der Zeit*

1886: Oskar Kokoschka born

1888: Theodor Storm died

1889: L. Anzengruber died; The *Freie Bühne* in Berlin (Otto Brahm); H. Sudermann: *Die Ehre*

1890: Gottfried Keller died; Holz and Schlaf: *Die Familie Selicke*; George: *Hymnen*

1891/2: Arno Holz: *Die Kunst, ihr Wesen und ihre Gesetze*

1892: Walt Whitman died

1895: Th. Fontane: *Effie Briest*; F. Wedekind: *Erdgeist*; A. Schnitzler: *Liebelei*

1898: Bert Brecht born; C. F. Meyer died; Th. Fontane died; Moscow Theatre founded (Stanislawski)

1900: Nietzsche died; Tolstoy: *Resurrection*

1901: Thomas Mann: *Buddenbrooks*; A. Strindberg: *The Dance of Death*

1905: Rilke: *Stundenbuch* publ.; Max Reinhardt: Director of the 'Deutsches Theater'

1906: Henry Ibsen died; Gerhart Hauptmann: *Und Pippa tanzt*

1907: Gorki: *Die Mutter*; George: *Der siebente Ring*; Agnes Miegel: *Balladen und Lieder*

1909: D. v. Liliencron died

1910: Tolstoy died; Björnstjerne Björnson died; Th. Däubler: *Nordlicht*

1911: C. Sternheim: *Die Hose*; F. v. Unruh: *Offiziere*

1912: Georg Heym d.; August Strindberg d.; Otto Brahm d.; R. Sorge: *Der Bettler*

1914(–18): World War I; Georg Trakl died; Christian Morgenstern died

1916: Arno Holz: *Phantasus* Folio Edition; G. Kaiser *Von Morgens bis Mitternachts*

1918: F. Wedekind died; Heinrich Mann: *Der Untertan*

1919: *Menschheitsdämmerung* (Anthology of Expressionism)

1921: E. Toller: *Masse Mensch*

1922: B. Brecht: *Trommeln in der Nacht*; H. v. Hofmannsthal: *Das Salzburger große Welttheater*

1924: Thomas Mann: *Der Zauberberg*; E. Barlach: *Die Sündflut*

1926: R. M. Rilke died; E. Barlach: *Der blaue Boll*

1927: Arnold Zweig: *Der Streit um den Sergeanten Grischa*

1928: Bertolt Brecht: *Dreigroschenoper*

1929: Arno Holz died; H. v. Hofmannsthal died; Alfred Döblin: *Berlin Alexanderplatz*

1933: Burning of books by the National Socialists; Stefan George died

1936: Maxim Gorki died

1938: Ernst Barlach died

1939(–45): World War II; B. Brecht: *Leben des Galilei*; E. Toller died

1942: C. Sternheim died; A. Mombert died; R. Musil died

1943: H. Hesse: *Das Glasperlenspiel*

1945: Else Lasker-Schüler died; Franz werfel d.; Josef Weinheber d.; Georg Kisaer d.

1946: Gerhart Hauptmann died; C. Zuckmayer: *Des Teufels General*

1947: Ricarda Huch died; Thomas Mann: *Doktor Faustus*; W. Borchert: *Draußen vor der Tür*

1950: Heinrich Mann died
1955: Thomas Mann died
1956: G. Benn died; B. Brecht died; Max Frisch: *Herr Biedermann und die Brandstifter*; Friedrich Dürrenmatt: *Der Besuch der alten Dame*
1957: Max Frisch: *Homo Faber*
1962: H. Hesse died; R. A. Schröder d.
1964: G. Britting died; Werner Bergengruen d.; Agnes Miegel d.
1965: Johannes Bobrowski died
1966: Hans Arp died
1967: R. Hochhuth: *Soldaten*
1968: P. Weiss: *Vietnam Discourse*

3

General Literary Bibliographies

Clemens Köttelwesch: *Bibliographie der deutschen Literaturwissenschaft*, 6 vols. ed. by H. W. Eppelsheimer; vol. I: 1945–53 (Eppelsheimer); vol. II: 1954–6 (Köttelwesch); vol. III: 1957–8 (Köttelwesch); vol. IV: 1959–60 (Köttelwesch); vol. V: 1961–2 (Köttelwesch), Frankfurt a.M.

B. Q. Morgan: *A Critical Bibliography of German Literature in English Translation: 1481–1927. With Supplement Embracing the Years 1928–1935*, Stanford University Press, California, 1938

J. Hansel: *Bücherkunde für Germanisten*, 1959; and *Personal Bibliographie zur deutschen Literaturgeschichte*, 1967.

W. P. Friedrich: *An Outline of German Literature*, New York, 1961, 2nd revised and enlarged ed.

Josef Körner: *Bibliographisches Handbuch des deutschen Schrifttums*, 4th ed., 1966, Bern

Deutsches Bücherverzeichnis, Graz, Austria

A Catalog of Books presented by Library of Congress Printed Cards, New Jersey, U.S.A.

Richard Mönnig: *Amerika und England im deutschen, österreichischen und schweizerischen Schrifttum der Jahre 1945–1949*, Stuttgart, 1951; and *Bibliography of Paperbound Books translated from the German and of Works on Germany*, Inter Nationes, Bonn, 1962

Hermann Kunisch: *Handbuch der deutschen Gegenwartsliteratur*, Munich, 1965; and *Kleines Handbuch der deutschen Gegenwartsliteratur*, 1967

Robert F. Arnold: *Allgemeine Bücherkunde zur neueren deutschen Literaturgeschichte*, 4th revised ed. by H. Jakob, 1966

Kürschners Deutscher Literatur-Kalender, 1967

Hermann Pongs: *Das Kleine Lexikon der Weltliteratur*, 6th ed., 1967

Gero von Wilpert: *Lexikon der Weltliteratur*, 2 vols., 1967

See also *Aufriß*, RLL, LW.

I am grateful to Professor V. Lange (Princeton) for a number of titles in my bibliographies.

4

General Works of Reference

(*a*) DRAMA

Theater heute, Zschft. ed. by Erhard Friedrich, Siegfried Melchinger, Hennig Rischbieter, Verlag Erhard Friedrich, Velber, nr. Hanover

Maske und Kothurn, ed. by the 'Institut für Theater-Wissenschaft', Vienna

Margret Dietrich: *Das moderne Drama*, Stuttgart, 1961

H. F. Garten: *Gerhart Hauptmann*, 1954; *Modern German Drama*, 1959

S. Melchinger: *Theater der Gegenwart*, Frankfurt a.M., 1956

Ronald Peacock: *The Art of the Drama*, 1957

Benno von Wiese (ed.): *Das deutsche Drama* (Von Barock bis zur Gegenwart), Interpretationen, 1958

Paul Fechter: *Das europäische Drama*, 3 vols., I, 1956–8

Ernst Alker: *Die deutsche Literatur im 19. Jhdt: 1832–1914*, Stuttgart, 1961; 1962 sec. rev. ed.

K. Guthke: *Geschichte und Poetik der deutschen Tragikomödie*, Göttingen, 1961

A. Müller and M. Schlien (eds.): *Dramen des Naturalismus*, Emsdetten, 1962

E. Ruprecht (ed.): *Literarische Manifeste des Naturalismus (1880–1892)*, 1962

Jost Schillemeit (ed.): *Deutsche Dramen von Gryphius bis Brecht*, Interpretationen, Fischer-Bücherei, 1965, vol. II

Heinz Kindermann: *Theatergeschichte Europas*, vol. VII, Salzburg, 1965; *Meister der Komödie*, Wien, 1952

P. Szondi: *Theorie des modernen Dramas*, 1956[1], 1959[2], Revidierte Ausgabe (edition Suhrkamp) 1963[1], 1967[4]; *Versuch über das Tragische*, Insel, 1961[1], 1964[2]; *Satz und Gegensatz*. Six Essays about Hofmannsthal, Th. Mann, Walter Benjamin, etc., Insel, 1964; *Hölderlin-Studien. Mit einem Traktat über philologische Erkenntnis*, Insel, 1967 (including Gattungspoetik und Geschichtsphilosophie)

Kindermann—Dietrich—Mühlher—Thurnher—Schmitz (ed.): *Dichtung aus Österreich* (Anthologie in 3 Bdn und einem Ergänzungsbd), Wien, 1966

Ingrid Bode: *Die Autobiographien zur deutschen Literatur, Kunst und Musik, 1900–1965*, Stuttgart, 1966

(b) NOVEL AND *Novelle*

H. Boeschenstein: *The German Novel 1939–1944*, Toronto, 1949

H. M. Waidson: *The Changing Pattern of the German Novel*, Inaugural Lecture, University College Swansea, 1961; *The Modern German Novel, a mid-twentieth century survey*, 1959

Roy Pascal: *The German Novel*, 1956; Paperback 1965

E. K. Bennett: *A History of the German Novelle*, 2nd ed. revised and continued by H. M. Waidson, 1961

W. E. Yuill: *Malice in Wonderland*, Contemporary Satire in Western Germany. Inaugural Lecture, University of Nottingham, 1967; *German Narrative Prose*, 2nd vol., 1966

R. Hinton Thomas: *Seventeen Modern German Stories*, 1965, ed. with Introduction and a Bibliographical Note

Johannes Klein: *Geschichte der deutschen Novelle von Goethe bis zur Gegenwart*, 1960, 4th ed.

Werner Welzig: *Der deutsche Roman im 20. Jahrhundert*, Stuttgart (Kröners Taschenausgabe)

Benno von Wiese: *Die deutsche Novelle von Goethe bis Kafka*, 2 vols., Interpretationen, 1963–4

R. R. Heitner (ed.): *The Contemporary Novel in Germany*, 1967

(c) LYRICAL POETRY

A. Closs: *Die neuere deutsche Lyrik bis zur Gegenwart*, Deutsche Philologie im Aufriß, ed. by W. Stammler, vol. II 1954, pp. 43–258; 1960, 2nd ed.; *The Genius of the German Lyric*, 2nd ed., Paperback, 1965; *Die freien Rhythmen in der deutschen Lyrik*, 1947; ed. *Reality and Creative Vision* (Symposium), 1963

E. Ermatinger: *Die deutsche Lyrik seit Herder*, 1921 ff., 3 vols.

L. Forster: *German Poetry 1944–1948*, 1949

R. Haller: *Geschichte der deutschen Lyrik vom Ausgang des Mittelalters bis zu Goethes Tod*, 1967

W. Kayser: *Die Geschichte der deutschen Ballade*, 1936

W. Killy: *20. Jahrhundert: Texte und Zeugnisse 1880–1933*, 1967

J. Klein: *Die deutsche Lyrik*, 1964, 2nd ed., 2 vols.

E. Lunding: *Wege zur Kunstinterpretation*, 1953; *Strömungen und Strebungen der modernen Literaturwissenschaft*, 1952

B. Markwardt: *Geschichte der deutschen Poetik*, 5th vol. 1967

Günther Müller: *Geschichte des deutschen Liedes*, 1925

P. Witkop: *Die deutschen Lyriker*, 1921 ff., 2 vols.

See also lists under paragraphs 7 and 10

5

Some Literary Journals and Magazines about the turn of the Nineteenth Century

1882–1884: *Kritische Waffengänge*, ed. by the brothers Heinrich (1855–1906) and Julius Hart (1859–1930), fought for a realistic theatre which at the same time was to present a big intellectual conflict

1885–1902: *Die Gesellschaft*, ed. by Michael Georg Conrad (1846–1927), co-eds.: C. Bleibtreu, Jacobowski. The models were Nietzsche and Wagner, etc.; attacked pseudo-dealings of the philistines; later also against the Berlin Naturalism

1887–1932: *Der Kunstwart*, ed. by Ferdinand Avenarius (1856–1923). He was a forward-looking guardian of tradition (Mörike, Hebbel, etc.) and champion of the best in contemporary literature, e.g. the works of Holz and G. Hauptmann
Avenarius also edited the *Hausbuch deutscher Lyrik* and poems of his own. Also:
Balladenbuch, repeatedly re-edited

1890 ff.: *Freie Bühne*, ed. by Otto Brahm (1856–1912), from 1891 ed. also by Wilhelm Bölsche, then Julius Hart, O. J. Bierbaum, Oskar Bie, etc.
from 1904: *Die neue Rundschau*

1892–1919: *Blätter für die Kunst*, ed. by Stefan George; see here p. 14

1892–1922: *Die Zukunft*, ed. by Maximilian Harden. (Ps. for Isidor Witkowski.) He was relentlessly attacked by the editor of *Die Fackel*. Harden, however, fought for the recognition of Ibsen, Tolstoy, Strinberg

1895–1900: *Pan*, ed. by O. J. Bierbaum, Bodenhausen, Meier-Gräfe, Flaischlen, etc. Aim = to educate the public to an appreciation of art and music and artistic book production. Contributors: Hartleben, H. v. Hofmannsthal, Holz, Maeterlinck, Verlaine, Kipling, etc.

1896 ff.: *Simplizissimus*, ed. by Verlag Albert Langen, ruthlessly satirical, against conceit, prudishness, bigotry and sanctimoniousness, amongst its contributors were: Altenberg, Dehmel, K. Kraus, D. v. Liliencron, Morgenstern, Rilke, Roda-Roda, Scheerbart, Schlaf, Wedekind etc.

1899–1902: *Die Insel*, ed. by Bierbaum, Heymel, R. A. Schröder; the aim of this journal was to support all truly creative production and intentions of the age. Contributors: Borchardt, Dehmel, Holz, Detlev von Liliencron, Rilke, Dauthendey, Walser, Wedekind, etc.

1899–1936: *Die Fackel*, ed. by K. Kraus (see p. 306); a much-feared and highly esteemed journal which from about 1912 he alone directed and wrote and published, as an independent, deadly weapon against Kerr, Harden, etc., against his own time and society, the 'huge swamp of phrases'. He denounced Wilhelm II and Franz Joseph who, to him, were war-mongers

1904–1914: *Der Charon*, founded by Otto zur Linde (1873–1938) and Rudolf Pannwitz (1881–   ), p. 320

1910–1932: *Sturm*, founded and ed. by H. Walden; see Expressionism

1911–1932: *Aktion*, founded and ed. by Franz Pfemfert; see Expressionism, p. 22

Cf. Fritz Schlawe: *Literarische Zeitschriften I. vl. 1885–1910; II. vl. 1910–1933;* 1961/2

6

Some Literary Journals and Magazines
of our Time

(For studies on specific aspects of German literature,
see also list of Abbreviations)

Akzente (Zeitschrift für Dichtung), ed. by W. Höllerer and
H. Bender, since 1967 ed. H. Bender

Antaios (Zweimonatsschrift), ed. by E. Jünger and Mircea Eliade

Frankfurter Hefte (Zschft. für Kultur u. Politik)

Kursbuch, ed. by H. M. Enzenberger

Literatur und Kritik, österr. Monatsschrift, ed. by G. Fritsch and
R. Henz

Lyrische Hefte, ed. by A. Astel

Manuskripte (Zschft. für Literature, Kunst u. Kritik), ed. by the
Forum Stadpark Graz

Merkur (Deutsche Zschft. für europ. Denken), ed. by H. Paeschke

Monat (Eine internationale Zschft.), Berlin-Dahlem

Neue Deutsche Hefte, ed. by J. Günther

Die Neue Rundschau, S. Fischer Verlag

Neues Forum (Internat. Zschft.)

Rot, texts ed. by M. Bense and Elisabeth Walther

Sinn und Form, most important East German literary journal,
Berlin; ed. by W. Girnus

Sprache im Technischen Zeitalter, ed. by W. Höllerer

Texte und Zeichen (literarische Zschft.), ed. by Alfred Andersch

Universitas (Zschft. für Wissenschaft, Kunst u. Literatur), ed. by
H. W. Bähr

Welt und Wort (literarische Monatsschrift), Heliopolis Verlag

Wort in der Zeit (Österr. lit. Zschft.), Wien; ed. by R. Henz und
G. Zerling

Zeitwende: Die neue Furche, Schriftleiter Wolfgang Böhme

German Studies, ed. by J. Hohnholz

German Literary Magazines, by P. Bridgwater, TLS April, June,
1968

7

Interpretations, Critical Essays and Literary Theories

Th. W. Adorno: *Noten zur Literatur*, 1958

Mein Gedicht ist mein Messer, Lyriker zu ihren Gedichten, ed. by
H. Bender, 1955

G. Benn: *Die Probleme der Lyrik*, 1951

P. Böckmann: *Formensprache*, 1966

C. M. Bowra: *Das Erbe des Symbolismus* (1943), German ed. 1947

Gedicht und Gedanke, ed. by H. O. Burger, 1942

E. Cassirer: *The Philosophy of Symbolic Forms*, 1953

A. Closs: *Medusa's Mirror*, 1957; *Urbild—Abbild—Sinnbild*, FuF.,
1960; *The shattered image, the wholeness of human experience and
the experimental character of contemporary German Poetry* (in 3
parts), Bombay, 1965; *Concealment and Revelation in Modern
German Lyrical Poetry*, see The Colston Research Society
Symposium on *Reality and Creative Vision in German Lyrical
Poetry*, 1963

Deutsche Lyrik von Weckherlin bis Benn, ed. Jost Schillemeit, 1965

H. Friedrich: *Die Struktur der modernen Lyrik*. Von Baudelaire
bis zur Gegenwart (Rowohlts deutsche Enzyklopädie, 25),
1956

R. D. Gray: *The German Tradition in Literature: 1871–1945*; and *An
Introduction to German Poetry*, 1965

M. Hamburger: *Reason and Energy*, 1957: and *Modern German
Poetry: 1910–1960. An Anthology with Verse Translations*, 1962;
and *From Prophecy to Exorcism: the premises of modern German
literature*, 1965

H. Hatfield: *German Literature: The major figures in context*, 1966.

C. Heselhaus: *Deutsche Lyrik der Moderne*, 1962, 2nd ed.

Deutsche Literatur im XX. Jahrhundert, ed. by H. Friedmann and
O. Mann, 1967, 5th ed.

Wege zum Gedicht, ed. by R. Hirschenauer and A. Weber, 1956

C. Hohoff: *Geist und Ursprung*, 1954

H. v. Hofmannsthal: *Der Dichter und diese Zeit* (1907), now in
Prosa, II, 1951, pp. 264–98

H. E. Holthusen: *Der unbehauste Mensch. Motive and Probleme der modernen Literatur*, 1951; *Ja und Nein* (Neue kritische Versuche), 1954; *Das Schöne und das Wahre* (Neue Studien zur modernen Literatur), 1958; *Plädoyer für den Einzelnen*, 1967

A. Holz: *Revolution der Lyrik*, 1899

G. R. Hocke: *Manierismus in der Literatur. Sprach-Alchimie und esoterische Kombinationskunst* (Rowohlts deutsche Enzyklopädie 82/83), 1959

K. A. Horst: *Die deutsche Literatur der Gegenwart*, 1957

K. R. Srinivasa Iyengar: *The Adventure of Criticism*, 1962

Interpretationen moderner Lyrik, ed. by the Fachgruppe Deutsch-Geschichte im Bayerischen Philologenverband, 1954

W. Jens: *Statt einer Literaturgeschichte*, 1957, 1958[2]; *Deutsche Literatur der Gegenwart* (Themen, Stile, Tendenzen), 1961

H. Kasack: *Mosaiksteine*, 1956

W. Kayser: *Das Groteske*. Seine Gestaltung in Malerei und Dichtung, 1957

W. Killy: *Wandlungen des lyrischen Bildes*, 1956, reprinted.

W. Kohlschmidt: *Dichter, Tradition und Zeitgeist*, 1965

A. Liede: *Dichtung als Spiel. Studien zur Unsinnspoesie an den Grenzen der Sprache*, 2 vols. 1963

K. Leonhard: *Moderne Lyrik. Monolog und Manifest*, 1963

R. N. Maier: *Das moderne Gedicht*, 1959

Mathematik und Dichtung, ed. by H. Kreuzer and R. Gunzenhäuser, 1965, cf. MLR IV. 1968

W. Mönch: *Das Sonett, Gestalt und Geschichte*, 1955

W. Muschg: *Die Zerstörung der deutschen Literatur*, 1956

J. Pfeiffer: *Wege zur Dichtung*, 1953

Poetik: (Siebente Folge des Jahrbuchs *Gestalt und Gedanke*), ed. by the Bavarian Academy, Munich, 1962. In it R. A. Schröder deals with poetry as 'gift of improvisation and of skilful craft'

H. Pongs: *Dichtung im gespaltenen Deutschland*, 1966; *Das Bild in der Dichtung*, I, 1960, 2nd revised ed.

H. Popper: *Reflections on form in German Poetry*, Trivium, 1966.

S. S. Prawer: *The 'Uncanny' in Literature*, 1965; *German Lyric Poetry*, 1952

H. Read: *The Forms of Things Unknown* (Essays towards an aesthetic philosophy), 1960

M. Reich-Ranicki: *Literatur der kleinen Schritte. Deutsche Literatur heute*, 1967

R. Samuel and R. H. Thomas: *Expressionism in German Life, Literature and the Theatre* (1910–24), 1939

A. Schirokauer: *Expressionismus der Lyrik* (1924), now in *Germanistische Studien*, 1957, pp. 19–117

F. A. Schmitt: *Stoff- und Motivgeschichte der deutschen Literatur*, 1965, 2nd ed. enlarged

F. J. Schneider: *Der expressive Mensch und die deutsche Lyrik der Gegenwart. Geist und Form moderner Dichtung*, 1927

George Steiner: *Language and Silence*. Essays, 1958–1966, 1967. *Triffst du nur das Zauberwort*. Stimmen von heute zur deutschen Lyrik, ed. by J. Petersen, 1961

K. Wais: *Igitur. Begegnungen Mallarmés mit seinen Vorgängern*, Comparative Literature Studies, 1967

Wladimir Weidle: *Les Abeilles d'Aristée*, 1954

Benno von Wiese: ed. of *Die deutsche Lyrik*, 2 vols. 1956

As to the general historical background cf. Golo Mann: *The History of Germany since 1789*, tr. by Marian Jackson, 1968, and T. L. Jarman: *The Rise and Fall of Nazi Germany*, 1955, re-ed.

8

Expressionism

Half a century after the rise of the German Expressionist era, we are experiencing a revival and a marked increase of important research and of editions (e.g. Professor A. D. Klarmann's and Werfel editions), exhibitions, monographs and bibliographies, representing the Expressionistic movement of 1910–24, see above list and:

A. D. Klarmann: *Expressionism in German Literature. A retrospect of a half century*, MLQ, March 1965, and the bibliography mentioned therein

C. Hill and R. Ley: *The Drama of German Expressionism* (A German–English Bibliography), University of North Carolina Press, Chapel Hill, 1960

Lyrik des Expressionistischen Jahrzehnts. Von den Wegbereitern bis zum Dada, introduced by G. Benn, Wiesbaden, 1955

Ahnung und Aufbruch. Expressionistische Prosa, ed. and introduced by Karl Otten, Darmstadt, 1957; Karl Otten (born 1889) dedicated this edition to the friends of his youth: Franz Blei, Robert Musil, Franz Pfemfert

Paul Raabe: *Die Zeitschriften und Sammlungen des literarischen Expressionismus* (Repertorium . . . 1910–1921), Stuttgart, 1964

Fritz Schlawe: *Literarische Zeitschriften 1910–1933*, Stuttgart, 1962

Harry Pross: *Literatur und Politik* (Geschichte und Programme der politisch-liter. Zschften im deutschen Sprachgebiet seit 1870), Freiburg i.B., 1963

Günter Erken: *Der Expressionismus*, in H. Kunisch's *Handbuch der deutschen Gegenwartsliteratur*, 647 ff., 1964

W. H. Sokel: *The Writer in extremis*, Stanford University Press, 1959

K. L. Schneider: *Expressionism in Art and Literature*, Amer. German Review, 1966

9

Existentialism

It is out of the question to give here an adequate bibliography of the vast literature on Existentialism. We therefore only merely offer titles of works or essays with special reference to our theme:

Søren Kierkegaard (1813–1855): *The Journals of Søren Kierkegaard*, ed. by Alexander Dru, London, 1938; *Kierkegaard*, by Walter Lowrie, London, 1938 (W. Lowrie gives us a glossary of Kierkegaard's terms); *Repetition*, tr. by W. Lowrie, Princeton, 1941

The Rev. Frederick Charles Copleston: *Existentialism and Modern Man*, 1948; *Contemporary Philosophy*, 1956; *A History of Philosophy* (Fichte to Nietzsche), 1963

Guido de Ruggiero: *Existentialism*, tr. by E. M. Cocks, ed. and introduced by Rayner Heppenstall, 1946

A. Closs: *Goethe and Kierkegaard*, MLQ, Seattle, Sept. 1949

Hans Jaeger: *Heidegger's Existential Philosophy and Modern German Literature*, PMLA, Sept. 1952; see also the bibliography of works by Heidegger and Jaspers

Jean Paul Sartre: *L'être et le néant*, 1943

The term Existentialism is used to cover various shades of philosophical thinking. There is an atheist existentialism (existence is born from NOTHING) as distinct from the Christian belief; there is a Catholic and a Protestant Existentialism; there is Sartre's view that God is absent and that man has nothing but his own will to rely on, e.g. his own free will in the choice of action: he must either shape his own destiny or perish. The responsibility lies in him alone.

Marxist determination is rejected, as the individual *cannot* win the freedom *in* society or *through* society, but only through him- or herself.

According to Father Copleston Heidegger is not, as has been often supposed, a preacher of heroic and tragic existence, but he carries on the analysis of the meaning of Being, which was pursued by philosophers like Aristotle and Hegel. Heidegger approaches the problem, however, in a new way, namely through an ontological analysis of man.

Jaspers, on the other hand, stands closer to Kierkegaard. For him, the chief function of philosophy is to break through the positivist mentality, to show that a purely scientific knowledge of all reality is unattainable, and to clarify for man his relationship to Being. For Jaspers 'Being' means ultimate Being as God, whereas for Heidegger, as for Aristotle, an analysis of the meaning of the term 'Being' logically precedes the raising of the problem of God's existence. If existence (i.e. our actual, particular life) precedes essence, i.e. the universal life, then the belief in the Platonic idea and a pre-established harmony is refuted.

But neither Heidegger nor Jaspers is an 'existentialist' in the same sense as Sartre.

Nietzsche's pronouncement : *God is dead* (cf. *Also sprach Zarathustra*, IV: 'Vom höheren Menschen') has been called by Rayner Heppenstall the 'greatest event in Western thought since the end of the 19th century'. It created a kind of metaphysical pornography (a 'self-indulgence in the muddy depths of life', Guido de Ruggiero, l.c.) and a language of new symbols, mainly based on Kierkegaard's philosophy and terminology: *repetition*, i.e. fresh start; '*the leap*': 'der Sprung', the 'acceptance' of one's fate (cf. Rilke's *Requiem*, etc.) as the means of gaining inner freedom; *existence* and the problem of feeling or of being guilty or not guilty (Kafka); and finally Kierkegaard's key-word: *anguish* (Angst): Nothingness engenders negatives: anxiety and a feeling of guilt. Omnes homines secundam naturam propagati nascuntur cum peccato, h.e. sine metu dei, sine fiducia erga deum et cum concupiscentia. . . . Kierkegaard, in spite of '*fear and trembling*', does not despair. He overcomes anguish by his belief in spiritual strength. The hour of despair is necessary for man's ultimate salvation. Sin and redemption are immanent in man's existence.

But Kierkegaard's rejection of compromise, his belief in suffering the tragic sense of our life as well as in the power of the '*example*' (of the divine person) is not shared by modern existentialists, who have emptied his philosophy of its religious foundation.

10

Lyrical Anthologies

Moderne Dichtercharaktere, ed. by W. Arent, 1884
Deutsche Lyrik seit Liliencron, ed. by H. Bethge, 1905
Im steinernen Meer. Großstadtgedichte, selected by O. Hübner and
    J. Moegelin, 1910
Der Kondor. Manifest jüngster Lyrik, ed. by K. Hiller, 1912
Die Aktionslyrik, vol. I: 1914–1916. Eine Anthologie, ed. by
    F. Pfemfert, 1916
Kameraden der Menschheit. Dichtungen zur Weltrevolution, ed. by
    L. Rubiner, 1919
Menschheitsdämmerung. Symphonie jüngster Dichtung, ed. by K. Pinthus,
    1919/20
Verkündigung, ed. by R. Kayser, 1921
Anthologie jüngster Lyrik, ed. by W. R. Fehse and K. Mann, 1927
*Das proletarische Schicksal. Ein Querschnitt durch die Arbeiterdichtung
    der Gegenwart*, ed. by H. Mühle, 1929
Das Gedicht. Blätter für die Dichtung, ed. by H. Ellermann, 1934 ff.
Die Ernte der Gegenwart, ed. by W. Vesper, 1940
De profundis. Deutsche Lyrik in dieser Zeit, ed. by G. Groll, 1946
Anthologie der Abseitigen, ed. by C. Giedion-Welcker, 1946
Ergriffenes Dasein. Deutsche Lyrik von 1900–1950, selected by
    H. E. Holthusen and F. Kemp, 1953 (1957 ff. enlarged ed.)
Das Gedicht. Jahrbuch zeitgenössischer Lyrik, ed. by R. Ibel, 1954–5 ff.
Deutsche Gedichte, ed. by Wiese-Echtermeyer, 1954
*Lyrik des expressionistischen Jahrzehnts. Von den Wegbereitern bis zum
    Dada*, introduced by G. Benn, 1955
*Die Lyrik des Expressionismus. Voraussetzungen, Ergebnisse und Grenzen,
    Nachwirkungen*, ed. by C. Heselhaus, 1956 (Deutsche Texte 5)
Transit. Lyrikbuch der Jahrhundertmitte, ed. by W. Höllerer, 1956
Dichtung moderner Maler, ed. by H. Platschek, 1956
Expeditionen (Deutsche Lyrik seit 1945), ed. by W. Weyrauch,
    1959
Deutsche Lyrik auf der anderen Seite, Ad den Besten, 1959
An den Wind geschrieben (Lyrik der Freiheit: 1933–1945), ed. by

Manfred Schlösser and Hans-Rolf Robertz, 1961, 2nd ed. Agora Series

Deutsche Lyrik. Gedichte seit 1945, ed. by H. Bingel, 1961

Aussichten—Junge Lyriker des deutschen Sprachraums, ed. by P. Hamm, 1966

Panorama moderner Lyrik deutschsprechender Länder, ed. by W. Hädecke and U. Miehe, 1966

Die Stimme Israels: deutsch-jüdische Lyrik 'nach 1933', ed. by Th. Röttger, 1966

Some English and American editions:

A. Closs and P. Williams (1957): *The Harrap Anthology of German Poetry*, several reprints; enlarged ed. in preparation

L. Forster: *The Penguin Book of German Verse*, 1959

W. Rose: *A Book of Modern German Lyric Verse 1890–1955*, 1960

Angel Flores: *An Anthology of German Poetry from Hölderlin to Rilke*, in English tr. with German originals, 1960, Anchor Books, New York

Michael Hamburger and Christopher Middleton: *Modern German Poetry 1910–60*, 1962

M. Bullock: ed. of *Expression. Poetry Quarterly*, current issues

P. Bridgwater: *Twentieth-Century German Poetry*, Penguin Books, 1963

Gertrude Clorius Schwebell: *Contemporary German Poetry*, Introduction by Professor V. Lange. *New Directions*, 1962; 1964 ff.

S. S. Prawer: *The Penguin Book of Lieder*, 1964, reprinted

E. Stahl: *The Oxford Book of German Verse*, revised 3rd ed., 1967

Christopher Middleton (ed.): *German Writing Today*, Penguin Books, 1967

Leading Contemporary German Authors of Works in Philosophy, Theology, Psychology, Aesthetics, Sociology, Economics and Journalism, etc.

As to the Bibliographies of influential physicists, mathematicians and great names such as Albert Schweitzer (1875–1965), Albert Einstein (1879–1955), W. K. Heisenberg (1901) etc., see the reference books: *Neue deutsche Biographie*, ed. by the Historische Kommission, Bayerische Akademie der Wissenschaften; *Die großen Deutschen*, ed. by H. Heimpel, Th. Heuss, B. Reifenberg; *Kürschner: Deutscher Gelehrten-Kalender*.

THEODOR W. ADORNO

Born 1903 in Frankfurt a.M., Sociologist, Professor at Frankfurt University. Emigrated in 1933. After the War returned to Germany and refounded with M. Horkheimer the Institute for Social Research.

Kierkegaard, Konstruktion des Ästhetischen, 1933; 1962
Dialektik und Aufklärung, together with Max Horkheimer, 1947
Philosophie der neuen Musik, 1949, 1958
Versuch über Wagner, 1952
Noten zur Literatur, I. 1958; II. 1961
Negative Dialektik, 1966

Professor Adorno also edited (1955) and characterized the works of the philosopher and friend:

WALTER BENJAMIN

Born 1892 in Berlin. Suicide 1940 in Portbou, on the French/Spanish border.

HERMANN BAHR

Born 1863 in Linz. Died 1934 in Munich. A powerful pioneer and spokesman on literary fashions. Contact with A. Holz and O. Brahm. A chameleon-like character whose many phases of transformation range from German Nationalism to Marxism, from an admiration of impressionism to an acceptance of Expressionism.

Kritik der Moderne, 1890
Die Überwindung des Naturalismus, 1891
Wiener Theater, 1899
Expressionismus, 1914

As to bibliography, see H. Kindermann, *Theatergeschichte Europas*, 1957
H. Bahr's comedy, *Das Konzert* (1909), is still a success on the contemporary stage.

KARL BARTH

Born 1886 in Basel. Professor of Theology at Bonn 1930–5; dismissed from his post when he refused the oath of absolute loyalty to the Führer. Professor of Theology in Basel since 1935, now Emeritus.

Some publications
Christliche Dogmatik, I. 1927 ff., II. 1940, III. 1945 ff., IV. 1953 ff.
Gotteserkenntnis und Gottesdienst nach 'schottischem Bekenntnis', 1938
(Engl. tr. 'The knowledge of God and the Service of God according to the teaching of the Reformation', 1938
Fürchte dich nicht! (sermons), 1949
The Doctrine of Reconciliation, 1956
Zeitkritische Aufsätze, Reden und Briefe von 1930–1960, ed. by K. Kupisch, 1961

MAX BENSE

Born 1910 in Straßburg. Professor at the Technische Hochschule in Stuttgart. In his approach to new interpretation of Kunst he seeks objective, i.e. numerical, criteria with which to measure proportions and relationships in works of art. He tries to apply methods used for *non*-literary matters to the literary genre and its language material. This leads him to a 'technological' rather than metaphysical aesthetics. His classification of 'texts' comprises texts relating to meaning or to non-romantic material: i.e. (*a*) constructive, logical, determined texts. (*b*) haphazard, mechanical, automatic texts.

Aesthetica, 4 vols., 1954–60
Theorie der Texte, 1962

FRANZ BLEI

Born 1871 in Wien. Died 1942 in New York. Popular writer, critic and translator. Author of not infrequently erotic and also frivolous stories and essays. Under the Ps. Peregrinus Steinhövel he wrote the satire of modern literature: *Das große Bestiarium der modernen Literatur*, 1920. No less amusing is his anthology: *Das Kuriositätenkabinett der Literatur*, 1924

Das Erotische (Essays), 1927
Schriften in Auswahl, 1960, (with bibliography), ed. by A. P. Gütersloh

MARTIN BUBER

Born 1878 in Wien. Died 1965 in Jerusalem. He held the Chair of the Science of Religion at Frankfurt University, left Germany in 1938. Professor (Emeritus) of Social Philosophy at the Hebrew University of Jerusalem. He translated (with Franz Rosenzweig) the Hebrew Bible into German, 1925 ff. In his philosophy Martin Buber advances the view that our existence is rooted in material as well as spiritual environment (*sozialer und geschichtlicher Raum*), which is our 'natural order', to which we are to respond with all our power.

Some of his publications in English
I and Thou, 1937
Israel and the World, 1948

Images of Good and Evil, 1952
The Eclipse of God, 1952

Werke, 3 vols., 1962
Martin Buber, sein Werk und seine Zeit (with bibliography), 1961

CARL JACOB BURCKHARDT

Born 1891 in Basel. He studied in Germany under Wölfflin and Husserl; friendship with Hugo von Hofmannsthal. High Commissioner of the League of Nations for Danzig, 1937–9. Member of the Institute des Sciences morales et politiques, 1949

Erinnerungen an Hugo von Hofmannsthal, 1940
Essays, 1951
Briefwechsel Hugo von Hofmannsthal—Carl J. Burckhardt, 1956
Betrachtungen und Berichte, 1964

ERNST ROBERT CURTIUS

Born 1886 in Thann (Alsace). Died 1956 in Rome. Literary historian, translator of Gide, T. S. Eliot, Browning, etc. Professor of Romance Studies at Bonn University. Next to Th. Mann, C. J. Burckhardt, A. Schweitzer, T. S. Eliot, A. Toynbee and H. v. Hofmannsthal one of the last true representatives of European Humanism, and one of the few eminent exponents of comparative literature studies, as manifested in:

Europäische Literatur und Lateinisches Mittelalter, 1949
Kritische Essays zur Europäischen Literatur, 1954, 2nd ed.
Ges. Aufsätze zur Romanischen Philologie, 1960

WILHELM DILTHEY

Born 1833 in Biebrich am Rhein. Died 1911 in Seis nr. Bozen (Bolzano). Founder of the theory of Geisteswissenschaften. According to Dilthey there are three types of philosophical concepts which correspond to three fundamental attitudes of life: (1) naturalism (intellect predominates), (2) idealism of freedom (will predominates), (3) objective idealism (feeling predominates).

Dilthey differentiates between *Erlebnis* (experience), *Ausdruck* (expression) and *Verstehen* (understanding).

Einleitung in die Geisteswissenschaften, 1883, 2nd ed. 1922
Das Erlebnis und die Dichtung, 1905, often re-ed.
Das Wesen der Philosophie (in the first vol. of *Kultur in der Gegenwart*), 1907
Der Aufbau der geschichtlichen Methode in den Geisteswissenschaften, 1910
Ges. Schriften, 1913 ff. and 1922 ff.

SIGMUND FREUD

Born 1856 in Freiberg, Moravia. Died 1939 in London. Emigrated to London in 1938. S. Freud studied the unconscious mental processes and their effect on our consciousness. He stressed not only the existence but also the importance of infantile sexuality.

Studien über Hysterie, 1895
Die Traumdeutung, 1900
Über Psychoanalyse, 1910
Massenpsychologie und Ich-Analyse, 1921
Theoretische Schriften, 1911–25, 1931
Schriften zur Neurosenlehre und zur psychoanalytischen Technik, 1913–1926, 1931

Ges. Schriften, ed. by A. Freud and A. J. Storfer, 1924 ff.
Die ges. Werke, 1952 ff.
Ernest Jones: *The Life and Work of Sigmund Freud*, 3 vols. 1953–5

FRIEDRICH GUNDOLF (Ps. for Gundelfinger, Ps. suggested by Stefan George)

Born 1880 in Darmstadt. Died 1931 in Heidelberg. Contributor to Stefan George's *Blätter für die Kunst* (1892–1919). In literature, Gundolf sought 'die geistige Gestalt' of each individual author, and he interpreted the poet (particularly Goethe) through the work rather than through a study of the psychology and personality of the writer.

Cäsar in der deutschen Literatur, 1904
Shakespeare und der deutsche Geist, 1911

Goethe, 1916 (several new editions)
Stefan George, 1920; 3rd ed., 1930
Shakespeare, sein Wesen und sein Werk, 1928
Romantiker, 1930

MARTIN HEIDEGGER

Born 1889 in Meßkirch, Baden. Emeritus Professor of Philosophy
in Freiburg i. Breisgau. Although Professor Heidegger disowns
any connexion with 'Existentialism', his main thinking being
dedicated rather to 'essence' than 'existence', he doubtlessly has
influenced German literature by his existential philosophy, cf.
his *Sein und Zeit:* accordingly, our existence is care and anxiety;
we are caught in the wheel of time and necessity; man's liberty
is twofold: to die in order to escape the monotony of existence, or
to transcend one's self.

Some publications:
Sein und Zeit, 1927
Existence and Being, 1949
Holzwege, 1950
Vorträge und Aufsätze, 1954
An Introduction to Metaphysics, 1960
Nietzsche, 1962

W. J. Richardson: *Heidegger* (Through phenomenology to
thought), 1965 (a learned and lucid exposition of the meaning of Heidegger's difficult language).

THEODOR HEUSS

Born 1884 in Brackenheim, Württemberg. Died 1963 in Stuttgart. In 1933 he was dismissed as lecturer on modern history.
Two years after the War he became Professor of Political Science
and Modern History. In 1949 elected President of the Federal
Republic of Germany by the First Federal Assembly; re-elected
for second term in 1954.

Some publications on the development of the German national
idea
Deutsche Nationalidee im Wandel der Geschichte, 1946

on German character
Deutsche Gestalten, 1948

on cultural policy
Kräfte und Grenzen einer Kulturpolitik, 1951

on changing perspectives
Das Bismarck-Bild im Wandel, 1951
Johann Peter Hebel, 1952
Hugo von Hofmannsthal, 1954
Schiller, 1955

EDMUND HUSSERL

Born 1859 in Proßnitz (now Prostejov), Moravia. Died 1938 in
Freiburg/Breisgau. Founder of Phenomenology, i.e. in contrast
to the simple observation of behaviour, the study of the varying
forms in which, according to our personal perception, objects
appear to our mind.

Ideen zu einer reinen Phänomenologie und phänomenologischen Philosophie,
1913
Vorlesungen zur Phänomenologie des inneren Zeitbewußtseins, ed. by
M. Heidegger, 1928

KARL JASPERS

Born 1883 in Oldenburg. Professor of Philosophy in Basel; now
Emeritus. He has justly been called 'the philosopher of humanity',
as he sees in the Togetherness of good human beings the way of
becoming human.

Allgemeine Psychopathologie, 1913; 1959 (7th ed.)
Die Psychologie und die Weltanschauungen, 1919; 1954 (4th ed.)
Die geistige Situation der Zeit, 1931; 1956 (6th ed.)
Philosophie (3 vols.), 1932; 1956 (3rd ed.)
Nietzsche, 1936; 1950 (3rd ed.)
Die Atombombe und die Zukunft des Menschen, 1958

Carl Gustav Jung

Born 1875 in Kesswyl (Switzerland). Died 1961 in Küßnacht bei Zürich. C. G. Jung rejected some of Freud's extreme theories about the sexual drive, and drew attention to the influence of the collective conscious.

Über den Begriff des kollektiven Unbewußten, 1935
Über den Archetypus mit besonderer Berücksichtigung des Animabegriffes, 1936 ff.
Über Mandalasymbolik, 1838 ff.
Psychologie und Alchemie, 1944 ff.
Ges. Werke, 1958 ff.

Erich von Kahler

Born 1885 in Prague; emigrated to the U.S.A. in 1938. Settled in Princeton (New Jersey). Interpreter of our time and its literature.

Über Recht und Moral (1911, Diss.)
Der deutsche Charakter in der Geschichte Europas, 1937
Die Verantwortung des Geistes, 1952
The Tower and the Abyss. An enquiry into the transformation of the individual, 1957
The Disintegration of Form in the Arts, 1968

Rudolf Kassner

Born 1873 in Groß-Pawlowitz in Moravia. Died 1959 in Sierre in the Swiss canton Wallis. Philosopher and pioneer in the field of physiognomic research; fundamentally in contrast to psychoanalysis. 'Einbildungskraft' is to him the creative centre in which simplicity and intellect are united; friend of R. M. Rilke.

Trs. of Plato (*Symposium, Phaidros, Phaidon*, etc.) and of Russian literature: Tolstoy, Dostoevsky, Gogol, Puschkin

Von den Elementen der menschlichen Größe, 1911
Zahl und Gesicht, 1919
Die Grundlagen der Physiognomik, 1922

Narziß oder Mythos der Einbildungskraft, 1928
Das physiognomische Weltbild, 1930
Physiognomik, 1932
Das inwendige Reich. Versuch einer Physiognomik der Ideen, 1953

Rudolf Kassner zum achtzigsten Geburtstag, ed. by A. C. Kensik and
D. Bodmer, 1953

ALFRED KERR (Ps. for Emanuel Kempner)

Born 1867 in Breslau; emigrated in 1933. Died 1948 in Hamburg.
Leading theatre critic; author of travel books and literary essays.
Particularly influential in his praise of Ibsen and Gerhart Haupt-
mann.

Die Welt im Drama (collection of reviews and criticisms), 5 vols.,
1917
Die Welt im Licht, Reisefeuilletons, 1920, 2 vols.

GRAF HERMANN KEYSERLING

Born 1880 in the castle Könno in Estland (Esthonia). Died 1946
in Aurach nr. Kitzbühel. Founded the 'Schule der Weisheit' (in
Darmstadt), aiming at a new fusion of man's intellect and soul.

Individuum und Zeitgeist, 1909
Das Reisetagebuch eines Philosophen, 1919
Das Spektrum Europas, 1928
Amerika: Der Aufgang einer neuen Welt, 1930
Das Buch vom persönlichen Leben, 1936

MAX KOMMERELL

Born 1902 in Münsingen (Württemberg). Died 1944 in Marburg/
Lahn. Professor for Germanistic at Frankfurt a.M. University and
then in Marburg/L. Translator, poet and scholar. Friendship
with E. R. Curtius, W. F. Otto and Stefan George whose circle
he, however, later left.

Dichter und Führer in der deutschen Klassik, 1928
Jean Paul, 1933

Gedanken über Gedichte, Essays, 1943
Geist und Buchstabe der Dichtung, 1944
Dichterische Welterfahrung, Essays, 1952

Briefe und Aufzeichnungen 1919–1944, aus dem Nachlaß, ed. by Inge
  Jens

EMIL LUDWIG (father's name: Hermann Cohn)

Born 1881 in Breslau. Had, since 1932, Swiss nationality. Died
1948 in Moscia (Ascona). Journalist, author and playwright; he
wrote popular biographies and histories. His successful lives of
great men were, however, considered controversial, because of his
cult of personalities and because of his subjective judgment: e.g.

Bismarck, 1926
Wilhelm II, 1926
Michelangelo, 1930
Gespräche mit Mussolini, 1932
Cleopatra, 1937
Roosevelt, 1938
Das Schicksal König Edwards VIII, 1939
Beethoven, 1943
Stalin, 1945
Der entzauberte Freud, 1946

GEORG (VON) LUKÁCS

Born 1885 in Budapest. He became responsible for education
under Béla Kun's revolutionary régime. After its collapse, he
went to Berlin. Friendship with Johannes Becher. In 1933 emigration to the U.S.S.R. Return (in 1945) to Budapest. Exponent
of 'Social Realism', but, under the influence of Stalin's ideologies,
accused of overrating the part played by bourgeois writers (Tolstoy, Balzac, Th. Mann, etc.) at the cost of the best proletarian
authors. During the insurrection of 1956, he was responsible for
Volksbildung in Imre Nagy's Cabinet. After having been deported by the Russians to Rumania, he was later allowed to go
back to Budapest.

Die Theorie des Romans, 1920, 3rd ed. 1965
Der Marxismus und die literarischen Theorien des 19. Jahrhunderts, 1937
Literatur und Demokratie, 1947
Karl Marx und Friedrich Engels als Literaturhistoriker, 1948
Die Eigenart des Ästhetischen, I. 1963
Deutsche Literatur in zwei Jahrhunderten, 1964
Von Nietzsche zu Hitler, Taschenbuchausgabe, 1966

RUDOLF PANNWITZ

Born 1881 in Crossen an der Oder. Left the Prussian Akademie in 1933, went to Switzerland. Was member of the Charon circle. Influenced by Nietzsche and Stefan George. In aesthetic perfection and beautiful forms he sees the most powerful counter-force against Nihilism. Beauty, according to him, is an artistic intensification, a 'Verdichtung' of the reality, not an escape from or negation of reality.

Die Krisis der europäischen Kultur, 1917
Kosmos Atheos, 1926
Die deutsche Idee Europa, 1931
Der Friede, 1950
Aufgaben Europas, 1956

WALTHER RATHENAU

Born 1867 in Berlin. Died 1922 in Berlin, assassinated. Industrialist, essayist, politician and scholar. In 1915 President of the AEG (Allgemeine Elektrizitäts-Ges.). In 1922 Reichsaußenminister. Mainly dealing with the problem of power and humanity, overpopulation and mechanization and of the loss of freedom in our life. We can, according to him, overcome this danger by a sense of true responsibility towards oneself and the community by inwardness ('Reich der Seele').

Zur Kritik der Zeit, 1912
Zur Mechanik des Geistes, 1913
Von kommenden Dingen, 1917
Die neue Gesellschaft, 1919

Ges. Schriften: 5 vols., 1918 and 1925; 6 vols. 1929

MAX SCHELER

Born in Munich. Died 1928 in Frankfurt a.M. Philosopher and sociologist.

Zur Phänomenologie und Theorie der Sympathiegefühle, 1913 (enlarged in 1923, under title *Wesen und Formen der Sympathie*)
Vom Ewigen im Menschen, 1921; (1923 enlarged)
Schriften zur Soziologie und Weltanschauungslehre, 4 vols., 1923–4
Die Wissensformen und die Gesellschaft, 1926

Ges. Werke, 1957 ff.

OSWALD SPENGLER

Born 1880 in Blankenburg/Harz. Died 1936 in Munich (suicide). In the triumph of the metropolis he saw the final annihilation of German culture and ultimately the death of all organic life.

Der Untergang des Abendlandes, 1918–22
Preußentum und Sozialismus, 1919–20
Der Mensch und die Technik, 1931
Jahre der Entscheidung, 1933

EDUARD SPRANGER

Born 1882 in Berlin. Died 1963 in Tübingen. Philosopher—most of his works went into many revised editions.

Wilhelm von Humboldt und die Humanitätsidee, 1909
Lebensformen, 1914 (many new editions)
Psychologie des Jugendalters, 1924
Kulturfragen der Gegenwart, 1953

H. W. Bähr (ed.): *Eduard Spranger. Sein Leben u. sein Werk* (Eine Gedenkschrift), 1964

RUDOLF STEINER

Born 1861 in Kraljewec. Died 1925 in Dornach, Switzerland.
Anthroposophist; founder of the 'Goetheanum' at Dornach.

Grundlinien einer Erkenntnistheorie der Goetheschen Weltanschauung, 1886
Goethe als Vater der neuen Ästhetik, 1888
Wahrheit und Wissenschaft, 1892
Goethes Weltanschauung, 1897
Theosophy, 1904
Vom Menschenrätsel, 1916
Von Seelenrätseln, 1917
Mein Lebensgang, 1924

MAX WEBER

Born 1864 in Erfurt. Died 1920 in Munich. (Brother of Alfred
Weber—author of the *Prinzipien der Geschichts- und Kultursozio-
logie*.) Max Weber was an influential political economist. He was
particularly interested in the problem of historical causation.
Against the Marxist idea of economic determinism and materialistic socialism he emphasized the importance of moral and
religious ideas, and he traced modern capitalism back to the
ethics of John Calvin and his followers.

M. Weber's main works are
Ges. Aufsätze zur Religionssoziologie, 1920–1
Wirtschaft und Gesellschaft, posth. 1922, enlarged ed. 1956; English
tr. *On law in economy and society*, 1954, 2nd ed.

LUDWIG WITTGENSTEIN

Born 1889 in Vienna. Died 1951 in Cambridge. 1930–6, fellow of
Trinity College, Cambridge. 1939–47, Professor of Philosophy.
Wittgenstein was mainly interested in language and the working
of language in the so-called 'language games'. According to
Wittgenstein it is the task of philosophy to clarify thought;
philosophy is an activity rather than a theory; metaphysical or
moral propositions cannot be expressed in language.

Tractatus logico-philosophicus, 1921 (German text), 1922 (German–
    English texts)
posth.: *Philosophical Investigations*, 1953
Remarks on the Foundations of Mathematics, 1956
Philosophische Untersuchungen, 1960
Philosophische Bemerkungen, 1964

WILHELM WORRINGER

Born 1881 in Aachen. Died 1965 in Munich. Art historian.

Abstraktion und Einfühlung; 1907 (dissertation), 1908 (book); 1948
    new ed.
Formprobleme der Gothik, 1911, 1930
Altdeutsche Buch-Illustration, 1912, 1921
Griechentum und Gotik, 1928
Formprobleme der Gegenwartskunst, 1948

Select Bibliography of Individual Authors

LEOPOLD AHLSEN

Born 1927 in Munich. He is considered to be a 'bayuwarischer Shaw'.

1960: *Raskolnikoff* published in *Theater Heute*
1964: *Sie werden sterben, Sire* published in *Theater Heute*; it deals with Everyman's fate, fear and certainty of death, a favourite theme of several modern plays; compare also Ionesco'a *Le roi se meurt* (*Exit the King*), where, however, the subject-matter is treated with deadly seriousness
1967: *Der arme Luther*

Several radio-plays
Philemon und Baukis, etc.

As to the above and other contemporary playwrights see also: Henning Rischbieter and Ernst Wendt in *Reihe Theater Heute*, 1965. Both authors single out three international successes (Welterfolge): R. Hochhuth: *Der Stellvertreter*, H. Kipphardt: *In der Sache J. Robert Oppenheimer*, P. Weiss: *Marat*.

ILSE AICHINGER

Born 1921 in Vienna. Married (since 1953) to G. Eich. Writer of sensitive but lucid rhythmic prose expressing her concern with the problematical reality of life. Prefers short story, Hörspiel and Dialogue for this purpose.

Novel
1948: *Die größere Hoffnung*

Short stories
1952: *Rede unter dem Galgen* (in Austria. *Der Gefesselte* in Germany, 1953)

1963: *Wo ich wohne* (including Dialogues and Verse)
1965: *Eliza, Eliza*

Radio-plays and dialogues
1953: *Knöpfe*
1957: *Zu keiner Stunde*
1961: *Besuch im Pfarrhaus*

Ian Hilton

PETER ALTENBERG Ps. for Richard Engländer

Born 1859 in Vienna. Died 1919 in Vienna. Bohemian, Impressionist, Kleinkünstler, 'Pointillist' and 'Aphorist', whose impressionist *feuilletons* and brief lyrical sketches have great charm.

1896: *Wie ich sehe*
1900: *Was der Tag mir zuträgt*
1909: *Bilderbögen des kleinen Lebens*
1912–13: *Semmering*

1947: *Briefe*, ed. by F. Glück

PETER PAUL ALTHAUS

Born 1892 in Münster. Died 1965. He was rightly compared with Morgenstern and Ringelnatz.

Poetry
1929: *Das vierte Reich*
1951: *In der Traumstadt*
1952: *Der Enzian*
1956: *Wir sanften Irren*

Comedy
1935: *Zauber der Stimme*

Also free adaptations and trs.
1923: *Mystische Lyrik aus dem ind. Mittelalter*
1927: *Altrussische Kirchenlieder*

Paul Alverdes

Born 1897 in Straßburg. From 1934 to 1944 with Benno von Mechow, editor of the Kulturzeitschrift *Das Innere Reich*, which during the Hitler regime was, to a certain extent, still trying to preserve a spirit of cosmopolitan attitude and humanity. After the War the author turned to writing and editing fairy-tales.

Poetry
1922: *Die Nördlichen*

Tragedy
1923: *Die feindlichen Brüder*

Radio-play
1933: *Die Freiwilligen* (dealing with the Langemarck tragedy)

Short Stories
1929: *Die Pfeiferstube*, his most famous Novelle which deals with the so-called Pfeifer—four wounded soldiers, three Germans and one Englishman—in a hospital; throat-wounds have impaired their speech
1933: *Der Kriegsfreiwillige Reinhold*
1942: *Jette im Wald*
1949: *Grimsbarts Haus*
1954: *Die Hirtin auf dem Felde*

Alfred Andersch

Born 1914 in Munich. Head of Radio-Essay, Stuttgart Radio, until 1958; at present free-lance author.

Autobiography
1952: *Die Kirschen der Freiheit*

Novels and stories
1957: *Sansibar oder der letzte Grund*
      Piazza san Gaetano
1958: *Geister und Leute*
1960: *Die Rote*

1962: *Wanderungen im Norden*
1963: *Ein Liebhaber des Halbschattens*
1967: *Efraim*

Radio-play
1965: *Fahrerflucht* (publ. in book-form)

Radio work
1959–60: *Marginalien*
1963: *Alte Peripherie*
1964: *Das scheintote Brügge*

Articles
1964–7: (in *Der Ruf*) *Texte und Zeichen*

Essays and critical writings
1965: *Die Blindheit des Kunstwerke und andere Aufsätze*

Turning from political journalism in 1947 after the occupying forces' ban on his periodical, *Der Ruf*, Andersch expresses in his literary work the Existentialist theory of man as an individual who forms his own life by active choice. Beginning with the autobiography and continuing throughout his works of fiction, Andersch takes as his central figure the individual who, by fleeing from his past, attempts to mould his life to his own ideals by choosing his future actions freely, rejecting the belief in predestined action.

Valerie Thornley Watson

LOU(ISE) ANDREAS-SALOMÉ

Born 1861 in St Petersburg. Died 1937 in Göttingen. The father of Louise von Salomé was a Russian general of German-Huguenot origin. She married the 'Iranist' F. C. Andreas; friendship with Nietzsche, Wedekind, Rilke; collaboration with S. Freud in Vienna; she believed in the psychotherapeutic treatment of disease, i.e. by hypnotic influence.

1892: *Ibsens Frauengestalten*
1894: *Fr. Nietzsche in seinen Werken*

1928: *R. M. Rilke* (ein Gedenkbuch)
1931: *Mein Dank an Freud* (Offener Brief)
1952: *Briefwechsel mit Rilke*

STEFAN ANDRES

Born 1906 in Breitwies near Trier.

Poetry
1933: *Die Löwenkanzel*
1935: *Der ewige Strom*
1948: *Requiem für ein Kind*
1950: *Der Granatapfel*

Novels
1932: *Bruder Luzifer*
1934: *Eberhard im Kontrapunkt*
      Die unsichtbare Mauer
1939: *Der Mann von Asteri*
1941: *Der gefrorene Dionysos* (1951: pub. under title *Die Liebes-
      schaukel*)
1947: *Die Hochzeit der Feinde*
1948: *Ritter der Gerechtigkeit*
1949–59: *Die Sintflut*, a novel trilogy (1949: *Das Tier aus der Tiefe*;
         1951: *Die Arche*; 1959: *Der graue Regenbogen*)
1953: *Der Knabe im Brunnen*
1954: *Die Reise nach Portiuncula*
1963: *Der Mann im Fisch*
1966: *Der Taubenturm*

Stories
1936: *El Greco malt den Inquisitor*
      Vom heiligen Pfäfflein Domenico
1937: *Moselländische Novellen*
1940: *Der olympische Frieden*
      Das Grab des Neides
1942: *Wir sind Utopia* (Cyrus Brook, 1954)
1943: *Wirtshaus zur weiten Welt*
1951: *Das goldene Gitter*
      Das Antlitz

1957: *Positano: Geschichten aus einer Stadt am Meer*
1960: *Die Verteidigung der Xanthippe*
1962: *Novellen und Erzählungen*

Drama

1946: *Ein Herz wie man's braucht*
1948: *Tanz durchs Labyrinth*
1950: *Gottes Utopia* (dramatization of *Wir sind Utopia*)
1952: *Der Reporter Gottes* (radio-play)
1955: *Die Touristen*
1956: *Das Lied vom roten Mantel* (radio-play)
1957: *Sperrzonen*
      Und Zeus lächelt

Studies

1950: Dempf, A.: *Theologische Romane: Jünger, Werfel, Andres* (Universitas)
1962: Hennecke, H. and others: *Stefan Andres: Eine Einführung in sein Werk* (Piper Verlag)

Stefan Andres infuses much of his richly imaginative fiction with the vivid humour of the Moselle valley in which he was born, while revealing in his work a strong sense of moral responsibility which has directed him towards such themes as that of his trilogy *Die Sintflut*, an ambitious attempt to translate into terms of utopian fantasy the rise and fall of Nazism. Utopian ideas also play a part in his most popular achievement, the novelle *Wir sind Utopia*, a moving tale of the Spanish Civil War. Andres spent the years 1937–49 in Positano, in Southern Italy, and his work often reflects his love of a country which he has come to regard as his second home.

T. J. Garrett

ERICH ARENDT

Born 1903 in Neuruppin. Lives in Berlin now; in 1933 he emigrated to Switzerland, and eventually to Colombia, South America. He had the reputation of being an 'aristocratic communist'. In his early poetry he is influenced by A. Stramm; his first poems appeared in *Sturm*; see p. 22.

Poetry

1951: *Trug doch die Nacht den Albatros*
1952: *Bergwindballade*
1957: *Gesang der sieben Inseln*
1959: *Flug-Oden*

Translations from: Pablo Neruda (Chilean poet, born 1904, Romantic, Revolutionary and Surrealist) and also from Rafael Alberti (born 1902, a Spaniard in exile, Buenos Aires, Argentine) from the Spaniard Miguel Hernández (born 1910, died 1942) and Nicolás Guillén (born 1902, Cuban).

HANS ARP

Born 1887 in Straßburg. Died 1966 in Basel. Sculptor and poet; lived in Meudon nr. Paris. In 1911 meeting with Kandinsky and the circle of the *Blaue Reiter*. In 1913 contributed to the journal *Sturm*. He, with H. Ball, R. Hülsenbeck, T. Tzara, M. Janco, became co-founder of the Dada-movement. 1916–19 *Dadaism* developed from the *Cabaret Voltaire* in Zürich. Hans Arp is a master of rearrangement of word material. The incongruous and unreasonable world is to him our normal existence. This is not a dream, also not surrealism, it is a conscious abdication of logic in order to escape logic for the sake of an absurd situation.

Poetry

1920: *Der vogel selbdritt*
     Die wolkenpumpe
1924: *Der Pyramidenrock*
1930: *Weißt du schwarzt du*
1939: *Muscheln und Schirme*
1953: *Wortträume und schwarze sterne* (ausgewählte Ged. 1911–52)
1960: *Mondsand*
1961: *Sinnende Flammen*
1963–4: *Ges. Gedichte*, I, II

HANS CARL ARTMANN

Born 1921 in St Achatz am Walde (on the Inn), Austria. Satirist, writer of parodies, anecdotes, burlesques and grotesques reminiscent of German Baroque style.

Poetry
1956: *XXV epigrammata, in teutschen alexandrinern gesetzt*
1958: *Med ana schwoazzn Dintn* in Viennese dialect
1966: *Verbarium*
1967: *Grünverschlossene Botschaft:—90 Träume*, illustrated by Ernst
      Fuchs

HERBERT ASMODI

Born 1923 in Heilbronn/Neckar. Author of comedies.

1958: *Pardon wird nicht gegeben*
1959: *Nachsaison*
1964: *Mohrenwäsche*

INGEBORG BACHMANN

Born 1926 in Klagenfurt. See p. 58 about Bachmann's imagery.

Poetry
1953: *Die gestundete Zeit*
1956: *Anrufung des großen Bären*
1958: *Nachtstücke und Arien.* Gedichte für ein Konzert von Hans
      Werner Henze

Radio-plays
1955: *Zikaden*
1958: *Der gute Gott von Manhattan*

Librettos
1960: Librettos for Hans Werner Henze, e.g. *The Prince of Hom-
      burg* (after H. v. Kleist's drama)
1963: *Der junge Lord*, satirical opera in two acts, libretto-text after
      a parable by Wilhelm von Hauff

Studies
1966: G. C. Schoolfield: *Ingeborg Bachmann*, in 'Essays on Con-
      temporary German Literature', vol. IV, *German Men of
      Letters*, ed. by B. Keith-Smith

The selected portraits in Klaus Nonnemann's edition: *Schriftsteller der Gegenwart*, 53 Porträts (1963), about contemporary (mainly West-German authors present rather critical assessments, in view of present-day high-power boosting of some authors, and are therefore well worth reading; see H. Daiber about Ingeborg Bachmann: 'Die Quantität der Lobpreisung überragt die Quantität der gepriesenen Arbeiten erheblich', 'Tant de bruit sur une omelette! Aber gute Omelettes sind selten . . .'

WOLFGANG BÄCHLER

Born 1925 in Augsburg. Connected with 'Group 47'.

Poetry
1950: *Die Zisterne*
1952–4: *Lichtwechsel*
1962: *Türklingel*. Balladen, Romanzen, Berichte

ERNST BARLACH

Born 1870 in Wedel (Holstein). Died 1938 in Rostock: Poet, play-wright, sculptor (particularly in wood), graphic artist.

Drama
1912: *Der tote Tag*; original title: *Blutgeschrei*
1918: *Der arme Vetter*
1920: *Die echten Sedemunds*
1924: *Sündflut*
1926: *Der blaue Boll*

Studies
1958: Willi Flemming *Ernst Barlach* (Wesen und Werk)
1961: P. Schurek: *Barlach, Eine Bildbiographie*
1964: Brian Keith-Smith: *Ernst Barlach* in *German Men of Letters*, vol. III, with a select bibliography, ed. by A. Natan

1956–9: *Ernst Barlach, Des dichterische Werk*, 3 vols.: I Drama, II and III Prose

EMIL BARTH

Born 1900 in Haan, Rheinland. Died 1958 in Düsseldorf.

Poetry
1928: *Totenfeier*
1933: *Ex voto*
1948: *Xantener Hymnen*
1952: *Nachtschatten* (poems in prose)
1956: *Tigermuschel*
1961: *Meerzauber* (posth.)

Novel
1951: *Enkel des Odysseus*

1960: *Ges. Werke*, 2 vols.

OTTO BASIL (Ps. Markus Hörmann)

Born 1901 in Vienna. Poet, essayist, translator, editor of the journals: *Plan* and *Das Wort*.

Poetry
1945: *Sternbild der Waage*
1947: *Apokalyptischer Vers*

Translations from Jean-Nicolas-Arthur Rimbaud and Upton Sinclair.

WALTER BAUER

Born 1904 in Merseburg an der Saale. Son of a worker. Emigrated to Canada in 1952, now lecturer in the German Department of University College, Toronto.

Poetry
1928: *Kameraden, zu euch spreche ich*
1929: *Stimme aus dem Leunawerk*
1943: *Gast auf Erden*
1948: *Dämmerung wird Tag*

1954: *Mein blaues Oktavheft*
1957: *Nachtwachen des Tellerwäschers*
1963: *Klopfzeichen*

Novels
1930: *Ein Mann zog in die Stadt*
1933: *Das Herz der Erde*
1950: *Besser zu zweit als allein*

Also author of stories, biographies, essays and radio-plays.

JOHANNES ROBERT BECHER

Born 1891 in Munich. Died 1958 in East Berlin. Since 1912 contributor to the journal *Aktion*. In 1917 he joined the USPD (Unabhängige sozialistische Partei Deutschlands), and in 1918 the Spartakus Bund, 1919 KPD (Kommunistische Partei Deutschlands). In 1928 the BPRS (Bund proletarisch-revolutionärer Schriftsteller) was founded and Becher was made its President; since 1935 in Russia, 1945–7 President of the *Kulturbund* which worked for the democratic re-establishment of Germany. He was with Paul Wiegler co-founder of the influential East German literary journal *Sinn und Form* (in 1949). 1954–6 First Minister for Culture in DDR. He is the author of the DDR *Nationalhymne*, music by H. Eisler.

Poetry
1914: *Verfall und Triumph*
1925: *Roter Marsch*
1931: *Der große Plan* (epic)
1946: *Heimkehr*
1949: *Nationalhymne der DDR*
1951: *Glück der Ferne—leuchtend nah*
1957: *Liebe ohne Ruh*

RICHARD BEER-HOFMANN

Born 1866 in Rodaun nr. Vienna. Died 1945 in New York. 1939, emigration to Switzerland and the U.S.A. After his death a Beer-Hofmann Gesellchaft was founded in New York. Playwright, poet, novelist, essayist, critic, producer. Contact with the Viennese circle of poets and writers: Bahr, Schnitzler, and above all H. v. Hofmannsthal.

As playwright he first made himself a name with *Graf von Charolais*, 1904 (an adaptation of Massinger's and Field's *The Fatal Dowry*, 1619)
1918: *Jaàkobs Traum*
1933: *Der junge David*
1936: *Vorspiel auf dem Theater zu König David*

Novel
1900: *Der Tod Georgs*

1963: *Ges. Werke*

Study
1947: Otto Oberholzer: *Richard Beer-Hofmann. Werk und Weltbild des Dichters*

EMIL BELZNER

Born 1901 in Bruchsal/Baden. Mainly novelist.

Novels
1933: *Kolumbus vor der Landung*
1940: *Ich bin der König!*
1953: *Der Safranfresser*
1956: *Juanas großer Seemann*

HANS BENDER

Born 1919 in Mühlhausen near Heidelberg. Co-editor of *Akzente*, from 1963 Chefredakteur of the journal *Magnum*. Editor of the Anthology *Mein Gedicht ist mein Messer*, 1955. Since 1962, with Rudolf de le Roi, Eduard Trier, Hermann Rinn, co-editor of the *Jahresring* (Beiträge zur deutschen Literatur und Kunst der Gegenwart).

Poetry
1957: *Lyrische Biographie*

Novel
1959: *Wunschkost*

Also author of short stories

GOTTFRIED BENN

Born 1886 in Mansfeld (Westpriegnitz). Son of a parson. Died
1956 in Berlin. See p. 28.

Poetry
1912: *Morgue*
1917: *Fleisch*
1927: *Ges. Gedichte*
1948: *Statische Gedichte*
1949: *Trunkene Flut*

Lecture
1951: *Probleme der Lyrik*, see also MLQ June 1954: *Substance and
    Symbol in Song*, p. 100 ff.
1955: Ed. with introduction: *Lyrik des expressionistischen Jahr-
    zehnts* (Von den Wegbereitern bis zum Dada)

Benn singles out the following 'pioneers' of expressionism: Mombert, Else Lasker-Schüler, Hadwiger, Stadler. He surveys ten
years of expressionist poetry — 1910–20:

for 1910: he mentions: Däubler, Schickele, Zech
for 1911: Heym, Jakob van Hoddis, Loerke, Werfel
for 1912: Benn, Blass, Drey, Friedländer, Rubiner
for 1913: Hasenclever, Kandinsky, Lichtenstein, Trakl, etc.

1956: *Ges. Gedichte* (on the occasion of his 70th birthday)
1957: *Ausgewählte Briefe*
1956, 1958: 2nd ed. *Gottfried Benn—Bibliographie 1912–1956*

Studies
1959 ff.: *Ges. Werke*, ed. by D. Wellershoff, 4 vols.

1961: F. Wood: *G. Benn's Attic Tryptich*, Germanic Rev., XXXVI
1962: *Die Kunst im Schatten des Gottes* (Für und wider Gottfried
          Benn), ed. by R. Grimm and Wolf-Dieter Marsch
1962: F. W. Wotke: *Gottfried Benn*
1964: Ian Hilton: *Gottfried Benn*, with a select bibliography in
          German Men of Letters, ed. by A. Natan.

WERNER BERGENGRUEN

Born 1892 in Riga. Died 1964 in Baden-Baden.

Novels

1927: *Das Kaiserreich in Trümmern*
1931: *Die Woche im Labyrinth*
1930: *Herzog Karl der Kühne*
1935: *Der Großtyrann und das Gericht* (English version, 1952: *A
          Matter of Conscience* (tr. by N. Cameron))
1940: *Am Himmel wie auf Erden*
1946: *Pelageja*
1949: *Das Feuerzeichen*
1952: *Der letzte Rittmeister* (English version, 1953: *The Last
          Captain of Horse*; a portrait of chivalry (tr. by E. Peters))
1954: *Die Rittmeisterin*
1961: *Der dritte Kranz*

Short stories

1927: *Das Buch Rodenstein*
1933: *Der Teufel im Winterpalais und andere Erzählungen*
1936: *Die drei Falken*
1939: *Der Tod von Reval; kuriose Geschichten aus einer alten Stadt*
1940: *Begebenheiten. Geschichten aus einem Jahrtausend*
1946: *Die Sultansrose*. Novellen
1947: *Sternenstand*. Novellen
1955: *Die Flamme im Säulenholz*. Novellen
1959: *Zorn, Zeit und Ewigkeit*

Poetry

1934: *Die Rose von Jericho*
1937: *Der ewige Kaiser*
1945: *Dies irae*

1950: *Die heile Welt*
1951: *Lombardische Elegie*

Autobiographical writings
1961: *Schreibtischerinnerungen*

Critical and miscellaneous writings
1939: *E. T. A. Hoffmann*
1949: *Römisches Erinnerungsbuch*

Study
1961: H. Bänziger: *Werner Bergengruen: Weg und Werk*, 2nd ed.

Bergengruen was a convert to Catholicism; his themes—the insecurity and transience of life and man's quest of permanence, man's imperfection and need of grace, the existence of purpose and order beyond the chaos and destruction on the surface of life—are expressed in traditional forms.

H. R. Klieneberger

ERNST BERTRAM

Born 1884 in Elberfeld. Died 1957 in Cologne. Greatly influenced by Stefan George. Professor of Germanistik in Cologne. Author of the Monograph on *Nietzsche. Versuch einer Mythologie*, 1918. Friendship with Carossa.

Poetry
1920: *Straßburg*
1922: *Der Rhein*
1925: *Nornenbuch*
1933: *Wartburg*
1934: *Griecheneiland*

PETER BICHSEL

Born 1935 in Lucerne.

Stories
1964: *Eigentlich möchte Frau Blum den Milchmann kennen*
1967: *Die Jahreszeiten*

HORST BIENEK

Born 1930 in Gleiwitz, Silesia; in 1951 he was deported to Siberia; returned in 1955.

Poetry
1957: *Traumbuch eines Gefangenen*

Stories
1959: *Nachtstücke*

Novel
1968: *Die Zelle*

OTTO JULIUS BIERBAUM

Born 1865 in Grüneberg, Silesia. Died 1910 in Kötzschenbroda nr. Dresden. Co-editor of the *Insel* and of *Pan*. Partner in the foundation of the Insel-Verlag and of the cabaret (*Überbrettl*) in Munich. Author of *Butzenscheibenlyrik*.

Short stories and novels
1892: *Studentenbeichten*
1896: *Pankrazius Graunzer*
1897: *Stilpe*, Roman aus der Froschperspektive
1898: *Kaktus und andere Künstlergeschichten*
1906 f.: *Prinz Kuckuck*, Leben, Taten, Meinungen und Höllen-
        fahrt eines Wollüstlings. 3 vols.

Poetry
1901: *Irrgarten der Liebe*; Verliebte, launenhafte und moralische
        Lieder, Gedichte and Sprüche

1912–17: *Ges. Werke*, ed. by M. G. Conrad and H. Brandenburg,
        10 vols.

WOLF BIERMANN

Born 1936 in Hamburg. Went to DDR in 1953; lives in East Berlin: see p. 47. Biermann, who lives by choice in East Berlin, has recently lost popularity in DDR. In his ballad about Villon he criticizes his Communist Party, and in *An die alten Genossen* he boldly attacks the new order and is impatient: 'Geduld ist mir die Hure der Feigheit . . .'

Poetry
1965: *Die Drahtharfe, Balladen, Gedichte, Lieder*; see pp. 47–8. A long-playing record of some of these songs appeared under the title: *Wolf Biermann, Ost, zu Gast bei Wolfgang Neuss, West* (PHILIPS Nr. 843 742 PY)

RUDOLF GEORG BINDING

Born 1867 in Basel. Died 1938 in Starnberg.

Poetry
1930: *Ausgewählte und neue Gedichte*

Stories
1912: *Opfergang*
1919: *Keuschheitslegende*
1921: *Unsterblichkeit.* This story of a flying ace has been inspired by the character and fate of Manfred von Richthofen
1932: *Moselfahrt aus Liebeskummer*
1935: *Wir fordern Reims zur Übergabe auf*

1954: *R. G. Binding, Ges. Werke*, 2 vols.

JOHANNES BOBROWSKI

Born 1917 in Tilsit. Died 1965 in Berlin.

Novels and Stories
1956: *Hans Clauert, der märkische Eulenspiegel* (children's book)
1964: *Levins Mühle*
1965: *Boehlendorff und Mäusefest* (short stories)
1966: *Litauische Claviere*

Essays
1967: *Selbstzeugnisse und Beiträge über sein Werk* (with bibliography)

Poetry
1961: *Sarmatische Zeit*
1962: *Schattenland Ströme*
1966: *Wetterzeichen*
1965: A selection from *Sarmatische Zeit* and *Schattenland Ströme* appeared in English: *Shadowland*

Study
1966: Patrick Bridgwater: *The Poetry of Johannes Bobrowski*; see *Forum for Modern Language Studies*, vol. II

The subject of Germany's relations with her Eastern neighbours was seen by Bobrowski as his principal theme. His interests included history and folklore. *Levins Mühle* is his main prose work.

H. M. Waidson

HEINRICH BÖLL

Born 1917 in Cologne.

Novels (and other prose fiction)
1949: *Der Zug war pünktlich* (English, *The Train was on Time*, 1956)
1950: *Wanderer, kommst du nach Spa . . .* (short stories; English, *Traveller, if you come to Spa——*, 1956)
1951: *Wo warst du, Adam?* (English, *Adam, where art Thou?*, 1955)
1953: *Und sagte kein einziges Wort* (English, *Acquainted with the Night*, 1954)
1954: *Haus ohne Hüter* (English, *The Unguarded House*, 1957)
1955: *Das Brot der frühen Jahre* (English, *The Bread of our Early Years*, 1957; annotated ed. by James Alldridge, 1965)
So ward Abend und Morgen (short stories)
1956: *Unberechenbare Gäste* (short stories)
1957: *Im Tal der donnernden Hufe* (shorter tale; English, 'In the valley of the thundering hooves', in *Absent without Leave, and other stories*, 1967)
1958: *Doktor Murkes gesammeltes Schweigen* (short stories; not wholly identical in content with '*Dokter Murkes gesammeltes Schweigen*' *and other stories*, annotated ed. by Gertrud Seidmann, introduction by H. M. Waidson, 1963; see also *Absent without Leave*)

1959: *Der Bahnhof von Zimpren* (short stories)
  Billard um halbzehn (English, *Billiards at Half-past Nine*, 1961)
1962: *Als der Krieg ausbrach. Als der Krieg zu Ende war* (short stories; English, 'Enter and exit', in *Absent without Leave*)
1963: *Ansichten eines Clowns* (English, *The Clown*, 1965)
1964: *Entfernung von der Truppe* (English, 'Absent without leave', in *Absent without Leave*)
1966: *Ende einer Dienstfahrt*

Drama
1961: Radio-plays in: *Erzählungen—Hörspiele—Aufsätze* (annotated ed. of *Vier Hörspiele*, by G. P. Sonnex, 1966)
1962: *Ein Schluck Erde*

Essays
1957: *Irisches Tagebuch* (annotated ed. by J. S. Robinson, 1967)
1961: Essays in: *Erzählungen—Hörspiele—Aufsätze*
1966: *Frankfurter Vorlesungen*

Studies
1962: *Der Schriftsteller Heinrich Böll*, Cologne and Berlin, 3rd ed. with bibliography
1964: Hermann Stresau, *Heinrich Böll*, Berlin
1966: W. E. Yuill, *Heinrich Böll*, in 'Essays on Contemporary German Literature', *German Men of Letters*, vol. IV, ed. by B. Keith-Smith

Heinrich Böll's gifts of powerful realism and emotional sensitivity are clearly marked in his short stories on themes from wartime Germany and the years immediately after, *Wanderer, kommst du nach Spa . . .*, and in his war novel, *Wo warst du, Adam?*, as well as in later work. Problems of family life in contemporary Germany are treated in *Und sagte kein einziges Wort*, *Haus ohne Hüter* and subsequently. A sense of humour and social satire are among the features of his short stories of the 1950s. A strong feeling of individualism is noticeable in the leading figures of subsequent works, such as *Ansichten eines Clowns*. Böll's work has been widely read and appreciated both in Germany and elsewhere.

H. M. Waidson

DIETRICH BONHOEFFER

Born in Breslau 1906. Evangelical pastor in Berlin; imprisoned because of opposition against National Socialism; executed in Flossenbürg on Good Friday, 9 April 1945; cf. W. H. Auden's poem *Friday's Child*, tr. by H. E. Holthusen, *Merkur*, Jan. 1967.

1946: *Auf dem Wege zur Freiheit* (Gedichte und Briefe aus der Haft), ed. by E. Bethge
1958: *Ges. Schriften*, ed. by E. Bethge, 4 vols.

RUDOLF BORCHARDT

Born 1877 in Königsberg. Died 1945 in Trins on the Brenner. Friendship with R. A. Schröder and H. von Hofmannsthal. Borchardt aimed at 'creative restoration' of poetry and culture which are rooted in the European tradition. He refers to the heritage of the three intellectual and artistic forces: archaic Greece, Rome, the Hohenstaufen period.

Poetry
1913: *Jugendgedichte*
1923: *Die Schöpfung aus Liebe*
1924: *Vermischte Gedichte*
1967: *Jamben*

Drama
1920: *Verkündigung*
1934: *Pamela*
1962: *Petra und das Tier*

Novels and epics
1923: *Poetische Erzählungen*
1929: *Das hoffnungslose Geschlecht*
1937: *Vereinigung durch den Feind hindurch*

Essays
1920: *Prosa I*
1928: *Handlungen und Abhandlungen*
1938: *Pisa*

1951: *Der leidenschaftliche Gärtner*
Tr. from Plato, Pindar, Aeschylos, Tacitus, Dante, Troubadours, Swinburne, etc.

1955 ff.: *R. Borchardt, Ges. Werks*, 8 vols.

Studies
1958: Silvio Rizzi: *Rudolf Borchardt als Theoretiker des Dichterischen*
1958: G. C. Bock: *Rudolf Borchardt. Eine Bibliographie*
1961: Werner Kraft: *R.B.—Welt aus Poesie und Geschichte*
1964: A. Wierzejewski: *R.B.'s Auffassung von der Dichtung (unter besonderer Berücksichtigung seines Dantebildes)*
1967: I. Sommer: *Untersuchungen zu R.B.'s Italien-Rezeption*
A. Wierzejewski

WOLFGANG BORCHERT

Born 1921 in Hamburg. Died 1947 in Basle.

Lyrical poetry
mainly from 1940 to 1946

Drama
1947: *Draußen vor der Tür*, Heimkehrerdrama.

Prose pieces
1947: *Die Hundeblume, Der Kaffee ist undefinierbar, Die drei dunklen Könige, An diesem Dienstag, Im Mai, im Mai, schrie der Kuckuck, Dann gibt es nur eins*
1949: *Das Gesamtwerk.* Mit einem biographischen Nachwort von Bernhard Meyer-Marwitz reprinted
1962: *Die traurigen Geranien und andere Geschichten aus dem Nachlaß.* Herausgegeben mit einem Nachwort von Peter Rühmkorf reprinted
1963: *Draußen vor der Tür*, ed. with an introduction, notes and a select vocabulary by P. B. Salmon, London

English trs.
1952: *The Prose Works of Wolfgang Borchert* by David Porter.

Introd. by Stephen Spender. London. (This vol. includes all works contained in *Das Gesamtwerk*, except the verse)

Study
1964: Hans Popper: *Wolfgang Borchert*. In *German Men of Letters*, vol. III

Borchert universalized conflicts, which reach far back into his childhood, by expressing them in the form of comment on postwar Germany. The buoyancy of his language derives from the interaction of a lyrical strain, the search for cosmic and social roots, with alienation, the ability to view each situation from the outside. Thus, with a mixture of fervour and irony, he faces up to universal guilt and cosmic fear, and searches for the possibility of love based on suffering.

H. Popper

FELIX BRAUN

Born 1885 in Vienna. Friendship with Hugo von Hofmannsthal. From 1939 to 1951 in England, now in Vienna.

Poetry
1909: *Gedichte*
1913: *Das neue Leben*
1919: *Hyazinth und Ismene*
       Das Haar der Berenike
1925: *Das innere Leben*

Drama
1917: *Tantalos*
1936: *Kaiser Karl V*
1953: *Rudolf der Stifter*

Novel
1927: *Agnes Altkirchner*, new version called *Herbst des Reiches*, 1957

Ed. of *Der tausendjährige Rosenstrauch* (Deutsche Gedichte aus 1000 Jahren), 1937 and 1949

Essays
1955: *Die Eisblume*

VOLKER BRAUN

Born 1939 in Dresden. Politically committed East German writer.

Poetry
1965: *Provokation für mich*
1966: *Vorläufiges*

BERTOLT BRECHT

Born 1898 at Augsburg. Died 1956 in East Berlin. 1918, military service. 1922, first performance of *Trommeln in der Nacht* in Munich. In 1924 Brecht becomes Dramaturge at Max Reinhardt's Deutsches Theater. 1933, emigration to Denmark, France, Russia, England, etc., and to the U.S.A. 1947, return to Europe (Switzerland). 1949, foundation of the *Berliner Ensemble*, which was directed by Brecht's wife, Frau Helene Weigel.

Poetry
1926: *Taschenpostille*
1927: *Hauspostille*
1943: *Gedichte im Exile*
1960 ff.: *Gedichte* Gesamtausgabe:

vol. I   1918–29: *Bertolt Brechts Hauspostille. Aus einem Lesebuch für Städtebewohner. Geschichten aus der Revolution.* 1960

vol. II   1913–29: *Unveröffentlichte und nicht in Sammlungen enthaltene Gedichte. Gedichte und Lieder aus Stücken.* 1960

vol. III   1930–3: *Lieder, Gedichte, Chöre. Die drei Soldaten. Die sieben Todsünden der Kleinbürger. Unveröffentlichte und nicht in Sammlungen enthaltene Gedichte. Gedichte und Lieder aus Stücken.* 1961

vol. IV   1934–41: *Svendborger Gedichte. Chinesische Gedichte. Studien. Gedichte aus dem Messingkauf. Zum Messingkauf gehörige Gedichte. Steffinische Sammlung.* 1961

vol. V   1934–41: *In Sammlungen nicht enthaltene Gedichte.* 1964

vol. VI   1941–7: *Gedichte im Exil; in Sammlungen nicht enthaltene Gedichte.* 1964

vol. VII   1948–56: *Buckower Elegien, Späte Gedichte.* 1964

vol. VIII   1913–56: *Nachträge.* 1965

vol. IX   1913–56: *Nachträge.* 1965

1965: *Bertolt Brecht. Selected Poems*, ed. by K. Wölfel, Oxford Univ. Press

Drama

Brecht's plays in a 12-vol. uniform ed. (Frankfurt a.M.):

vol. I   *Baal* (1922). *Trommeln in the Nacht* (1922). *Im Dickicht der Städte* (1927). (Erste Stücke) 1957

vol. II: *Leben Eduards des Zweiten von England* (1924, together with L. Feuchtwanger). *Mann ist Mann* (1927). (Erste Stücke) 1957

vol. III: *Die Dreigroschenoper* (1934, first performance 1928). *Aufstieg und Fall der Stadt Mahagonny* (1929). *Das Badener Lehrstück vom Einverständnis* (1928–29). (Stücke f.d. Theater am Schiffbauerdamm, Bd. 1) 1958

vol. IV: *Die heilige Johanna der Schlachthöfe* (1932). *Der Jasager, der Neinsager* (1929–30). *Die Maßnahme* (1931). (Stücke f.d. Theater am Schiffbauerdamm, Bd. 2) 1955

vol. V: *Die Mutter* (1932, a dramatization of Gorki's novel). *Die Ausnahme und die Regel* (written in 1930; 1937). *Die Horatier und die Kuriatier* (1934). (Stücke f.d. Theater am Schiffbauerdamm, Bd. 3) 1957

vol. VI: *Die Rundköpfe und die Spitzköpfe* (1938). *Furcht und Elend des Dritten Reiches* (1938). (Stücke aus dem Exil, Bd. 1) 1957

vol. VII: *Die Gewehre der Frau Carrar* (1937). *Mutter Courage und ihre Kinder* (written in 1939). *Das Verhör des Lukullus* (written in 1939). (Stücke aus dem Exil. Bd. 2) 1957

vol. VIII: *Leben des Galilei* (written in 1938–9; second version performed in 1957). *Der gute Mensch von Sezuan* (written in 1938–42). (Stücke aus dem Exil, Bd. 3) 1957

vol. IX: *Herr Puntila und sein Knecht Matti* (written in 1940). *Der aufhaltsame Aufstieg des Arturo Ui* (1941). *Die Gesichte der Simone Machard* (written in 1941–3 with L. Feuchtwanger). (Stücke aus dem Exil, Bd. 4) 1957

vol. X: *Schweyk im Zweiten Weltkrieg* (written in 1941–4). *Der kaukasische Kreidekreis* (1948). *Die Tage der Commune* (1948–9). (Stücke aus dem Exil, Bd. 5) 1957 vol. XI: Bearbeitungen I: *Die Antigone* des Sophokles (1948). *Der Hofmeister*, nach Lenz (1950). *Coriolan*, nach Shakespeare (1952–3), 1959

vol. XII: Bearbeitungen II: Der Prozess der *Jeanne d'Arc* zu Rouen 1431, nach Seghers (1952), *Don Juan*, nach Molière (1952). *Pauken und Trompeten*, nach Farquhar (1955). 1959

See *Deutsches Schriftstellerlexikon von den Anfängen bis zur Gegenwart*, by Günter Albrecht, Kurt Böttcher, Herbert Greiner-Mai, Paul Günter Krohn. 1961. Volksverlag Weimar

A 20-vol. ed. of Brecht's works, 1967, has been made available by the Suhrkamp Verlag

Studies

Bertolt Brecht in Selbstzeugnissen und Bilddokumenten, dargestellt von M. Kesting, Rowohlts Monographien, with photographs throughout the text

1957: Sinn und Form: 2. Sonderheft: *Bertolt Brecht*

1959: J. Willett: *The Theatre of Bertolt Brecht. A study of eight aspects*, with 109 illustr., 1967, rev. 3rd ed.

1959: M. Esslin: *Brecht, a Choice of Evils. A critical study of the man and his opinions*, London

1960: R. Geissler: *Zur Interpretation des modernen Dramas: Brecht—Dürrenmatt—Frisch*

1960: R. Grimm: *Bertolt Brecht—Die Struktur seines Werkes*; 1965, 4th ed.

W. Haas: *Bert Brecht*. A monograph in series 'Köpfe des XX. Jhdts'

1961: R. Gray: *Brecht*, London

1962: H. Hultberg: *Die ästhetischen Anschauungen Bertolt Brechts*, Copenhagen, 1962

1963: R. Ruland: *The American plays of B. Brecht*, American Quarterly, XV

1965: *Bertolt Brecht: Der Messingkauf Dialogues*, trs. with informative notes. By *Messingkauf* (purchase of brass) Brecht means sketches, poems and notes in dialogue form on dramaturgical questions; cf. also Brecht's *Kleines Organ für das Theater*, here p. 84

1966: Inter Nationes: *Bertolt Brecht*, by E. Wendt, E. Leiser, K. Völker, M. Walser; with Bibliography, Bad Godesberg

WILLI BREDEL

Born 1901 in Hamburg. 1917 member of the Spartakus Union; in 1933 in the KZ; in 1935 emigrated to Russia where with B. Brecht and L. Feuchtwanger he ed. the journal *Das Wort*; returned to DDR in 1945.

Novels

1935: *Die Prüfung* (about his experiences in the KZ)
1941–53: trilogy: *Verwandte und Bekannte*
1941: *Die Väter*
1949: *Die Söhne*
1953: *Die Enkel*
1959: *Ein neues Kapitel*

1944, 1948: *Ernst Thälmann, Beitrag zu einem politischen Lebensbild*

GEORG BRITTING

Born 1891 in Regensburg. Died 1964 in Munich, see p. 56

Poetry

1935: *Der irdische Tag*
1939: *Rabe, Roß und Hahn*
1942: *Lob des Weines*
1947: *Begegnung*
1951: *Unter hohen Bäumen*

Stories

1933: *Die kleine Welt am Strom*
1941: *Der Schneckenweg*
1953: *Afrikanische Elegie*

His only novel

1932: *Lebenslauf eines dicken Mannes, der Hamlet hieß*

1948: *Lyrik des Abendlandes*, ed. together with H. Hennecke,
      C. Hohoff and K. Vossler.

1957–61: *Gesamtausgabe*, 6 vols., amongst them 2 vols. of poems.

Study
1962: Dietrich Bode: *Georg Britting. Geschichte seines Werkes*, with a preface by F. Sengle

HERMAN BROCH

Born 1886 in Vienna. The son of a Jewish textile manufacturer. Entered the family firm, played until 1928 a leading part in Austrian industrial relations, then turned to intellectual pursuits and literature. Arrested in 1938 by National Socialists, spent his time in prison sketching his most important novel, *Der Tod des Vergil*. Released through the intervention of foreign friends, among them James Joyce, he settled in America. Turned increasingly to psychological studies (Professorship at Yale, 1950). Died at New Haven, 1951.

Broch's mission as he saw it was to combat modern ethical disintegration (which he depicted directly in his novel trilogy *Die Schlafwandler* and by analogy in *Vergil*) with the resources of the intellectual disciplines, psychology, literature and mysticism. His philosophy is basically a Platonic striving for unity.

In his best-known work, *Der Tod des Vergil*, which is the inner monologue of the dying poet reflecting on present and past experiences, the problem is whether or not he should hand over to Augustus his manuscript of the *Aeneid*; Vergil's doubts are of the ethical rightness of such an act of self-assertion, not the aesthetic value of his work. In deciding to accede to his friend's desire to possess the *Aeneid* he achieves an ethically acceptable act which symbolizes Broch's view of the primacy of moral values in human relationships. In this, his best work, Broch succeeds, despite a tendency to excessive diffuseness and obscurity, in creating a style which in itself is a revelation of his hero's situation as well as a vehicle for his thoughts.

Novels
1931/1932/1964: *Die Schlafwandler* (trilogy)
1933: *Die unbekannte Größe*
1945: *Der Tod des Vergil*
1950: *Die Schuldlosen*

Study

1966: J. J. White: *Broch, Virgil, and the cycle of history*, Germanic Rev., XLI

J. B. Bednall

KARL BRÖGER

Born 1886 in Nuremberg. Died 1944 in Nuremberg. This patriotic *Arbeiterdichter* became famous for his *Bekenntnis* which ends with much-recited lines (see also p. 319):

> . . . Daß dein ärmster Sohn auch dein getreuester war,
> Denk es, o Deutschland.

Poetry

1918: *Soldaten der Erde*
1924: *Deutschland*

ARNOLT BRONNEN (really Bronner)

Born 1895 in Vienna. Died 1959 in East Berlin. 1935: Dramaturge of the Reichs-Rundfunk-Gesellschaft in Berlin, later in opposition to the regime.

Drama

1920: *Vatermord;* this 'father-son' tragedy caused a sensation
1924: *Katalaunische Schlacht*
1926: *Reparationen*
1929: *Michael Kolhaas*
1941: *Gloriana*

Reportage

1956: *Deutschland—Kein Wintermärchen*

Autobiography

1954: *Arnolt Bronnen gibt zu Protokoll* (in the form of a trial)
1960: *Tage mit Bertolt Brecht* (memoirs)

1958: *Ausgewählte Dramen*

FERDINAND BRUCKNER (Ps. for Theodor Tagger)

Born 1891 in Vienna. Died 1958 in Berlin. Emigrated to the U.S.A. before the War. Playwright, translator, essayist. During the First World War he edited the journal *Marsyas*. A few years after the World War he founded the Renaissancetheater in Berlin.

Drama
1926–8: *Die Krankheit der Jugend*
1928: *Die Verbrecher*
1930: *Elisabeth von England*
1931: *Timon;* the 3rd final version of *Timon* appeared under the title *Timon und das Gold* in 1956
1933–4: *Die Rassen*
1936–7: *Napoleon der Erste*
1942–6 (written in 1942, performed in 1946): *Heroische Komödie*
1951–2: *Pyrrhus and Andromade*
1957: *Der Kampf mit dem Engel*

Poetry
1944: *Negerlieder*

Study
1962: dissertation (Bristol University) by A. J. Harper: *Ferdinand Bruckner's historical dramas*

FRANZ BÜCHLER

Born 1904 in Straßburg. Poet and mainly play-wright.

Drama
1938: *August der Starke*
1939: *Herzog Bernhard*
1952: *Theseus*
1961: *Ree, Wind, Iris (Trilogy)*

Essay
1942: *Über das Tragische*

CHRISTINE BUSTA (Ps. for Christine Dimt)

Born 1915 in Vienna. Interpreter, teacher, now librarian. Busta's aim is, as she says, to transform fear, terror and guilt into joy, love and redemption.

Poetry
1951: *Der Regenbaum*
1955: *Lampe und Delphin* (the dolphin is symbol of healing power)
1958: *Die Scheune der Vögel*
1959: *Die Sternenmühle* (poetry for children)
1965: *Unterwegs zu älteren Feuern*

ELIAS CANETTI

Born 1905 in Bulgaria. Descendant of Spanish Jews. Educated in Germany and Austria, where he lived until 1938, when he moved to Paris and then London, where he still lives. Principal interest is study of crowd psychology.

Publications
1935: *Die Blendung*, Vienna (3rd ed. Munich, 1963)
1960: *Masse und Macht*
1964: *Dramen*
1965: *Aufzeichnungen 1942–1948*

English translations
1946: *Auto-da-Fé (Die Blendung)*, London, 2nd ed. 1962; Penguin Books, 1965
1962: *Crowds and Power (Masse und Macht)*, London

Studies
1962: Erich Fried: Introd. to *Welt im Kopf*, Vienna
1965: Idris Parry: *Elias Canetti's novel 'Die Blendung'*, in *Essays in German Literature*, vol. I, London, Institute of Germanic Studies
1966: Urs Jenny: *Von Vätern und Göttern: Canetti, Merkur*, xx, 3
Idris Parry

HANS CAROSSA

Born 1878 in Bad Tölz. Died 1956 in Rittsteig, nr. Passau.

1910: *Gedichte* (various enlarged editions appeared, from 1938 entitled *Ges. Gedichte*)

1913: *Dr Bürgers Ende* (from 1930 entitled *Die Schicksale Dr. Bürgers*)

1922: *Eine Kindheit* (A)

1924: *Rumänisches Tagebuch*

1928: *Verwandlungen einer Jugend* (B)

1931: *Der Arzt Gion*

1933: *Führung und Geleit*

1938: *Geheimnisse des reifen Lebens*

1941: *Das Jahr der schönen Täuschungen* (C)

1948: *Aufzeichnungen aus Italien*

1951: *Ungleiche Welten* (at the end of this work there appeared the short story *Ein Tag im Spätsommer 1947*, which appeared separately with a new title in 1956 as *Die Frau vom guten Rat*)

1955: *Der Tag des jungen Arztes* (D)

In January 1957 the four autobiographical volumes (A, B, C and D) appeared under the title *Geschichte einer Jugend*.

Study

Further bibliographical information is obtainable from the introduction of Clair Baier: *Selections from Hans Carossa*, 1960 or from Albert Langen: *Hans Carossa, Weltbild und Stil*, 1955

All of Carossa's writing, even where it purports to be fictional, is in essence autobiography (or veiled autobiography). Nevertheless this very human and humane writer, whilst producing a straightforward, if poetic, description of fact, conceives every happening, every person and thing of which he speaks as having symbolic meaning.

Clair Baier

PAUL CELAN (Ps. for Paul Antschel)

Born 1920 in Czernowitz (Bucovina); now naturalized Frenchman.

Poetry
1948: *Sand aus den Urnen*
1952: *Mohn und Gedächtnis*
1955: *Von Schwelle zu Schwelle*
1959: *Sprachgitter*
1963: *Niemandsrose*
1967: *Atemwende*

He wrote also paraphrasing translations of Apollinaire, Rimbaud, Valéry, etc.

Study
1966: S. S. Prawer: *Paul Celan*, in Essays on 'Contemporary German Literature', vol. IV, *German Men of Letters*, l.c.

HANS CHLUMBERG (Ps. for Hans Bardach Edler von Chlumberg)

Born 1897 in Vienna. Died 1930 in Leipzig.

Drama
1930: *Wunder um Verdun* (the dead of the First World War rise and settle accounts with the surviving generation)

HERMANN AUGUST CLAUDIUS

Born 1878 in Langenfelde in Holstein. Great-grandson of Matthias Claudius. Author of Low German and High German folksongs.

1912: *Mank Muern* (Zwischen Mauern)

Also author of 'workers' songs'
1914: *Hörst du nicht den Eisenschritt?*

Biography
1938: *Matthias Claudius*

1957: *Ges. Werke*, 2 vols.

HEDWIG COURTHS-MAHLER

Born 1867 in Nebra, nr. Querfurt. Died 1950 in Rottach-Egern on the Tegernsee. Most prolific author of bourgeois 'Kitsch' stories, sentimental 'Schundromane' which were even more popular than E. Marlitt's (Eugenie John's) nineteenth century novels.

C.-M. wrote over two hundred novels, e.g. *Gib mich frei, Ich will, Mein liebes Mädel, Eine andre wirst du küssen*, etc. Some appeared in instalments, for instance as serialized issues in the *Hausfrau* and other women's magazines. See also DLL.

FRANZ THEODOR CSOKOR

Born 1885 in Vienna. Emigrated in 1938 to Poland, Rumania and Jugoslavia, returned to Vienna after the War. Mainly playwright. At the early stages of his career influenced by G. Büchner and Expressionism.

Drama
1917: *Die Sünde wider den Geist*
1918: *Die rote Straße*
1926: *Gesellschaft der Menschenrechte* (about G. Büchner)
1930–6: *Europäische Trilogie*
1930: *Besetztes Gebiet*
1936: *Dritter November 1918* (about the collapse of the Austrian army)
1946: *Der verlorene Sohn*
1954: (Trilogy): *Olymp und Golgatha* (period between Caesar's assassination and Christ's Crucifixion): (1) *Pilatus*, (2) *Caesars Witwe*, (3) *Kalypso*
1965: *Die Kaiser zwischen den Zeiten* (Dramatisches Diptychon mit einem Prolog und einem Epilog) contrasting the last persecutor of the early Christians (Diocletian) with their first protector (Constantine)

Poetry
1944: *Das schwarze Schiff* (about his emigration)

Prose
1955: *Auf fremden Straßen* (about his Odyssey through Poland and the Balkans)

THEODOR DÄUBLER

Born 1876 in Triest (then Austria). Died 1934 in St Blasien, Black Forest. Befriended by Barlach. See p. 28.

Poetry
1910: the lyrical epic *Das Nordlicht*, his chief work
1915: *Der sternhelle Weg*
1916: *Hymne an Italien*
      Sternenkind
1924: *Attische Sonette*

MAX DAUTHENDEY

Born 1867 in Würzburg. Died 1918 in Malang (Java). Sensitive poet, prose writer and painter, literary contacts with Richard Dehmel and Stefan George.

Neo-Romantic poems
1893: *Ultra-Violett*
1907: *Singsangbuch*
1911: *Die geflügelte Erde*

Stories
1909–10: *Lingam*
1911: *Die acht Gesichter am Biwa-See* (Japanische Liebesgeschichten)
1924: *Erlebnisse auf Java*

1925: *Ausgew. Ges. Werke*. 6 vols.
1930 ff.: *Ges. Werke.*, 9 vols.

RICHARD DEHMEL

Born 1863 in Wendisch-Hermsdorf, Mark Brandenburg. Died 1920 in Blankenese, nr. Hamburg. See p. 5.

Poetry
1891: *Erlösungen*
1893: *Aber die Liebe*
1896: *Weib und Welt*

1897: *Die Verwandlungen der Venus*
1900: *Fitzebutze* (together with Paula Dehmel)

Epic
1903: *Zwei Menschen*, a poetic novel about man and woman; their
    individual happiness sinks in a greater universal fate

Drama
1895: *Der Mitmensch*, a tragi-comedy
1917: *Die Menschenfreunde*

1906–7: *Ges. Werke*, 10 vols.
1922–3: *Ausgewählte Briefe*, 2 vols.

Studies
1932: Paul von Hagen: *Richard Dehmel. Die dichterische Kom-
    position seines lyrischen Gesamtwerks*
1963: P. J. Schindler: *Richard Dehmel. Dichtungen, Briefe, Doku-
    mente*, ed.

FRITZ DIETTRICH

Born 1902 in Dresden. Died 1964 in Kassel.

Poetry
1930: *Gedichte*
1934: *Der attische Bogen*
1936: *Mythische Landschaft*
1940: *Die Hirtenflöte*
    Güter der Erde. Oden
1952: *Der Lichtgott singt*

HEIMITO VON DODERER

Born 1896 in Weidlingau, Vienna. Died 1966 in Vienna.

Novels (and other prose fiction)
1924: *Die Bresche. Ein Vorgang in vierundzwanzig Stunden* (shorter
    tale)
1930: *Das Geheimnis des Reichs*

1938: *Ein Mord den jeder begeht*

1940: *Ein Umweg*

1951: *Die erleuchteten Fenster oder die Menschwerdung des Amtsrates Julius Zihal*

    Die Strudlhofstiege oder Melzer und die Tiefe der Jahre

1953: *Das letzte Abenteuer* (shorter tale)

1956: *Die Dämonen* (English, *The Demons*, 1961)

1958: *Die Posaunen von Jericho* (shorter tale)

1959: *Die Peinigung der Lederbeutelchen* (short stories)

1962: *Die Merowinger oder Die totale Familie*

1963: *Die Wasserfälle von Slunj*

1966: *Unter schwarzen Sternen* (includes *Das letzte Abenteuer* and *Die Posaunen von Jericho* with other short fiction)

Verse

1957: *Ein Weg im Dunkeln*

Essays

1930: *Der Fall Gütersloh*

1958: *Österreich. Bilder seiner Landschaft und Kultur* (ed. with an introduction)

1959: *Grundlagen und Funktion des Romans*

1964: *Tangenten. Tagebuch eines Schriftstellers 1940–1950*

Study

Dietrich Weber, *Heimito von Doderer. Studien zu seinem Romanwerk*, Munich, 1963.

The novel *Das Geheimnis des Reichs* reflects the experiences of a group of prisoners of war in Siberia during and after the First World War. *Ein Mord den jeder begeht*, in a contemporary setting, and *Ein Umweg*, taking place in seventeenth century Austria, exemplify the author's treatment of the theme of personal development. The full variety and vitality of Doderer's work are demonstrated in *Die Strudlhofstiege* and *Die Dämonen*; the author's comments (in *Tangenten*) on these novels as he was working on them indicate their central importance for him. *Die Wasserfälle von Slunj*, the first part of a 'novel no. 7', again offers a broad and vivid panorama of Austrian life.

H. M. Waidson

ALFRED DÖBLIN

Born 1878 in Stettin. Died 1957 in Emmendingen, nr. Freiburg i.B.

Novels

1912: *Der schwarze Vorhang*
1915: *Die drei Sprünge des Wang-lun*
1920: *Wallenstein*
1924: *Berge, Meere und Giganten*
1929: *Berlin Alexanderplatz*
1934: *Babylonische Wandrung*
1935: *Pardon wird nicht gegeben*
1937-8: *Südamerika-Roman* (I. 1937, *Die Fahrt ins Land ohne Tod*; II. 1938, *Der blaue Tiger*)
1948-50: *November 1918* (I. 1948, *Verratenes Volk*; II. 1949, *Heimkehr der Fronttruppen*; III. 1950, *Karl und Rosa*)
1956: *Hamlet oder Die lange Nacht nimmt ein Ende*

Stories

1913: *Die Ermordung einer Butterblume* (collection)
1917: *Die Lobensteiner reisen nach Böhmen* (collection)
1920: *Die Flucht aus dem Himmel*
1925: *Die beiden Freundinnen*
1934: *Sommerliebe*
1946: *Der Oberst und der Dichter*
1948: *Heitere Magie* (two stories: *Reiseverkehr mit dem Jenseits* and *Märchen vom Materialismus*)
1962: *Der Tierfreund oder Das zweite Paradies*

A prolific writer of great range and talent, Döblin is an important figure in the development of the German novel in the first half of the century. His works include *Novellen*, plays, a long verse epic, essays on philosophical, political and literary topics, in addition to the novels, which represent his major achievement. In the novels he makes use of historical, contemporary and exotic material, and incorporates many of the stylistic features of the modern novel. *Berlin Alexanderplatz*, a virtuoso description of proletarian *Großstadt* life, highly original in both content and form, must be considered one of the outstanding novels in the language. The mythical elements, together with the mystical and visionary strain, of many of the novels may partly explain Döblin's failure to gain wide popular success.

The stories, most of which were written early in his career, have been largely overshadowed by the novels, but it was, in fact, in the shorter prose form that Döblin's reputation was first made. Many of the stories in the two main collections (1913 and 1917) were first published in the Expressionist journal *Der Sturm*, and broke new ground in their subject-matter and technique. The most striking features of Döblin's stories are, on the one hand, their thematic originality and variety—he conducts explorations into the subconscious impulses of the psyche, and particularly its pathological aspects, exposing what lies beneath the surface of bourgeois morality—and, on the other, their stylistic diversity—employing naturalist, symbolist and Expressionist techniques, he adapts the traditional forms of the *Märchen*, the legend and the mystery-story, among others, for his purpose. Much of this work deserves attention for its intrinsic merits, as well as for the insight it gives into Döblin's work as a whole.

D. S. Low

HILDE DOMIN

Born 1912 in Cologne. 1940–52 in the Dominican Republic, then in the U.S.A.; returned to Germany in 1954.

Poetry
1959: *Nur eine Rose als Stütze*
1962: *Rückkehr der Schiffe*
1964: *Hier*

1966: ed. *Doppelinterpretationen: Das zeitgenössische deutsche Gedicht zwischen Autor und Leser*

TANKRED DORST

Born 1925 in Sonneberg, Thüringia; see p. 102.

Drama
1960 (first performance): *Die Kurve*
1964 (publ. in *Theater Heute*): *Die Mohrin*

Influenced by B. Brecht and by F. Dürrenmatt.

FRIEDRICH DÜRRENMATT

Born 1921 in Konolfingen, Canton Berne, Switzerland.

Drama

1947: *Es steht geschrieben*
1948: *Der Blinde*
1949: *Romulus der Große* (annotated ed. by H. F. Garten, 1962;
  English, in *Four Plays* 1964)
1951: *Der Prozeß um des Esels Schatten* (radio-play)
1952: *Nächtliches Gespräch* (radio-play)
  Die Ehe des Herrn Mississippi (English, in *Four Plays*, 1964)
1953: *Stranitzky und der Nationalheld* (radio-play)
  Ein Engel kommt nach Babylon (English, in *Four Plays*, 1964)
1954: *Herkules und der Stall des Augias* (radio-play)
1955: *Das Unternehmen der Wega* (radio-play)
1956: *Der Besuch der alten Dame* (annotated ed. by Paul Kurt
  Ackermann, 1961; English, *The Visit*, 1962)
1957: *Abendstunde im Spätherbst* (radio-play)
1959: *Frank der Fünfte*
1960: *Der Doppelgänger* (radio-play)
1962: *Die Physiker* (annotated ed. by Arthur Taylor, 1966;
  English, in *Four Plays*, 1964)
1966: *Der Meteor*

Novels

1950: *Der Richter und sein Henker* (annotated ed. by Leonard
  Forster, 1962; English, *The Judge and his Hangman*, 1954)
1951: *Der Verdacht* (annotated ed. by Leonard Forster, 1965;
  English, *The Quarry*, 1962)
1952: *Die Stadt* (shorter prose)
1955: *Grieche sucht Griechin* (English, *Once a Greek*, 1965)
1956: *Die Panne* (English, *A Dangerous Game*, 1960); annotated ed.
  of *Die Panne* and *Der Tunnel* by F. J. Alexander, 1967
1958: *Das Versprechen* (annotated ed. by Leonard Forster, 1967;
  English, *The Pledge*, 1959)

Essays

1966: *Theater-Schriften und Reden* (edited by Elisabeth Brock-
  Sulzer)

Studies

1960: Hans Bänziger: *Frisch und Dürrenmatt*, Berne and Munich
1960: Elisabeth Brock-Sulzer, *Dürrenmatt. Stationen seines Werkes*, Zürich
1962: Werner Oberle and others: *Der unbequeme Dürrenmatt*, Basle
1964: H. M. Waidson: *Friedrich Dürrenmatt*. In *German Men of Letters*, vol. III

The drama of the Swiss author Dürrenmatt is stark, challenging and often paradoxical. Plays such as *Der Besuch der alten Dame* and *Die Physiker* have made a wide, international impact. His writing on drama is stimulating. In his fiction he has usually chosen to write detective stories; *Das Versprechen* is subtitled: *Requiem auf den Kriminalroman*.

H. M. Waidson

KASIMIR EDSCHMID (Ps. for Eduard Schmid)

Born 1890 in Darmstadt. Died 1966 in Vulpera, Switzerland; famous as an Expressionist prose-writer; also novelist and essayist; later author of travel books, etc.

Poetry

1911: *Verse, Hymnen, Gesänge*
1913: *Bilder* (lyrische Projektionen)
1919: *Stehe von Lichtern gestreichelt* (*Die Silbergäule*)

Novellen

1915: *Die sechs Mündungen*
1915–16: *Das rasende Leben*
1916: *Timur*
1952: *Der Bauchtanz*

Novels

1920: *Die achatnen Kugeln*
1923: *Der Engel mit dem Spleen*
1926: *Die gespenstigen Abenteuer des Hofrat Brüstlein*
1932: *Die Großen der Erde*
1937: *Der Liebesengel*, several reprints
1950: *Wenn es Rosen sind, werden sie blühen* (about Büchner)

1958: *Drei Kronen für Rico* (about the young Hohenstaufen Frederick II)
1946, 1964: *Das gute Recht*

Essays
1919: *Über den Expressionismus in der Literatur und die neue Dichtung*
1920: *Die doppelköpfige Nymphe*
1961: *Lebendiger Expressionismus*
1962: *Portraits und Denksteine*

His early prose is characterized by dithyrambic rhythms and rich imagery, often cosmic in scope. Events, in the main, function for the display of instincts and emotions, on which attention is focused, as they harbour the forces which create, and give direction to, the human personality. Their physical forms of expression provide the basis for experience; but again and again they get transformed into intellectual energy and spiritual aspiration. Thus they range from brutal self-assertion to sacrificial love, sometimes switching from one attitude to another, sometimes alternating between these different attitudes and their respective levels of expression. And whether they fulfil or pervert their essential creative nature, they always exemplify, within human nature, cosmic forces, just as human brotherhood is an instance of the larger cosmic unity of existence.

Since about 1923, travel books and historical and documentary novels have played an increasingly significant part in Edschmid's work. He now depicts the physical and social environment of his characters with painstaking accuracy, so that we are given a comprehensive view of the three-cornered struggle between natural forces, social demands and instinctual drives. In this the individual has to try and find a meaningful pattern of living, and above all to preserve that core of personal integrity and human dignity, which is in continual danger on account of pressures from without and perversion from within, thus jeopardizing the chances—and, indeed, the worthwhileness—of survival. In fact, this central issue, together with the themes and character-types clustered around it, can be traced through all stages of Edschmid's development, as a comparison of specific motifs and symbols will show. In the last works, however, his central concern has been with the problems of awareness of guilt, justice and mercy.

H. Popper

ALBERT EHRENSTEIN

Born 1886 in Vienna. Died 1950 in New York. Discovered and furthered by Karl Kraus; contributed to Herwarth Walden's *Sturm.*

Poetry
1914: *Die weiße Zeit*
1916: *Der Mensch schreit*
1917: *Die rote Zeit*
1920–1: *Wien*
1931: *Mein Lied*

1924: *China klagt* (Nachdichtungen revolutionärer chinesischer Lyrik aus drei Jahrtausenden)

Novel
1911: *Tubutsch*, illustrated by his friend Oskar Kokoschka

1961: *Albert Ehrenstein: Gedichte und Prosa*, ed. and introduced by Karl Otten, with bibliography

1961: *Albert Ehrenstein. Ausgewählte Aufsätze*, ed. by M. Y. Ben-gavriêl

GÜNTER EICH

Born 1907 in Lebus an der Oder. Author in Group 47; lived in Oberbayern; now in Austria; married Ilse Aichinger.

Poetry
1930: *Gedichte*
1948: *Abgelegene Gehöfte*
1949: *Untergrundbahn*
1955: *Botschaften des Regens*
1964: *Zu den Akten*
1966: *Anlässe und Steingärten*

Radio-plays (the main themes are the purification of man through his readiness for sacrifice, and man's return to the preconscious state of Nature):

1953: *Träume* (Vier Spiele)
1953–4: *Die Mädchen aus Viterbo*
1955: *Zinngeschrei*
1958: *Stimmen* (Sieben Hörspiele)
   Allah hat 100 Namen
1964: *In anderen Sprachen* (Vier Hörspiele)

Studies
1966: F. M. Fowler: *Günter Eich*, in 'Essays on Contemporary
   German Literature', vol. IV, *German Men of Letters*
1965: A. Zimmermann: *Das lyrische Werk Günter Eichs* (Versuch
   einer Gestaltanalyse). Erlangen-Nürnberg Univ. Diss.,
   Offset-Fotodruck

HERBERT EISENREICH

Born 1925 in Linz/Donau, Austria: friendship with H. von
Doderer; mainly story-writer, novelist and essayist.

Stories
1957: *Böse schöne Welt*
1965: *Liebesgeschichten*

Novel
1953: *Auch in ihrer Sünde*

Radio-play
1955: *Wovon wir leben und woran wir sterben*

Essays
1960: *Geist und Fleisch*
1964: *Reaktionen*

GERRIT ENGELKE

Born 1890 in Hanover. Died 1918 nr. Cambrai, France (shortly
before the end of World War I). He was discovered as a poet by
R. Dehmel, who introduced him to the literary circle: *Werkleute
auf Haus Nyland*—a community (Bund der Werkleute) founded
with J. Kneip and W. Vershofen by Josef Winckler (born 1881 in
Rheine, Westfalen); see H. Lersch, p. 319, also p. 400.

  The circle met at J. Winckler's ancestral 'Haus Nyland'. They were disciples of R. Dehmel and guided by the principle of nobility of labour and by their belief in a possible balance between personal freedom and our modern industrial development and between working-men and management. The journal of *Haus Nyland* called *Quadriga* aimed at a reconciliation of humanity and technology.

Gerrit Engelke is one of the best German 'worker-poets'. His poems appeared posthumously under the title: *Rhythmus des neuen Europa*, 1921, ed. by his friend Jakob Kneip.

1960: *Gerrit Engelke: Das Gesamtwerk*

HANS MAGNUS ENZENSBERGER

Born 1929 in Kaufbeuren (Allgäu). Now living in Berlin and Norway.

Poetry
1957: *verteidigung der wölfe*
1960: *landessprache*
1962: *Gedichte*
1964: *blindenschrift*

1958: ed. of: *Clemens v. Brentano—Gedichte, Erzählungen, Briefe*

1960: ed. the Anthology: *Museum der modernen Poesie*
1961: *Allerleirauh* (Viele schöne Kinderreime ges. von H. M. Enzensberger)
Clemens Brentanos Poetik (based on H. M. E.'s dissertation, 1955)

Essays
1962: *Einzelheiten*

1965 ff.: Editor of the journal *Kursbuch*

Studies
1966: P. Bridgwater: *Hans Magnus Enzensberger*, in 'Essays on Contemporary German Literature', vol. IV, *German Men of Letters*, l.c., see also GLL, October 1967.

PAUL ERNST

Born 1866 in Elbingerode, Harz. Died 1933 in St Georgen, Styria, Austria.

Prose works

(a) Short stories

1902: *Altitalienische Novellen*

1903: *Prinzessin des Ostens*

1921: *Erdachte Gespräche*

1926: *Komödianten-und Spitzbubengeschichten* as well as many others subsequently collected in (1930) *Romantische Geschichten*

1930: *Lustige Geschichten*
      Geschichten zwischen Traum und Tag

1931: *Frühe Geschichten* (four of the 19 vols. of Ges. Schriften published 1928-31 by Georg Müller, Munich)

(b) Novels

1904: *Der schmale Weg zum Glück*

1916: *Saat auf Hoffnung*

1923: *Grün aus Trümmern*

1926: *Der Schatz im Morgenbrotstal*

1931: *Das Glück von Lautental*

(c) Autobiography

1928: *Jugenderinnerungen*

1930: *Jünglingsjahre*

(d) Criticism

1906: *Der Weg zur Form*

1912: *Ein Credo*

1923: *Tagebuch eines Dichters*

1942: *Völker und Zeiten im Spiegel ihrer Dichtung*

Dramatic works

1898: *Lumpenbagasch, Im Chambre Separée*

1905: *Demetrios*

1908: *Canossa*

1909: *Brunhild*

1913: *Der Heilige Crispin*

1915: *Preußengeist*

1917: *Yorck*
1922: *Chriemhild*

Verse epic
1923–8: *Kaiserbuch*

Studies
1935: A. Potthoff: *Paul Ernst. Einführung in sein Leben und Werk*, Munich
1938: K. Cunningham: *Paul Ernst's Theory of the Novelle* in 'German Studies' presented to H. G. Fiedler, Oxford
W. W. Chambers: *Paul Ernst's Conception of the nature and role of the Poet* in MLR, vol. 44

Ernst's reputation rests on his *Novellen*, which are carefully composed, unpretentious and interesting as tales. He did, however, devote his main energies to the drama which he regarded as the paramount literary form and has left a significant amount of stimulating dramatic criticism. In theory and in practice he opposed Naturalism as a neo-Classic.

W. Walker Chambers

HERBERT EULENBERG

Born 1876 in Mühlheim (Ruhr). Died 1949 in Düsseldorf-Kaiserswerth. 1906–9 Dramaturge in Düsseldorf.

Drama
1901: *Leidenschaft*
1918: *Krieg dem Krieg*, two one-act plays
1932: *Thomas Münzer*
1934: *Tilman Riemenschneider*

HANNS HEINZ EWERS

Born 1871 in Düsseldorf. Died 1943 in Berlin. Under E. A. Poe's literary influence.

Novels
1910: *Der Zauberlehrling*
1913: *Alraune*

1920: *Vampir*
1922: *Der Geisterseher*, a continuation of Schiller's novel

1905: Essay on *Edgar Allan Poe*

HANS FALLADA (Ps. for Rudolf Ditzen)

Born 1893 in Greifswald. Died 1947 in Berlin. He stayed in Germany during the Third Reich. His literary fame mainly rests on his three novels:

1920–30: *Bauern, Bonzen und Bomben*
1932: *Kleiner Mann—was nun?*
1934: *Wer einmal aus dem Blechnapf frißt*

Stories
1936: *Hoppelpoppel, wo bist du*
1938: *Geschichten aus der Murkelei*

Novel
1947: *Jeder stirbt für sich allein* (about the resistance movement)

LION FEUCHTWANGER

Born 1884 in Munich. Died 1958 in Pacific Palisades, California.

Novels
1910: *Der tönerne Gott*
1923: *Die häßliche Herzogin*
1925: *Jud Süß*
1929: *Erfolg*
1932: *Der jüdische Krieg*
1933: *Die Geschwister Oppermann*
1935: *Die Söhne*
1936: *Der falsche Nero*
1940: *Exil*
1942: *Der Tag wird kommen* (also as *Das gelobte Land*)
1943: *Die Brüder Lautensack*
1945: *Simone*
1947–8: *Die Füchse im Weinberg* (also as *Waffen für Amerika*)
1951: *Goya oder der arge Weg der Erkenntnis*

1952: *Narrenweisheit oder Tod und Verklärung des Jean-Jacques
        Rousseau*
1955: *Die Jüdin von Toledo* (also as *Spanische Ballade*)
1957: *Jefta und seine Tochter*

Dramatized novel
1920: *Thomas Wendt*

Drama
1916: *Vasantasena*
      Warren Hastings, Gouverneur von Indien (adapted in collabor-
        ation with Brecht in 1925 as *Kalkutta, 4. Mai*)
1918: *Jud Süß*
      Die Kriegsgefangenen
      Friede (from Aristophanes: *Acharnians* and *Eirene*)
      Appius und Virginia (from John Webster)
1921: *Der Amerikaner oder die entzauberte Stadt*
1923: *Der holländische Kaufmann*
1924: *Leben Eduards des Zweiten von England* (from Marlowe, in
        collaboration with Brecht)
1927: *Die Petroleum-Inseln; Wird Hill amnestiert?*
1948: *Wahn, oder der Teufel in Boston*
1956: *Die Witwe Capet*

Poetry
1928: *PEP, J. L. Wetcheeks amerikanisches Liederbuch*

Short stories
1903: *Die Einsamen. Zwei Skizzen*
1934: *Marianne in Indien und sieben andere Erzählungen*
1946: *Venedig (Texas) und 14 andere Erzählungen*
1949: *Odysseus und die Schweine*

Essays, memoirs, etc.
1937: *Moskau 1937*
1942: *Unholdes Frankreich*
1956: *Centum Opuscula*
1961: *Das Haus der Desdemona*

Studies

1946–7: V. Wittner: *Lion Feuchtwanger*, Schweizer Annalen 3

1954: *L. Feuchtwanger zum 70. Geburtstag. Worte seiner Freunde.* Berlin (contains a detailed Bibliography)

1959: W. Jahn: *Die Geschichtsauffassung Lion Feuchtwangers in seiner Josephus-Trilogie*, Rudolstadt

1959: *Lion Feuchtwanger* (Schriftsteller der Gegenwart, No. 2), Berlin (3rd ed.)

1964: W. Yuill: *Lion Feuchtwanger*, in 'German Men of Letters', vol. III, l.c.

W. E. Yuill

OTTO FLAKE (Ps. Leo F. Kotta)

Born 1880 in Metz. Died 1963 in Baden-Baden. Author of essays, dramas, stories, novels, biographies (Ulrich von Hutten, Marquis de Sade) and histories (Kaspar Hauser, Klemens von Metternich).

Essays

1924: *Zum guten Europäer*

Novels

1922: *Ruland*

1922–8: the *Ruland Epos*, Bildungsroman in 5 vols.

1924: *Der gute Weg*

1926: *Villa U.S.A.*

1928: *Eine Kindheit* (1st version under the title *Das Freitagskind*, 1913)

1928: *Freund aller Welt*

1931: *Christa*, Kinderroman

1946 and 1963: *Die Deutschen*

1946–8: *Fortunat*, 4 vols. in one: 1960

WALTER FLEX

Born 1887 in Eisenach. Died 1917 in a cavalry attack against the Russians on the island of Oesel. Through his death his person became a symbol of heroism for Germans.

Poetry
1910: *Im Wechsel*
1915: *Vom großen Abendmahl*

Stories
1916: *Der Wanderer zwischen beiden Welten*

1925, 1936: *Ges. Werke*, 2 vols.

Study
1928: J. Klein: *Walter Flex*

HANS FRANCK

Born 1879 in Wittenburg, Mecklenburg. Died 1963 on Landgut Frankenhorst. Son of a tiler. Mainly influenced by H. v. Kleist, F. Hebbel and Paul Ernst.

Drama
1910: *Der Herzog von Reichstadt*

Legend
1919: *Lady Godiva*, dramatische Legende

Autobiography
1929: *Mein Leben und Schaffen*

Novels
1937: *Annette*, biogr. novel about Droste-Hülshoff
1938: *Die Stadt des Elias Holl* (appeared 1921 under title *Das dritte Reich*
1942: *Mecklenburgische Sagen*
1953: *Marianne*, biogr. novel about Marianne v. Willemer
1958: *Letzte Liebe* (Goethe and Ulrike v. Lewetzow)
1960: *Cantate* (S. Bach)

Stories
1955: *Die vier großen B*, Bach, Beethoven, Brahms, Bruckner.

Bruno Frank

Born 1887 in Stuttgart. Died 1945 in Beverley Hills, U.S.A. Friendship with Thomas Mann and Lion Feuchtwanger.

Poetry
1905: *Aus der goldenen Schale*

Novels
1926: *Trenck*. Roman eines Günstlings
1934: *Cervantes* (biographical)

Short stories
1916: *Himmel der Enttäuschten*

Drama
1927: *Zwölftausend*, about the barter of soldiers by German princes

Leonhard Frank

Born 1882 in Würzburg. Died 1961 in Munich. Pacifist, influenced by S. Freud, etc. During the First World War he emigrated to Switzerland and before the Second World War to the U.S.A.; afterwards returned to Germany.

Novels
1914: *Räuberbande*; this first novel is perhaps his best; it received the Fontane Prize (boys who later become good citizens, rebel against society)
1924: *Der Bürger*
1929: *Bruder und Schwester*, incest-novel
1949: *Die Jünger Jesu*

Stories
1917: *Der Mensch ist gut*
1927: *Karl und Anna*; this love-story was his greatest success; it is a Heimkehrergeschichte, later dramatized and also filmed

1957: *Ges. Werke*, 6 vols.

Gustav Frenssen

Born 1863 in Barlt, Holstein. Died 1945 in Barlt. Author of novels about North Germany.

His most famous novels
1901: *Jörn Uhl*
1906: *Hilligenlei*

Story
1922: *Der Pastor von Poggsee*

Erich Fried

Born 1921 in Vienna. Now in London. Translator of works by Dylan Thomas and T. S. Eliot, Graham Greene, Shakespeare, etc.

Poetry
1958: *Gedichte*
1963: *Reich der Steine*
1964: *Warngedichte*
1965: *Überlegungen*
1966: *und Vietnam und*
1967: *Anfechtungen*

Max Frisch

Born 1911 in Zurich. Architect and journalist, now wholly dedicated to literature.

Drama
1944: *Santa Cruz*
1946: *Die chinesische Mauer*, a farce, new version 1955
1949: *Als der Krieg zu Ende war*
1951: *Graf Öderland* (eine Moritat), new version 1961
1953: *Don Juan und die Liebe zur Geometrie* (Komödie)
1956: *Biedermann und die Brandstifter* (Ein Lehrstück ohne Lehre, Hörspiel)   1958: Stage play

1962: *Andorra* (Stück in 11 Bildern)
    Max Frisch: Stücke, 2 vols., Suhrkamp Verlag
1967: *Biografie: ein Spiel*

Novels

1954: *Stiller*, 1956 published, English title: *I'm not Stiller*, Penguin
    Books
1957: *Homo Faber*
1950: *Tagebuch 1946–1949*
1964: *Mein Name sei Gantenbein*

Study

1964: Martin Esslin: *Max Frisch* in 'German Men of Letters',
    vol. III, l.c.

WALTER HELMUT FRITZ

Born 1929 in Karlsruhe. Mainly poet, but also story-writer and translator from the French of Jean Follain, Alain Bosquet, etc.

Poetry

1956: *Achtsam sein*
1958: *Bild und Zeichen*
1963: *Veränderte Jahre*
1966: *Die Zuverlässigkeit der Unruhe*

GUNTER BRUNO FUCHS

Born 1928 in Berlin. Poet, satirist, founder of the gallery *Zinke*. He had a variety of occupations: labourer, clown, graphic artist and printer.

Poetry

1957: *Nach der Haussuchung*
1960: (poetry and prose) *Brevier eines Degenschluckers*
1965: *Pennergesang: Gedichte und Chansons*
1967: *Blätter eines Hof-Poeten*

FRANZ FÜHMANN

Born 1922 in Rokytnice, Riesengebirge. His Russian war prison from 1945 to 1949 brought about an inner change; now settled in DDR.

1953: *Die Fahrt nach Stalingrad*: this lyric epic is about his three-fold contacts with Stalingrad: as soldier, as prisoner of war, as friend

Poetry
1953: *Die Nelke Nikos*
1957: *Aber die Schöpfung soll dauern*
1962: *Die Richtung der Märchen*

War stories
1959: *Stürzende Schatten*

1962: Book for children: *Lustiges Tier—A B C*
1967: (*Ges. Erzählungen*) *König Ödipus*

Louis Fürnberg (Ps. 'Nuntius')

Born 1909 in Iglau, Moravia. Died 1957 in Weimar. Abandoning on health grounds early training in ceramics. Fürnberg took up journalism. As member of the Czecho-Slovak Communist Party from 1928 he worked on *International Literature*, *Gegenangriff*, *Links-front*, etc. From 1932 to 1936 he played a leading part in the *Agitproptruppe*, was imprisoned by the Nazis in 1939, but escaped to Palestine. Returning in 1946 Fürnberg was successively on the Czech Ministries of Information and of Education. From 1954 settled in Weimar, he was Deputy Director of the Nat. For-schungs-u. Gedenkstätten d. dt. Lit. and member of the editorial board of *Weimarer Beiträge*.

After the very popular *Songs und Gedichte*, 1933, for which the poet also composed the tunes, Fürnberg's collections of poetry show increasing versatility and growing assurance in form and ideology: examples are *Hölle Haß und Liebe*, 1943, *Die spanische Hochzeit*, 1948, *Wanderer in den Morgen*, 1951, *Das wunderbare Gesetz*, 1956. Tenderly personal evocation of a lullaby (*Wiegenlied in der Fremde*) contrasts with the challenge of *Gang durch die Heide* and *Ein Lied für meine Kinder* (where the hymnic quality character-istic of F.'s poetry shows formal kinship with the vigour and resolve of hymn writers of the seventeenth century). *Bruder Namenlos/Ein Leben in Versen*, 1947, is seen as documentation of F.'s own progress towards socialist humanism.

Mozart-Novelle, 1947, and *Begegnung in Weimar* are examples of a remarkably sensitive prose-style. Further editions of most of the works have been posth. published by Dietz, Berlin. Some of F.'s German trs. of Czech poetry appeared in 1961.

Studies

1967: *Weimarer Beiträge*, p. 355 ff. about F.'s correspondence with Arnold Zweig

W. F. Mainland

LUDWIG ANTON SALOMON FULDA

Born 1862 in Frankfurt a.M. Died 1939 in Berlin, suicide. Friendship with P. Heyse.

Drama

1893: *Der Talisman*
1910: *Herr und Diener*
1920: *Des Esels Schatten*
1924: *Die Gegenkandidaten*
1932: *Der neue Harem*

GERD GAISER

Born 1908 in Oberriexingen (Württemberg). Extensive travels and art studies have left their mark on his work which contains a contemporary realism, yet also a certain ambivalence. A note of resignation creeps in, but gentle humour is also observable. The irony of fate and the need for human sympathy and understanding is emphasized. Considerable linguistic inventiveness and mastery of lyrical evocative prose.

Novels

1950: *Eine Stimme hebt an*
1953: *Die sterbende Jagd*
1955: *Das Schiff im Berg*
1958: *Schlußball*

Short story collections
1949: *Zwischenland*
1956: *Revanche*
Einmal und oft
1959: *Gib acht in Domokosch*
1960: *Am Paß Nascondo*
1965: *Gazelle, grün*

Essays
1959: *Sizilianische Notizen*

His work is partly tr. into English.

Ian Hilton

PETER GAN (Ps. for Richard Moering)

Born 1894 in Hamburg. Emigrated before the War, now again living in Hamburg.

Poetry
1935: *Die Windrose*
1949: *Die Holunderflöte*
1956: *Schachmatt*
1961: *Die Neige*
1965: *Das alte Spiel*

Great virtuosity and clarity of expression in traditional verseform; poems about Gustav Schwab, Philipp Otto Runge, etc., and in memoriam E. R. Curtius, Rudolf Borchardt and Ernst Bertram.

LUDWIG ALBERT GANGHOFER

Born 1855 in Kaufbeuren. Died 1920 in Tegernsee. His popular novels mainly deal with life in the Bavarian Alps.

1880: Volksstück: *Der Herrgottschnitzer von Ammergau* (together with H. Neuert)

Some of his most successful novels
1894: *Die Martinsklause*

1895: *Schloß Hubertus*
1904: *Der hohe Schein*

1906–21: *Ges. Schriften*, 40 vols.; see also DLL

STEFAN GEORGE

Born 1868 at Büdesheim. Died 1933 in Minusio nr. Locarno.

Bio-bibliographical dates
(For these, with slight alterations, I am indebted to the late
E. K. Bennett's *Stefan George* in the 'Studies in modern European literature and thought', 1954.)
1886–9: *Von einer Reise: Zeichnungen in Grau: Legenden* (published
under the title *Die Fibel*, 1901)
1890: *Hymnen*
1891: Meeting with H. v. Hofmannsthal in Vienna
Pilgerfahrten, tr. of Baudelaire, privately circulated
1892: *Algabal*, limited edition, *Blätter für die Kunst* (1892–1919)
1895: *Die Bücher der Hirten und Preisgedichte: der Sagen und Sänge;
und der Hängenden Gärten*
1897: *Das Jahr der Seele*
1900: *Der Teppich des Lebens und die Lieder von Traum und Tod. Mit
einem Vorspiel*
1906: *Maximin, ein Gedenkbuch*, privately published
1907: *Der Siebente Ring*
1909: Tr. of Shakespeare's Sonnets
1912: Tr. of passages from *La Divina Commedia*
1914: *Der Stern des Bundes*
1928: *Das Neue Reich*
1933: George leaves Germany for Switzerland
Death at Minusio

Studies
About Stefan George's 'Third Humanism' and the heritage of
Goethe in the Twentieth Century see ÉG, Sept. 1949 and MLQ,
Sept. 1949, essays on the occasion of the bicentenary of Goethe's
birth.

Friedrich Gundolf: *George* (an idolatrous interpretation of the
poet), 1920

Edna Lowrie Duthie: *L'Influence du Symbolisme français dans le Renouveau Poétique de l'Allemagne*, 1933

Eduard Lachmann: *Die ersten Bücher Stefan Georges*, 1933

Willi Koch: *Stefan George—Weltbild, Naturbild, Menschenbild*, 1933

Ernst Morwitz: *Die Dichtung Stefan Georges*, 1934

Edward Jaime: *Stefan George und die Weltliteratur*, 1949

Robert Boehringer, *Mein Bild von Stefan George*, 1951, 1968[2]

Leni, Asbeck-Stansberg: *Stefan George—Gestalt und Werk*, 1951

Ulrich K. Goldsmith: *Stefan George. A study of his early work*, Univ. of Colorado Studies, 1959

E. M. Butler: *The Tyranny of Greece over Germany* (Chap. 8), 1935

Sir Maurice Bowra: *The Heritage of Symbolism* (Chap., 'Stefan George'), 1943

Cyril Scott: *Die Tragödie Stefan Georges* (L. Hempe Verlag), 1952

August Closs: *Medusa's Mirror* (Studies in German Literature), 1957

H. Arbogast: *Die Erneuerung der deutschen Dichtersprache in den Frühwerken Stefan Georges*, 1967, Cologne

Translations into English
Cyril Scott: *Selected Poems*, 1910
Valhope and Morwitz: *Selected Poems*, 1944

RAINER MARIA GERHARDT

Born 1927 in Karlsruhe. Died 1954, suicide. Co-editor of the magazine *fragmente*.

Poetry
1950: *Der Tod des Hamlet*
1952: *Umkreisung*

JENS GERLACH

Born 1926 in Hamburg. He went to East Germany in 1953. Author of poems, film scripts, radio-plays and chanson for Agitprop (Agitation-Propaganda). Influenced by G. Heym and B. Brecht.

Poetry

1953: *Der Gang zum Ehrenmal*
Ich will deine Stimme sein

1956: Ed. of *Gedichte aus Ost und West*

FRANZ KARL GINZKEY (Ps. Heinrich Hege)

Born 1871 in Pola. Died 1963 in Vienna. Prolific poet, author of numerous stories and several novels.

Poetry
1906: *Das heimliche Läuten*
1917: *Befreite Stunde*

Novels
1908: *Jakobus und die Frauen*
1912: *Der von der Vogelweide*
1916: *Der Gaukler von Bologna*

1948: Autobiography: *Der Heimatsucher*

REINHARD GOERING

Born 1887 in Schloß Bieberstein, nr. Fulda. 1936, suicide in Flur Bucha, nr. Jena.

Plays
1917: Expressionist drama: *Seeschlacht*. The events during the battle of the Skaggerak are reflected in the fates of seven sailors in the munition-tower of a battleship
1919: *Scapa Flow*
1930: *Die Südpolexpedition des Kapitän Scott*

1961: *Prosa, Dramen, Verse*. Preface by D. Hoffmann

ALBRECHT GOES

Born 1908 in Langenbeutingen, Württemberg.

Principal works
1950: *Unruhige Nacht* (Erzählung), annotated ed. by A. E. Hammer, London, 1965

1954: *Das Brandopfer* (Erzählung), annotated ed. by A. R. Robinson, London, 1958. Engl. tr. by M. Hamburger, 1956

Some other titles
1956: *Ruf und Echo*, 25 essays and addresses written between 1951 and 1955
1958: *Gedichte*, a selection of 103 poems by Goes
1959: *Von Mensch zu Mensch*, a new and enlarged ed. of 19 essays written between 1937 and 1951
1961: *Die guten Gefährten*, a new ed. of 23 essays and addresses written between 1937 and 1958

Albrecht Goes has made his mark in three different literary fields —the poem, the essay and the prose tale (*Erzählung*), his central theme in most cases being the cause of humanity and Christian values. This comes out most effectively in the two prose-works which have made him internationally famous, namely *Unruhige Nacht* and *Das Brandopfer*, each dealing with incidents from the war years of 1939–45, the former on the Eastern Front and the latter inside Germany under Nazi rule.

A. R. Robinson

WOLFGANG GOETZ

Born 1885 in Leipzig. Died 1955 in Berlin. Theatre critic, Feuilletonist, since 1945 ed. of the *Berlinerhefte für geistiges Leben*.

Drama
1925: *Neidhardt von Gneisenau*
1936: *Der Ministerpräsident*

Novel
1926: *Das Gralswunder*

Biogr. works on Schiller, Goethe, Mozart

IWAN (or YVAN) GOLL (Ps. for Isaac Lang; other Ps.: Iwan Lassang, Tristan Torsi, Johannes Thor, etc.).

Born 1891 in St Dié in the Vosges. Died 1950 in Paris. He wrote in French and German until 1930, when he wrote almost entirely in French. Friendship with Romain Rolland and James Joyce and members of the Apollinaire circle. In the Journal *Surréalism*, he advocated Cubism in literature, about 1924. In 1939 he emigrated to New York. His wife, Claire Goll, tr. many of his works. He founded the French-American Journal *Hemisphères* 1943–6, to which André Breton, Henry Miller, Saint-John Perse contributed whilst he was in New York.

Poetry (in German)
1914: *Films*
1918: *Der neue Orpheus*
1928: *Die siebente Rose*
1954: *Abendgesang* (posth.)

1960: *I. Goll: Dichtungen* (Lyrik, Prosa Drama), ed. by C. Goll

Drama
1920: *Die Unsterblichen*. Goll here reveals himself as a forerunner
　　　　of the present-day Theatre of the Absurd
1924: *Der Stall des Augias*

JOACHIM VON DER GOLTZ

Born 1892 in Obersasbach, Baden.

1922: *Vater und Sohn*, drama dealing with Frederick II's relationship with his father

EUGEN GOMRINGER

Born 1925 in Bolivia. Poetry: *Konstellationen*, 1953, 1960, 1963.
1960: founder of the series *Konkrete Poesie—poesia concreta*. The avant-garde has in E. Gomringer, H. Heissenbüttel (see p. 274) and F. Mon (see p. 96) its extreme exponents. The years 1950–60 witnessed the foundation of several international, literary groups some wildly pretentious, some mainly political or commercial, and a few genuinely seeking new modes of expression. It is impossible to forecast the fate of the many novelties. Here it must suffice if we but briefly refer to some representative titles such as: *The Vienna Group, Concrete Poetry, Situationist International, Group*

Zero, Movens, moreover *Lettrism, Permutationelle Kunst* (influenced by Max Bense), *Ultimismus,* etc. The newest of the new is *Neodadaismus,* the avante-garde of the avant-garde! Some of the excesses in their art and poetry are exposed in the following passage:

'We see the consequences today at every step; the new sculptor displays heaps of scrapmetal or assembles large grocery boxes, Rauschenberg exhibits clean white canvasses as his early works, and an enthusiastic critic, John Cage, praises them as "landing-places for lights and shadows". The composer of "concrete" music produces the noises of machines and the streets, and I hear that there is even a music of silence—three musicians appear on the podium, stand there, and do nothing at all. The dramatist produces the noises of a boys' school lavatory and displays its obscene scribblings. More seriously Marc Saporta produces a "shuffle novel", No. 1, where the pages are loose and unnumbered and can be read in any order. All distinctions between art and reality have fallen. All arts tend toward self-abolition. Some of these acts or works obviously need not be taken seriously. They are elaborate hoaxes as old as Dada or as Marcel Duchamp, who submitted under the title "Fountain" a hospital urinal to the Independent Show in New York in 1917. I hope I am not suspected of lack of sympathy with modern art, the avant-garde, or experimentation when I judge that art, in these symptoms, has reached the zero point and is about to commit suicide.' (René Wellek, in CL, Eugene, Oregon, vol. XVII, 1965, No. 4.)

GÜNTER GRASS

Born 1927 in Danzig. See p. 102. Controversial novelist, poet and dramatist. His powerful and biting fiction surveys Germany of the last forty years. Master of extravagant invention and linguistic ingenuity. His training as sculptor and draughtsman is reflected in his concern for shape and images.

Novels and novelle
1959: *Die Blechtrommel* (brought him international recognition)
1961: *Katz und Maus*
1963: *Hundejahre*

Poetry
1956: *Die Vorzüge der Windhühner*

1960: *Gleisdreieck*
1967: *Ausgefragt*

Plays
1956: *Hochwasser*
1957: *Noch zehn Minuten bis Buffalo*
       Onkel, Onkel
1966: *Die Plebejer proben den Aufstand* (first major theatrical venture)

Essay
1968: *Über das Selbstverständliche*

Studies
1966: Idris Parry: *The Special Quality of Hell*, Listener, LXXV
1967: Idris Parry: *Aspects of G. Grass's Narrative Technique*, Forum
       for Mod. Lang. Studies III

His fiction and much of his verse is available in English translation.

Ian Hilton

HANS GRIMM

Born 1875 in Wiesbaden. Died 1959 in Lippoldsberg on the Weser.

Novel
1926: *Volk ohne Raum*

Short stories
1913: *Südafrikanische Novellen*
1916: *Der Gang durch den Sand*
1918: *Der Ölsucher von Duala*
       Die Olewagen-Saga
1930: *Der Richter in der Karu und andere Geschichten*
1934: *Lüderitzland*
1936: *Des Elefanten Wiederkehr*

Autobiographical writings
1950: *Rückblick*
1951: *Leben in Erwartung; meine Jugend*
1960: *Suchen und Hoffen; aus meinem Leben, 1928–34*

Critical and miscellaneous writings

1913: *Afrikafahrt-West*

1929: *Das deutsche Südwesterbuch*

1950: *Die Erzbischofschrift; Antwort eines Deutschen,* English version, 1952: *The answer of a German; an open letter to the Archbishop of Canterbury* (tr. by L. Hudson)

Grimm's writings, some of which are politically tendentious, record the world of Boers and African natives, of German and English colonizers in South Africa among whom he had worked for thirteen years, in a style modelled on that of the Icelandic sagas.

H. R. Klieneberger

ALBERT PARIS GÜTERSLOH (Ps. for Albert Conrad Kiehtreiber)

Born 1887 in Vienna. Varied activities as writer, artist, actor and director in Berlin, Vienna and Munich. Best known (after early fame as Expressionist novelist) as painter. In disfavour under National Socialists (ban on 'decadent' artistic activities); later revival of literary work, for which he is best known now. Gütersloh is difficult to classify on account of the many-sided nature of his art (corresponding to his own view of the world as a many-faceted phenomenon which it is the duty of the artist to depict with a simple joy in his task, whatever the difficulties; for only the individual can transmit his own unique view). Friend and mentor of Doderer.

Essays

1911: *Egon Schiele. Versuch einer Vorrede*

1921: *Die Vision vom Alten und vom Neuen*

1926: *Die Bekenntnisse eines modernen Malers*

Novels

1910: *Die tanzende Törin*

1962 (begun 1935): *Sonne und Mond*

Stories

1947: *Die Fabeln vom Eros*

1962: *Laßt uns den Menschen machen*

J. B. Bednall

MARTIN GUMPERT

Born 1897 in Berlin. Died 1955 in New York. Began as Expressionist, contributed to *Aktion*; friendship with Thomas Mann.

Poetry
1921: *Heimkehr des Herzens*

ALEXANDER XAVER GWERDER

Born 1923 in Thalwil, Switzerland. Died 1952; suicide in Arles,
Provence. See also H. R. Hilty, p. 280. His moral and artistic
masters were Nietzsche and Benn. Friendship with K. Krolow,
who dedicated to him the *Elegien auf den Tod eines jungen Dichters*.

Poetry
1951: *Blauer Eisenhut*
1955: *Dämmerklee*
1959: *Land über Dächer*

PETER HACKS

Born 1928 in Breslau. Student in Munich; not until 1955 in
DDR; playwright under the influence of Brecht, particularly in
his Marxian reinterpretations of historical events; also author of
radio-plays, essays, etc. Ed. of *Theater Heute*, 1955–63.

Drama
1954: *Eröffnung des indischen Zeitalters* (Columbus is depicted as the
        enemy of feudalism)
1955: *Die Schlacht bei Lobositz*
1958: *Der Müller von Sanssouci*
1962: *Die Sorgen und die Macht*, a comedy about life in an East
        German factory
1965: *Moritz Tassow*, a comedy about collective farming and the
        collapse of Tassow's Communist Utopia
1968: *Amphitryon*

WOLFGANG HÄDECKE

Born 1929 in Weissenfels, Saale. Left the DDR for the BRD in
1958, because of political attacks on his poems.

Poetry

1958: *Uns stehen die Fragen auf*
1963: *Leuchtspur im Schnee*

PETER HÄRTLING

Born 1933 in Chemnitz. Since 1962 editor of the journal *Monat*. Jamin is the key-figure in his poetry = the Romantic dreamer with a clown's cap. His power lies in the witchcraft of the poetic word, which can turn reality into unreality and make the dead laugh; it can, with a childlike imagination and wilfulness, withdraw from the horror of life into a fairy world.

Poetry

1953: *Poems und Songs*
1955: *Jamins Stationen*
1958: *Unter den Brunnen*
1962: *Spielgeist—Spiegelgeist*

Novels

1959: *Im Schein des Kometen*
1964: *Niembsch oder der Stillstand* (biogr. novel)

Anthology

1966: *Vergessene Bücher*

RUDOLF HAGELSTANGE

Born 1912 in Nordhausen (Harz). Lives in Unteruhldingen am Bodensee.

Poetry

1945–6: *Venezianisches Credo*
1952: *Ballade vom verschütteten Leben*
1953: *Zwischen Stern und Staub*
1962, 1964: *Lied der Jahre*

Novel

1959: *Spielball der Götter*

1957: *How do you like America* (travel descriptions)

Studies

About the *Ballad of the Buried Life* see p. 44 and A. Closs: *The Genius of the German Lyric*, pp. 362–3, l.c.; also the LW, 1968: vol. II, *Werke*, ed. by G. v. Wilpert, and Herman Salinger's tr. of the *Ballad of the Buried Life*, University of North Carolina Press, 1962.

MAX HALBE

Born 1865 in Güttland, nr. Danzig. Died 1944 in Burg, nr. Neuötting, Oberbayern. Friendship with Frank Wedekind and Ludwig Thoma; author of the naturalist dramas:

1890: *Freie Liebe*
1893: *Jugend*
1897: *Mutter Erde*, etc.

Max Halbe also wrote a novel about Optiz: *Die Friedensinsel*, 1944

Max Halbe: *Ges. Werke*, 7 vols., 1917–23; and 13 vols., 1945

ENRICA FREIIN VON HANDEL-MAZZETTI

Born 1871 in Vienna. Died 1955 in Linz. In her historical novels this catholic author courageously denounces religious fanaticism.

Novels

1906: *Jesse und Maria* (probably her best work)
1910: *Die arme Margaret*
1912–14: Trilogy: *Stephana Schwertner*
1928: *Johann Christian Günther* (biographical novel); see also DLL

PETER HANDKE

Born 1942 in Griffen, Carinthia, Austria. Lives in Germany now. Writer of fascinating plays of words, without plots and without real characters.

Drama

1964: *Weissagung*
1965: *Selbstbezichtigung*
1966: *Publikums Beschimpfung*
1968: *Kaspar*

Novel
1966: *Die Hornissen*
1967: *Der Hausierer*, Kriminalroman told by a hawker

ERNST HARDT

Born 1876 in Graudenz. Died 1947 in Schönhausen. Influenced by Stefan George. Hardt treats old legends with Neo-Romantic turgid morbidity.

Drama
1907: *Tantris der Narr*. Isolde is handed naked over to the lepers by King Mark; about the Tristan theme see Bibliography in vol. I *Introductions* and KLW
1911: *Gudrun*. Gudrun loves the man who tears her from the beloved
1913: *Schirin und Gertraude*, based on the theme of the Graf von Gleichen with his two wives

JOHANN JACOB HARINGER

Born 1898 in Dresden. Emigrated to Switzerland in 1938. Died 1948 in Zürich.

Poetry
1919 and 1921: *Die Kammer*
1946: *Das Fenster*
1962: *Lieder eines Lumpen*

FELIX HARTLAUB

Born 1913 in Bremen. Died 1945, missing in Berlin. Son of the art-historian Gustav F. Hartlaub. As his *Tagebuchblätter* prove, Felix Hartlaub was a highly gifted writer whose life was, unfortunately, cut all too short.

1955: *Gesamtwerk*, ed. by Geno(veva) Hartlaub

His sister Geno(veva), born 1915 in Mannheim, is a novelist and storywriter

WALTER HASENCLEVER

Born 1890 in Aachen. In 1933 emigrated to France. Died 1940, suicide in the internment camp Les Milles, France. Friendship with Kurt Pinthus, Franz Werfel, Max Reinhardt, Oskar Kokoschka, Ernst Toller, Kurt Tucholsky, Jean Giraudoux and others.

Drama

1914: *Der Sohn*. Expressionist drama about father and son. The father is described as symbol of reaction

1917: *Antigone*. Kreon is politically interpreted as a kind of William II

1929: *Ehen werden im Himmel geschlossen* (comedy)

1963: *Ausgewählte Werke: Gedichte, Dramen, Prosa*, ed. and introd. by Kurt Pinthus

CARL HAUPTMANN

Born 1858 in Bad Ober-Salzbrunn, Silesia. Died 1921 in Schreiberhau, Riesengebirge, Silesia. (Brother of Gerhart Hauptmann.) Author of a few Naturalist dramas, but his masterpiece is the artist-novel: *Einhart der Lächler*, 1907.

GERHART HAUPTMANN

Born 1862 in Obersalzbrunn, Silesia. Died 1946 in Agnetendorf, nr. Schreiberhau; buried on Hiddensee, Baltic.

Drama

1889: *Vor Sonnenaufgang*
1890: *Das Friedensfest*
1891: *Einsame Menschen*
1892: *Die Weber*
       Kollege Crampton
1893: *Der Biberpelz*
       Hanneles Himmelfahrt
1896: *Florian Geyer*
       Die versunkene Glocke
1898: *Fuhrmann Henschel*

1900: *Schluck und Jau*
     Michael Kramer
1901: *Der rote Hahn*
1902: *Der arme Heinrich*
1903: *Rose Bernd*
1906: *Und Pippa tanzt*
1911: *Die Ratten*
1912: *Gabriel Schillings Flucht* (written in 1905–6)
1913: *Festspiel in deutschen Reimen*
1914: *Der Bogen des Odysseus*
1917: *Winterballade*
1920: *Der weiße Heiland*
     Indipohdi
1926: *Dorothea Angermann*
1932: *Vor Sonnenuntergang*
1933: *Die goldene Harfe*
1935: *Hamlet in Wittenberg*
1941 ff.: *Atridentetralogie*
1942: *Magnus Garbe*
1952: *Herbert Engelmann* (written in 1924)

Prose

G. Hauptmann's narrative writings are, in comparison to his dramatic work, all too often underestimated, but there are masterpieces amongst them such as *Bahnwärter Thiel* and above all *Der Ketzer von Soana*.

1887: *Fasching* (Novelle)
1888: *Bahnwärter Thiel* (Novelle)
1890: *Der Apostel* (story)
1908: *Griechischer Frühling* (Reisetagebuch)
1910: *Der Narr in Christo Emanuel Quint* (novel)
1912: *Atlantis* (novel)
1918: *Der Ketzer von Soana* (Novelle)
1924: *Die Insel der großen Mutter* (novel)
1930: *Buch der Leidenschaft* (novel)
1944: *Mignon* (Novelle)

Poetry

1885: *Promethidenlos* (an unsuccessful imitation of Byron's *Childe Harold*)

1921: *Anna* (Versepos)
1928: *Till Eulenspiegel* (Versepos)
1942: *Der große Traum* (Versepos)

Studies

1954: H. F. Garten: *Gerhart Hauptmann*, Cambridge
1957: M. Sinden: *Gerhart Hauptmann*: the prose plays, Toronto
1957: J. M. Veale: *Gerhart Hauptmann's concept of the Grail story*, Dissertation, Bristol
1964: *Hauptmann, Centenary Lectures*, ed. by K. G. Knight, London
1964: Neville E. Alexander: *Studien zum Stilwandel im dramatischen Werk Gerhart Hauptmanns*, Stuttgart

Some English text editions and annotations
S. D. Stirk: *Bahnwärter Thiel* and *Fasching*
Pamela Reilly: *Die versunkene Glocke*
F. Stopp: *Die Weber*
Charlotte Jolles: *Einsame Menschen*
Brigitte E. Schatzky: *Gerhart Hauptmann Vor Sonnenaufgang* (Soziales Drama), 1964, with introductory notes on dialect and biographical data, to which I am indebted for the above lists.
Gerhart Hauptmann und die Antike, Felix A. Voigt, revised and ed. by W. Studt, 1965

With Gerhart Hauptmann, the world of myth and magic and that of naturalism and rationality, poetic dream and concern with society are in constant conflict, but those two spheres are in his finest works a unity.

GEORG ALBRECHT HAUSHOFER

Born 1903 in Munich. Son of Karl Haushofer who was founder and professor of *Geopolitics*. Georg Albrecht Haushofer became adviser to R. Hess and after Hess's flight to England he was arrested but soon set free; in 1944 again arrested; in 1945 shot at the Moabit prison in Berlin. In the Moabit prison he wrote the *79 Moabiter Sonnette*, 1946, posth. The MS was found in the hand of the dead poet.

Drama
1934: *Scipio*
1938: *Sulla*
1939: *Augustus*

MANFRED HAUSMANN

Born 1898 in Cassel. Novels, short stories, lyric poetry, plays in verse and prose, essays, trs. of Japanese and Chinese verse.

Novels
1928: *Lampioon küßt kleine Mädchen und Birken*
1929: *Salut gen Himmel*
1932: *Abel mit der Mundharmonika*
1937: *Abschied von der Jugend*
1953: *Liebende leben von der Vergebung*
1961: *Fünf Romane*, omnibus edition containing the above

Poetry
1949: *Die Gedichte*

Short stories
1956: *Der Überfall*. Ges. Erzählungen
         Was dir nicht angehört (ed. by R. Hargreaves, with intro-
         duction, notes and vocabulary, Harrap, 1962)
                                                            R. Hargreaves

BERNT VON HEISELER

Born 1907 in Brannenburg am Inn, Upper Bavaria. Son of Henry von Heiseler. Essayist, poet, playwright, prose-writer.

1932: *Henry von Heiseler. Sein Weg in den Werken*

Drama
1941: *Cäsar*
1945: *Hohenstaufentrilogie*
1947: *Philoktet*
1949–51: *Schauspiele*, 3 vols.

Poetry
1940, 1949, 1957: *Gedichte*
1950: *Spiegel im dunklen Wort*
1955: *Allerleirauh* (Märchen, Balladen und erzählende Gedichte)

Monographs
1939: *Kleist*
1959: *Schiller*

Novelle
1938: *Katharina*
1940: *Apollonia*

Novel
1952: *Versöhnung*, cf. *Medusa's Mirror* by A. Closs, 1957 and GLL, July 1954
1964: *Das verschwiegene Wort*

1959-63: Ed. of *Der Kranich*, ein Jahrbuch für die dramatische, lyrische und epische Kunst

Essays
1939 and 1954: *Ahnung und Aussage*

HENRY VON HEISELER

Born 1875 in Petersburg. Died 1928 in Brannenburg, Upper Bavaria. Mainly playwright and poet (under the influence of Stefan George).

1937-8: *Ges. Werke*, ed. by B. von Heiseler, 3 vols.

HELMUT HEISSENBÜTTEL

Born 1921 in Rüstringen, nr. Wilhelmshaven. Influenced by L. Wittgenstein's philosophy of language; in Group 47. Poet, literary critic, author of experimental landscapes of words. He creates word-chains, often deprived of their grammatical function within a sentence; the words themselves become autonomous and behave like playful atoms, turning round themselves. The very identity of the actual objects becomes illusory, causality is eliminated and replaced by a pattern of analogies and associations. The conventional grammatical sequence suggests a special order and relationship between subject and object. This relationship is overthrown by the experimental texts, and it is also called in question by the present reinterpretation of reality; see also E. Gomringer, p. 261.

Poetry
1945–55: *Kombinationen*
1956: *Topographien*
1960 ff.: *Textbuch I* (1960), *II* (1961), *III* (1962), *IV* (1964), *V* (1965), *VI* (1967)

1966: *Über Literatur*

Other extreme examples of playful word-artistry can be found in Gerhard Rühm's 'visuelle texte' (Textbilder), 'skripturale malerei' and 'textmontagen'; e.g. *rhythmus r*, or *reihe kurzer stücke 1955–57*. They remind one of the *Textbuch* by H. Heissenbüttel and also of E. Fried's skilfully suggested equivocalness of meaning but only to a certain degree. G. Rühm (born 1930), who is also from Vienna and nine years younger than E. Fried, is obviously attempting the impossible when trying to present his audiovisual texts. He differentiates between texts for hearing and texts for reading: see *Wort in der Zeit*, 1964, 2.

Another Viennese artist, Ernst Jandl (born 1925), occasionally succeeds, by using the single vowel 'E' (in the *E-Series*) throughout a text, in erecting an impressive artifice: 'Henker messen'; see E. Jandl's *Lange Gedichte*, *Reihe 'Rot'*, ed. by M. Bense and Elisabeth Walther, Text 16, 1964, and p. 289.

RUDOLF HENZ (Ps. R. Miles)

Born 1897 in Göpfritz, Lower Austria.

Poetry
1929: *Unter Brüdern und Bäumen*
1945: *Wort in der Zeit*

1951: *Der Turm der Welt*, an epic in terza rima, perhaps his best lyrical work and at the same time a document of our immediate past

Novels
1932: *Die Gaukler*
1935: *Dennoch Mensch*
1939: *Die Hundsmühle*

Drama
1937: *Kaiser Joseph II*
1954: *Die große Entscheidung*, a Paulus-Drama

STEPHAN HERMLIN

Born 1915 in Chemnitz (now Karl-Marx Stadt). 1936 he emigrated to Palestine and Switzerland. 1945 returned to Germany; in East Berlin now.

Poetry
1945: *Wir verstummen nicht*
1947: *Zweiundzwanzig Balladen*
1949: *Stalin*
1956: *Dichtungen*

Stories
1950: *Die Zeit der Gemeinsamkeit*

1957: a vol. of his collected *Nachdichtungen*

MAX HERRMANN-NEISSE

Born 1886 in Neisse. Died 1941 in London. Contact with Oskar Loerke and Carl Hauptmann. In his voluntary emigration he suffered the maddening agonies of human and artistic frustration. He felt like his 17th/18th cent. compatriot Christian Günther, unhappy and lonely, struck down by fate. The portraits of his huge cranium with the gnarled forehead and his dwarfish body were made by artists such as Georg Grosz.

Poetry
1941: (posth.) *Letzte Gedichte*
1946: *Heimatfern*, a selection of his poems

Study
1966: R. Lorenz: *Max Herrmann-Neisse*

FRITZ VON HERZMANOVSKY-ORLANDO

Born 1877 in Wien. Died 1954 in Meran. Writer of grotesque, kafkaesque visions, friend of Alfred Kubin. During his lifetime only *Der Gaulschreck im Rosennetz* appeared (1928).

1957–63: Fritz von Herzmanovsky: *Ges. Werke*, ed. by Friedrich
Torberg
    vol. I: *Der Gaulschreck im Rosennetz* (story)
    vol. II: *Maskenspiel der Genien* (novel)
    vol. III: *Lustspiele und Ballette*
    vol. IV: *Cavaliere Huscher und andere Erzählungen*

HERMANN HESSE

Born 1877 in Calw. Died 1962 in Montagnola. Nobel Prize winner in 1946 for his novels. From a Swabian pietistic background and considerably interested in Indian and eastern thought. Crises in the formative years and at the First World War—when he was a pacifist—led to semi-retirement from life in 1919. Besides novelist, also well-known essayist, sensitive and talented lyric-poet and water-colourist. His writings, which reflect his love of painting and music, are humanistically inclined and rather autobiographical, mirroring various stages of his spiritual odyssey and the painful awareness of the tensions between traditional values and modern life.

Novels
1904: *Peter Camenzind*
1906: *Unterm Rad*
1910: *Gertrud*
1914: *Rosshalde*
1919: *Demian*

1927: *Steppenwolf*
1943: *Glasperlenspiel*

Stories
1899: *Eine Stunde hinter Mitternacht*
1907: *Hermann Lauscher* and *Diesseits*
1908: *Nachbarn*
1912: *Umwege*
1915: *Knulp*
1916: *Schön ist die Jugend*
1917: *Kinderseele*
1919: *Märchen* (expanded 1946)
1920: *Klein und Wagner*
       Klingsors letzter Sommer
1922: *Siddhartha*
1930: *Narziss und Goldmund*
1932: *Morgenlandfahrt*
1933: *Kleine Welt*
1935: *Fabulierbuch*
1945: *Traumfährte*

Poetry
1899: *Romantisch Lieder*
1911: *Unterwegs*
1915: *Musik des Einsamen*
1921: *Ausgewählte Gedichte*
1929: *Trost der Nacht*
1934: *Vom Baum des Lebens* (and 1952)
1936: *Stunden im Garten* (Idyll)
1937: *Neue Gedichte*
1942: *Die Gedichte* (and 1947)
1961: *Stufen*

Essays and miscellaneous writings
1913: *Aus Indien*
1919: *Zarathustras Wiederkehr*
1920: *Wanderung*
       Blick ins Chaos
1925: *Kurgast*
1927: *Die Nürnberger Reise*

1928: *Betrachtungen*
1929: *Eine Bibliothek der Weltliteratur*
1937: *Gedenkblätter* (expanded 1959)
1946: *Der Europäer*
 Krieg und Frieden
 Dank an Goethe
1949: *Frühe Prosa*
1951: *Späte Prosa*
1955: *Beschwörungen*
1963: *Späte Prosa*

1925 ff.: *Ges. Werke*
1952: *Ges. Dichtungen*, 6 vols.
1957: *Ges. Schriften*, 7 vols.

Studies
1965: Th. Ziolkowski: *The Novels of Hermann Hesse*
 E. Rose: *Faith from the Abyss*

Much of his work has been tr. into English and American

Ian Hilton

MAX REINE HESSE

Born 1885 in Wittlich. Died 1952 in Buenos Aires.

Novels:
1933: *Morath schlägt sich durch*
 Morath verwirklicht einen Traum
1937–50: (Trilogy) *Dietrich Kattenburg*

OTTO HERMANN HEUSCHELE

Born 1900 in Schramberg, Black Forest. 1923–6 Lektor at the Deutsche Verlagsanstalt; mainly essayist, poet, editor of anthologies (e.g. *Lasset die Klage*, 1953, and *Wir stehen in Gottes Hand*, 1955), and story-writer. Friendship with Reinhold Schneider. Spätromantiker in the twentieth century.

Poetry
1931: *Licht übers Land*
1933: *Groß war die Nacht*
1941: *Feuer des Himmels*
1954: *Gaben der Gnade*

GEORG HEYM

Born 1887 in Hirschberg, Silesia. Died 1912, drowned whilst skating on the Havel, Berlin. Powerful visionary, expressionistic poetry, some of which is published in *Menschheitsdämmerung*.

1922: *Dichtungen*, ed. by K. Pinthus and E. Loewenson
1960 ff.: *Gesamtausgabe*, ed. by K. L. Schneider, 4 vols.

G. Heym's poem *Umbra vitae* appeared in an English and French verse-tr. in *Ohne Haß und Fahne: No Hatred and No Flag: Sans Haine et sans Drapeau*, ed. by W. G. Deppe, Christopher Middleton and Herbert Schönherr, Hamburg, 1959; see p. 319.

STEFAN HEYM (Ps. for Hellmuth Fliegel)

Born 1913 in Chemnitz (Karl Marx-Stadt). Emigrated in 1933. Wrote in English and German; since 1952 in DDR. Mainly author of dramas and novels.

Drama
1935: *Die Hinrichtung*
1937: *Gestern/Heute/Morgen*

Novels
1942: *Hostages;* German title: *Der Fall Glasenapp*
1948: *The Crusaders;* German title: *Kreuzfahrer von heute*
1953: *Goldsborough*

KURT HEYNICKE

Born 1891 in Liegnitz. Several of his Expressionist poems appeared in *Menschheitsdämmerung*, l.c.

Poetry

1917: *Rings fallen Sterne*
1918: *Gottes Geigen*
1920: *Das namenlose Angesicht*
1937: *Das Leben sagt Ja*

Author of several film texts (*Drehbücher*) for UFA.

WOLFGANG HILDESHEIMER

Born 1916 in Hamburg. 1933 emigrated to Palestine; now in Poschiavo, Graubünden. Connected with the Group 47. Author of radio-plays, stories, comedies. In his playful ironical sketches he treats the phenomenon of simulation and semblance in society, the fate of counterfeiters, social and aesthetic blacklegs.

Drama

1955: *Der Drachenthron,* comedy, based on the Turandot story
1958: *Spiele, in denen es dunkel wird,* collection of one-act plays
1960: Radio-play, *Herr Walsers Raben*
1963: *Die Verspätung:* Ein Stück in zwei Teilen

Novel

1965: *Tynset:* Eine Utopie

H. R. HILTY

Born 1925 in St Gallen, Switzerland. Editor of *Hortulus* and of several anthologies of poetry. Mainly poet, novelist, essayist. He edited poems by Alexander Xaver Gwerder, see p. 265.

Poetry

1948: *Nachtgesang*
1956: *Eingebrannt in den Schnee*
1959: *Daß die Erde uns leicht sei*

Novel

1962: *Parsifal*

ROLF HOCHHUTH

Born 1931 in Eschwege, nr. Kassel. Now living at Riehen, nr. Basel.

Drama

1963: *Der Stellvertreter* (*The Representative*). About this play cf. p. 98.

1967: *Soldaten.* Also this play has been inspired by the author's belief that history reveals itself in the powerful masters of events. Characters such as Schiller's Wallenstein, Posa, etc., are obviously R. Hochhuth's models and idols. Two historical occurrences are the main theme of the above drama: the bombing of civilians (in Dresden) and the alleged murder of General Sikorski, see p. 100.

FRITZ HOCHWÄLDER

Born 1911 in Vienna. Emigrated to Switzerland. Main themes of his dramas: guilt and purification, justice and revenge. He became internationally known through his drama: *Das heilige Experiment* (1943, publ. 1947): ed. with notes by J. R. Foster, London, 1957; a play about the violent dissolution of the order of the Jesuits in Paraguay. English title: *The Strong are Lonely;* French title: *Sur la terre comme au ciel.*

Donadieu (composed in 1953): This tragedy has been inspired by C. F. Meyer's ballad: *Die Füße im Feuer;* the closely knit drama is centred in the conflict between the Huguenot Donadieu and the Royalist Dubosc. Donadieu (Don à Dieu) renounces the right of revenge which is finally carried out by Lavalette, Dubosc's companion: ed. with notes by C. B. Johnson, London, 1967.

1967: *Der Befehl,* a TV play

Hochwälder also composed farcical plays such as *Der Himbeerpflücker,* 1965, which is a weak variation of Gogol's *Government Inspector.*

1959 ff.: *Ges. Dramen*

JAKOB VAN HODDIS (Ps. for Hans Davidsohn)

Born 1887 in Berlin. Expressionist, contributor to *Sturm* and *Aktion*. Mentally ill since 1914, deported in 1942, missing since then.

His poem *Weltende* appeared in 1911 and is according to Benn one of the very best expressionist poems.

1958: *Weltende. Ges. Dichtungen*, ed. by Paul Pörtner

WALTER HÖLLERER

Born 1922 in Sulzbach-Rosenberg, Oberpfalz. Professor for Literaturwissenschaft in the Techn. Hochschule, Berlin; Vorstand of the Institute for 'Sprache im Technischen Zeitalter'; co-editor of the journal *Akzente* 1954–67; editor of the journal *Sprache im technischen Zeitalter* since 1961. Editor of *Transit* (Lyrikbuch der Jahrhundertmitte) 1956.

Poetry
1952: *Der andere Gast*. The title is significant: the empirical ego
is different from the lyrical ego. The other world, 'das
Widerspiel', i.e. artistic reality, is contrasted with our
outwardly experienced or purely descriptive reality

HUGO VON HOFMANNSTHAL (Ps. Loris)

Born 1874 in Vienna. Died 1929 in Rodaun, nr. Vienna. First literary contacts and friendship with H. Bahr, A. Schnitzler, Stefan George (H. v. H. contributed to the *Blätter für die Kunst*); later literary contacts also with Rilke and Rudolf Kassner, R. A. Schröder, Anton Wildgans, Rudolf Borchardt, Max Reinhardt.

Lyric poetry
1907–10: *Die ges. Gedichte*
1922: *Gedichte*
1934: *Nachlese der Gedichte*

Dramatic works

1891: *Gestern*

1897: *Der weiße Fächer*
Das kleine Welttheater

1900: *Der Tor und der Tod* (1893 first publ. in *Der Modern Musenalmanach*)
Der kaiser und die Hexe

1892–1901: *Der Tod des Tizian*

1904: *Elektra* ('frei nach Sophokles')
Das gerettete Venedig, based on Thomas Otway's *Venice preserved* (1682)

1908: *Christinas Heimreise*

1911: *Jedermann*

1920–1: *Der Schwierige*

1922: *Das Salzburger große Welttheater*

1927: *Der Turm*, altered stage version (1st version 1925)

Operntexte

1911: *Der Rosenkavalier*

1912: *Ariadne auf Naxos*

1919: *Die Frau ohne Schatten*

1927: *Die ägyptische Helena*

1929: *Arabella*

Prose works

1932: *Andreas oder die Vereinigten*

Special editions

Loris, Prose Works of the early years of Hugo von Hofmannsthal, with an epilogue by Max Mell

Ges. Werke, 1923–4 (6 vols.), and 1934 (3 vols.)

Ges. Werke in separate sections, edited by Herbert Steiner, Bermann-Fischer Publishing House, Stockholm, 1945 ff., now S. Fischer, Frankfurt a.M., 15 vols.

Studies

1926, 1954, 1964: *Briefwechsel, mit Richard Strauss*

1929: *Hugo von Hofmannsthal—Buch der Freunde* (Tagebuch-Aufzeichnungen) (with an epilogue by R. A. Schröder); now in *Aufzeichnungen*, 1959

1930: Max Kommerell: *Hugo von Hofmannsthal*

1938: K. J. Naef: *Hugo von Hofmannsthal, Leben und Werk*, with a bibliography by Herbert Steiner

1938, 1953: *Briefwechsel mit Stefan George*

1942: Mary E. Gilbert: *Der Tor und der Tod*, Blackwell, Oxford

1953: I. Parry: *Werther and Lord Chandos*, Publ. of the Engl. Goethe Soc., XXXIII

1954: *Hugo von Hofmannsthal-Rudolf Borchardt*, Correspondence

1955: *Hofmannsthal, Selected Essays*, ed. by Mary E. Gilbert, Blackwell, Oxford

1956: *Hugo von Hofmannsthal—Carl J. Burckhardt*, Correspondence

1957: *Jedermann, Hugo von Hofmannsthal*, ed. by Margaret Jacobs, Nelson's German Texts. *Jedermann* is based principally on the fifteenth century morality play *Everyman*

1962: M. Hamburger: *Selected Plays and Libretti of H. v. Hofmannsthal*, New York

1962: W. H. Rey: *Weltentzweiung und Weltversöhnung in Hofmannsthals griechischen Dramen*, Philadelphia

1963: E. Schwarz: *Hofmannsthal und Calderon*, Harvard Univ. Press

Hofmannsthal. Studies in Commemoration, University of London, Institute of Germanic Studies

1964: M. Hamburger: *Hugo v. Hofmannsthal: Zwei Studien*, Göttingen

1966: *H. von Hofmannsthal: Bibliographie des Schrifttums, 1892–1963* ed. by Horst Weber

1967: *Hugo von Hofmannsthal. Arthur Schnitzler, Briefwechsel*, ed. by Therese Nickel und Heinrich Schnitzler

G. Erken: *Hofmannsthals dramatischer Stil*, Tübingen

HANS EGON HOLTHUSEN

Born 1913 in Rendsburg, Schleswig-Holstein. 1961–4 Director of the Goethe-Haus in New York; see also p. 41.

Poetry

1947: *Klage um den Bruder*

1949: *Hier in der Zeit*

1952: *Labyrinthische Jahre*

Novel

1956: *Das Schiff*, Aufzeichnungen eines Passagiers

Essays

1951: *Der unbehauste Mensch*
1958: *Das Schöne und das Wahre*
1961: *Kritisches Verstehen*
1968: *Plädoyer für den Einzelnen*

ARNO HOLZ

Born 1863 in Rastenburg, East Prussia. Died 1929 in Berlin.

Poetry

1885: *Buch der Zeit* (Lieder eines Modernen)
1898: *Phantasus*, 2 little vols.
1916: *Phantasus*, Folio ed.

Drama

1896: *Sozialaristokraten*
1905: *Traumulus* (with O. Jerschke)
1908: *Sonnenfinsternis*
1913: *Ignorabimus*

Literary satires and imitations

1902 ff.: *Blechschmiede* (Literaturkritik)
1903–4: *Dafnis. Lyrisches Portrait aus dem 17. Jahrhundert* (a brilliant recreation of poetry in Baroque style)

Novellen (written with Joh. Schlaf, under the Ps. Bjarne P. Holmsen): *Papa Hamlet*

Play (also together with Joh. Schlaf): *Die Familie Selicke*

Sammelband by A. Holz and Joh. Schlaf, 1892: *Neue Gleise*

Theory

1891: *Theory of 'Konsequenter Naturalismus'*
1892: *Die Kunst, ihr Wesen und ihre Gesetze*
1899: *Revolution der Lyrik*

1924–5 ff.: *Das Werk*, 10 vols.
1961–4: *Werke*, ed. by W. Emrich, 7 vols.

Study
1960: A. Closs: *Die neuere deutsche Lyrik vom Barock bis zur Gegen-
        wart*, in *Aufriß*, see also RLL: *Freie Rhythmen*, and
        MLN, 1950 Nov.

RICARDA HUCH

Born 1864 in Brunswick. Died 1947 in Frankfurt a.M.

Poetry
1891: *Gedichte*
1907: *Neue Gedichte*
1913: *Liebesgedichte*
1944: *Herbstfeuer*

Novels and stories
1893: *Erinnerungen von Ludolf Ursleu dem Jüngeren* (in English tr.
        Eros Invincible, New York, and *Unconquered Love*, London,
        1931)
1896: *Der Mondreigen von Schlaraffis*
1897: *Teufeleien*
1899: *Fra Celeste und andere Erzählungen*
1902: *Aus der Triumphgasse*
1903: *Vita somnium breve* (in 1913 appeared under the title
        Michael Unger)
1906: *Die Verteidigung Roms* (in English tr. *Defeat*, 1928)
1907: *Der Kampf um Rom* (in English tr. *Victory*, 1929)
1910: *Der letzte Sommer*
        Das Leben des Grafen Federigo Confalonier
1912–14: *Der Große Krieg in Deutschland* (in 1937 appeared under
        the title *Der Dreißigjährige Krieg*)
1938: *Frühling in der Schweiz* (Jugenderinnerungen)
1943: *Weiße Nächte* (Novelle)

Essays and critical works
1899: *Blütezeit der Romantik*

1902: *Ausbreitung und Verfall der Romantik* (appeared as *Die Romantik*, 1908)
1904: *Gottfried Keller*
1916: *Luthers Glaube*
1919: *Der Sinn der Heiligen Schrift*
1921: *Entpersönlichung*
1946: *Urphänomene*

Studies
1950: Maries Baum: *Leuchtende Spur. Das Leben Ricarda Huchs*
1951: Else Hoppe, *Ricarda Huch. Weg, Persönlichkeit, Werk*
1966: Wilhelm Emrich: Introduction (Vol. 1) to *Ricarda Huch. Ges. Werke*

This remarkably versatile writer succeeds in combining the rôles of artist and scholar. Very much aware of the cultural traditions of the past, she is especially indebted, in her creative works, both to the Romantics and the later nineteenth century realists, in particular Keller. It is generally considered that her genius expresses itself best in her historical works, where again she combines accuracy and poetic imagination in her recreation and interpretation of the outstanding events and personalities of the past.

Sheila Jones

PETER HUCHEL

Born 1903 in Berlin-Lichterfelde. From 1949 to 1962 Chefredakteur of the East German Literary journal *Sinn und Form*.

Poetry
1948: *Gedichte* (Sammelband)
1963: *Chausseen, Chausseen*
1967: *Die Sternenreuse* (Gedichte 1925–47)

Peter Huchel's nature poetry—an essentially mournful, yet not really elegiac lyric—has a direct appeal to the readers which, to some degree like Bobrowski's verse, is rare in contemporary poetry.

It is also different from the 'Naturlyrik' by K. Krolow or

W. Lehmann, or from Loerke's Song of Nature: 'Gesang der Dinge'.

RICHARD HUELSENBECK (Ps. for Charles R. Hulbeck)

Born 1892 in Frankenau, Hessen-Nassau. 1936 emigrated to the U.S.A. Psychiatrist and a founder of the 'Bürgerschreck' Dadaism.

1920: *Manifest—Der neue Mensch*
      En avant Dada (Geschichte des Dadaismus)

Poetry
1954: *Die Antwort der Tiefe*

Memoirs
1957: *Mit Witz, Licht und Grütze; auf den Spuren des Dadaismus*

HANS HENNY JAHNN

Born 1894 in Hamburg. Emigrated to Denmark, farmer on the island of Bornholm; after the war returned to Germany. Died 1959 in Hamburg.

Author of tragedies
1919: *Pastor Ephraim Magnus*, the theme of the artist's bondage
      as human being imprisoned in the sinful flesh
1925: *Medea*, theme of the ageing once-beautiful woman and
      also of mixed marriage
1934: *Armut, Reichtum, Mensch und Tier*, first performance 1948
1955: *Thomas Chatterton*

Novels
1929: *Perrudja*
1949 ff.: Romantrilogie: *Fluß ohne Ufer*
      1. *Das Holzschiff*
      2. *Die Niederschrift des Gustav Anias Horn, nachdem er*
         neunundvierzig Jahre alt geworden war
      3. *Epilog*
1956: *Die Nacht aus Blei*

ERNST JANDL—see H. Heissenbüttel, p. 273

In June 1965 at the Royal Albert Hall, E. Jandl orchestrated and spoke his own so-called sound-poems. His most successful technique is that of radiophonic effects achieved by slowing down or accelerating the movement of the tapes, e.g. in *Schmerz durch Reibung (Pain through Friction)* with its funny mixture of pushing and yelping noises: Fr-Fr-Fr-Frau-au-au . . . *or* the comical repetitions in *Niagara Falls*: Niagaaaaa; ra; felle . . . In 1966 appeared E. Jandl's *Laut und Luise* with an epilogue by H. Heissenbüttel.

UWE JOHNSON

Born 1934 in Cammin, Pommern.

Novels
1959: *Mutmaßungen über Jakob*
1961: *Das dritte Buch über Achim*
1965: *Zwei Ansichten*

English trs. (by Ursule Molinaro)
1963: *Speculations about Jakob* (London, New York)
1964: *The Third Book about Achim* (New York)

Shorter narrative pieces
(*a*) 1963: Collected in the volume: *Karsch und andere Prosa*
Jonas zum Beispiel (the Old Testament prophet; earlier version: *Besonders die kleinen Propheten*, 1962)
Osterwasser, Beihilfe zum Umzug, Geschenksendung, keine Handelsware (these concern the characters of *Mutmaßungen über Jakob*); *Eine Reise wegwohin, 1960* (a sequel to *Das dritte Buch über Achim*)
(*b*) 1965: Published in Kursbuch I: *Eine Kneipe geht verloren* (an excursus or commentary on *Zwei Ansichten*)

Criticism
1961: *Berliner Stadtbahn* (in *Merkur*, Aug. 1961)
1965: *Auskünfte und Abreden zu 'Zwei Ansichten'* (*auf Fragen von Mike S. Schoelman*) (in *Dichten und Trachten*, 26, 2. Halbjahr, 1965)

Translations
1959: Melville, *Israel Potter, His Forty Years in Exile*
1963: John Knowles, *A Separate Peace* (*In diesem Land*)

Studies
1962: Horst Bienek, *Werkstattgespräche mit Schriftstellern. Mit 15 Photos auf Tafeln*
1962: Herbert Ahl, *Literarische Portraits*
1963: Marcel Reich-Ranicki, *Deutsche Literatur in West und Ost. Prosa seit 1945*

Uwe Johnson is reputedly the first novelist to choose the divided Germany as his theme. He is concerned with showing how human personality is violated, as the frontier cuts ruthlessly across all lines of communication. For it results in the estrangement of the two communities from each other, as each of them imposes its own system of moral values, social attitudes and use of language on its citizens, regardless of the individual's possible sense of integrity. This can only be grasped by means of patient, objective cross-examination of characters at crucial moments in their daily life. Thus the form of each work unfolds in the course of a conversation, in which narrator and audience are *together* engaged in uncovering what each system of concepts and attitudes either parades as self-evident, or wilfully ignores. This approach also explains Johnson's style, which he derives from the spoken word, and his use of alienation and emblematic images.

H. Popper

HANNS JOHST

Born 1890 in Seerhausen bei Oschatz, Saxony. 1935–45 President of the Reichsschriftumskammer and the German Academy; he began as an Expressionist.

Poetry
1924: *Lieder der Sehnsucht*

Drama
1916: *Der junge Mensch—Ein ekstatisches Szenarium* about the conflict between generations: between pupil and teacher

1917: *Der Einsame*; about Christian Dietrich Grabbe
1927: *Thomas Paine*
1933: The National Socialist drama *Schlageter*

In spite of Johst's political commitment it cannot be denied that his earlier dramas show exceptional promise and indeed achievement. His poetry, in its earlier stages, enjoyed the unreserved praise of a man of unusual taste and integrity, Oskar Loerke: 'Dieses schöne Gedichtheft vom Wachstum des Kindes vor seiner Geburt, vom Wachstum in der Mutter, im Vater, in der Welt. Wer kein Stein ist, wird die Innigkeit . . . mitempfinden.'

PETER JOKOSTRA

Born 1912 in Dresden. Now living in Linz am Rhein; in his affirmation of the elemental nature akin to J. Bobrowski.

Poetry
1958: *An der besonnten Mauer*
1960: *Magische Straße*
1961: *Hinab zu den Sternen*
1967: *Die gewendete Haut*

1964: *Ohne Visum*, anthology of writers who fled from East Germany

ERNST JÜNGER

Born 1895 in Heidelberg; 1912 in the Foreign Legion; 1914–18 war service in the German army, storm-troop officer; 1918 Sept., award of the Pour Le Mérite; 1939 rejoins army; 1940 in Paris; 1942–3 in Russia; since 1951 living in Wilflingen, Württemberg. The most important achievement in Ernst Jünger's work is his so-called 'magischer Realismus', i.e. an artistic expression in which ratio and mystery ('Vernunft und Zauber') merge into a unique, new dimension. Ernst Jünger sees himself as the great-grandson of an Idealistic, and the grandson of a Romantic, and son of a Materialistic age. According to him, Classicism has become an empty shell, Romanticism has burnt itself out, Materialism offers to an artist mere surface-reliefs (see his

Strahlungen, p. 16). By the side of the rational explanation of life he seeks to penetrate the realm of dark forces which reach beyond the range of our ordinary knowledge.

Works

1920: *In Stahlgewittern,* tr. by B. Creighton: *The Storm of Steel,* 1929
1929: *Das abenteuerliche Herz,* Traum—Tagebuch—Aufzeich-nungen
1932: *Der Arbeiter*
1934: *Über den Schmerz*
1939: (novel) *Auf den Marmorklippen,* tr. by S. O. Hood, 1947
1945: *Der Friede,* tr. by S. O. Hood, 1948
1949: *Strahlungen. Tagebücher 1941–1945*
(novel) *Heliopolis. Rückblick auf eine Stadt*
1951: *Der Waldgang*
1954: *Die Sanduhr,* Essays
1957: (novel) *Gläserne Bienen*
1958: *Mantrana. Einladung zu einem Spiel*
1959: *Zeitmauer*
1967: *Subtile Jagden,* a book of reminiscences

1960 ff.: *Ernst Jünger: Werke,* 10 vols.
        Antaios. Zweimonatsschrift, ed. by E. Jünger and Mircea Eliade

Studies

1953: J. P. Stern: *Ernst Jünger. A writer of our time.* (*Studies in Modern European Literature and Thought*)
1953: Karl O. Paetel: *Ernst Jünger. Eine Bibliographie*

FRIEDRICH GEORG JÜNGER

Born 1898 in Hanover. Brother of Ernst Jünger; now living in Überlingen/Bodensee.

Poetry

1937: *Der Taurus*
1940: *Der Missouri*
1946: *Der Westwind*

1947: *Die Silberdistelklause*
       Das Weinberghaus
1948: *Die Perlenschnur*
1952: *Iris im Wind*
1954: *Ring der Jahre*, which contains some of his earlier books of
       poems

Essays

1936: *Über das Komische*
1946: *Die Perfektion der Technik*
1952: *Rhythmus und Sprache im deutschen Gedichte*

Novels

1954: *Der erste Gang*
1956: *Zwei Schwestern*

1967: *Ges. Erzählungen*

ERICH KÄSTNER

Born 1899 in Dresden.

Poetry

1928: *Herz auf Taille*
       Lärm im Spiegel
1930: *Ein Mann gibt Auskunft*
1932: *Gesang zwischen den Stühlen*
1948: *Kurz und bündig*

Stories

1928: *Emil und die Detektive* (in English tr. 1930)
1931: *Fabian. Die Geschichte eines Moralisten* (in English tr. 1932)
       Pünktchen und Anton (in English tr. *Annaluise and Anton*, 1932)
1933: *Das fliegende Klassenzimmer* (in English tr. 1934)
1934: *Emil und die drei Zwillinge* (in English tr. 1935)
       Drei Männer im Schnee (in English tr. 1935)
1935: *Die verschwundene Miniatur* (in English tr. *The Missing
       Miniature: or The Adventures of a sensitive Butcher*, 1936)
1938: *Georg und die Zwischenfälle*, appeared as *Der kleine Grenz-
       verkehr*, 1949 (in English tr. *A Salzburg Comedy*, 1950)

1949: *Die Konferenz der Tiere* (tr. *The Animals' Conference*, 1949)
    Das doppelte Lottchen (tr. *Lottie and Lisa*, 1950)
1957: *Als ich ein kleiner Junge war*

Drama
1930: *Leben in dieser Zeit*
1956: *Die Schule der Diktatoren*

Miscellaneous
1948: *Der tägliche Kram* (Chansons und Prosa 1945–8)
1952: *Die kleine Freiheit* (Chansons und Prosa 1949–52)
1963: *Let's face it. Poems* tr. ed. by P. Bridwater

Studies
1957: J. Winkelmann: *The poetic style of Erich Kästner*
1959: Hermann Kesten: Introduction to Kästner's *Ges. Schriften in sieben Bänden* (Cologne)
1966: W. Lough: *Als ich ein kleiner Junge war* (London)
1966: L. Enderle: *Erich Kästner*, Reinbek

Kästner is, on his own admission, a moralist, who satirizes the social and political follies of his times. This didactic element also reveals itself, to a lesser degree, in his delightful children's books, for which he is best known.

Sheila Jones

FRANZ KAFKA

Born 1883 in Prague. Died 1924 in Kierling nr. Vienna. Rediscovered after the Second World War and considered one of the most influential writers in twentieth century literature. Experienced isolation at home and as a German-speaking Jew in Prague. His fondness for diaries and memoirs point to existential preoccupations. Potential as a writer recognized early on, but much of his work remained fragmentary. The sense of futility and cross-purpose complexity is basically reflected. Concerned with setting down his nightmare world of the imagination, but the concrete image is preferred. His language is precise, even though the work as a whole may appear intricate and posing many extra-literary questions.

Novels
1925: *Der Prozeß*
1926: *Das Schloß*
1927: *Amerika*

Short stories
1913: *Der Heizer*
Betrachtung
1916: *Das Urteil*
Die Verwandlung
1919: *In der Strafkolonie*
Ein Landarzt
1924: *Ein Hungerkünstler*
1931: *Beim Bau der chinesischen Mauer*

1935–7: *Ges. Schriften*, 6 vols.
1946 ff.: *Ges. Schriften*, 10 vols.
1946–8: *Ges. Werke*, 9 vols.
1952: *Briefe an Milena*
1961: *Erzählungen*

Most of Kafka's work has been tr. into English.

Studies
1953: I. Parry: *Kafka and Gogol*, GLL, VI
1958: A. Flores and H. Swander: *Franz Kafka Today*, Univ. of Wisconsin Press
1960: G. Anders: *Franz Kafka* (English ed.)
1962: R. Gray: *Kafka: A Collection of Critical Essays*
H. Politzer: *Franz Kafka: Parable and Paradox*
R. Freedman: *Kafka's obscurity: The illusion of Logic in Narrative*, Modern Fiction Studies, VIII
1965: I. Parry: *Kafka, Rilke, and Rumpelstiltskin*, The Listener, LXXIV
1966: W. H. Sokel: *Franz Kafka*, Columbia University

Ian Hilton

Georg Kaiser

Born 1878 in Magdeburg. Emigrated to Switzerland. Died 1945 in Ascona. Influenced by Wedekind and Sternheim.

Drama (Stücke, Bühnenspiele):
1905: *Rektor Kleist*, Tragi-comedy
1906: *Der Zentaur*
1910: *König Hahnrei*
1912: *Von Morgens bis Mitternachts*
1912-13: *Die Bürger von Calais*
1914: *Europa*, Spiel und Tanz in 5 Aufzügen
1917: *Die Koralle*
1918: *Gas I*
1918-19: *Gas II*
1919: *Hölle = Weg = Erde*
1924: *Kolportage*
1925: *Gats*
1926: *Der mutige Seefahrer* (written 1910)
1927: *Der Präsident* (a revised version of *Der Kongreß*, 1905)
1929: *Mississippi*
1937-8: *Der Gärtner von Toulouse*
1938: *Napoleon in New Orleans*
1942: *Die Spieldose*
1944: *Pygmalion* (1948 in *Griechische Dramen*)
  Bellerophon (1948, in *Griechische Dramen*)

Studies
1957: B. J. Kenworthy: *Georg Kaiser*, Oxford; a searching study which is built up on the two poles of Kaiser's work: his relatively objective social criticism and his flight into the subjective
1960: Wolfgang Paulsen: *Georg Kaiser. Die Perspektiven seines Werkes*, Tübingen

Hermann Kasack

Born 1896 in Potsdam. Died 1966 in Stuttgart.

Novels
1947: *Die Stadt hinter dem Strom*

1952: *Das große Netz*
1953: *Fälschungen*

Stories
1949: *Der Webstuhl*

Already well known between the Wars as a poet, Kasack made his mark as a narrative writer after 1945, with a number of *zeitkritisch* novels and stories. *Die Stadt hinter dem Strom*, an allegorical vision of a devastated zone (Europe), occupied by 'dead souls', and controlled by remote and absolute authorities, has an oppressive quality reminiscent of Kafka. Neither this work, however, nor the long satirical novel *Das große Netz*, is wholly satisfactory as a novel. *Fälschungen*, which describes a case of artistic forgery, is more modest in scope, and perhaps his most successful narrative work.

Studies
1966: *Hermann Kasack*, by W. F. Mainland, in 'Essays on Contemporary German Literature'

D. S. Low

MARIE LUISE KASCHNITZ (Freifrau von Kaschnitz-Weinberg)

Born 1901 in Karlsruhe.

Poetry
1947: *Gedichte*
1952: *Ewige Stadt*
1957: *Neue Gedichte*
1962: *Dein Schweigen—meine Stimme*
1965: *Ein Wort weiter*. This title indicates the key-note of Frau Kaschnitz's mature poetry: lament must be transcended by hope: 'Halte nicht ein bei der Schmerzgrenze / Halte nicht ein / Geh ein Wort weiter / Einen Atemzug / Noch über dich hinaus / Greif dir im Leeren / Die Osterblume . . .
1966: *Überallnie* (selected poems 1928–65) with Nachwort by K. Krolow. This edition shows M. L. Kaschnitz's

artistic development from her neo-classic poetry to a contemporary awareness of personal commitment and the demands of a collective age

Essays
1945: *Menschen und Dinge*
1963: *Wohin denn ich* (Erinnerungs- und Notizbuch)

Stories
1960: *Lange Schatten*

Biographical novel
1949: *Gustave Courbet* (Roman eines Malerlebens)

RUDOLF KASSNER

Born 1873 in Groß-Pawlowitz, Moravia. Died 1959 in Sierre, Kanton Wallis.

Short stories
1902: *Der Tod und die Maske*

Autobiographical writings
1938: *Buch der Erinnerung*
1946: *Die zweite Fahrt*
1949: *Umgang der Jahre*

Critical and miscellaneous writings
1900: *Die Mystik, die Künstler und das Leben; über englische Dichter und Maler im 19. Jahrhundert*
1903: *Der indische Idealismus*
1904: *Die Moral der Musik*
1908: *Melancholia; eine Trilogie des Geistes*
1911: *Von den Elementen der menschlichen Größe*
1914: *Die Chimäre*
1918: *Der Umriß einer universalen Physiognomik*
1919: *Zahl und Gesicht*
1922: *Die Grundlagen der Physiognomik*
1930: *Das physiognomische Weltbild*
1932: *Physiognomik*

1936: *Von der Einbildungskraft*
1938: *Der Gottmensch*
1947: *Das neunzehnte Jahrhundert; Ausdruck und Größe*
1951: *Die Geburt Christi*
     Von der Eitelkeit
1953: *Das inwendige Reich; Versuch einer Physiognomik der Idee*

In his numerous essays and studies Kassner, who rejected the rational-discursive method of modern science and philosophy, sought an intuitive, visionary perception of the organic unity of all cultural and ethical phenomena: in his later work he tried to formulate his vision in Christian terms.

H. R. Klieneberger

BERNHARD KELLERMANN

Born 1879 in Fürth. Died 1951 in Potsdam. Novelist and essayist. Vice-President of DDR *Kulturbund* in 1945. A most successful writer at the time of the First World War. Influenced early by neo-romanticism but preferred treating social critical themes. His stories are frequently graphic and exciting, but uneven.

Novels
1904: *Yester und Li*
1906: *Ingeborg*
1909: *Der Tor*
1910: *Das Meer*
1913: *Der Tunnel* (perhaps his most successful work)
1920: *Der neunte November*
1925: *Die Brüder Schellenberg*
1932: *Die Stadt Anatol*
1935: *Lied der Freundschaft*
1938: *Das blaue Band*
1948: *Totentanz*

Short stories
1922: *Die Heiligen*
1923: *Schwedenklees Erlebnis*
1934: *Jangtsekiang*

Reports and essays

1910: *Ein Spaziergang in Japan*
1915: *Der Krieg im Westen*
1916: *Der Krieg im Argonnerwald*
1928: *Auf Persiens Karawanenstrassen*
1929: *Der Weg der Götter. Indien, Klein-Tibet, Siam*
1940: *Meine Reisen in Asien*
1945: *Was sollen wir tun?*
1952: *Aufsätze, Briefe und Reden 1945–51*

1958 ff.: *Ausgewählte Werke*, 6 vols.

Much of his fiction has been tr. into English.

Ian Hilton

HERMANN KESTEN

Born 1900 in Nürnberg. Emigrated to New York; lives in Rome now.

Novel

1928: *Josef sucht die Freiheit*
1936 ff.: *Trilogy on Spain*
        (*a*) *Ferdinand und Isabella* (1936), subtitle: *Sieg der Dämonen* (1952)
        (*b*) *König Philipp II* (1938), subtitle: *Ich der König* (1950)
        (*c*) *Um die Krone. Der Mohr von Kastilien* (1952)
1939: *Die Kinder von Guernica*

Biography
1952: *Casanova*

1958: *Ges. Werke*

HEINER KIPPHARDT

Born 1922 in Silesia.

1962: *Der Hund des Generals*, a play influenced by the Brecht theatre.

1964: *In der Sache J. Robert Oppenheimer.* The play is based on documents recorded during Professor Oppenheimer's trial, see also Urs Jenny: *In der Sache Oppenheimer* (in *Theater Heute*, Nov. 1964); this drama was originally written for TV, and it is in its present form hardly suitable to prove an artistic success on the stage, as it is rather a case story than a stage drama. It is lacking in convincing characters and, above all, in individual and original language

1965: *Joel Brand. Die Geschichte eines Geschäfts.* The suggested deal is the exchange of a million of Jews for ten thousand lorries, see p. 102

1964: *Die Ganovenfresse. Zwei Erzählungen*

KLABUND (Ps. for Alfred Henschke). This pseudonym is a contraction of Kla(bautermann) and (Vaga)bund. 'Klabund', according to the author, means transformation.

Born 1890 in Crossen (Oder). Died 1928 in Davos, Switzerland. Friendship with G. Benn. Klabund's reputation is not so much based on his novels (about Mohammed, Rasputin, Borgia, etc.) but on his drama: 1924: *Der Kreidekreis*; cf. B. Brecht's later *Der Kaukasische Kreidekreis.*

Klabund also wrote poems and free translations or adaptations. His power of empathy is shown in e.g. *Li-Tai Pe*, 1916. He seems to be particularly gifted in being able to project himself into a foreign literary form and atmosphere.

1930: *Ges. Werke*, 6 vols.; new ed. 1951 ff.

JOCHEN KLEPPER

Born 1903 in Beuthen on the Oder. Died 1942 in Berlin.

Novels
1933: *Der Kahn der fröhlichen Leute*
1937: *Der Vater; Roman des Soldatenkönigs*
1951: *Die Flucht der Katharina von Bora; aus dem Nachlaß herausgegeben von K. Pagel*

Poetry
1937: *Du bist als Stern uns aufgegangen; Gedichte*
1938: *Kyrie; geistliche Lieder*

Autobiographical writings
1955: *Unter dem Schatten deiner Flügel; aus den Tagebüchern der Jahre 1932–1942*
1958: *Überwindung; Tagebücher und Aufzeichnungen aus dem Kriege*

Critical and miscellaneous writings
1940: *Der christliche Roman*
1960: *Nachspiel; Erzählungen, Aufsätze, Gedichte*

Klepper's novel *Der Vater* interprets the tragic inner conflict suffered by King Frederick William I of Prussia in terms of the existential paradoxes of Luther's theology. Klepper's diaries record in detail and with unfailing veracity the world of the Third Reich—until December 1942 when Klepper chose to die, together with his Jewish wife and stepdaughter who were facing deportation.

H. R. Klieneberger

KURT KLUGE

Born 1886 in Leipzig. Died 1940 in Lüttich. Novelist, sculptor and brass-founder; master of humorous stories; a modern Jean Paul.

Novels
1934: *Der Glockengießer Christoph Mahr*
1938: *Der Herr Kortüm*. This novel, his main literary success, arose out of his two former novels: 1934: *Die silberne Windfahne*, and 1937: *Das Flügelhaus*
1940: *Die Zaubergeige*

WOLFGANG KOEPPEN

Born 1906 in Greifswald. Journalist, actor, author of travel-stories and novels.

Novels
1935: *Die Mauer schwankt*
1951: *Tauben im Gras*
1953: *Das Treibhaus*
1954: *Der Tod im Rom*

OSKAR KOKOSCHKA

Born 1886 in Pöchlarn, Austria. Went into exile in 1938. Painter, draughtsman, stage designer, poet, playwright.

Drama
1911: *Der brennende Dornbusch*
1917: *Hiob*
1919: *Orpheus und Eurydike*

Stories
1962: The volume of stories: *Spur im Treibsand* appeared in an
      English tr. under the title *A Sea ringed with visions*

Study
1964: W. I. Lucas: *Oskar Kokoschka*, in *German Men of Letters, III*

BARBARA KÖNIG

Born 1925 in Reichenberg; chiefly story-writer.

Stories
1958: *Das Kind und sein Schatten*

Novels
1961: *Kies*   1965: *Die Personenperson*

ANNETTE KOLB

Born 1875 in Badenweiler, of French mother who was a pianist, and a Bavarian father. Emigrated in 1933 to Paris and then to New York, later back to Paris. Friendship with René Schickele and Thomas Mann. Literary contact also with Rilke. Her stories are to a great extent autobiographical.

Essays
1906: *Sieben Studien: l'âme âux deux patries*
1929: *Versuch über Briand*

Novels

1913: *Das Exemplar*
1934: *Die Schaukel*
1947: *König Ludwig II. von Bayern und Richard Wagner*

Monographs

1937: *Mozart*
1941: *Franz Schubert, sein Leben*

ERWIN GUIDO KOLBENHEYER

Born 1878 in Budapest. Died 1962 in Solln, nr. Munich. Found great response in the Third Reich; see p. 34.

Novels

1908: *Amor dei* (a Spinoza-novel)
1910: *Meister Joachim Pausenwang*
1917–25: Paracelsus-Trilogy: (1) 1917: *Die Kindheit des Paracelsus*, (2) 1921: *Das Gestirn*, (3) 1925: *Das dritte Reich*
1927: *Das Lächeln der Penaten*
1938: *Das gottgelobte Herz* (about Margarete Ebner)

Poetry

1929: *Lyrisches Brevier*

Geschichtsroman

1934: *Gregor und Heinrich*

Drama

1903: *Giordano Bruno*
1929: *Die Brücke*

Theory

1925: *Bauhütte* (Grundzüge einer Metaphysik der Gegenwart)

Studies

1953: Franz Koch: *Kolbenheyer*
1957: *Ges. Werke*, 14 vols.

GERTRUD KOLMAR (Ps. for Gertrud Chodziesner)

Born 1894, in Berlin. Daughter of a Jewish lawyer from Kolmar in Posen. 1943 deported, missing since then.

Poetry
1934: *Preußische Wappen*
1938: *Die Frau und die Tiere*
1955: *Das lyrische Werk*, enlarged with bibliography, ed. by Hilde Wenzel, 1960

Story
1965: *Eine Mutter*

PAUL KORNFELD

Born 1889 in Prague. Died 1942 in the KZ Lodz, Poland. He was an Expressionist writer until about 1922.

Tragedy
1918: *Verführung* (written 1913)
1919: *Himmel und Hölle*

Comedy
1922: *Der ewige Traum*
1926: *Kristian oder die gelbe Rose*

Novel
1957: (posth.) *Blanche oder das Atelier im Garten*

KARL EMERICH KRÄMER (Ps. George Forestier)

Born 1918 in Düsseldorf; see L. Forster, *GLL*, 1956.

Poetry
1952: *Ich schreibe mein Herz in den Staub der Straße*
    Stark wie der Tod ist die Nacht, ist die Liebe
1958: *Nur der Wind weiß meinen Namen*

THEODOR KRAMER

Born 1897 in Niederhollabrunn, Lower Austria. 1939 emigrated to England. Died 1958 in Vienna. Influenced by Trakl and Brecht.

Poetry

1928: *Die Gaunerzinke*
1931: *Wir lagen in Wolhynien im Morast*
1936: *Mit der Ziehharmonika*
1946: *Die untere Schenke*
1956: *Vom schwarzen Wein*, selected poems

KARL KRAUS

Born 1874 in Gitschin, Böhmen. Died 1936 in Vienna. Author of unsparing satires and critic of bourgeois hypocrisy. 1899–1936 Journal: *Die Fackel*. His public support of Dollfuss through whom K. Kraus seemed to have hoped to avert Hitler's annexation of Austria, lost him a number of Socialist friends. About 1933 he began to write a Fackel-Heft as an attack on the Third Reich which, however, did not appear until 1952 under the title: *Die dritte Walpurgisnacht*; see p. 80.

1919: 2 vols. *Weltgericht*
1922: *Die letzten Tage der Menschheit*
1952 ff.–1964: *Ges. Werke*, ed. by H. Fischer, 12 vols.
vol. I: *Die dritte Walpurgisnacht*
vol. II: *Die Sprache*
vol. III: *Beim Wort genommen* (Sprüche und Widersprüche—
            pro Domo et Mundo)
vol. IV: *Widerschein der Fackel*
vol. V: *Die letzten Tage der Menschheit* (Tragödie)
vol. VI: *Literatur und Lüge*
vol. VII: *Worte in Versen*
vol. VIII: *Untergang der Welt durch schwarze Magie*
vol. IX: *Unsterblicher Witz*
vol. X: *Mit vorzüglicher Hochachtung*
vol. XI: *Sittlichkeit und Kriminalität*
vol. XII: *Die chinesische Mauer*
1964: Comprehensive bibliography in *Nachrichten aus dem Kösel-Verlag*

Studies

1964: Helmut Arntzen: *Deutsche Satire des 20 Jahrhunderts,* with special reference to the formal perfection in K. Kraus's artistic satire

1966: Caroline Kohn: *Karl Kraus*

1968: F. Field: *The Last Days of Mankind. Karl Kraus and his Vienna*

MAX KRETZER

Born 1854 in Posen (Poznan). Died 1941 in Berlin. 'Naturalist' novelist.

Novels

1888: *Meister Timpe,* his most famous work
1897: *Das Gesicht Christi*
1906: *Was ist Ruhm*
1909: *Mut zur Sünde*
1913: *Mädchen aus der Fremde*

ERNST KREUDER

Born 1903 in Zeitz, nr. Leipzig.

Novels

1948: *Die Unauffindbaren*
1959: *Agimos oder Die Weltgehilfen*

Stories

1939: *Die Nacht des Gefangenen* (collection)
1944: *Das Haus mit den drei Bäumen* (collection)
1946: *Die Gesellschaft vom Dachboden*
1954: *Herein ohne anzuklopfen*
1963: *Spur unterm Wasser*

Kreuder's novels and stories, closely similar in style, are a unique compound of *Märchen* and mystery-story, though with an underlying seriousness—his characters are engaged in a search for the truth, or reality, which lies behind routine everyday existence.

An imaginative writer in the Romantic tradition, whose work, however, reveals a tendency to mannerism.

D. S. Low

KARL KROLOW

Born 1915 in Hanover. Mainly lyrical poet, translator; influenced by Loerke and W. Lehmann. 1960–1 Gastdozent für Poetik at the University of Frankfurt a.M. His six guest-lectures are contained in the revised ed.: *Aspekte zeitgenössischer deutscher Lyrik*, 1961.

Poetry
1943: *Hochgelobtes, gutes Leben*
1948: *Gedichte*
      Heimsuchung
1949: *Auf Erden*
1952: *Die Zeichen der Welt*
1954: *Wind und Zeit*
1956: *Tage und Nächte*
1959: *Fremde Körper*
1962: *Unsichtbare Hände*
1965: *Ges. Gedichte*

1948: *Nachdichtungen aus fünf Jahrhunderten französischer Lyrik*
1957: *Die Barke. Phantasie*, Übertragungen zeitgenössischer Lyrik

Some of Krolow's later poetry seems to divorce Ego and Nature from his refined artistry of words which claim their own autonomy of magic existence, see pp. 42 and 53.

1966: *Poetisches Tagebuch*

HERMANN KÜKELHAUS

Born 1921 in Essen. This promising poet died 1944 in a Berlin military lazaret.

1947: *Gedichte* (posth.)

GÜNTER KUNERT

Born 1929 in Berlin. Lives in East Berlin; furthered by J. R. Becher, influenced by B. Brecht.

Poetry
1950: *Wegschilder und Mauerinschriften*
1961: *Tagwerke*
1963: *Erinnerung an einen Planeten*
1966: *Der ungebetene Gast*

A comparison of G. Kunert's poem: *Ikarus 64* with the beginning of Goethe's *Harzreise im Winter* and A. Wolfenstein's *Im Bestienhaus* brings out in full relief the poet's response to the changes of time. In contrast to Goethe's soaring self-assurance A. Wolfenstein's vision is heavily weighed down by the burden of matter, but G. Kunert, in spite of all physical and cultural ballast which hampers us, calls for a new start to new horizons:

> 'Dennoch breite die Arme aus und nimm
> einen Anlauf für das Unmögliche . . .'

Stories
1964: *Tagträume*

Novel
1967: *Im Namen der Hüte*, based on a Grimm fairty-tale; the hero Heinrich finds out people's characters and thoughts by putting their hats on his head

ISOLDE KURZ

Born 1853 in Stuttgart (daughter of the author Hermann Kurz). Died 1944 in Tübingen. Friendship with painters and scholars: Arnold Böcklin, Adolf von Hildebrand, Hans von Marées, etc.

Poetry
1889: *Gedichte*

Stories
1890: *Florentiner Novellen*
1895: *Italienische Erzählungen*

Novel

1922: *Nächte von Fondi*

1931: (autobiogr. novel) *Vanadis. Der Schicksalsweg einer Frau*

Autobiography

1938: *Die Pilgerfahrt nach dem Unerreichlichen*

1925: *Ges. Werke* 6 vols.; see also DLL

FRIEDO LAMPE

Born 1899 in Bremen. Died 1945 in Klein-Machnow, nr. Berlin (shot by the Russians by mistake).

Novels

1933: *Am Rande der Nacht*
1937: *Septembergewitter*

Stories

1946: *Von Tür zu Tür*

1950: *Aus dem Nachlaß*
1955: *Das Gesamtwerk*

Study

1961: Lionel Thomas: *Friedo Lampe and his Work*, GLL, XIV, pp. 194–203

Lampe's short novel *Am Rande der Nacht* explores the activities of various characters on an autumn night in his native Bremen; his masterpiece, the longish story *Septembergewitter*, is a skilled exploitation of the 'tranche de vie' approach in which a melancholy awareness of life's transient beauty and evil predominates.

L. H. C. Thomas

PETER MARTIN LAMPEL

Born 1894 in Schönborn, Silesia. Emigrated in 1933 to Switzerland and eventually to the U.S.A.; now living in Hamburg. Playwright, novelist and painter.

Drama
1928: *Revolte im Erziehungshaus*
1929: *Giftgas über Berlin*
1930: *Wir sind Kameraden*
1931: *Vaterland*
1951: *Flucht vor uns selber*

Story
1955: *Wir fanden den Weg*

Novel
1929: *Verratene Jungen*

ODA LANGE, see ODA SCHAEFER, p. 356

ELISABETH LANGGÄSSER

Born 1899 in Alzey, Rheinhessen. Died 1950 in Rheinzabern.

Novels
1933: *Proserpina*
1936: *Der Gang durch das Ried*
1946: *Das unauslöschliche Siegel*
1950: *Die märkische Argonautenfahrt* (English version, 1953: *The Quest*, tr. by J. B. Greene)

Short stories
1932: *Grenze, besetztes Gebiet*
      Das Triptychon des Teufels
1938: *Rettung am Rhein*
1947: *Der Torso*
1949: *Das Labyrinth*

Poetry
1924: *Der Wendekreis des Lammes*
1935: *Die Tierkreisgedichte*
1947: *Der Laubmann und die Rose*
1948: *Kölnische Elegie*

Critical and miscellaneous writing
1961: *Das Christliche der christlichen Dichtung*

Elisabeth Langgässer's poetry explores the correspondence between the pagan mysteries, embodied in classical mythology, and the mysteries of the Catholic faith; the tension between the unredeemed natural world and the world of grace is the recurrent theme of her prose-fiction.

H. R. Klieneberger

ELSE LASKER-SCHÜLER

Born 1869 (not 1876, as usually stated) in Wuppertal-Elberfeld. Died 1945 in Jerusalem. First marriage with the Berlin doctor J. B. B. Lasker; second marriage (1901–11) with Herwarth Walden (Georg Levin); eccentric character; in her religious verse akin, in some degree, to Rilke and Expressionists; friendship with Peter Hille, Georg Grosz, R. Dehmel, Karl Kraus, O. Kokoschka, Theodor Däubler, G. Benn, Franz Marc, F. Werfel, Kurt Pinthus and other writers or artists.

Poetry
1902: *Styx*, her first collection of poems
1911: *Meine Wunder*
1913: *Hebräische Balladen*; it was, by the author, considered her main work
1917: *Ges. Gedichte*
1943: *Mein blaues Klavier*

Essays, memoirs, stories, etc.
1906–7: *Das Peter Hille Buch*
1908: *Die Nächte der Tino von Bagdad*
1912: *Mein Herz*. Ein Liebesroman mit Bildern und wirklich lebenden Menschen
1913: *Essays*
       Gesichte
1916–17: *Der Malik* (later subtitle: *Ein Kaiserroman*)
1921: *Briefe Peter Hilles an Else Lasker-Schüler*
1925: *Ich räume auf: Meine Anklage gegen meine Verleger*
1932: *Arthur Aronymus. Geschichte meines Vaters*
1937: *Hebräerland*

Studies
1919–20: *Gesamtausgabe*, 10 vols.

1951: *Lasker-Schüler: Dichtungen und Dokumente*, ed. by E. Ginsberg
1959–62: *Ges. Werke*, ed. by F. Kemp and W. Kraft

CHRISTINE LAVANT (Ps. for Christine Habernig), maiden name Thonhauser

Born 1915 in Groß-Edling nr. St Stefan, Lavanttal, Carinthia. The ninth and last child of a miner; now in St Stefan in the Lavanttal. Furthered by Paula Grogger; influenced by Rilke, particularly in her early poetry of 1949.

Poetry
1949: *Die unvollendete Liebe*
1956: *Die Bettlerschale*
1959: *Spindel im Mond*
1962: *Der Pfauenschrei*

Stories
1948: *Das Kind*
1952: *Baruscha*, Drei Erzählungen

Study
1965: W. V. Blomster: *Christine Lavant*, Symposium, XIX

GERTRUD VON LE FORT

Born 1876 in Minden, Westphalia. 'The greatest metaphysical writer of the twentieth century' (Zuckmayer). A christian apologist presenting her views symbolically and imaginatively. The themes of *Reich*, *Kirche* and *Frau* figure centrally in her work, which is characterized by its neo-classical language and simplicity of style.

Novels
1928: *Der römische Brunnen* (*Das Schweißtuch der Veronika* Pt 1)
1930: *Der Papst aus dem Ghetto*
1938: *Die Magdeburgische Hochzeit*
1946: *Der Kranz der Engel* (*Das Schweißtuch der Veronika* Pt 2)

Short stories
1931: *Die Letzte am Schafott*

1940: *Die Abberufung der Jungfrau von Barby*
1943: *Das Gericht des Meeres*
1947: *Die Consolata*
1950: *Die Tochter Farinatas*
1954: *Am Tor des Himmels*
1957: *Der Turm der Beständigkeit*
1961: *Das fremde Kind*
1964: *Die Tochter Jephthas*
1967: *Das Schweigen*

Poetry
1924: *Hymnen an die Kirche*
1932: *Hymnen an Deutschland*
1949: *Gedichte* (enlarged 1953)

Essays and miscellaneous writings
1934: *Die Ewige Frau*
1947: *Unser Weg durch die Nacht*
1951: *Aufzeichnungen und Erinnerungen*
1962: *Aphorismen*
1966: *Die Hälfte des Lebens*

1956: *Erzählende Schriften* 3 vols.
1966: *Erzählungen*

Much of her work is available in English or American tr., see II, *German Men of Letters*, l.c.

Ian Hilton

WILHELM LEHMANN

Born 1882 in Puerto Cabello, Venezuela. His father was a Lübeck merchant. At the age of three, the poet was taken to Germany; friendship with Oskar Loerke and Moritz Heimann (Ps. Hans Pauli), who was Lektor of the 'Verlag der Moderne', S. Fischer in Berlin, and a playwright (cf. *Heimann: Nachgelassene Schriften*, ed. by O. Loerke, 1926). W. Lehmann lives at Eckernförde in Schleswig-Holstein, where he taught until his retirement in 1947.

Poetry

1935: *Antwort des Schweigens*
1942: *Der grüne Gott*
1946: *Entzückter Staub*
1950: *Noch nicht genug*
1954: *Überlebender Tag*
1957: *Meine Gedichtbücher*
1962: *Abschiedslust*
1967: *Sichtbare Zeit. Gedichte aus den Jahren 1962–1966*

Novels

1916: *Der Bilderstürmer*
1918: *Die Schmetterlingspuppe*
1921: *Weingott*

Stories

1912: *Cardenio und Celinde*. Eine Liebesgeschichte (in *Pan* Wochen-
 schrift ed. by Alfred Kerr, vol. II)
1915: *Der bedrängte Seraph* (in *Der neue Merkur*)
1922: *Vogelfreier Josef*
1923: *Der Sturz auf die Erde*
1928: *Verführerin. Trösterin*
1933: *Die Hochzeit der Aufrührer*
1938: *Die Aufführung*
1948: *Das Gelächter*
1949: *Der stumme Laufjunge*

Essays

1947: *Bewegliche Ordnung*
1956: *Dichtung als Dasein*
1961: *Kunst des Gedichts*

1962: *Sämtliche Werke*, 3 vols.

Studies

1966: D. A. Scrase: *Wilhelm Lehmann*, in 'Essays on Contemporary
 German Literature', IV, *German Men of Letters*, l.c.

D. Scrase

HANS LEIFHELM

Born 1891 in München-Gladbach. Died 1947 in Riva on the Gardasee. Friendship with H. Lersch.

Poetry
1926: *Hahnenschrei*
1933: *Gesänge von der Erde*
1949: *Lob der Vergänglichkeit* (posth.)

HANS KARL HERMANN GOTTFRIED LEIP

Born in 1893 in Hamburg. Son of a sailor. Poet, novelist, graphic artist; now living in Switzerland.

Novels
1923: *Der Pfuhl*, about Hamburg after the First World War
1925: *Godekes Knecht*, a novel which was praised by Thomas Mann. The Low German Klaus Störtebeker and Godeke Michelson (frequently heroes in dramas, novels and songs) were the leaders of the so-called 'Vitalienbrüder' about 1395–1401
1932 and 1954: *Jan Himp und die kleine Brise*
1954: *Der große Fluß im Meer*, story about the gulf-stream

Poetry
Hans Leip is the author of the popular song: *Lili Marleen*, written in 1915
1948: *Frühe Lieder* (Auswahl)

Chronicle
1959: *Bordbuch des Satans*, about freebooting

Study
1958: R. Italiaander: *Hans Leip und sein Werk*

JOSEF LEITGEB

Born 1897 in Bischofshofen (Salzburg). Died 1952 at Innsbruck.

Poetry
1935: *Musik der Landschaft*

1943: *Vita somnium breve*
1953: *Sämtliche Gedichte*, with Introduction by H. Graf

Novels
1934: *Kinderlegende*
1936: *Christian und Brigitte*

Stories
1959: *Abschied und fernes Bild*, posth., ed. by F. Punt, with
bibliography

SIEGFRIED LENZ

Born 1926 in Lyck, East Prussia. Prose-writer and dramatist. Recurrent themes are persecution and man alone with his conscience. Sharp, clear realistic prose, often with ironic undertones.

Novels
1951: *Es waren Habichte in der Luft*
1953: *Duell mit dem Schatten*
1957: *Der Mann im Strom*
1959: *Brot und Spiele*
1963: *Stadtgespräch*

Short stories
1955: *So zärtlich war Suleyken*
1958: *Jäger des Spottes*
1960: *Das Feuerschiff*
1964: *Lehmanns Erzählungen oder So schön war mein Markt*
1965: *Der Spielverderber*

Drama
1962: *Zeit der Schuldlosen*
1964: *Das Gesicht*

In above both plays the author deals with the problem that every one of us is potentially a dictator. Facial resemblance (in *Das Gesicht*) enables a hairdresser to act as a double to the tyrant.

Ian Hilton

RUDOLF LEONHARD (Ps. Robert Lanzer)

Born 1889 in Lissa (Poland). Died 1953 in East Berlin. Pacifist, but shortly after the First World War joined the revolutionary forces. Essayist, novelist, Expressionist poet, playwright, and translator (of Anatole France).

Poetry

1914: *Barbaren* (Ballads)
1918: *Polnische Gedichte*
1921: *Spartakus-Sonette*
1925: *Das nackte Leben* (Sonetten-Sammlung), 1948, 2nd ed.
1947: *Deutsche Gedichte*

1947: *Plaidoyer pour la démocratie allemande*, Paris

Drama

1929: *Das Floß der Medusa*
1933: *Traum*
1936: *Führer und Co, eine politische Komödie*
1945-6: tragedy *Geiseln*

Stories

1938: *Der Tod des Don Quijote* (about the Civil War in Spain)

1961 ff.: *Werkausgabe*, 4 vols.

ALEXANDER LERNET-HOLENIA

Born 1897 in Vienna. Cavalry officer on Russian front in First World War. Experience of collapse of Hapsburg Monarchy had a decisive influence upon his thought and works. Achieved recognition after War as poet, dramatist (mainly comedy) and novelist. Influenced by Rilke, Hugo von Hofmannsthal and Viennese theatrical tradition. His novels are polished, swift, fond of exploring unlikely romantic subjects and situations, the nature of personal identity and the psychology of eros. Most successful are the war stories, which reveal a profound nostalgia for his vanished Austria. His novel *Die Standarte* (1934) is, like Joseph Roth's *Radetzkymarsch* (1932), or Franz Werfel's *Barbara oder die Fröm-*

migkeit (1929) an important document of the disintegrating Monarchy.

Other novels
1941: *Mars im Widder*
1942: *Beide Sizilien*
1964: *Götter und Menschen*

Poetry
1921: *Pastorale*
1927: *Das Geheimnis Sankt Michaels*
1933: *Die goldene Horde*
1946: *Germanien*

Drama
1926: *Demetrius*
1927: *Österreichische Komödie*
     Ollapotrida
1934: *Die Frau des Potiphar*

J. B. Bednall

HEINRICH LERSCH

Born 1889 in München-Gladbach. Settled in Bodendorf/Ahr. Died 1936 in Remagen. Boilermaker and coppersmith. He became a member of the *Bund der Werkleute auf Haus Nyland*; see also G. Engelke, p. 243, and K. Bröger, p. 228. In the Third Reich his war-poem: *Soldatenabschied*, with the refrain: 'Deutschland muß leben, und wenn wir sterben müssen', found wide response, but it would be unjust to call Lersch a Chauvinist. He believed in world-brotherhood and desired peace for his country and for the whole of mankind.

Poetry
1914: *Abglanz des Lebens*
1918: *Deutschland*
1924: *Wir Volk*
1925: *Mensch im Eisen*

Lersch's poem *Brüder* appeared in an English and French verse-tr. in *Ohne Haß und Fahne*, l.c.; see p. 279.

1966: *Ausgewählte Werke*, ed. by J. Klein, 2 vols.; the 1st vol. contains Lersch's poems, the 2nd vol. his *Erzählungen und Briefe*

ALFRED LICHTENSTEIN

Born 1889 in Berlin. Died 1914 nr. Vermandevillers, on the Somme. Influenced by J. van Hoddis. His poem *Die Dämmerung*, which appeared in the *Simplizissimus* in 1911, is, like J. van Hoddis's *Weltende* (1911), one of the very first German Expressionist poems; cf. Gottfried Benn: *Probleme der Lyrik*, 1951. At the same time in the above poem A. Lichtenstein's predilection for grotesque presentation of objects is already evident.

1962: *Ges. Gedichte*, ed. (with bibliography) by Klaus Kanzog

FREIHERR DETLEV VON LILIENCRON

Born 1844 in Kiel. Died 1909 in Alt-Rahlstedt, nr. Hamburg. Mainly lyrical poet and German Impressionist of creative originality.

Epic
1896–1908: *Poggfred. Kunterbuntes Epos in 29 Kantussen*

Poetry
1883: *Adjutantenritte und andre Gedichte*
1890: *Der Haidegänger und andere Gedichte*

Short stories
1895: *Kriegsnovellen*

Novel (auto-biographical)
1908: *Leben und Lüge*

1910–20: *Ges. Werke*, 8 vols., ed. by Richard Dehmel

OTTO ZUR LINDE

Born 1873 in Essen. Died 1938 in Berlin Lichterfelde. Founder of the circle of poets: 'Charon', with Rudolf Pannwitz. Otto zur

Linde's poetry and 'Charon' publications are unfortunately still not fully recognized.

1910–25: *Ges. Werke*, 10 vols.

I.	*Thule Traumland*
II.	*Lieder der Liebe und Ehe*
III.	*Stadt und Landschaft*
IV.	*Charontischer Mythos*
V.	*Wege, Menschen und Ziele*
VI.	*Das Buch Abendrot*
VII/VIII.	*Lieder des Leids*
IX/X.	*Denken, Zeit und Zukunft*

1911: *Arno Holz und der Charon*. In this treatise he settles accounts with Holz's theory of the '*Phantasus-Zeile*'; see p. 4.

ERNST LISSAUER

Born 1882 in Berlin. Died 1937 in Vienna. Author of the notorious *Haßgesang gegen England* (1914), a poem of which he could hardly feel proud, particularly in 1933 when he, being a Jew, emigrated to Vienna. Soon after 1920 his poetry became non-political, and rather unsuccessfully he turned to drama, e.g. dealing with *Eckermann*, 1921; *Luther und Thomas Münzer*, 1929.

HERMANN LÖNS

Born 1866 in Kulm, West Prussia. Died 1914, nr. Loivre nr. Reims.

Poetry

1911: *Der kleine Rosengarten* (Volkslieder); *Mein blaues Buch* (Balladen und Romanzen); *Lieder und Lautensatz*, music composed by Ernst Licht, 1916

Descriptions of heathland

1901: *Mein grünes Buch*
1907: *Mein braunes Buch* (Haidbilder)

Novels

1910: *Der Wehrwolf*, a peasant-chronicle, time: the Thirty Years War, place: the Lüneberg Heath; his most famous novel, based on the hero's motto that God helps those who help themselves

1911: *Das zweite Gesicht* (Künstlerroman)
1924: *Sämtliche Werke*, ed. by Fr. Castelle, 8 vols.

1959: Stanley Radcliffe: *Hermann Löns*, ed.

OSKAR LOERKE

Born 1884 in Jungen an der Weichsel (Vistula). Died 1941 in Berlin-Frohnau. In 1917 Lektor with S. Fischer-Verlag; 10 years later he became Permanent Secretary in the Section 'Dichtkunst' of the Prussian Academy—a post which at the time of 'mischief' (Unheil) he was deprived of.

Poetry
1911: *Wanderschaft* (the first of his 7 vols. of poems)
1916: *Gedichte*
1921: *Die heimliche Stadt*
1926: *Der längste Tag*
1929: *Pansmusik*
1930: *Atem der Erde*
1934: *Der Silberdistelwald*

1965: *Oskar Loerke: Der Bücherkarren (Besprechungen)* (a collection of Loerke's weekly book reviews in the Berlin *Börsen-Courier*), ed. by Hermann Kasack

HANS LORBEER

Born 1901 in Kleinwittenberg. Poet, novelist and playwright.

Poetry
1925: *Gedichte eines jungen Arbeiters*
1927: *Lenin, Liebknecht, Luxemburg* (Sprechchor)
1948: *Die Gitterharfe*

Novels
Romantrilogie (about Luther):
(a) 1956: *Das Fegefeuer*

(*b*) 1959: *Der Widerruf*
(*c*) 1964: *Die Obrigkeit*

Drama
1931: *Phosphor*

JOACHIM MAASS

Born 1901 in Hamburg. Emigrated to the U.S.A. before the Second World War, where he became professor of modern German literature; chiefly novelist.

Novels
1930: *Bohème ohne Mimi*
1932: *Der Widersacher*
1935: *Die unwiederbringliche Zeit*
1939: *Ein Testament*
1945: *Das magische Jahr*
1952: *Der Fall Gouffé* (which is considered his chief prose work)

1957: *Kleist, die Fackel Preußens* (Lebensgeschichte)

JOHN HENRY MACKAY

Born 1864 in Greenock, Scotland. Since his second year living in Germany. Died 1933 in Berlin. Influenced by Max Stirner's philosophy of anarchism and by German Naturalistic writers, cf. Arno Holz's drama *Sozialaristokraten*, 1896; cf. H. Holz.

Poetry
1887: *Sturm*

Biography
1898: *Max Stirner, sein Leben und sein Werk*

1911: *Ges. Werke* (8 vols.)

1928: *Werke*

HEINRICH MANN

Born 1871 in Lübeck (brother of Thomas Mann). Died 1950 in Los Angeles.

Novels

1893: *In einer Familie*
1900: *Im Schlaraffenland*
1902–3: Trilogy *Die Göttinnen* (*Diana, Minerva, Venus*)
1903–4: *Die Jagd nach Liebe*
1905: *Professor Unrat*
1907: *Zwischen den Rassen*
1910: *Die kleine Stadt*
1914–18: *Der Untertan*
1917: *Die Armen*
1925: *Der Kopf*
1927: *Mutter Marie*
1928: *Eugénie*
1931: *Die große Sache*
1932: *Ein ernstes Leben*
1935: *Die Jugend des Königs Henri Quatre*
1937: *Die Vollendung des Königs Henri Quatre*
1943: *Lidice*
1949: *Der Atem*
1950: *Empfang bei der Welt*

Dramatized novel

1962: *Die traurige Geschichte von Friedrich dem Großen*

Short stories

1897: *Das Wunderbare*
1904–5: *Flöten und Dolche*
1905–6: *Schauspielerin*
1906: *Stürmische Morgen*
1908: *Die Bösen*
1910: *Das Herz*
1911: *Rückkehr vom Hades*
1920: *Die Ehrgeizige*
1923: *Kobes; Der Jüngling*
1924: *Abrechnungen*
1926: *Liliane und Paul*
1929: *Sie sind jung*

Dramas

1910: *Variété; Der Tyrann; Die Unschuldige* (one-acters)

1911: *Schauspielerin*
1912: *Die große Liebe*
1913: *Madame Legros*
1916: *Brabach*
1918: *Der Weg zur Macht*
1923: *Das gastliche Haus*

Essays, speeches, memoirs, etc.

1915: *Zola*
1919: *Macht und Mensch*
1923: *Diktatur der Vernunft*
1932: *Das öffentliche Leben; Das Bekenntnis zum Übernationalen*
1933: *Der Haß*
1945: *Ein Zeitalter wird besichtigt*

(A more detailed bibliography will be found in the Berlin periodical *Aufbau*, vol. 6, 1950)

Studies

1946: K. Lemke: *Heinrich Mann. Zu seinem 75. Geburtstag*, Berlin
1949: V. Mann: *Wir waren fünf. Bildnis der Familie Mann*, Constance
1951: H. Jhering: *Heinrich Mann*, Berlin
1956: A. Kantorowicz: *Heinrich und Thomas Mann*, Berlin
1962: U. Weisstein: *Heinrich Mann*, Tübingen
1963: W. E. Yuill: *Heinrich Mann*, in *German Men of Letters*, l.c. vol. II, London
1967 ff.: E. Zenker: *Heinrich Mann—Bibliographie*

W. E. Yuill

THOMAS MANN

Born 1875 in Lübeck. Son of a merchant. Settled in Munich as writer (1901); a convinced supporter of the German cause in 1914–18 War, his liberal views compelled him to leave Germany when the National Socialists came to power. Reached America in 1939 via France and Switzerland, settled in California. Returned to Switzerland in 1952. Died 1955 in (Zürich-Kilchberg). Mann is universally recognized as the greatest German novelist of this century, modern despite the fact that the intellectual, philosophical and artistic tradition from which he emerged and to which he freely acknowledged his debt stretched right back to the Classicism of Goethe and included as chief formative influences the philosophy of Schopenhauer and Nietzsche and the music-drama of Wagner.

It was from these sources that he induced the intellectual problem which is the chief concern of his early works (*Buddenbrooks, Tonio Kröger, Der Tod in Venedig*): the predicament of the artist whose intuitive penetration of the surface of reality upon which the bourgeois is content to live makes him first unhappy in and, later, unfit for the society of his fellows; a situation which is rendered more poignant if, as human being, he feels drawn towards the world and its happy children. In a succession of works which reveal structural mastery, as well as experimenting with several interesting techniques (leitmotiv, stylistic parody), Mann grapples with this problem, which he can never really be said to have solved.

J. B. Bednall

Novels

1901: *Buddenbrooks*

1909: *Königliche Hoheit*

1922: *Die Bekenntnisse des Hochstaplers Felix Krull* (fragment), later ed. 1954, film 1957

1924: *Der Zauberberg*

1933–43: *Joseph und seine Brüder* (tetralogy):

1933: *Die Geschichten Jaakobs*

1934: *Der junge Joseph*

1936: *Joseph in Ägypten*

1943: *Joseph der Ernährer*

1939: *Lotte in Weimar* (a Goethe-novel)

1947: *Doktor Faustus*

1951: *Der Erwählte*

Novellen and stories

1898: *Der kleine Herr Friedemann*

1903: *Tristan*, and *Tonio Kröger*

1912: *Der Tod in Venedig*

1919: *Herr und Hund* (Ein Idyll)

1921: *Wälsungenblut*

1926: *Unordnung und frühes Leid*

1930: *Mario der Zauberer*
1940: *Die vertauschten Köpfe* (Indische Legende)
1953: *Die Betrogene*

Speeches, essays and criticisms
1910: *Versuch über das Theater* and *Der alte Fontane*
1915: *Friedrich und die große Koalition*
1918: *Betrachtungen eines Unpolitischen*
1923: *Goethe und Tolstoi*
1930: *Die Forderung des Tages* (Reden und Aufsätze aus den Jahren 1925–1929)
1935: *Leiden und Größe der Meister. Neue Aufsätze* (about Goethe, R. Wagner, A. v. Platen, Th. Storm, etc.)
1937: *Ein Briefwechsel* (correspondence with the Dean of Bonn, Faculty of Arts, on the occasion of Th. Mann's loss of his Ehrendoktorat)
1938: *Schopenhauer*
1939: *Die Kunst des Romans*
1948: *Neue Studien* (about Nietzsche, Dostoyevsky, etc.)
1950: *Lob der Vergänglichkeit*

Eds. of letters and works
1961: *Briefe 1889–1936*, ed. by Erika Mann
1963: *Briefe 1937–1947*, ed. by Erika Mann
       Wagner und unsere Zeit, ed. by Erika Mann

1938: *Stockholmer Gesamtausgabe*
1960: *Ges. Werke*, 12 vols., Frankfurt a.M.

Studies
1958: Erich Heller: *The ironic German. A study of Thomas Mann*
1959: extensive bibliography, by H. Bürgin (with W. A. Reichart and Erich Neumann): *Das Werk Thomas Manns*
1964: H. Hatfield: *Thomas Mann: A Collection of Critical Essays*
1965: *Thomas Mann. Eine Chronik seines Lebens*, ed. by H. Bürgin and H.-O. Mayer
1966: A. W. Riley: *Three Cryptic Quotations in Thomas Mann's 'Felix Krull'*, Journal of English and Germanic Philology, LXV
1967: *Thomas Mann Studies*, vol. II, ed. by K. W. Jonas and I. B. Jonas. This volume has been designed not only to bring

the bibliographical record of critical literature on Mann up to date, but also to enlarge the scope of Volume I.

HANS MARCHWITZA

Born 1890 in Scharley, nr. Beuthen, Upper Silesia. Died 1965 in DDR. He was a miner in the Ruhr during the First World War. Shortly after the First World War he became a member of the USPD (Unabhängige Sozialistische Partei Deutschlands) and in 1920 a member of the KPD (Kommunistische Partei Deutschlands); emigrated in 1933; after 1950–1 Botschaftsrat of the DDR in Prague. Author of political-didactic prose.

His trilogy
1934: *Die Kumiaks*
1952: *Die Heimkehr der Kumiaks*
1959: *Die Kumiaks und ihre Kinder*
highly praised in the official circles of DDR

1947: Autobiographical novel: *Meine Jugend*

GEORG MAURER

Born 1907 in Sächsisch-Regen, Siebenbürgen. Poet and translator (from Rumanian literature); in his hymnic verse influenced by Hölderlin.

Poetry
1936: *Ewige Stimmen*
1948: *Gesänge der Zeit* (Hymnen und Sonette)
1953: *Zweiundvierzig Sonette*
1955: *Die Elemente* (free-rhythmic verse)
1959: *Poetische Reise*
1961: *Drei Strophen Kalender*
1962: *Gedichte* (Neue Auswahl)
1965: *Variationen*

KARL MAY (Ps. Karl Hohenthal, E. v. Linden, etc.)

Born 1842 in Hohenstein–Ernstthal, Sachsen. Died 1912 in Radebeul, nr. Dresden. Author of stories of adventure and heroism, e.g. his much-read novels for the young: *Winnetou*, 3 vols.; *Old Surehand*, 4 vols.; *Im Reiche des silbernen Löwen*, 4 vols., etc.

Karl May's glorification of courage, friendship and human sympathy won him many readers in Germany and abroad. His novels are again reprinted and tr. into many languages; see also DLL.

FRIEDERIKE MAYRÖCKER

Born 1924 in Vienna.

Poetry
1964: *rot 18*
1965: *texte*
1966: *Tod durch Musen*

CHRISTOPH MECKEL

Born 1935 in Berlin. He, like Günter Grass, is poet as well as graphic artist.

Poetry
1956: *Die Tarnkappe*
1958: *Hotel für Schlafwandler* (mit vier Ätzungen des Verfassers)
1959: *Nebelhörner*
1962: *Wildnisse*
1964: *Gedichtbilderbuch* (elf Bilder und elf Gedichthandschriften)
1967: *Bei Lebzeiten zu singen*

Prose
1961: *Im Land der Umbramauten.* This is a twilight region, a grotesque world of anxiety and terror: whole forests, railway stations and houses begin to move from their ground, but a sense of playfulness redeems the senselessness of a macabre scene

WALTER MEHRING

Born 1896 in Berlin. Author of satirical poems and political cabaret chansons; connected with Herwarth Walden's 'Sturm' and the Berlin Dada movement; friendship with Kurt Tucholsky; emigrated to the U.S.A., now living in Ascona; see p. 19.

Poetry

1929: *Die Gedichte, Lieder und Chansons des W.M.*
1962: *Neues Ketzerbrevier*, a cross-section of his satirical ballads and songs

Novel

1960: *Müller, Chronik eines teutschen Stammbaums*, with drawings by Fritz Fischer. This travesty of the story of a German pedigree is a reprint of the 1935 edition: *Müller. Die Chronik einer deutschen Sippe von Tacitus bis Hitler*

1952: enlarged ed. 1964: *Die verlorene Bibliothek. Autobiographie einer Kultur*
1959: *Berlin-Dada*

ERNST MEISTER

Born 1911 in Hagen-Haspe, Westphalia. He was called the author of a 'Kandinsky-poetry'; he is, unfortunately, far less known than those writers who crave to monopolize literary fashion nowadays, yet Meister's mastery of dialectic word-artifices puts him by the side of most refined craftsmen of the poetic *chiffre* in the contemporary scene.

Poetry

1932: *Ausstellung*
1953: *Unterm schwarzen Schafpelz*
1957: *Fermate*
      . . . und Ararat
1962: *Flut und Stein*
1964: *Gedichte 1932–64*

MAX MELL

Born 1882 in Marburg an der Drau. Author of popular mystery plays in which the religious conversion of criminals is brought about by the purity of a human soul.

Drama
1923: *Das Apostelspiel*
1927: *Das Nachfolge-Christi-Spiel*

Max Mell not only blends the religious with the criminal elements in man but also the old myths with modern interpretation: e.g. in his tragedies:

1932: *Die Sieben gegen Theben*
1944: *Der Nibelunge Not*
1951: *Kriemhilds Rache*
1955: *Jeanne d'Arc*

1962: *Ges. Werke: Prosa, Dramen, Verse*, 4 vols.

GUSTAV MEYRINK (Ps. for Gustav Meyer)

Born 1868 in Vienna. Died 1932 in Starnberg, Oberbayern. Author of grotesque novels and short stories; contributor to the *Simplizissimus*. Famous for his *Golem* novel, 1915: Golem (Hebr. = embryo) is the creation of a Rabbi who gives life to his figure of clay; it cannot speak; Meyrinck's Golem, with a Mongolian face, reappears after a period of thirty-three years and represents the ghetto spirit of the Jews in Prague.

Other novels
1916: *Das grüne Gesicht*
1921: *Der weiße Dominikaner*

Short, satirical stories
1909 ff.: *Des deutschen Spießers Wunderhorn*

KARL MICKEL

Born 1935 in Dresden. Now living in East Berlin. He is with Adolf Endler the co-editor of the Anthology: *In diesem besseren Land*, which appeared in DDR, and in which W. Biermann is unfortunately ignored; see W. Biermann, p. 47.

Poetry
1967: *Vita nova mea*

AGNES MIEGEL

Born 1879 in Königsberg. Died 1964 in Salzuflen, nr. Bielefeld, buried in Bad Nenndorf, nr. Hanover. Friendship with Lulu von Strauss und Torney and with Baron von Münchhausen. Agnes Miegel is considered the greatest German ballad-writer of the twentieth century.

Poetry
1901: *Gedichte*
1907: *Balladen und Lieder*
1927: *Ges. Gedichte*

Stories
1926: *Geschichten aus Altpreußen*
1949: *Die Blume der Götter*
      Apotheose
1951: *Der Federball*
1962: *Heimkehr*

1953–5: *Ges. Werke*, 7 vols.; see also KLW
1967: Anni Porreck: *Agnes Miezel*

ERIKA MITTERER (married Petrowsky)

Born 1906 in Vienna. Contact with Rilke; see Rilke's *Briefwechsel in Gedichten mit Erika Mitterer*, 1950.

Poetry
1930: *Dank des Lebens*
1935: *Gesang der Wandernden*
1946: *Zwölf Gedichte 1933–1945*

WALTER VON MOLO

Born 1880 in Sternberg (Mähren). Died 1958 in Murnau, Oberbayern. Author of several important historical-biographical novels:

1912–16: *Der Schiller Roman*, 4 vols.:
      I. *Ums Menschentum*
      II. *Im Titanenkampf*

III. *Die Freiheit*
IV. *Den Sternen zu*
1922, 1924: *Fridericus-Rex*—Trilogie *Der Roman meines Volkes*:
    I. *Fridericus*
    II. *Luise, Königin von Preußen*
    III. *Das Volk wacht auf*

Other novels
1925: *Bobenmatz*
1928: *Bruder Luther*
1931: *Friedrich List*
1950: *Die Affen Gottes*

Autobiography
1957: *So wunderbar ist das Leben*

ALFRED MOMBERT

Born 1872 in Karlsruhe. Died 1942 in Winterthur, Switzerland. Mombert, like Wolfskehl, felt deeply rooted in his Jewish and German cultural heritage. His arrest in 1940 and his rescue from the concentration camp (by his friend Hans Reinhart who gave him asylum in Winterthur) are depicted as a cosmic struggle between Sfaira (the old poet) and a daemon.

Poetry
1896: *Der Glühende*
1897: *Die Schöpfung*
1901: *Der Denker*
1905: *Die Blüte des Chaos*
1909: *Der himmlische Zecher*

Dramatic trilogy
1907–11: *Aeon*:
    (1) *Aeon der Weltgesuchte*
    (2) *Aeon zwischen den Frauen*
    (3) *Aeon vor Syrakus*

Myth
1936–42: *Sfaira der Alte*

1963: *Alfred Mombert: Dichtungen*, Gesamtausgabe, 3 vols.

In his imagery and concept of myth A. Mombert shows a certain affinity to Blake and Nietzsche.

FRANZ MON (Ps. for Franz Löffelholz)

Born 1926 in Frankfurt a.M.

Poetry
1959: *artikulationen*
1960: *protokoll an der kette*
1962: *verläufe*

Mon is an admirer of Dadaism, Surrealism and of Kurt Schwitters. His grotesques have the characteristics of a highly conscious collage; see also Gomringer, and pp. 95-6.

CHRISTIAN MORGENSTERN

Born 1871 in Munich. Died 1914 in Meran. He was the son of a landscape painter; almost only known for his playful, nonsense poems, but also master of serious poetry. Under the influence of R. Steiner, Schopenhauer, Nietzsche, Dehmel, etc.

Poetry
1905: *Galgenlieder*
1906: *Melancholie*
1910: *Palmström*
     Einkehr
1911: *Ich und Du* (Sonette, Ritornelle, Lieder)

1928: *Die Schallmühle* and 1960: *Aphorismen und Sprüche*, ed. posth.
    by Margarete Morgenstern

ARMIN MÜLLER

Born 1928 in Schweidnitz. Since 1945 in Weimar. Author of politically committed poems:

1953: *Seit jenem Mai*
1959: *Das weiße Schiff*

KARL CHRISTIAN MÜLLER (Ps. Teut Ansolt)

Born 1900 in Saarlouis. Tr. of modern English lyrical poetry.

Poetry
1929: *Kranz des Jünglings*
1954: *Wünschelrute*
1966: *Die Sandrose* (Gesänge). It is symbol of the desert (of time)
    and of fertility

Story
1943: *Bibelschreiber*

BÖRRIES FREIHERR VON MÜNCHHAUSEN (Ps. H. Albrecht)

Born 1874 in Hildesheim. Died 1945, suicide, in Windischleuba
nr. Altenburg, Saxony. His models were Theodor Fontane and
Moritz von Strachwitz, but he was perhaps more effective as a
theorist than a writer of ballads. In his *Meisterballaden* (1923) he
expounds his own views on the 'Ballade'.

Poetry
1911: *Herz im Harnisch*
1916: *Die Standarte*
1924: *Das Balladenbuch*, enlarged ed. 1950
1928: *Idyllen und Lieder*

ROBERT MUSIL

Born 1880 in Klagenfurt of old Austrian officer and civil service
family. Father professor at Brno Technical University. Military
academy with view to career as officer, but left to study engineering. Appointments at various Technical Academies at Brno,
Stuttgart and Vienna. Studied philosophy in Berlin, wrote
dissertation on epistemological subject. Published first book in
1906, thereafter wrote steadily but slowly: his most celebrated
work, the huge novel *Der Mann ohne Eigenschaften*, remained unfinished. Served as Austrian officer from 1914 to 1918, afterwards

discharged various civil service appointments. Left Germany for Vienna in 1933, settled in Zürich and then Geneva in 1938. Died 1942 in Geneva.

Musil's work has been slow to appear and his fame as one of the most significant modern European novelists is of recent date. His most important external experience seems to have been the decay of modern European culture, symbolized for him in the collapse of Austria-Hungary (the 'Kakanien' of his major novel). Musil has not only succeeded in limning the physiognomy of an epoch: he has also given artistic shape to his own feeling that possible, as well as real, spatial and temporal existents and relationships have an equal ontological—and therefore aesthetic—validity.

Novels
1906: *Die Verwirrungen des Zöglings Törless*
1930, 1933, 1943: *Der Mann ohne Eigenschaften*

Novellen
1911: *Die Vereinigungen*
1924: *Drei Frauen*
1952 ff.: *Ges. Werke*, 4 vols.

Study
1961: Burton Pike: *Robert Musil: an introduction to his work*
1966: H. W. Reichert: *Nietzschean influence in Musil's Der Mann ohne Eigenschaften*, German Quarterly, XXXIX
1968: Elizabeth J. Boa: *Austrian Ironies in Musil's Drei Frauen*, MLR, Jan.
    Elisabeth Stopp: *Musil's 'Törless'. Content and Form*, MLR, Jan.

J. B. Bednall

FRANZ NABL

Born 1883 in Lautschin (Bohemia). Austrian writer concerned with the presentation of human behaviour in cold objective terms with occasional surrealist undertones.

Novels
1908: *Hans Jäckels erstes Liebesjahr*

1911: *Ödhof* (perhaps still his best-known work)
1917: *Das Grab des Lebendigen* (*Die Ortliebschen Frauen*, 1936)
1921: *Die Galgenfrist*
1935: *Ein Mann von gestern*

Short stories
1911: *Narrentanz*
1919: *Der Tag der Erkenntnis*
1923: *Die Augen*
1935: *Das Meteor*
1937: *Der Fund*
1943: *Kleine Freilichtbühne*
1946: *Mein Onkel Barnabas*
1962: *Der erloschene Stern*

Drama
1925: *Trieschübel*

Autobiographical writings
1938: *Steirische Lebenswanderung*
1963: *Die zweite Heimat*

Ian Hilton

ALFRED NEUMANN

Born 1895 in Lautenburg (West Prussia). Died 1952 in Lugano.
Emigrated 1933; author of historical novels. Internationally
known for his story (1925): *Der Patriot* (the patriotic murderer of
the mad Tsar Paul I commits suicide). The work was later filmed
(with Emil Jannings) and dramatized.

Novels
1926: *Der Teufel*
1927: *Die Rebellen* (the Italian irredenta revolt against the Austrian regime)

Romantrilogie on Napoleon III
1934: *Neuer Caesar*
1936: *Kaiserreich*
1941: *Die Volksfreunde*

ROBERT NEUMANN

Born 1897 in Vienna. Emigrated in 1934; took English nationality; lives at Locarno. Writing both in English and in German.

Literary parodies and satires
1927: *Mit fremden Federn*
1932: *Unter falscher Flagge*

Novels
1929: *Sintflut* (theme: the inflation in Austria)
1930, 1952: *Hochstapler-Novelle*; new title: *Die Insel der Circe*
1939 (in English), 1945 (in German): *An den Wassern von Babylon*

WOLF VON NIEBELSCHÜTZ

Born 1913 in Berlin. Died 1960 in Düsseldorf. An original personality, opposed to '*Blut-und-Boden-Literatur*' as well as to cerebral language experiments in contemporary lyrical poetry.

Poetry
1939: *Preis der Gnaden*
1942: *Die Musik macht Gott allein*
1962: *Gedichte und Dramen* (posth.)

Novels
1949: *Der blaue Kammerherr*, in four parts
1959: *Die Kinder der Finsternis*

FRIEDRICH NIETZSCHE

Born 1844 in Röcken, nr. Lützen. Died 1900 in Weimar. See p. 1 ff. In 1869 professor of classical philology in Basel; friendship with R. Wagner; since 1889 struck down by madness.

1871: *Geburt der Tragödie aus dem Geiste der Musik*
1873–5: *Unzeitgemäße Betrachtungen*
1878: *Menschliches, Allzumenschliches*
1880: *Morgenröte. Gedanken über die moralischen Vorurteile*
1881–6: *Die fröhliche Wissenschaft*
1883–5: *Also sprach Zarathustra*

1884–8: *Der Wille zur Macht*
1886: *Jenseits von Gut und Böse*
1888: *Der Antichrist*
   Der Fall Wagner
   Ecce Homo
   Dionysos—Dithyramben

1906 ff.: *Werke*, ed. by E. Förster-Nietzsche and R. Oehler,
   11 vols.
1933 ff.: *Hist krit. Ed.*, Nietzsche-Archiv

Studies
1918: Ernst Bertram: *Versuch einer Mythologie*
1926: Ludwig Klages: *Die psychologischen Errungenschaften
   Nietzsches*
1931: A. Bäumler: *Nietzsche, der Philosoph und Politiker*

HANS ERICH NOSSACK

Born 30 Jan. 1901 in Hamburg.

Stories
1947: *Nekyia. Bericht eines Überlebenden*
1948: *Interview mit dem Tode* (shorter prose); 2nd ed. 1950, entitled *Dorothea*
1955: *Spätestens im November*
1956: *Spirale. Roman einer schlaflosen Nacht*
1958: *Der jüngere Bruder*
1961: *Nach dem letzten Aufstand*
1963: *Begegnung im Vorraum* (collected tales)
1964: *Das kennt man*
1965: *Das Testament des Lucius Eurinus*

Drama
1949: *Die Rotte Kain*
1956: *Die Hauptprobe*
1963: *Ein Sonderfall*

Poetry
1947: *Gedichte*

Essays

1966: *Die schwache Position der Literatur* (collected talks and essays)

Studies

1962: Horst Bienek: *Werkstattgespräche mit Schriftstellern*
1963: Marcel Reich-Ranicki: *Deutsche Literatur in West und Ost*
1965: P. Prochnik: *Controlling Thoughts in the Work of Hans Erich Nossack* (GLL), Oct.
1966: Brian Keith-Smith: *Hans Erich Nossack* (Essays on Contemporary German Literature, IV)

The author's disillusionment with post-war society is reflected in the desperate efforts of the individual to establish a personal identity. In the struggle against rationalization a visonary world emerges, based on instinctive spiritual values rather than social or religious ideologies.

P. H. Hubsch

ROSE NYLAND

Born 1929 in Chemnitz. Emigrated to Norway and Sweden. 1951 returned to DDR; politically committed poems:
1959: *Genoße Mensch*
1961: *Und waren dennoch Sieger*

ANDREAS OKOPENKO

Born 1930 in Košice, Czechoslovakia

Poetry
1957: *Grüner November*
1963: *Seltene Tage*

Story
1967: *Die Belege des Michael Cetus*

DR OWLGLASS (Ps. for Hans Erich Blaich)

Born 1873 in Leutkirch (Allgäu). Died 1945 in Fürstenfeldbruck, nr. Munich. Chefredakteur of the *Simplizissimus* for several years. He tr. Aristophanes: *Vögel*: also Rabelais, Master of humorous and subtle poems; has a predilection for eccentricities.

Poetry
1904: *Der saure Apfel*
1910: *Gottes Blasebalg*
1917: *Käuze*

ALFONS PAQUET

Born 1881 in Wiesbaden. Died 1944 in Frankfurt. Author of several travel books about England, America, Russia, etc. Founder of the so-called *Bund rheinischer Dichter*, of which he was Director until 1933, but he did not emigrate. Paquet sings of the mystery of the towns, which he calls 'the proudest fruits of Nature'.

Drama
1927: *William Penn*

Poetry
1902: *Lieder und Gesänge*
1912: *Held Namenlos*
1956: *Gedichte*, ed. by A. von Bernus

RUDOLF PAULSEN

Born 1883 in Berlin. Member of the '*Charon*' circle under Otto zur Linde; see p. 320.

Poetry
1911: *Gespräche des Lebens*
1924: *Die kosmische Fibel*
1955: *Träume des Tritonen*
1964: *Schwarz und Weiß auf blauem Grunde*

1934: *Kunst und Glaube, Briefe an einen jungen Maler*

ERNST PENZOLDT

Born 1892 in Erlangen. Died 1955 in Munich. Poet, sculptor, painter, novelist and playwright.

Poetry
1922: *Der Gefährte*

Novels

1928: *Der arme Chatterton*

1930: *Die Powenzbande* (his most successful novel)

1934: *Kleiner Erdenwurm*

1938: *Die Leute aus der Mohrenapotheke* (new version of his novel: *Der Zwerg*, 1927)

Story

1941: *Korporal Mombour*; its film title: *Es kommt ein Tag*, 1950

Drama

1946: *Die verlorenen Schuhe*, comedy which later appeared under the title *Der Diogenes von Paris*, 1948

1949–62: *Ges. Schriften*, 4 vols.

1966: Ernst Penzoldt's *The treasure*, tr. by A. J. Pomerans, ed. by W. E. Yuill: *German Narrative Prose*, 2nd vol., London

ALFONS PETZOLD

Born 1882 in Vienna. Died 1923 in Kitzbühel, Tirol. Most notable Austrian 'worker poet'; influenced by Rilke; befriended by Felix Braun.

Poetry

1912: *Der Ewige und die Stunde*

1915: *Volk, mein Volk*

1916: *Der stählerne Schrei*

1919: *Der Dornbusch* (Soziale Gedichte)

1922: *Gesang von Morgen bis Mittag* (Auswahlband)

Novels

1913: *Erde*

1920: *Das rauhe Leben*, autobiographical

FRANZ PFEMFERT

Born 1879 in East Prussia. Died 1954 in Mexico. 1911 founder of the journal *Aktion*; not committed to any particular party but enemy of militarism and nationalism. Anarchist, pacifist, Spartakist, later Trotskyist. The early contributors to Pfemfert's *Aktion* were: Heym, van Hoddis, Stadler, Lichtenstein, and Blass, but Ernst Blass (born 1890 in Berlin, died 1939 in Berlin) soon preferred Stefan George's disciplined verse-form to Expressionism.

P. Raabe: *Die Aktion ed. by Franz Pfemfert 1911–14*, 1961; and *Die Zeitschriften und Sammlungen des literarischen Expressionismus*, 1964

HEINZ PIONTEK

Born 1925 in Kreuzburg, Silesia. Mainly poet, also essayist and story-writer; see p. 42 and p. 371.

Poetry
1952: *Die Furt*
1953: *Die Rauchfahne*
1957: *Wassermarken*
1962: *Mit einer Kranichfeder*
1966: *Klartext*

Novel
1967: *Die mittleren Jahre* (Piontek's first novel)

1949: Ed. *Aus meines Herzens Grunde* (Evangelische Lyrik aus vier Jahrhunderten)
1960: tr. *John Keats: Gedichte*

THEODOR PLIVIER (really Plievier)

Born 1892 in Berlin. Many jobs in many parts of the world, including Australia and South America. Sailor during First World War, took part in Wilhelmshaven meeting in 1918, then activities as left-wing publicist during 1920s. Emigrated to Russia in 1933, returned to East Germany in 1945; settled on Lake Constance. Died 1955 at Avegno (Lugano). His novels are based mainly on personal experience and conform to the doctrinaire social realism he avowed. The episodic and didactic tendencies which are his main weakness as a writer prove well adapted for depicting the fate of the German 6th Army in *Stalingrad*, his best (and internationally known) work.

Novels

1929: *Des Kaisers Kuli*
1932: *Der Kaiser ging, die Generäle blieben*
1945: *Stalingrad*
1952: *Moskau*
1954: *Berlin*

J. B. Bednall

JOHANNES POETHEN

Born 1928 in Wickrath, Niederrhein.

Poetry

1952: *Lorbeer über gestirntem Haupt*
1956: *Risse des Himmels*
1958: *Stille im trockenen Dorn*
1966: *Wohnstadt zwischen den Atemzügen*

PAULA VON PRERADOVIČ (married name P. Molden)

Born 1887 in Vienna. Died 1951 in Vienna. Grand-daughter of the Croatian poet P. v. Preradovič. Author of the text of the *National Anthem* of the second Republic of Austria; see GLL 1954.

Poetry

1933: *Dalmatinische Sonette*
1946: *Ritter, Tod und Teufel*
1950–2: *Ges. Gedichte*, 3 vols.

Stories

1940: *Pave und Pero*. Her only novel; life-story of her ancestors
1950: *Königslegende*

KUNE RAEBER

Born 1922 in Klingnau, Switzerland; mainly lyrical poet.

Poetry

1950: *Gesicht im Mittag*
1957: *Die verwandelten Schiffe*

1960: *Gedichte*
1963: *Flußufer*

FRIEDRICH RASCHE

Born 1900 nr. Radeberg nr. Dresden. Died in 1965 in Hanover. Poet, essayist, story-writer; since 1945 Feuilleton-Chef of the *Hannoversche Presse*. His literary output is small but of fine quality.

Poetry
1949: *Gedichte*
1967 (posth.): *Aus allen Winden*

Novellen
1948: *Die Gehenkten*. Fünf Geschichten; amongst these stories the first *Untergang eines Orchesters* symbolizes the apocalyptic era through which his own generation in Germany and the whole of Europa had to pass; the author depicts the destruction of an orchestra through their conductor—a demon incarnate

HANS REHBERG

Born 1901 in Posen. Died 1963 in Duisburg. Mainly playwright, whose models were Grabbe, Büchner, H. von Kleist, etc. Acknowledged by the 'Third Reich'.

Drama
Author of the cycle of dramas about Prussian rulers:
1934: *Der große Kurfürst*
1935: *Friedrich I*
      Friedrich Wilhelm I
1936: *Friedrich der Große*

and the tragedies
1949: *Elisabeth und Essex*
1950: *Wallenstein*
1956: *Rembrandt*

HANS JOSÉ REHFISCH (Ps. Georg Turner, René Kestner)

Born 1891 in Berlin. Died 1960 in Schuls, Switzerland (Unterengadin). Emigrated to London, became President of 'Club 43'.

Later he went to New York, then returned to Germany. Mainly playwright.

Drama

1920: *Der Chauffeur Martin*

1929: (together with Wilhelm Herzog) *Die Affäre Dreyfus*
Pietro Aretino

1938: *The Iron Road* (German version, 1952)

1955: *Oberst Chabert* (Heimkehrer-Tragödie), based on Balzac's story

Novels

1951: *Die Hexen von Paris*

1959: *Lysistratas Hochzeit*

1944: he edited a Symposium: *In Tyrannos* (Four centuries of Struggle against Tyranny in Germany, with chapters on Hutten (from whom the motto of the edition is taken), Thomas Münzer, Leibnitz, Lessing, Hegel, Büchner, Boerne and Heine, 1848, Karl Marx, Ferdinand Lassalle, Bebel, Liebknecht, Nietzsche, Spartacus, Karl Kraus, Rahel Varnhagen and Rosa Luxemburg, etc.)

MAX REINHARDT

Born 1873 in Baden, nr. Vienna. Died 1943 in New York. 1933 emigration. Max Reinhardt the producer and theatre manager intuitively understood and exploited the pleasure man takes in anything theatrical. 1924 he became Director of the 'Theater in der Josephstadt' and created the so-called 'Josephstädter Theaterstil'. In the U.S.A. Reinhardt founded a school of actors and theatre directors at Hollywood. He produced his grandiose artistic spectacles in or outside cathedrals (e.g. the Salzburger Festspiele), in Baroque mansions or in halls, i.e. 1911, Vollmoeller's *Mirakel*, in London, Olympia Hall; cf. 1930: *Die Spielpläne Max Reinhardts 1905–1930*, ed. by Franz Horch, and 1961: H. Jhering: *Von Reinhardt bis Brecht. Vier Jahrzehnte Theater und Film*, 3 vols.

CHRISTA REINIG

Born 1926 in Berlin. Art historian and poet.

Poetry
1960: *Die Steine von Finisterre*
1963: *Gedichte*

Stories
1965: *Drei Schiffe* (Prosa-Auswahl)

Radio-play
1968: *Das Aquarium*

There is a Brechtian spite in many of her ballads and parodies and witheringly cold observations: e.g.

> '. . . Ich bin so eingewohnt in mist
> und achte nicht mehr auf behausung.
> Wenn goethezweihundertjahrgeburtstagsfeier ist
> Dann geh ich gerade zur entlausung . . .'

ERICH MARIA REMARQUE (real name Erich Paul Remark)

Born 1898 at Osnabrück. Took part in First World War, then various jobs, finally became journalist. Started writing novels in 1920, achieved world fame with *Im Westen nichts Neues* (1929), a report on the 'lost generation' of the War. This most famous of anti-war novels achieves its effects by the objective portrayal of the impact of trench warfare upon a sensitive youth, told from the unheroic, anti-militaristic, ranker's point of view. Its weakness lies in the self-defeating effect of piling on excessive distressing detail. As in Remarque's later novels, the human power of survival in extreme situations (inflation, emigration, National Socialism) is depicted. Remarque settled in New York in 1939, became an American citizen in 1947.

Other novels of his
1931: *Der Weg zurück*, filmed as *The Way Back*
1946: *Arc de Triomphe*
1963: *Die Nacht von Lissabon*

J. B. Bednall

HANS WERNER RICHTER

Born 1908 in Bansin auf Usedom (Pomerania). Son of fisherman. Book-trade in Berlin, 1933 emigrated to Paris, served in Second World War (American P.o.W.); edited (1947) periodical *Der Ruf* (banned by Occupying Powers); founder in September 1947 of 'Group 47'; at present living in Munich. Novels written in neo-realistic style known to the Group as 'Kahlschlag'; deal mostly with immediately post-war experiences.

Novels
1949: *Die Geschlagenen*
1951: *Sie fielen aus Gottes Hand*
1953: *Spuren im Sand*
1959: *Linus Fleck oder der Verlust der Würde*

J. B. Bednall

WERNER RIEGEL

Born 1925 in Danzig. Died 1956 in Hamburg.

Poetry
1956: *Heiße Lyrik*, together with Peter Rühmkorf
1961: *Gedichte und Prosa*

WERNER RIEMERSCHMID

Born 1895 in Maria Enzersdorf, Lower Austria; died 1967; story-writer, playwright, but mainly poet.

Poetry
1936: *Das verzauberte Jahr*
1942: *Der Bote in Zwielicht*
1953: *Ergebnisse* (Gedichte und Aphorismen)
1965: Steinbrüche

RAINER MARIA RILKE

Born 1875 in Prague. Died 1926 in the Sanatorium Val-Mont; see p. 6.

Poetry
1894: *Leben und Lieder*

1896: *Larenopfer*
1897: *Traumgekrönt*
1898: *Advent*
1899–1903: *Das Stundenbuch* (in drei Büchern), publ. 1905
1898–1906: *Das Buch der Bilder*, 1902 first ed.
1907–8: *Neue Gedichte* (in two parts)
1908–9: *Das Requiem*
1912: *Das Marienleben*
1912–22: *Duineser Elegien* and *Sonette an Orpheus*
1935: *Poèmes Français*
1927, 1934: *Späte Gedichte*
1906–26: *Gedichte*, publ. 1953 (*Poems 1906–26*, tr. and introduced
    by J. B. Leishman, 1957)

Stories, descriptions and novels
1902: *Worpswede*
1903–7: *Auguste Rodin* (in two parts)
1904: *Geschichten vom lieben Gott*
1904–10: *Die Aufzeichnungen des Malte Laurids Brigge*
1906: *Die Weise von Liebe und Tod des Cornets Christoph Rilke*
    (written 1899)

Briefe
An einen jungen Dichter (Fr. X. Kappus)
An eine junge Frau (Lisa Heise)
Briefwechsel with Lou Andreas-Salomé (see p. 204)
Fürstin Marie von Thurn und Taxis, André Gide, Katharina
    Kippenberg, Benvenuta (Magda von Hattingberg), etc.

Some of Rilke's own translations
1908: *Elizabeth Barrett-Brownings Sonette nach dem Portugiesischen*
1913: *Portugiesische Briefe* (*Marianna Alcoforado*)
1913–19. *Michelangelo: Sonette*
1923–5: *Paul Valéry: Gedichte*
1927: *Paul Valéry: Eupalinos oder die Architektur*

Studies
1966: Ingeborg Schnack, ed. *Rilkes Leben und Werk im Bild*
    E. Zinn, ed. *Sämtliche Werke in sechs Bänden*
    K. Altheim, ed. R. M. Rilke: *Briefe*

1931: *Rainer Maria Rilke. A Study in Poetry and Mysticism*, by Federico Olivero

1938: *Rilke's Apotheosis*, by Eudo C. Mason
Rainer Maria Rilke. Aspects of his Mind and Poetry, ed. by William Rose and C. Craig Houston, with an introduction by Stefan Zweig

1941: *Rainer Maria Rilke*, by E. M. Butler, re-ed. 1946

1943: *The Heritage of Symbolism*, by C. M. Bowra, pp. 56–97, 'Rainer Maria Rilke'

1949: *Rilke. Man and Poet*, by Nora Wydenbruck

1957: *Rainer Maria Rilke's Poetic Vision*, by A. Closs, in *Medusa's Mirror*

1957: I. Parry: *Malte's Hand*, GLL, XI

1959: H. J. Weigand: *Rilke's 'archäischer Torso Apollos'*, Monatshefte, LI

1960: H. F. Peters: *Rainer Maria Rilke; Masks and the Man*, Seattle

1965: *Rainer Maria Rilke's Duineser Elegien*, ed. with notes and introduction by E. L. Stahl, Blackwell's German Texts

The discerning notes and introductions in J. B. Leishman's trs. are indispensable to the Rilke scholars.

JOACHIM RINGELNATZ (Ps. for Hans Bötticher)

Born 1883 in Wurzen, Saxony. Died 1934 in Berlin. 'Ringelnatz' means ringed snake, water-adder, or also little seahorse. He is the poet of everyday trivialities. Not only subject-matter, but also the form of much of the cynical 'Asphalt' poetry is at the mercy of Ringelnatz's clownery.

1912: *Schnupftabakdose* (Stumpfsinn in Versen), together with R. J. M. Seewald

1923: *Kuttel Daddeldu*

1952: *Ausgewählte Gedichte*

1953: *Rororingelnatz*

Study

1964: *Joachim Ringelnatz in Selbstzeugnissen und Bilddokumenten*, by Herbert Günther

LUISE RINSER

Born 1911 in Pitzling, Upper Bavaria. The conflict—particularly for the woman—between passion and conscience is a recurring theme in her work, in which the Christian-humanist note becomes increasingly stronger.

Novels
1948: *Die Stärkeren*
1950: *Mitte des Lebens*
1953: *Daniela*
1955: *Der Sündenbock*
1957: *Abenteuer in der Tugend* (together with *Mitte des Lebens*) forms
        Nina, 1961
1962: *Die vollkommene Freude*
1966: *Ich bin Tobias*

Short stories
1940: *Die gläsernen Ringe*
1946: *Erste Liebe*
1948: *Jan Lobel aus Warschau*
1956: *Ein Bündel weißer Narzissen*
1959: *Geh fort, wenn du kannst*
1962: *Vom Sinn der Traurigkeit*
1964: *Septembertag*

Essays and miscellaneous writings
1946: *Gefängnistagebuch*
1960: *Der Schwerpunkt*
1964: *Über die Hoffnung*

Ian Hilton

HEINZ RISSE
Born 1898 in Düsseldorf.

Novels (and other prose fiction)
1948: *Irrfahrer*
1950: *Wenn die Erde bebt* (English, *The Earthquake*, 1953)
1951: *So frei von Schuld*
1953: *Dann kam der Tag*
        Belohne dich selbst (short stories)

1956: *Große Fahrt und falsches Spiel*
1958: *Buchhalter Gottes* (short stories)
1959: *Die Schiffschaukel* (short stories)
1962: *Fort geht's wie auf Samt* (short stories)
1963: *Ringelreihen*
n.d.: *Macht und Schicksal einer Leiche*

Autobiography
1968: '*Jahrgang 1898*' (in the vol. *Jahr und Jahrgang 1898*), ed. Joachim Karsten

Themes such as order and chaos, justice and revenge, crime and punishment, providence and chance are unfolded with narrative tension in Heinz Risse's novels and tales.

H. M. Waidson

KARL RÖTTGER

Born 1877 in Lübbecke in Westphalia. Died in 1942. Friendship with Otto zur Linde and co-editor of the *Charon*; poet, playwright, novelist; author of *Christuslegenden*.

Poetry
1909: *Wenn deine Seele einfach wird*
1912: *Die Lieder von Gott und dem Tod*

1958: *Ausgewählte Werke*, ed. by Hella Röttger and Hanns Martin Elster

PETER ROSEGGER

Born 1843 in Krieglach (Styria), Austria. Son of poor peasants. Died 1918 in Krieglach. A most popular author, Heimatdichter; stories on customs and people of his country. Since 1876 until his death editor of the monthly journal *Heimgarten*.

Poetry
1870: his first book of poems *Zither und Hackbrett* (poems in the dialect of Upper Styria)

Some of his most popular stories
1875: *Die Schriften des Waldschulmeisters*

1877: *Waldheimat. Erinnerungen aus der Jugendzeit*
1883: *Der Gottsucher* (novel, 2 vols.)
1885: *Bergpredigten*
1902: Stories: *Als ich noch der Waldbauernbub war* (3 vols.)
1908: *Alpensommer*

1913 ff.: *Ges. Werke*, 40 vols.; see also KLW and DLL

EUGEN ROTH

Born 1895 in Munich. His early work is reminiscent of Expressionist lyrical form.

Poetry
1918: *Die Dinge, die unendlich uns umkreisen*
1921: *Erde, der Versöhnung Stern*
1922: *Der Ruf.* Vaterländische Sonette
1959: *Heitere Verse*
1964: *Der letzte Mensch*

JOSEPH ROTH

Born 1894 in Schwabendorf, Volhynia, of Jewish-Slavonic
origin. Died 1939 in Paris. After serving two years (1916–18) in
the War, Roth worked as a journalist in Vienna and from 1921 in
Berlin; from 1923 to 1932 he was a regular contributor to the
Frankfurter Zeitung. Emigrated from Germany in 1933 and lived
mainly in a Paris hotel until 1939, when he died, an alcoholic, in
a hospital for the poor.

Novels
1924: *Hotel Savoy*
      Die Rebellion
1927: *Die Flucht ohne Ende*
1928: *Zipper und sein Vater*
1929: *Rechts und Links*
1930: *Hiob*
1932: *Radetzkymarsch*
1934: *Tarabas*
1935: *Die Hundert Tage*

1936: *Beichte eines Mörders*
1937: *Das falsche Gewicht*
1938: *Die Kapuzinergruft*
1939: *Die Geschichte von der 1002. Nacht*
1966: *Der stumme Prophet*

Studies
1956: Hermann Kesten: *Einleitung zu Joseph Roths Werken* (Band 1)
1957: Karl August Horst: *Joseph Roths Schattenlinie* (in *Merkur*, 110. 11. Heft 4)
    Franz Schonauer: *Über den Dichter Joseph Roth* (in *Akzente*, 4)

In his novels Roth describes the fate of people who lived in the Austro-Hungarian Empire, and particularly its eastern provinces, during the opening decades of the twentieth century. His characters range from aristocratic soldiers to impoverished Jewish teachers. In spite of the variety of their occupations they have three things in common: they are all subjects of the Austrian monarchy, they are all involved in the Great War, and they all experience loneliness. These three factors are inseparable, for the War brought about the end of the monarchy and thus destroyed the values which lent meaning to their lives. In the only novel, which is not set at all in Eastern Europe, *Die 100 Tage*, Roth deals once again with the love and loyalty of a subject to the Emperor, Napoleon. Roth's main interest is in the fate of human beings and not in politics.

G. L. Jones

LUDWIG RUBINER

Born 1881 in Berlin. Died 1920 in Berlin. Contributor to *Die Aktion* and *Die weißen Blätter*.

Poetry
1916: *Das himmlische Licht*

Essays
1917: *Der Mensch in der Mitte*

1919: ed. of *Kameraden der Menschheit*

PETER RÜHMKORF

Born 1929 in Dortmund. Poet in 'Group 47'. Ruthless satirist and parodist. Under the Ps. 'Leslie Meier' he attacked severely German post-war poets and critics; he was editor of the much-read and feared Hamburger Studenten-Kurier *Konkret*. With Enzensberger he is one of the influential 'angry young men' of present-day Germany.

1956: with Werner Riegel—author of the poems: *Heiße Lyrik*,
cf. W. Stammler's *Aufriß*, l.c., 2nd vol., 2nd ed., p. 344 f.
1959: in *Irdisches Vergnügen in G*, he parodies B. H. Brockes' style
1962: *Kunststücke: 50 Gedichte nebst einer Anleitung zum Widerspruch*
1961: A monograph on Wolfgang Borchert

Rühmkorf is master in making fun of literary treasures. Thus also Klopstock's magnificent *Zürchersee* Ode does not escape Rühmkorf's debunking verse:

'Schön ist, Mutter Natur, deiner Erfindung Pracht
mit entspanntem Munde gepriesen,
schöner ein künstlich Gebiß' . . .

His recent collection of pop-songs and gutter poetry: *Über das Volksvermögen—Exkurse in den literarischen Untergrund*, 1967, is an amusing and refreshing attack on bourgeois inhibitions and taboos; in an appendix some Sixth-Form lyrics, so-called *Primanerverse*, are added; see also p. 19.

NELLY SACHS

Born 1891 in Berlin. Now in Stockholm; was saved during the War by Prince Eugen of Sweden and Selma Lagerlöf, shortly before the latter's death (1940). Nobel Prize in 1966. Sachs' writing is inspired by her vision of the historical privileges and 'blessings' of the Jewish people, i.e. to have to suffer more than the other races, and that it is the persecuted ones who are in God's Grace; hatred and revenge must not and cannot be the fundaments of a new and happier future.

Poetry
1946: *In den Wohnungen des Todes*
1949: *Sternverdunkelung*

1961: *Fahrt ins Staublose*, collected poems
1962: *Zeichen im Sand* (scenic poems or 'poetic plays')
1964: *Glühende Rätsel*

Drama
1951: *Mysterienspiel Eli*, a mystery of the sorrows of Israel, tr. into
   English by Christopher Holme

1961: *Nelly Sachs zu Ehren*, contributions by I. Aichinger,
   G. Eich, H. M. Enzensberger, H. Kasack, etc.

ERNST VON SALOMON

Born 1902 in Kiel. Involved in the Walther Rathenau murder,
1922; five years' hard labour.

Autobiography
1931: *Die Geächteten*

Autobiographical novel:
1951: *Der Fragebogen*

ODA SCHAEFER (O. Lange)

Born 1900 in Berlin. First married to the painter Albert Schaefer,
second marriage to Horst Lange.

Poetry
1939: *Die Windharfe*
1946: *Irdisches Geleit*
1959: *Grasmelodie*

Author of radio-plays, e.g.
Mozart auf der Reise nach Prag, after Mörike's Novelle
Die schöne Magelone
Gösta Berling

WILHELM SCHÄFER

Born 1868 in Ottrau, Hesse. Died 1952 in Überlingen am Bodensee.

Friendship with R. Dehmel; writer of short stories and master oɪ anecdotes; essayist. Ed. of the magazine *Die Rheinlande*.

Stories
1908: *Anekdoten*
        Rheinsagen
1913: *Die unterbrochene Rheinfahrt*
1925: *Hölderlins Einkehr*

Essays and interpretations
1922 and 1953: *Die Dreizehn Bücher der deutschen Seele*
1933: *Deutsche Reden*; about Dürer, Pestalozzi, Goethe, Beethoven, etc.
1934: *Mein Leben*. Autobiography

1937–43: C. Höfer: *W. Schäfer—Bibliographie*, 2 vols.

ALBRECHT SCHAEFFER

Born 1885 in Elbing, West Prussia. Died 1950 in Munich. Poet, essayist, prose-writer. He went voluntarily to the U.S.A. in 1939. Died in the year of his return to Germany; see p. 46.

Stories
1918: *Gudula*
        Josef Montfort

'Bildungsroman'
1920–1: *Helianth* (Bilder aus dem Leben zweier Menschen von heute und aus der norddeutschen Tiefebene), 3 vols. (shortened to 2 vols. 1928)

Lyrical epic
1920: *Raub der Persephone* (Eine attische Mythe)
1922: *Parzival* (Ein Versroman in drei Kreisen). Antiquity and Christianity, e.g. Odysseus and Parzival (who, however, has really little in common with Wolfram's conception of the hero) are amongst the favourite themes in A. Schaeffer's work

In his *Aphaia. Der Weg der Götter, Völker und Zahlen* (1937) the subject-matter of the dialogues of the three pupils of Socrates (Plato—Nikias—Parmenides) is the temple of the goddess Aphaia on the island Aigina.

A. Schaeffer believed in determination of our world by a transcendental force, and he quotes accordingly the religious statement: 'Credo quia praeclarum.' The motto to his *Parzival* is significantly a line from the mystic Angelus Silesius = 'Mensch, was du liebst, in das wirst du verwandelt werden'.

A. Schaeffer interprets the world as the creation of the Spirit whose medium on earth is the poet; cf. his *Mythos* (*Abhandlungen über die kulturellen Grundlagen der Menschheit*), ed. by Walter Ehlers, Veröffentlichungen der Deutschen Akademie für Sprache und Dichtung, 1958, published with a 'Zeittafel' and an A. Schaeffer-bibliography.

PAUL SCHALLÜCK

Born 1922 in Warendorf/Westphalia. Mainly novelist and author of radio-plays.

Novels
1951: *Wenn man aufhören könnte zu lügen*
1953: *Ankunft null Uhr zwölf*
1959: *Engelbert Reineke*

Radio-plays
1954: *Unsichtbar*
1961: *Nächtliche Gespräche*
1962: *Hand und Name*

Stories
1955: *Weiße Fahnen im April*

EDZARD SCHAPER

Born 1908 in Ostrowo, Posen.

Novels
1934: *Die Insel Tütarsaar*
1935: *Die sterbende Kirche*

1949: *Der letzte Advent*

1940: *Der Henker* (reprinted 1956 under title *Sie mähten gewappnet die Saaten*

1950: *Die Freiheit des Gefangenen*

1951: *Die Macht der Ohnmächtigen* (published together 1961 under title *Macht und Freiheit*)

1954: *Der Gouverneur oder Der glückselige Schuldner*

1957: *Attentat auf den Mächtigen*

1961: *Der vierte König*

1963: *Der Aufruhr des Gerechten: eine Chronik*

Stories

1965: *Ges. Erzählungen*, including especially:

1950: *Der große, offenbare Tag*

1952: *Hinter den Linien*

Das Christkind aus den großen Wäldern

1962–3: *Dragonergeschichte*

Studies

1952: Max Wehrli: *Edzard Schaper*, in Schaper, E., *Untergang und Verwandlung: Betrachtungen und Reden* (also includes complete bibliography of Schaper's works up to 1952)

1954: Karl Josef Hahn: *Der Erzähler Edzard Schaper*, *Deutsche Rundschau* 4

1955: Helmut Uhlig: *Edzard Schaper*, in Friedmann, H. and Mann, O., *Christliche Dichter der Gegenwart*

1959: Franz Lennartz: *Edzard Schaper*, *Deutsche Dichter und Schriftsteller unserer Zeit*, 8th ed.

In addition to the novels and stories for which he is best known—he was awarded the Fontane-Preis of the City of Berlin in 1953—Schaper's work includes essays, lectures, radio-plays, editions, introductions, and translations of Northern European authors. The Baltic countries, which were the home of his choice 1930–40, provide the background for many of his works.

Schaper's outlook is eminently Christian and he sees not only the problematic situation of modern man but also the hope of a solution: he shows that there is an inner freedom which can be attained in captivity, even at the expense of physical freedom (as in *Die Freiheit des Gefangenen, Hinter den Linien*), that there is wealth which does not depend on material possessions (e.g. the hidden treasure in *Die Insel Tütarsaar*, the beggar's wealth in *Die Legende vom vierten König*) and a power, the power of faith, which manifests itself most strongly when the isolated individual feels weakest of all (e.g. in *Die Macht der Ohnmächtigen*) for 'Nur der Allmächtige schenkt auch in die leeren Hände und in einen tauben Sinn' (*Der vierte König*). A slight inclination to preach is counterbalanced by a welcome streak of humour in the style of some of Schaper's recent works (*Attentat auf den Mächtigen, Der Aufruhr des Gerechten*).

Teresa M. Kinnear

RICHARD VON SCHAUKAL

Born 1874 in Brünn, Moravia. Died 1942 in Vienna. In his early poetry influenced by Impressionism and French Symbolism.

Poetry
1893: *Gedichte*
1897: *Meine Gärten* (subtitle 'Einsame Verse')
1898: *Tristia*
1926: *Gezeiten der Seele*

Stories
1906: *Eros Thanatos*

1960 ff.: *Ges. Werke*

RUTH SCHAUMANN (married name: R. Fuchs)

Born 1899 in Hamburg. Poet, graphic artist, sculptor, painter. Inspired by genuine love of humanity. Rooted in the European tradition, her verse is in striking contrast to the highly intellectual contemporary poetry.

Poetry
1920: *Die Kathedrale*
1927: *Der Rebenhang*
1937: *Der Siegelring*
1949: *Ländliches Gastgeschenk*

Novels and stories
1932: *Amei. Eine Kindheit*, autobiographical novel
1956: *Die Frau des guten Schächers*, stories
1959: *Die Haarsträhne*, novel

PAUL SCHEERBART (Ps. Bruno Küfer)

Born 1863 in Danzig. Died 1915 in Berlin. Humorist and 'kosmischer Schwärmer', pamphleteer with a predilection for the paradox and the absurd. About the end of the nineteenth century he became the founder of the '*Verlag deutscher Phantasten*'. His influence can be traced in Hans Arp's Dada-verse and also in J. Ringelnatz's nonsense-poetry.

Novels
1901: *Die Seeschlange*
1913 and 1964: *Lesabéndio. Ein Asteroiden-Roman mit 14 Zeichnungen von Alfred Kubin*

Poetry
1909 and 1963: *Katerpoesie*

RENÉ SCHICKELE

Born 1883 in Oberehnheim (Alsace). Died 1940 in Vence (France). Much-travelled journalist and prominent Expressionist. Directly concerned with the publication of the journals *Stürmer* and *Das neue Magazin für Literatur*, and editor of *Weiße Blätter* (1913–20). His pacifist beliefs forced him to emigrate to Switzerland (1915–1919). Emigrated again in 1933, to France. The peculiar position of the Alsatian is presented in his writings, which themselves reflect this French/German approach in form and are marked by a sense of rhythm and humour.

Novels and stories
1909: *Der Fremde*
1911: *Meine Freundin Lo*
1913: *Das Glück*
1914: *Trimpopp und Manasse*
       Benkal, der Frauentröster

1915: *Aissé*
1920: *Die Mädchen*
1925: *Maria Capponi*
1927: *Blick auf die Vogesen*
1929: *Symphonie für Jazz*
1931: *Der Wolf in der Hürde* (forming with Maria Capponi and
      Blick auf die Vogesen the trilogy: *Das Erbe am Rhein*)
1933: *Die Witwe Bosca*
1937: *Die Flaschenpost*
1938: *Le retour* (Heimkehr, 1939)

Poetry
1902: *Sommernächte*
1915: *Mein Herz, mein Land*

Drama
1914: *Hans im Schnakenloch*
1920: *Am Glockenturm*

Essays and miscellaneous writings
1913: *Schreie auf dem Boulevard*
1919: *Die Genfer Reise*
      Der 9. November
1922: *Wir wollen nicht sterben*
1932: *Die Grenze*
1934: *Liebe und Ärgernis des D. H. Lawrence*

1960: *Werke*, 3 vols.

Ian Hilton

HANS SCHIEBELHUTH

Born 1895 in Darmstadt. Died 1944 in East Hampton, Long
Island. A virtuoso in most of the lyric forms cultivated by the
expressionists but not in immediate contact or close ideological
sympathy with the expressionist mainstream. A few poems
authentically record impressions of the trenches and hospitals
of the 1914 war. His mature poetry ranges from the powerfully
erotic to the apocalyptic-visionary style, though without much
metaphysical seriousness. He is perhaps at his best in his lighter

manner, in his whimsical, humorous but often satirically incisive 'ballads'.

1912: *Die Klänge des Morgens*
1919: *Der kleine Kalender*
1920: *Der Hakenkreuzzug. Neodadaistiche Ungedichte*
1921: *Wegstern*
1933: *Schalmei vom Schelmenried*

Posthumous collections
1966: I *Gedichte 1916–1936, Übertragungen*
1967: II *Prosa, Briefe, Theaterkritiken*
　　　　(Vols. 20 and 21 of 'Agora. Eine humanistische Schriften-reihe'), ed. by Manfred Schlösser (II contains a very full bibliography)

N. Horton Smith

JOHANNES SCHLAF

Born 1862 in Querfurt in Saxony. Died 1941 ibid. For many years a friend and collaborator of A. Holz. Essays on: (*a*) Walter Whitman, (*b*) Verhaeren, (*c*) Maurice Maeterlinck, (*d*) Friedrich Nietzsche, etc.

Novellen and dramatic sketches (with A. Holz)
1889: *Papa Hamlet*
1890: *Familie Selicke*
1892: *Neue Gleise*

Prosa-Lyrik
1892: *In Dingsda*
1894–5: *Frühling.* Both texts are models of Impressionist descriptions of nature

Drama
1892: *Meister Oelze*

His first Romantrilogie
(*a*) 1900: *Das dritte Reich*
(*b*) 1901: *Die Suchenden*
(*c*) 1902: *Peter Bojes Freite*

His second Romantrilogie
(a) 1904: *Der Kleine*
(b) 1908: *Der Prinz*
(c) 1909: *Am toten Punkt*

Poetry
1930: *Das Spiel der hohen Linien*

ARNO SCHMIDT

Born 1914 in Hamburg.

Stories
1949: *Leviathan*
1953: *Die Umsiedler*

Novels
1956: *Das steinerne Herz*
1963: *Nobodaddy's Kinder* (Trilogy):
   Aus dem Leben eines Fauns
   Brand's Haide. Schwarze Spiegel

Essays and stories
1959: *Rosen und Porree*
1965: *Die Ritter vom Geist. Von vergessenen Kollegen*
1966: *Trommler beim Zaren* (essays, reviews, stories)

Trs. from J. F. Cooper, Wilkie Collins, W. Faulkner, Peter Fleming, E. A. Poe, etc.

Criticism
1959: *Berechnungen I* and *II*

In *Berechnungen* I and II Arno Schmidt expounds his method of exercising the writer's craft. It constitutes the most crucial moment in the general activity of using language to describe the world and to present its existence vividly and lucidly ('Beschreibung und Durchleuchtung der Welt durch das Wort'), without which no control of the environment would be possible.

The traditional narrative moulds (letter novel, diary, etc.), which arose from the narrator's social frame of reference (conversation and monologue; viewing situations from the inside or the outside), have become insufficient for 'developing the forms of prose which will correspond exactly to certain ever recurring types of processes of the consciousness or modes of experience'.

Schmidt's narrative technique thus consists in an elaboration of the traditional 'I-narrative', and at first sight it is reminiscent of Wieland on the one hand, and writers such as Jean Paul on the other, who do not disguise, either the framework of conversation (including monologue), or the loose texture of association of ideas and images from which all experience is built up.

The portrayal of this fragmentary state of conscious experience is contrasted with the 'whitewashing' which occurs in Goethe's prose, whose 'pleasant illusion of a *fully efficient* life without gaps . . . does not in any way do justice to reality'.

Schmidt, on the other hand, seeks to do so by stringing together 'small units of experience, both internal and external', like pearls on a string. Their aggregate re-creates in each case a panorama taken from past history or the present day, or a time after the next (nuclear) world war. The general intention is the typical satirist's pulling down of idols and uncovering self-deception and hypocrisy, in order to clear the ground for a truthful appraisal of man in the 'Era of Physics'.

H. Popper

WILHELM SCHMIDTBONN (Ps. for Wilhelm Schmidt)

Born 1876 in Bonn. Died 1952 in Bad Godesberg. Musically gifted.

Drama

1908: *Der Graf von Gleichen* (theme = the man with two wives)
1909: *Der Zorn des Achilles*
1915: *Die Stadt der Besessenen*, this Wiedertäufersspiel is about the Anabaptists and their excesses at Münster

ERNST SCHNABEL

Born 1913 in Zittau. Author of radio-plays, travel stories and novels. Now in the Norddeutscher Rundfunk.

Novels
1939: *Die Reise nach Savannah*
1941: *Nachtwind*

Travel stories
1955: *Die Erde hat viele Namen*

Report
1958: *Anne Frank—Spur eines Kindes* (tr. into many languages)

ANTON SCHNACK

Born 1892 in Bieneck, Lower Franconia. Started as an Expressionist but is essentially Romantic.

Poetry
1919: *Strophen der Gier*
1936: *Die Flachenpost*
1948: *Mittagswein*

Novels
1936: *Zugvögel der Liebe*
1937: *Der finstere Franz*

Stories
1936: *Die Verstoßenen*
1954: *Die Reise aus Sehnsucht*

FRIEDRICH SCHNACK

Born 1888 in Bieneck, Lower Franconia.

Poetry
1920: *Das kommende Reich*
1938: *Ges. Gedichte*

Novels
1922: *Die goldenen Äpfel*
1927 & 1951: *Die Orgel des Himmels*
1956: *Aurora und Papilio*

Also author of travel-books and popular Naturbücher.

GEORG SCHNEIDER

Born 1902 in Coburg.

Poetry
1925: *Die Barke*, under George's influence
1953: *Sieben Töne*
1960: *Atem der Jahre*

Trs.
1955: *Französische Volkslieder und Chansons*
1962: *William Shakespeare: Lieder aus den Dramen*

REINHOLD SCHNEIDER

Born 1903 in Baden-Baden. Died 1958 in Freiburg i.B.

Novels
1938: *Las Casas vor Karl V; Szenen aus der Konquistadorenzeit* (English
    version, 1948: *Imperial Mission*, tr. by W. Oden)
1956: *Die silberne Ampel*

Short stories
1953: *Der fünfte Kelch; Erzählungen*
    Das getilgte Antlitz; Erzählungen

Drama
1948: *Der Kronprinz; politisches Drama*
1950: *Der große Verzicht*
1951: *Die Tarnkappe*
1952: *Innozenz und Franziskus*

Poetry
1954: *Die Sonette von Leben und Zeit, dem Glauben und der Geschichte*

Historical writings
1930: *Das Leiden des Camões, oder Untergang und Vollendung der
    portugiesischen Macht*
1931: *Philipp der Zweite, oder Religion und Macht*
1933: *Die Hohenzollern; Tragik und Königtum*
1936: *Das Inselreich; Gesetz und Größe der britischen Macht*

Autobiographical writings

1954: *Verhüllter Tag*
1958: *Winter in Wien*

Critical and miscellaneous writings

1931: *Portugal; ein Reisetagebuch*
1940: *Macht und Gnade*
1946: *Die Stunde des heiligen Franz von Assisi* (English tr. 1953, by
     J. Meyer)
1953: *Herrscher und Heilige*
     Über Dichter und Dichtung
1955: *Erbe und Freiheit*
1958: *Pfeiler im Strom*

Schneider's works embody a tragic vision of life which for some
years he tried to harmonize with the Catholic faith to which he
returned in 1937. During the Nazi era he attempted to rouse the
consciences of Germans in sonnets which were circulated clan-
destinely.

H. R. Klieneberger

ARTHUR SCHNITZLER

Born 1862 in Vienna. Died 1931 in Vienna. Doctor of medicine
and author. Impressionist of Viennese atmosphere. Master of the
nuance, the so-called 'Kleinkunst'. His work is mainly dedicated
to and rooted in the atmosphere of dying Vienna, e.g. the
dramatic scenes: *Anatol*, cycle of seven dialogues (1893):

(a) *Die Frage an das Schicksal*
(b) *Weihnachtseinkäufe*
(c) *Abschiedssouper*, etc.
1895: *Liebelei*
1899: *Der grüne Kakadu*—perhaps Schnitzler's most effective
     'Revolutionsdrama', based on the events of 14 July 1789;
     enacted murder is turned to real murder
1900: *Der Reigen* (written 1896–7) consists of 10 dialogues—
     various individual love-affairs of men and women
1901: *Der Schleier der Beatrice*
1904: *Der einsame Weg*
1912: *Professor Bernhardi*

Novels
1908: *Der Weg ins Freie*
1928: *Therese* (Chronik eines Frauenlebens)

1912: *Ges. Werke*, 8 vols.
1922–6: 9 vols.
1955: *Meisterdramen*
1961: *Die erzählenden Schriften*, 2 vols.

According to a notice in *Welt & Wort* (July 1965) A. Schnitzler's works are coming out in a 'Lizenzausgabe' in the DDR.

Studies
1963: *Arthur Schnitzler* by H. B. Garland in 'German Men of Letters', l.c.
   H. W. Reichart and Herman Salinger: *Studies in Arthur Schnitzler*, Centennial Memorial Volume, Chapel Hill, University of North Carolina Press
1966: R. H. Allen: *An annotated Arthur Schnitzler Bibliography*, Chapel Hill, University of North Carolina Press

WOLFDIETRICH SCHNURRE

Born 1920 in Frankfurt a.M.

Novels and stories
1953: *Sternstaub und Sänfte. Die Aufzeichnungen des Pudels Ali*
1958: *Eine Rechnung, die nicht aufgeht* (short stories)
   Als Vaters Bart noch rot war (short stories)
1959: *Das Los unserer Stadt*
1960: *Man sollte dagegen sein* (short stories)
1963: *Funke im Reisig* (short stories)
1964: *Ohne Einsatz kein Spiel* (short stories)

Essays
1962: *Berlin. Eine Stadt wird geteilt*
1964: *Schreibtisch unter freiem Himmel*

Poetry
1956: *Kassiber*

1957: *Abendländler*
1964: *Kassiber und neue Gedichte*

Radio-plays
1967: *Spreezimmer möbliert*

Much of Wolfdietrich Schnurre's work is set in Berlin, where he grew up from 1928 onwards. His versatility and power as a writer are displayed particularly in the short story.

H. M. Waidson

KARL SCHÖNHERR

Born 1867 in Axams, Tirol. Died 1943 in Vienna. Mainly playwright:

1907: *Erde*. Like Nature itself the old peasant Grutz feels renewed by touching the earth and does not give place to his son, who cannot marry until his father dies
1910: *Glaube und Heimat*
1915: *Weibsteufel*
1916: *Frau Suitner*, a tragedy of the ageing sterile wife, who commits suicide
1923: *Es*

1948: *Ges. Werke*, 2 vols.

ERNST SCHÖNWIESE

Born 1905 in Vienna. Ed. of the literary journal *Das Silverboot*.

Poetry
1947: *Der siebenfarbige Bogen*
Ausfahrt und Wiederkehr
1953: *Requiem in Versen*
1957: *Der Alte und Junge Chronos*
1962: *Baum und Träne*

ALBERT ARNOLD SCHOLL

Born 1926 in Wetter an der Ruhr. Author of poetry, essays and radio-plays.

Poetry
1953: *Die gläserne Stadt*
1960: *Keiner zu Hause*

Radio-play
1956: *Reise in die Gegenwart*

A. A. Scholl is one of the 'Fünf junge Lyriker': H. Piontek, W. Höllerer, George Forestier, P. Celan and A. A. Scholl, in H. E. Holthusen's *Ja und Nein* (Neue kritische Versuche), 1954.

WILHELM VON SCHOLZ

Born 1874 in Berlin. Conservative, rooted in classical culture and literature; with Willy Andreas, co-founder and co-editor of *Die Großen Deutschen*. He also edited works by Minnesingers, Heinrich Suso, Eichendorff, Droste-Hülshoff; Calderon 'Nachdichtungen', etc.

Drama
1905: *Der Jude von Konstanz*, a tragedy about the baptized Jew in the Middle Ages
1906: *Meroe*
1910: *Die vertauschten Seelen*
1924: *Die gläserne Frau*

Novel
1926: *Perpetua*

Theory
1956: *Das Drama, Wesen und Darstellung der dramatischen Kunst*

Autobiography
1934: *Mein Leben*
1964: *Mein Theater*

1924: *Ges. Werke*, 5 vols.
1944: *Die Gedichte:* Gesamtausgabe

FRIEDRICH SCHREYVOGL

Born 1899 in Mauer, nr. Vienna. Chefdramaturg of the Wiener Burgtheater. Critic, playwright, poet, essayist.

Poetry
1918: *Klingen im Alltag*
1921: *Flöte am Abend*

Drama
1920: *Der zerrissene Vorhang* (Dramenzyklus)
1921: *Auferstehung*
1926: *Das brennende Schiff*
1933: *Habsburgerlegende*
1937: *Der Gott im Kreml* (about Demetrius)
1941: *Die kluge Wienerin* (one of his most successful comedies)

Novels:
1921: *Der Antichrist*
1929: *Tristan und Isolde*
1938: *Die Nibelungen*
1954: *Das fremde Mädchen*

RUDOLF ALEXANDER SCHRÖDER

Born 1878 in Bremen. Died 1962 in Wiessee, Upper Bavaria. In 1899–1900 with Otto Julius Bierbaum co-founder of the reputable and influential journal *Insel*.

Poetry
1899: *Unmut. Ein Buch Gesänge*
1900: *Empedokles*
1906: *Elysium*
1910: *Deutsche Oden*
1930: *Mitte des Lebens*
1940: *Die weltlichen Gedichte*
1949: *Die geistlichen Gedichte*
1952 ff. *Ges. Werke*, 8 vols.

R. A. Schröder was an accomplished translator from Greek: Homer; Latin: Cicero, Horace, Virgil; French: Molière, Racine,

Corneille; English: Shakespeare, Pope's *The Rape of the Lock*,
T. S. Eliot's *Murder in the Cathedral*; Flemish: Guido Gezelle,
Stijn Streuvels (Frank Lateur), etc.

Essays

1932: *Racine und die deutsche Humanität*
1936: *Dichtung und Dichter der Kirche*
1939: *Die Aufsätze und Reden*
1949: *Goethe und Shakespeare*

Studies

1938: *Werke und Tage* (Festschrift on his 60th birthday)
1958: *An R. A. Schröder, von M. Bodmer, C. H. Burckhardt, Th. Heuss, O. v. Taube*
1963: *Dem Dichter zum Gedächtnis*

A. Wierzejewski

HANS DIETER SCHWARZE

Born 1926 in Münster, Westphalia.

Poetry

1952: *Quersumme*
1956: *Flügel aus Glas*
1960: *Clowns*

KARL SCHWEDHELM

Born 1915 in Berlin. At present directing the section *'Literatur'* in
'Der Süddeutsche Rundfunk'.

Poetry

1955: *Fährte der Fische*

KURT SCHWITTERS

Born 1887 in Hanover. Died 1948 in Ambleside, England.
Painter, sculptor, poet; he belonged to the circle of the Dadaists;
emigrated in 1933. 1919–20 founder of the terms: *'Merz-Kunst'*,
and *'Merzwortwerk'*.

Poems
1918–22: *Die Blume Anna*, see particularly the poem: *An Anna
          Blume* (from *Sturm*, X, 1919)

> 'O du, Geliebte, meiner siebenundzwanzig Sinne, ich
> liebe dir!—Du deiner dich dir, ich dir, du mir.
> —Wir?
> Das gehört (beiläufig) nicht hierher . . .'

1965: *Anna Blume und ich: die gesammelten 'Anna Blume' Texte*, ed.
      by Ernst Schwitters, Arche

Study
1967: W. Schmalenbach: *Kurt Schwitters—Leben und Werk*,
      Cologne

ANNA SEGHERS (Ps. for Netty Radvanyi)

Born in Mainz in 1900.

Novels
1932: *Die Gefährten*
1933: *Der Kopflohn*
1935: *Der Weg durch den Februar*
1937: *Die Rettung*
1942: *Das siebte Kreuz* (1942 English version, 1943 German
      version)
1941: *Transit* (1941 English version, 1948 German version)
1949: *Die Toten bleiben jung*
1959: *Die Entscheidung*

Stories
1928: *Der Aufstand der Fischer von St Barbara*
1930: *Auf dem Weg zur Amerikanischen Botschaft* (collection)
1953: *Der Bienenstock* (collection)
1958: *Brot und Salz* (collection)
1961: *Das Licht auf dem Galgen*

Anna Seghers emerged as a writer of considerable talent in the
late 1920s. A member of the Communist Party since 1928 (and
now living in East Germany), she has consistently written from

an ideological viewpoint, which has not, however—except perhaps in some of her most recent works—diminished the literary quality of her writing. Her best novel, *Das siebte Kreuz*, a masterly account of an escape from a Nazi concentration camp before the War, is rightly regarded as a classic of its sort.

D. S. Low

INA SEIDEL

Born 1885 in Halle.

Novels and Novellen
1922: *Das Labyrinth*
1923: *Sterne der Heimkehr*
1930: *Das Wunschkind*
1938: *Lennacker*
1940: *Unser Freund Peregrin*
1954: *Das unverwesliche Erbe*
1959: *Michaela*

Poetry
1919: *Gedichte*
1927: *Neue Gedichte*
1929: *Der volle Kranz*
1937: *Ges. Gedichte*

Autobiography
1935: *Meine Kindheit und Jugend*

Biographies
1944: *Achim von Arnim, Bettina Brentano, Clemens Brentano*

Prolific writer of novels, stories and poems. The novels tend to be psychological studies of human, usually women's problems within a literary group or the family (e.g. *Das Labyrinth*, *Das Wunschkind*). *Lennacker* analyses the rehabilitation of an officer after World War I. High standing as a lyric poet.

Biography
1956: K. A. Horst: *Ina Seidel*

L. H. C. Thomas

REINHARD JOHANNES SORGE

Born 1892 in Berlin-Rixdorf. Died 1916 nr. Ablaincourt/Somme, in the First World War. Influenced by Nietzsche's *Also sprach Zarathustra*, Stefan George and Alfred Mombert. Famous for his tragedy: *Der Bettler* ('Eine dramatische Sendung'), 1912, which is considered one of the first if not the first German Expressionist drama. *Der Bettler*, at the same time, marks the end of Sorge's Expressionism. He turned away from Nietzsche and was converted to Catholicism: see his *Gericht über Zarathustra*, 1912; *Der Sieg des Christos*, 1914; and *Metanoeite!* ('turn back, repent'), 1914.

1925: *Nachgelassene Gedichte*
1962 ff.: *Sämtliche Werke*, 3 vols., ed. by H. G. Rötzer

CARL SPITTELER

Born 1845 in Liestal, Canton Bern. Died 1924 in Luzern. Received the Nobel Prize in 1919.

Epics
1880–1: *Prometheus und Epimetheus*
1900 ff.: *Olympischer Frühling*, 4 vols.; revised ed. 1910

Poetry
1889: *Schmetterlinge*
1906: *Glockenlieder*

1906: *Imago* (Prosaerzählung), which gave the title to the psycho-analytical journal *Imago*

Study
1922: W. Adrian: *The Mythologie in Carl Spittelers Olympischem Frühling*

ERNST STADLER

Born 1883 in Kolmar, Alsace. Died 1914 in Zaandvoorde, Belgium. Influenced by Stefan George and Hugo von Hofmannsthal. His early poems appeared under the title *Präludien*, 1905, but by 1914 he developed into an Expressionist poet:

1914: *Der Aufbruch*

1954: *Ernst Stadler, Dichtungen*, 2 vols., ed. by K. L. Schneider

HERMANN STEHR

Born 1864 in Habelschwerdt, nr. Glatz. Died 1940 in Oberschrei-
berhau.

Novels
1900: *Leonore Griebel*
1905: *Der begrabene Gott*
1909: *Drei Nächte*
1918: *Der Heiligenhof*
1924: *Peter Brindeisener*
1929: *Nathanael Maechler*
1933: *Die Nachkommen*
1944: *Damian oder Das große Schermesser*

Short stories
1898: *Auf Leben und Tod*
1899: *Der Schindelmacher*
1916: *Das Abendrot*
1921: *Die Krähen*
1926: *Der Geigenmacher*
1929: *Mythen und Mären*
1931: *Meister Cajetan*

Play
1904: *Meta Konegen*

Poetry
1920: *Das Lebensbuch*
1936: *Der Mittelgarten*

Autobiographical writings
1934: *Mein Leben*

Critical and miscellaneous writings
1936: *Das Stundenglas; Reden, Schriften, Tagebücher*

The Silesian Hermann Stehr developed from Naturalist beginnings into an author of fiction in which a peasantry, aware of the preternatural and disposed towards an unorthodox Christian mysticism, is extolled in opposition to the—supposedly—soul-destroying world of urban industrial civilization.

H. R. Klieneberger

CARL STERNHEIM

Born 1878 in Leipzig. Died 1942 in his castle near Brussels. His target in some of his best dramas is the philistine:

1910–11: *Die Hose* (written in 1909–10), exposes the servility of a subaltern whose wife loses her knickers in public, when the royal party of the Emperor passes by

1912: *Die Kasette*

1913: *Bürger Schippel* (the proletarian who becomes bourgeois)

1914: *Der Snob* (a comedy about an upstart, who is prepared to forgo his identity)

1916: *Tabula rasa* (attack on a social democratic party politician)

1919: *Die Marquise von Arcis*, based on Diderot's play, tr. into English by Ashley Dukes, was performed in London in 1935 under the title *The Mask of Virtue*, with Vivien Leigh as Henriette. The Marquise of Pomeraye in the play suspects that the Marquis's passion for her has vanished. She lays him a trap by introducing him to the prostitute Henriette, but the Marquis ennobles Henriette by making her his wife. She is depicted as 'the new woman' in a depraved society

1963 ff.: *Das Gesamtwerk*, ed. by W. Emrich, 8 vols.

1964 ff.: *Ges. Werke*, ed. by F. Hofmann, 6 vols.

Studies

1965: *Carl Sternheim*, by W. Wendler

Select bibliography in *Carl Sternheim* by R. Beckley, in *German Men of Letters*, vol. II, l.c.

AUGUST STRAMM

Born 1874 in Münster in Westphalin. Died 1915 in Russia. From about 1914 his dramas take on a pronounced Expressionist form.

Drama
1914: *Sancta Susanna*
      Haidebraut
1915: *Erwachen*
      Kräfte

Poetry (posth.)
1917: *Die Menschheit*
1919: *Tropfblut*

1963: *Das Werk*, complete ed. of Stramm's *Werke*, by R. Radrizani, with bibliography

EMIL STRAUSS

Born 1866 in Pforzheim. Died 1960 in Freiburg im Breisgau.

Novels
1901: *Der Engelwirt*
1904: *Kreuzungen* (love crosses the hero's life)
1912: *Der nackte Mann* (historical novel)
1934: *Das Riesenspielzeug*, his most important Bildungsroman——a call 'back to nature' in view of the moral and intellectual breakdown of our civilization at the end of the nineteenth century
1940: *Lebenstanz*

Novellen and stories
1912: *Der Schleier*
1915-16: *Der Spiegel*
1945-7: *Dreiklang*, Novellenzyklus

1955: *Ludens. Erinnerungen und Versuche*

1949 ff.: *Ges. Werke*

LULU VON STRAUSS UND TORNEY

Born 1873 in Bückeburg. Died 1956 in Jena. Wife of the publisher Eugen Diederichs. A distinguished German ballad-writer. Her favourite themes are Frisian and Lower Saxon history and landscape.

Poetry
1898: *Gedichte*
1902: *Balladen und Lieder*
1926: *Reif steht die Saat* (Lyrische Gesamtausgabe)

Novels
1907: *Lucifer, Roman aus der Stedingerzeit* (13th century). Stedinger is the name for the Oldenburg Marschbauern. Their struggle for liberty and the cruel crusade against them in 1234 have served as a stirring theme in several German dramas, stories and epics
1911 and 1937: *Der Judashof*, a novel about a Low German hereditary farm

LUDWIG STRAUSS

Born in 1892 in Aachen. Died 1953 in Jerusalem.

Poetry
1918: *Wandlung und Verkündigung*
1952: *Heimliche Gegenwart* (Gedichte von 1933–50)

ERWIN STRITTMATTER

Born 1912 in Spremberg, Niederlausitz. President of the East German Writers' Association.

Drama
1954: *Katzgraben* (Bauernkomödie)
1961: *Die Holländerbraut*

Novels
1950: *Ochsenkutscher*
1954: *Tinko*

1957: *Der Wundertäter*
1963: *Ole Bienkopp* (a picaresque novel)

Hermann Sudermann

Born 1857 in Matziken im Memelland. Died 1928 in Berlin.
Alfred Kerr and Hermann Bahr were Sudermann's relentless
opponents.

Drama
1889: *Die Ehre* which made him world-famous. A play about
      the relative values of honour
1890: *Sodoms Ende*
1893: *Heimat*; Magda was played by Eleonore Duse
1896: *Teja*

Novels
1887: *Frau Sorge*
1888: *Der Katzensteg* (English tr., *Regina or The Sins of the Fathers*,
      by Beatrice Marshall, 1905)

Stories
1917: *Litauische Geschichten*

1923: *Dramatische Werke*, 6 vols.

As to Sudermann's dramatic work, see Professor W. F. Mainland
in *German Men of Letters*, vol. II, where the clash between Sudermann's social and moral problems and character study is fully
revealed.

Wilhelm Szabo

Born 1901 in Vienna.

Poetry
1933: *Das fremde Dorf*
1940: *Im Dunkel der Dörfer*
1954: *Herz in der Kelter*

Otto Freiherr von Taube

Born 1879 in Reval. Tr. from Russian, French, Italian, Spanish, Portuguese, English, etc.

Poetry
1908: *Gedichte und Szenen*
1937: *Wanderlieder*

Frank Thiess

Born 1890 in Eluisenstein, nr. Uexküll (Livonia). Studied in Germany, fought in First World War, turned to journalism and literary activity, settled in Austria 1933–52, was intermittently in difficulties with the National Socialists, but refused to emigrate (debate with Thomas Mann on the merits of 'inner emigration'). Prolific and internationally esteemed novelist in the popular vein, writing disciplined prose under the acknowledged influence of Goethe, who later turned to historical novels of a new type depicting in scholarly detail great events in world history and cultural epochs, seen from the point of view of the philosopher of history.

Novels
1921: *Der Tod von Falern*
1934: *Der Weg zu Isabelle*
1936: *Tsushima*
1937: *Stürmischer Frühling*
1941: *Das Reich der Dämonen*
1959: *Die griechischen Kaiser*
1961: *Sturz nach oben*

J. B. Bednall

Ludwig Thoma (Ps. Peter Schlemihl)

Born 1867 in Oberammergau. Died 1921 in Rottach (Tegernsee). Since 1897 editor of *Simplizissimus*. Satire against philistines. Powerfully realistic characterization of Bavarian peasants, particularly of the Dachau region.

Poetry
1901: *Grobheiten* (*Simplicissimus Gedichte*)
1903: *Neue Grobheiten*

Satirical stories
1904 ff.: *Lausbubengeschichten*
1906: *Tante Frieda* (Neue Lausbubengeschichten)

Novels
1911: *Der Wittiber* (perhaps his finest 'peasant novel')
1922: *Der Ruepp*

1966: *The Girl from India*, story tr. by R. Thonger; ed. by W. E.
Yuill in *German Narrative Prose*, 2nd vol., London

1922: *Ges. Werke*, 7 vols.; and 1956, 8 vols.

JESSE THOOR (Ps. Peter Karl Höfler)

Born 1905 in Berlin. Died 1952 in Lienz. Emigrated first to Brno
(1938), then to London in 1939. His verse combines religious
vision with stark realism. His mastery of the sonnet-form has
rightly been compared with that of the Baroque poet Andreas
Gryphius.

Poetry
1948: *Sonette*
1956: *Die Sonette und Lieder*, ed. by Alfred Marnau, Deutsche
Akademie, Darmstadt

1965: ed. Michael Hamburger: *Jesse Thoor: Das Werk. Sonette,
Lieder, Erzählungen*

ERNST TOLLER

Born 1893 in Samotschin, nr. Bromberg. Died 1939 in New York
(suicide in the New York hotel 'Mayflower'). He took part in the
November revolution (1918) of the workers; after Kurt Eisner's
death he became Chairman of the USPD (Unabhängige Sozialistische Partei Deutschlands) and Commander of the Räterepub-
lik; then five years' imprisonment: 1919–24.

Poetry
1921: *Gedichte der Gefangenen*
1924: *Das Schwalbenbuch*

1924–33: much abroad; 1933 in exile. Several of his tragedies
are Expressionist 'Stationen-Dramen' for propaganda
purpose.

Drama
1919: *Die Wandlung*
1920: *Masse Mensch*
1922: *Maschinenstürmer*
1923: *Der deutsche Hinkemann*
1927: *Hoppla, wir leben*
1930: *Feuer aus den Kesseln* (Historisches Schauspiel)
1932–3: *Die blinde Göttin* (English version: *Blindman's Buff*, by
E. Toller and Denis Johnson, 1938)
1939: *Pastor Hall*, tr. into English by Stephen Spender and Hugh
Hunt, 1947, Deutsches Bühnen MS. (acting script)

1934: (Prose) *I was a German* (Toller's autobiography), New York

1961: *Ernst Toller: Prosa, Briefe, Dramen, Gedichte*

Study
1964: Richard Beckley: *Ernst Toller* (with a select bibliography—
also of English trs.) in *German Men of Letters*, IIIrd vol., l.c.

FRIEDRICH TORBERG (Ps. for Kantor–Berg)

Born 1908 in Vienna. Friendship with Broch, Kraus, Werfel, etc.;
emigrated to Switzerland, France and finally to the U.S.A. Since
1951 again in Vienna. Critic, poet, novelist and translators.
Co-editor of the monthly magazine *Forum*.

Poetry
1929: *Der ewige Refrain*

Novels
1930: *Der Schüler Gerber absolviert*, new ed. 1954

1948: *Hier bin ich, mein Vater*. A novel about the fate of Jews in Hitler Germany
1950: *Die zweite Begegnung*. A novel about Bohemia under Communist rule

1962 ff.: *Ges. Werke*, 4 vols.

GEORG TRAKL

Born 1887 in Salzburg. Died 1914 in Cracow hospital (probably suicide with cocaine drugs); see p. 13. Mainly poetry.

1913: *Gedichte*
1915: *Sebastian im Traum*
1917: *Die Dichtungen*
1920: *Der Herbst des Einsamen*
1928: *Die Dichtungen*
1945: *Die Dichtungen, Gesamtausgabe*, Die Arche
1933: *Gesang des Abgeschiedenen* (Gedichte)
1939: *Aus goldenem Kelch* (Die Jugenddichtungen)
1947: *Offenbarung und Untergang* (Die Prosadichtungen)
1949: *Nachlaß und Biographie* (Gedichte, Briefe, Bilder, Essays)

Studies
Wolfgang Schneditz: *Georg Trakl in Zeugnissen der Freunde*, 1951
Walter Ritzer: *Trakl-Bibliographie*, 1956
A. Closs: *Georg Trakl, Austrian Poet* (in '*New Road*, 1946'), ed. by Fred Marnau, with translations of Trakl-poems by Ernst Sigler
Irene Morris: *George Trakl*, GLL, 1949
K. L. Schneider: *Der bildhafte Ausdruck in den Dichtungen G. Heyms, G. Trakls und E. Stadlers*, 1968, 3rd ed.

KURT TUCHOLSKY (several Ps. = Theobald Tiger, Peter Panter, Ignaz Wrobel, Kaspar Hauser)

Born 1890 in Berlin. He was 'ausgebürgert' in 1933. Died 1935 (suicide) in Hindas, nr. Göteborg, Sweden. Satirist, author of chansons; contributor to the *Weltbühne, Vossische Zeitung*, etc.

1914: *Der Zeitsparer* (Grotesken)
1919: *Fromme Gesänge*
1920: *Träumereien an preußischen Kaminen*

1912: *Rheinsberg* (Ein Bilderbuch für Verliebte)
1931: *Schloß Gripsholm* (love-story)

1960–2: *Ges. Werke*, 3 vols., ed. by M. Gerold-Tucholsky and
F. J. Raddatz

FRANZ TUMLER

Born 1912 in Gries, nr. Bozen (Bolzano). Now living in Austria,
mainly author of 'Zeitromane' and 'Heimkehrer' stories.

Stories
1937: *Die Wanderung zum Strom*
1939: *Der Soldateneid*
1959: *Der Mantel*

Novels
1949: *Der alte Herr Lorenz*
1950: *Heimfahrt*
1953: *Ein Schloß in Österreich*
1956: *Ein Schritt hinüber*
1965: *Aufschreibung aus Trient*

FRITZ VON UNRUH

Born 1885 in Koblenz. Son of a Prussian General, educated with
Hohenzollern Princes in a Military College; became pacifist, and
emigrated to France and U.S.A. The central themes of his works
are the stark reality of the First World War and the responsibility
of the individual within the human community. Ecstatic, Expressionist language.

Drama
1911: *Offiziere*
1913: *Louis Ferdinand, Prinz von Preußen*
1913–14: *Stürme*, published and performed in 1922

Tragödientrilogie
1917: *Ein Geschlecht*
1920: *Platz*
1936: *Dietrich*

Novels

1919: *Opfergang* (about the horror of the battle of Verdun),
written in 1916

1947: *The End is not yet* (German version 1949: *Der nie verlor*, a
'Hitler-novel')

Study

1964: W. F. Mainland: *Fritz von Unruh*, with Select Bibliography,
in 'German Men of Letters', III., l.c.

FRITZ USINGER

Born 1895 in Friedberg (Hessen). In his poetry under Hölderlin's
and George's influence.

Poetry

1918: *Der ewige Kampf*
1920: *Große Elegie*
1927: *Irdisches Gedicht*
1931: *Das Wort*
1937: *Die Geheimnisse*
1942: *Hermes*
1948: *Hesperische Hymnen*
1955: *Fest der Geister*
1957: *Niemands Gesang*

Essays

1940: *Medusa*

Study

1947: Gertrud Bäumer: *Der Dichter Fritz Usinger*

KLARA VIEBIG

Born 1860 in Trier. Died 1952 in Berlin. The landscapes of the
Eifel to the Rhineland are favourite themes in her naturalistic
stories, see KLW: Naturalismus.

Novels

1900: *Das Weiberdorf*
1902: *Die Wacht am Rhein*

1904: *Das schlafende Heer*
1932: *Menschen unter Zwang*

1919–22: *Ausgewählte Werke*, 8 vols.; see also DLL

Karl Gustav Vollmoeller

Born 1878 in Stuttgart. Died 1948 in Los Angeles. Happened to be in U.S.A. in 1939; first interned, lived later in New York and California. Literary friendship with Stefan George and D'Annunzio, wrote for the *Blätter für die Kunst*, and the *Insel-Almanach*. Author of neo-romantic macabre and lyrical dramas, such as:

1903: *Catharina, Gräfin von Armagnac* (influenced by H. v. Hofmannsthal's *Frau im Fenster*)
1911: *Wieland*
Mirakel, produced by Max Reinhardt; see M. Reinhardt, p. 346.

Georg von der Vring

Born 1889 in Brake (Unterweser). Died 1968 in Munich. Painter and poet, author of several radio-plays and translator of Verlaine, Maupassant, Blake, etc.

Poetry
1925: *Südergast*
1933: *Das Blumenbuch*
1942: *Octoberrose*
1947: *Verse für Minette*
1954: *Kleiner Faden blau*
1956: *Die Lieder des Georg von der Vring: 1906–56*
1961: *Der Schwan*

Novels
1927: *Soldat Suhren* (War-diary in form of a novel)
1948: *Magda Gött*

Karl Heinrich Waggerl

Born 1897 in Bad Gastein, Austria. Mainly author of popular stories and novels.

Novels

1930: *Brot*
1931: *Schweres Blut*
1934: *Mütter*

Stories

1936: *Kalendergeschichten*
1946: *Die Pfingstreise*

HERWARTH WALDEN (Ps. for Georg Levin)

Born 1878 in Berlin. Since 1941 missing in Russia (probably Siberia). Editor of the *Sturm*, to which Heynicke and Stramm, etc., contributed. The first issue of H. Walden's *Sturm* appeared on 3 March 1910. See also p. 22.

MARTIN WALSER

Born 1927 in Wasserburg on the Bodensee. Author of parodies, grotesques and satires. His dramas and novels tend to be overloaded by laboured dialectics. His main vehicle of dramatic progress is the critical enquiry by discussion; see also Hdb. A keytheme is the inability of the artist to convey in words events and the meaning of these experiences, e.g. in the novel *Das Einhorn* about love or rather sex.

Novels

1957: *Ehen in Philippsburg*
1960: *Halbzeit*
1966: *Das Einhorn*. The hero is commissioned by a womanpublisher to write a novel about love. In an affair with her he collects relevant material

Drama

1961: *Der Abstecher* (*Detour*), comedy; radio-play since 1963
1962: *Eiche und Angora. Eine deutsche Chronik*. Satire about the Wohlfahrt State with its privileged bosses and under-privileged classes, and the recrudescence of evil nationalism
1963: *Überlebensgroß Herr Krott. Requiem für einen Unsterblichen*, a play about servility and power. Here again the problem

of a new outbreak of Nazism. The ruthless captain of
industry, though tired of life, cannot die; he must live
on, as none of the underlings can replace him. The alle-
gory is transparent: capitalism goes on; it is immortal.

1964: *Der schwarze Schwan*. About the problem of responsibility
and guilt. Use of the analytical method; the deeds of the
fathers are seen and judged through the eyes of the sons:
'Was ein Vater tut, das hätte auch der Sohn getan,
wenn's an ihm gewesen wäre.' The son is ready to take
upon himself the responsibility for his father's crimes if in
his own nature he discovers the possibility and tendency
of committing them. But the brilliantly constructed idea
is spoiled by an unconvincing character

Several radio-plays

Essays
1965: *Erfahrungen und Leseerfahrungen*. This vol. contains the
important study about contemporary drama: *Imitation
or Realism*

ROBERT WALSER

Born 1878 in Biel. Died 1956 in Herisau, Canton Appenzell. He
died on Christmas Day, in the course of a walk, taken from the
hospital where he had been resident since about 1933.

Novels (and other prose)
1904: *Fritz Kochers Aufsätze* (shorter prose)
1907: *Geschwister Tanner*
1908: *Der Gehülfe*
1909: *Jakob von Gunten*
1917: *Der Spaziergang* (English, *The Walk and other stories* (1957))
1918: *Poetenleben* (shorter prose)
1925: *Die Rose* (shorter prose)
1953: *Dichtungen in Prosa* (ed. by Carl Seelig and others)

Poetry
1909: *Gedichte*, 3rd ed. with preface by Carl Seelig (1944)
1958: *Unbekannte Gedichte*, ed. with postscript by Carl Seelig

Studies

1960: K. J. W. Greven: *Existenz, Welt und reines Sein in Werk Robert Walsers* (Diss. Cologne)

1963: H. M. Waidson: *Robert Walser*, in: 'German Men of Letters', vol. II, l.c.

The Swiss author Robert Walser lived for much of the time between 1905 and 1913 in Berlin, and this was the most fertile period of his writing. Apart from his three novels and *Der Spaziergang*, his most distinctive work, with its polished, impressionistic style, lies in the prose sketch and the short story.

H. M. Waidson

JAKOB WASSERMANN

Born 1873 in Fürth. Died 1934 in Alt-Aussee (Steiermark). Enjoyed great success in the twenties and thirties and often compared then with Thomas Mann. His novels examined the causes of the moral sickness of man and revealed a basic faith in humanity. A strong narrator of fertile imagination. His plots are often involved, the form dramatic, sometimes sensational.

Novels

1897: *Die Juden von Zirndorf*
1900: *Die Geschichte der jungen Renate Fuchs*
1908: *Caspar Hauser oder die Trägheit des Herzens*
1910: *Die Masken Erwin Reiners*
1915: *Das Gänsemännchen*
1919: *Christian Wahnschaffe*
1925: *Laudin und die Seinen*
1928: *Der Fall Maurizius*
1930: *Etzel Andergast*
1934: *Joseph Kerkhovens dritte Existenz*

Short stories

1903: *Der niegeküßte Mund*
1906: *Die Schwestern*
1911: *Der goldene Spiegel*
1922: *Oberlins drei Stufen*
1923: *Das Gold von Caxamalca*
1926: *Der Aufruhr um den Junker Ernst*

Essays and other writings
1921: *Mein Weg als Deutscher und Jude* (poignant autobiography)
1928: *Lebensdienst*

1920–2: *Wendekreis* (novels and short stories), 4 vols.
1944–8: *Ges. Werke*, 7 vols.

Much of his fiction has been tr. into English.

Ian Hilton

FRANK WEDEKIND

Born 1864 in Hanover. Died 1918 in Munich. A twentieth century Rousseau who praises physical strength and beauty (see Alex Natan, vol. II, 'German Men of Letters'). Forerunner of Impressionism and Expressionism; but mainly Surrealist. Anti-Naturalist who preaches freedom of sexual instincts: man is adventurer, woman is a formidable feline creature.

Drama
1891: *Frühlings Erwachen*
1895: *Erdgeist*
1900: *Marquis von Keith*
1901: *König Nicolo oder So ist das Leben*
1904: *Die Büchse der Pandora*
      Hidalla
1906: *Totentanz*
1912: *Franziska*
1914: *Simson oder Scham und Eifersucht*

1912–21: *Ges. Werke*, 9 vols., ed. by A. Kutscher, R. Friedenthal
1924: *Ges. Briefe*, 2 vols., ed. by F. Strich
      Ausgew. Werke, 5 vols., ed. by F. Strich
1954 ff.: *Ges. Werke* (*Neuausgabe*), by H. Maier

Lulu (based on the two tragedies: *Erdgeist* and *Die Büchse der Pandora*) is the title of the opera by Alban Berg, who at the time of his early death (1935) left the last act in sketch form. 'Lulu' is not merely an erotic character but an archetypal figure expressing man's sexual urge.

JOSEF WEINHEBER

Born 1892 in Vienna. Died 1945 in Kirchstetten, Lower Austria (suicide? through overdose of sleeping pills). After his death the *Josef Weinheber Gesellschaft* in Vienna was founded to further the author's literary work.

Poetry

1920: *Der einsame Mensch*
1923: *Von beiden Ufern*
1926: *Boot in der Bucht*
1934: *Adel und Untergang*; see GRM 1937
1935: *Wien wörtlich*
1936: *Späte Krone*
1937: *O Mensch, gib acht* (Ein erbauliches Kalenderbuch für Stadt- und Landleute)
1938: *Zwischen Göttern und Dämonen*
1939: *Kammermusik*
1947: *Hier ist das Wort*

Selections of poems

1935: *Vereinsamtes Herz*
1937: *Selbstbildnis*
1944: *Dokumente des Herzens*

Studies

1935: *Josef Weinheber, Persönlichkeit und Schaffen*, ed. by Adolf Luser
1940: *Josef Weinheber im Bilde*, by Lenz Grabner und Otto Stibor
1942: *Josef Weinheber*, by F. Koch
1953-6: Josef Weinheber: *Sämtliche Werke*, ed. by J. Nadler and H. Weinheber, 5 vols.
1966: *Josef Weinheber: Gedichte*, selected by F. Sacher, Geleitwort und Zeittafel by F. Jenaczek

GÜNTHER WEISENBORN (Ps. Eberhard Foerster, Christian Munk)

Born 1902 in Velbert (Rhineland). Collaborated with B. Brecht.

Drama

1928: antiwar drama *U-Boot S4* (also radio-play)

1945: *Die Illegalen* (resistance drama)
1949: *Ballade vom Eulenspiegel, vom Federle und von der dicken Pompanne*; its style reminds one of Brecht's epic drama

Novels
1935: *Das Mädchen von Fanö* (Liebesroman), filmed in 1937
1961: *Der Verfolger*

LEO WEISMANTEL

Born 1888 in Obersinn (Rhön). Died 1964 in Jugenheim (Bergstraße), south of Darmstadt. Humanist and author of religious works. Mainly novelist and playwright.

Romantrilogie about the Rhön region: *Vom Leben und Sterben eines Volkes*:
1. 1928: *Das alte Dorf*
2. 1932: *Die Geschichte des Hauses Herkommer*
3. 1933: *Das Sterben in den Gassen*
This trilogy appeared in a new version (1943) under the title: *Das Jahr von Sparbrot, Die Leute von Sparbrot, Tertullian Wolf*

Künstlerromane:
1936: *Dill Riemenschneider*
1938: *Leonardo da Vinci*
1939: *Gericht über Veit Stoss*
1940–3: Trilogy *Mathis-Nithart, der fälschlich Matthias Grünewald genannt wurde*
1950: *Albrecht Dürers Brautfahrt ins Leben* and *Der Junge Meister*

Drama
1919: *Die Reiter der Apocalypse*, three one-act plays
1921: *Der Totentanz*

ERNST WEISS

Born 1884 in (Brünn) Brno, Moravia. 1940 suicide in Paris. His work shows certain affinities to that of Kafka, Musil, and particularly Thomas Mann (*Zauberberg*). A much-neglected writer.

Novels

1928: *Der Aristokrat*, reissued in 1966; original title: *Boetius von Orlamünde*. The scene is laid in a boarding-school for aristocrats; description of the final collapse of an unreal, decadent world

1931: *Georg Letham. Arzt und Mörder*

1937: *Der arme Verschwender*

1963: *Der Augenzeuge* (written in 1939); the story of a doctor who cured the Führer Adolf Hitler of his hysterical blindness and sleeplessness in 1918

KONRAD WEISS

Born in 1880 in Rauenbretzingen, nr. Schwäbisch-Hall, Württemberg. Died 1940 in Munich. He was art-critic to the monthly magazine *Hochland*, up to 1920; since 1920 contributor to the *Münchener Neueste Nachrichten*.

Poetry:

1918: *Tantum dic verbo*

1921: *Die cumäische Sibylle*

1929: *Das Herz des Wortes*

1939: *Das Sinnreich der Erde*

1961: *Gedichte 1914–39*

PETER WEISS

Born 1916 in Nowawes, nr. Berlin. Emigrated to England and finally to Sweden; has Swedish citizenship; returned to Berlin.

Drama

1963: *Nacht mit Gästen—Eine Moritat* (grotesque Schauderdrama), father and mother are murdered by a robber-guest. The children open the gold chest but find nothing but beetroots

1964: *Die Verfolgung und Ermordung Jean Paul Marats, dargestellt durch die Schauspielgruppe des Hospizes zu Charenton unter Anleitung des Herrn de Sade*

1965: *Die Ermittlung* (Oratorio)

1967: *Gesang vom lusitanischen Popanz* (Stück mit Musik in 2 Akten, in *Theater heute*)
1968: *Vietnam Discourse*

Stories
1960: *Der Schatten des Körpers des Kutschers*
1961: *Abschied von den Eltern* (autobiographical)
1962: *Fluchtpunkt* (autobiographical)
1963: *Das Gespräch der drei Gehenden*

See also p. 101.

FRANZ WERFEL

Born 1890 in Prague. Died 1945 in Beverley Hills, California.

Novels, Novellen and stories
1920: *Spielhof*
      Die schwarze Messe (fragment of a novel in *Genius*)
      Nicht der Mörder, der Ermordete ist schuldig
1923: *Verdi*
1927: *Der Tod des Kleinbürgers*
      Geheimnis des Menschen
1928: *Abituriententag*
1929: *Barbara oder die Frömmigkeit*
1931: *Die Geschwister von Neapel*
1933: *Die vierzig Tage des Musa Dagh* (1939)
1937: *Höret die Stimme* (Jeremias-Roman)
1939: *Der veruntreute Himmel*
1941: *Eine blaßblaue Frauenschrift*
      Das Lied von Bernadette (1947)
1946: *Stern der Ungeborenen*

Drama
1911: *Der Besuch aus dem Elysium*
1915: *Die Troerinnen* (after Euripides)
1917: *Die Mittagsgöttin* (originally part of the book of poems: *Gerichtstag*)
1920: *Spiegelmensch*
1921: *Bocksgesang*

1922: *Schweiger*
1924: *Juarez und Maximilian*
1926: *Paulus unter den Juden*
1930: *Das Reich Gottes in Böhmen*
1935: *Der Weg der Verheißung*
1945: *Jakobowsky und der Oberst* (Komödie einer Tragikomödie)

Poetry
1911: *Der Weltfreund* (1918, Nachdruck)
1913: *Wir sind* (Neue Gedichte)
1915: *Einander* (Oden und Lieder)
1917: *Gesänge aus drei Reichen*
1919: *Der Gerichtstag* (Gedichte in 5 Büchern)
1921: *Ariel*
1922: *Beschwörungen*

Essays
1931: *Realismus und Innerlichkeit*
1932: *Können wir ohne Gottesglauben leben?*
1935: *Schlaf und Erwachen*
1938: *Von der reinsten Glückseligkeit des Menschen*
1948: *Ges. Werke in Einzelbänden*, ed by Adolf D. Klarmann

Lists kindly supplied by Professor A. D. Klarmann

Deutsche Textbücher for the foll. Verdi-operas
1926: *Macht des Schicksals*
1929: *Simone Baccanegra*
1932: *Don Carlos*

Ed.
1926: *Verdi-Briefe*

Trs.
1920: Otakar Březina: *Winde von Mittag nach Mitternacht* (with Emil Sandek)
1923: Otakar Březina: *Baumeister am Tempel* (with Otto Pick)
Otakar Březina: *Musik der Quellen* (with Emil Sandek)

Studies
1961: Lore B. Foltin: *Franz Werfel*, Univ. of Pittsburg Press

1962: Henry A. Lex: *The unwordly character in the Works of Franz Werfel*. Diss. Univ. of Pennsylvania, Philadelphia
1964: W. H. Fox: *Franz Werfel* (in 'German Men of Letters', III)
1967: A. D. Klarmann: *Franz Werfel—das lyrische Werk*

WOLFGANG WEYRAUCH

Born 1907 in Königsberg, East Prussia. Author in 'Group 47'; poet, essayist, journalist and author of radio-plays. In his style he aims at naked directness and baldness of expression, the so-called 'Kahlschlag', combined with avant-garde form-experiments.

Poetry
1950: *An die Wand geschrieben*
1956: *Gesang, um nicht zu sterben*
       Nie trifft die Finsternis
1963: *Die Spur: neue Gedichte*

1959: Ed. *Expeditionen*, an anthology of German lyrical poetry since 1945

Stories
1959: *Mein Schiff das heißt Taifun*
1962: *Dialog mit dem Unsichtbaren* (Sieben Hörspiele)
1963: *Das grüne Zelt* (Zwei Hörspiele)
1966: *Etwas geschieht*

ERNST WIECHERT

Born 1887 in Kleinort, East Prussia. Died 1950 in Uerikon on Lake Zürich.

Novels
1916: *Die Flucht*
1922: *Der Wald*
1924: *Der Totenwolf*
1925: *Die blauen Schwingen*
1926: *Der Knecht Gottes Andreas Nyland*
1929: *Die kleine Passion; Geschichte eines Kindes*
1931: *Jedermann; Geschichte eines Namenlosen*

1932: *Die Magd des Jürgen Doscocil* (English version, 1947: *The Girl and the Ferryman*, tr. by E. Wilkins and E. Kaiser)

1934: *Die Majorin* (English version, 1936: *The Baroness*, tr. by P. and T. Blewitt)

1939: *Das einfache Leben* (English version, 1954, by M. Heynemann)

1945-7: *Die Jerominkinder* (English version, 1951: *The Earth is our Heritage*, tr. by R. Maxwell)

1950: *Missa sine nomine* (English version, 1953, by M. Heynemann and M. B. Ledward)

Short stories
1928: *Der silberne Wagen*
1930: *Die Flöte des Pan*
1934: *Der Todeskandidat*
1936: *Das heilige Jahr*

Autobiographical writings
1936: *Wälder und Menschen; eine Jugend*
1945: *Der Totenwald; ein Bericht* (English version, 1947: *The Forest of the Dead*, tr. by U. Stechow)
1949: *Jahre und Zeiten; Erinnerungen*

Critical and miscellaneous writings
1946: *Drei Reden; Der Dichter und die Jugend* (1933)
   Der Dichter und die Zeit (1935)
   Rede an die deutsche Jugend (1945) (English version, 1948: *The Poet and his Time;* three addresses, tr. by I. Taeuber)

Study
1947: H. Ebeling, *Ernst Wiechert; das Werk des Dichters*

In his later novels, which are set in an East Prussian rural milieu, Wiechert denounces modern civilization and the intellectual outlook associated with it and celebrates a life of labour, close to the soil; but the cult of suffering and of sympathy with suffering in his writings separates him from the Nazi authors of the 'Blood and Soil' school. Wiechert's public protests against Nazism led to his imprisonment in the concentration camp of Buchenwald in 1938.

H. R. Klieneberger

ANTON WILDGANS

Born 1881 in Vienna. Died 1932 in Mödling, nr. Vienna. Director of Wiener Burgtheater for several years.

Poetry
1909: *Herbstfrühling*
1911: *Und hättet der Liebe nicht*

Drama
1914: *Armut*
1916: *Liebe*
1918: *Dies irae*

Epic
1927: *Kirbisch und der Gendarm, die Schande und das Glück*

1948 ff.: *Kritische Gesamtausgabe*, ed. O. Rommel; see also DLL

JOSEF WINCKLER

Born 1881 in Rheine, Westphalia. Co-founder of the literary circle 'Werkleute auf Haus Nyland', which furthered the art and industry of the working man; see also Engelke, p. 243. He was famous for his novel *Der tolle Bomberg* (1924) about a mad and overweening Westphalian aristocrat Baron von Bomberg.

His *Eiserne Sonette* appeared first in *Quadriga*, Journal of the Haus Nyland, and then, in 1914, in book-form.

1957: *Ges. Gedichte*

EUGEN GOTTLOB WINKLER

Born 1912 in Zürich. Died 1936, suicide in Munich. His artistic models are particularly Verlaine and Rilke.

1956: *Dichtungen, Gestalten und Probleme Nachlaß*, collected works, ed. by W. Warnach, H. Rinn, J. Heitzmann

GABRIELE WOHMANN (née Guyot)

Born 1932 in Darmstadt. Author of novels, stories, radio-plays, essays and criticism.

Novels
1958: *Jetzt und nie*
1965: *Abschied für länger*

Stories
1958: *Mit einem Messer*
1960: *Sieg über die Dämmerung*

Radio-plays
1965: *Die Gäste*
1966: *Große Liebe*

FRIEDRICH WOLF

Born 1888 in Neuwied (Rhein). Died 1953 in Lehnitz, nr. Berlin.
He joined the Communist Party before 1933, emigrated, and re-
turned in 1945 to (East) Germany. F. Wolf is considered (after
Brecht) the most representative playwright in East Germany.

1929: *Cyankali*, a play about the Abtreibungsparagraph (abortion
       paragraph)
1933: *Professor Mamlock*, a drama about the persecution of the
       Jews
1950: *Bürgermeister Anna* (Bauernkomödie)

1960 ff.: *Ges. Werke*, 16 vols., ed. by Else and W. Pollatschek

ALFRED WOLFENSTEIN

Born 1883 in Halle, Saale. Died in 1945, suicide in Paris. Trs.
from Nerval, Rimbaud, Verlaine.

Poetry
1914: *Die gottlosen Jahre*
1917: *Die Freundschaft*
1919: *Menschlicher Kämpfer*

Drama
1923: *Mörder und Träumer*
1929: *Die Nacht vor dem Beil*

Stories
1918: *Der Lebendige*
1937: *Die gefährlichen Engel*

KARL WOLFSKEHL

Born 1869 in Darmstadt. Died 1948 in Auckland, New Zealand. Long friendship with Stefan George, but Wolfskehl's style is in great contrast to George's disciplined form.

Poetry
1903: *Ges. Dichtungen*
1927: *Der Umkreis*
1950: *Hiob oder die vier Spiegel*
      Sang aus dem Exil

1960: *Ges. Werke*, ed. by Margot Ruben and Claus Victor Bock, 2 vols.
1966: *Karl Wolfskehl. Briefe und Aufsätze, 1925–1933*

Wolfskehl, like Mombert (see bibliography, p. 333), was tragically bound up with Germany's cultural heritage. As a refugee he still tried to uphold his belief in a nobility of the mind and the affinity between the Jewish and German tradition in the country of his birth. He writes: 'I have lost my homeland in which I . . . have been settled since Charlemagne. . . . I have the Rhine in my bones, like the Mediterranean from which I originated and with which I have formed new ties, completing the cycle.'

KONRAD WÜNSCHE

Born 1928 in Zwickau.

Drama
1964: *Vor der Klagemauer*
      Der Unbelehrbare und andere Stücke; see *Theater Heute*, Feb. 1964
1966: *Jerusalem Jerusalem*, a play about the first crusade

Poetry
1963: *Lyrik. Schemen entsprechend*

PAUL ZECH (Ps. Timm Borah or Paul Robert: for reviews of his own works!)

Born 1881 in Briesen, nr. Thorn, West Prussia. Died 1946 in Buenos Aires, Argentine.

Poetry
1913: *Schwarz sind die Wasser der Ruhr*
1914: *Die eiserne Brücke*
1929: *Rotes Herz der Erde*. Selection of ballads and songs
1948: *Sonette aus dem Exil*

Stories
1946: *Die schwarze Orchidee*
1956: *Die grüne Flöte von Rio Beni*
Menschheits Dämmerung, l.c., contains a short bibliography and
    P. Zech's *Selbstbildnis*

WERNER ZEMP

Born 1906 in Zurich. Died 1959 in Mendrisio. Spätklassiker, admirer of Mörike and Stifter, etc.

Poetry
1943: *Gedichte* (1954: sec. ed. enlarged)
1956: *Das Hochtal*
1967: *Das lyrische Werk. Aufsätze. Briefe*; ed. by Verena Haefeli

1967: Verena Haefeli: *Werner Zemp. Das Problem einer deutschen 'poésie pure'*; see G 1968, II, 444 and 478

ALBIN ZOLLINGER

Born 1895 in the Zürcher Oberland. Died 1941 in Zürich.

Poetry
1933: *Gedichte*
1936: *Sternfrühe*
1939: *Stille des Herbstes*
    Haus des Lebens

Novels

1939: *Die große Unruhe*
1940: *Pfannenstiel* (Geschichte eines Bildhauers)
1942: *Bohnenblust oder die Erzieher* (Second part of *Pfannenstiel*)

1961 ff.: *Ges. Werke*, 4 vols.

CARL ZUCKMAYER

Born 1896 in Nackenheim, Rheinhessen. He went into exile in 1938: to England, Switzerland, and finally the U.S.A. Now living in Switzerland; see p. 87.

Drama

1925: *Der fröhliche Weinberg*, a rustic comedy
1927: *Schinderhannes*
1928: *Katharina Knie*
1929: *Kakadu-Kakada* (Ein Kinderstück)
1931: *Der Hauptmann von Köpenick* (Ein deutsches Märchen)
1934: *Der Schelm von Bergen*
1946: *Des Teufels General*
1948: *Barbara Blomberg*
1950: *Gesang im Feuerofen*
1955: *Das kalte Licht*

1929: Film-text: *Der blaue Engel*, with Emil Jannings and Marlene Dietrich as actors; based on Heinrich Mann's novel *Professor Unrat*

Novels

1936: *Salwàre oder die Magdalena von Bozen*
1937: *Ein Sommer in Österreich*

Essays

1959: Centenary essays about Schiller and Gerhart Hauptmann: *Ein Weg zu Schiller*
1962: *Ein voller Erdentag*

Poetry

1948: *Gedichte 1916–1948*

Autobiography
1966: *Als wär's ein Stück von mir*

1960: *Ges. Werke*, 4 vols.

Studies
1960: I. Engelsing-Malek: *Amor Fati in Zuckmayers Dramen*
P. Meinherz: *Carl Zuckmayer. Sein Weg zu einem modernen Schauspiel*
1960: A. R. Robinson: *Der Seelenbräu*
1961: H. F. Garten: *Der Hauptmann von Köpenick*
1962: C. B. Johnson: *Des Teufels General*
1963: D. Barlow: *Carl Zuckmayer. Three Stories*
1964: Sheila Rooke: *Carl Zuckmayer* in 'German Men of Letters', l.c., vol. II
See also W. E. Yuill: *German Narrative Prose*, 2nd ed. 1966, pp. 146/7.

ARNOLD ZWEIG

Born 1887 in Groß-Glogau, Silesia. Novelist, essayist and dramatist. Emigrated to Palestine in 1933 and returned to Berlin in 1948. Former President of the East German Academy of Arts and one of the most celebrated of DDR writers. Influenced early by impressionism but turned to socialist and pacifist ideals. Planned a series of novels covering the German scene between the Wars. His work tends to be on a large scale: dramatic and detailed, yet controlled and straightforward.

Novels
1927: *Der Streit um den Sergeanten Grischa* (his best-known work)
1931: *Junge Frau von 1914*
1932: *De Vriendt kehrt heim*
1935: *Erziehung vor Verdun*
1937: *Einsetzung eines Königs*
1938: *Versunkene Tage* (*Verklungene Tage*, 1950)
1947: *Das Beil von Wandsbeck*
1954: *Die Feuerpause*
1957: *Die Zeit ist reif*
1963: *Traum ist teuer*

Short stories
1912: *Die Novellen um Claudia*
1919: *Benarône*
1923: *Söhne. Zweites Geschichtenbuch*
1925: *Frühe Fährten*
1928: *Pont und Anna*

Plays
1914: *Ritualmord in Ungarn* (*Die Sendung Semaels*, 1918)
1921: *Das Spiel vom Sergeanten Grischa*
1939: *Bonaparte in Jaffa*

Essays
1925: *Lessing, Kleist, Büchner*
1927: *Caliban oder Politik und Leidenschaft*
1933: *Bilanz der deutschen Judenheit* (expanded 1960 and 1964)
1961: *Baruch Spinoza*

1952: *Der Elfenbeinfächer* (selected short stories)
1955: *Der Regenbogen* (selected short stories)
1956: *Soldatenspiele* (plays)
1957: *Früchtekorb. Jüngste Ernte* (essays)
1957 ff.: *Ausgewählte Werke*
1959: *Essays. Erster Band*
1961: *Novellen 1907–1955*, 2 vols.

Some of his work has been trs. into English

Ian Hilton

STEFAN ZWEIG

Born 1881 in Vienna. Died 1942 in Persepolis (Rio de Janeiro). Much-travelled and successful as biographer and writer of short stories, in which he penetrated into human character, as befitted an admirer of Freud. Also translator, lyric poet and dramatist. Humanist and pacifist beliefs are reflected in his work.

Poetry
1901: *Silberne Saiten*
1906: *Die frühen Kränze*

Plays
1907: *Tersites*
1917: *Jeremias*
1926: *Volpone* (adaptation of Ben Johnson's *Volpone*)

Novel
1938: *Ungeduld des Herzens*

Short stories
1911: *Erstes Erlebnis*
1920: *Angst*
1923: *Amok*
1927: *Verwirrung der Gefühle*
1929: *Kleine Chronik*
1937: *Der begrabene Leuchter*
1941: *Schachnovelle*
1948: *Legenden*

Biographies, essays and other writings
1905: *Verlaine*
1910: *Verhaeren*
1919: *Fahrten*
1920: *Romain Rolland*
       Drei Meister (Balzac, Dickens, Dostoyevsky)
1921: *Marceline Desbordes-Valmore*
1924: *Frans Masareel*
1925: *Der Kampf mit dem Dämon* (Hölderlin, Kleist, Nietzsche)
1927: *Sternstunden der Menschheit* (expanded 1936 and 1943)
1928: *Drei Dichter ihres Lebens* (Casanova, Stendhal, Tolstoy)
       (which together with *Drei Meister* and *Der Kampf mit
       dem Dämon* form *Baumeister der Welt*, 1935)
1929: *Joseph Fouché*
1932: *Marie Antoinette*
       Die Heilung durch den Geist (Mesmer, Baker-Eddy, Freud)
1935: *Maria Stuart*
       Triumph und Tragik des Erasmus von Rotterdam
1936: *Castellio gegen Calvin*
1937: *Begegnungen mit Menschen, Büchern, Städten*
1938: *Magellan*
1941: *Brasilien*

1942: *Amerigo*
　　　Die Welt von gestern (a poignant autobiography)
1948: *Balzac*

1924: *Ges. Gedichte*
1937: *Gesamtausgabe des erzählerischen Werkes*, 2 vols.
1943: *Zeit und Welt* (Ges. Aufsätze und Vorträge, 1904–40)
1960: *Ausgewählte Werke*, 2 vols.
1964: *Die Dramen*

Bibliography
1946: Friederike Maria Zweig: *Stefan Zweig*, English ed.

Ian Hilton

APPENDIX

GERMAN MUSIC

To help the reader seeking accessible editions of music written before 1800 as much use as appropriate has been made of two sources:

(1) HAM = Davison and Apel, *Historical Anthology of Music* in 2 volumes, Vol. II beginning at No. 182 (Oxford University Press)
(2) CW = Das Chorwerk. Small volumes of music under the general editorship of F. Blume (Möseler Edition Novello)

Gramophone catalogues change too frequently for a printed discography to be very useful, but valuable and relevant discs can be found in the History of Music in Sound (O.U.P. & H.M.V. & H.M.S.) and in the Archive series of the Deutsche Grammophon Gesellschaft.

The excisions necessary to reduce the glorious history of German music to one chapter will strike the reader (as they do the writer) not as surgery but as butchery. In choosing where to begin one finds only sporadic materials for the task—music whose haphazard survival can hardly give a balanced picture—and the attempt to discover what may be specifically 'German' about this music is a ticklish, if not foolhardy, task. But one is supported by the musical folk-consciousness of the Germans themselves in choosing as starting point the Easter Sequence *Victimae Paschali laudes* (HAM 166) by Wipo (c. 1000–c. 1050) who was chaplain to Conrad II. This noble melody, bold in its range (an octave and a fourth) and in its frequent thirds and larger intervals, yet intricate in the workmanship of considered repetitions of short figures, remained a German heritage for five centuries, its most telling phrases reappearing in print in 1513 as the tune 'Christ ist erstanden'—one of Luther's favourites and the subject of one of the few extended preludes in Bach's *Orgelbüchlein*.

It is this boldness and craftsmanship, together with a directness of utterance and of rhythm which stem from the German language, as opposed to the greater suppleness of French and the invitation to elongation which Latin vowels extend, which we shall meet constantly as a German trait. But above all this is the capacity to absorb foreign styles and forms and to transform them by the infusion of a uniquely energetic expressive power. One must wait until the second half of the eighteenth century before claiming with certainty a German hegemony in initiating as well as carrying out new musical designs. But before this the German composers are not chameleons or fashion-mongers. They bide their time, like Walt Whitman's boy in *Sea Drift*, 'absorbing, translating' and then when native fire has remoulded the materials they create late but virtually new works from the melting-pot.

In the middle ages the main centre of musical creativity was France. In the early fifteenth century it was the Burgundian court, though not without the strong and acknowledged sweetening influence of the Englishman John Dunstable, the prevalence of whose music on the continent of Europe was arguably the only important and lasting consequence of the battle of Agincourt. As the fifteenth century proceeded the leadership passed to a line of Netherlands composers (meaning not just the present Netherlands but all the 'low countries') whose culminating figure was Josquin des Prés (c. 1450–1521). But so great was the ascendancy of the Netherlands composers that they continued both as style-setters and as musical directors in the most influential centres in Europe till almost the end of the sixteenth century. Even then German musicians achieved no dominant position, for it was the sudden outburst of Italian composers of genius at the century's end which ensured the predominance of Italian styles—with occasional forays from the reinvigorated French—for the whole of the seventeenth century at least.

In the long period from the twelfth century to the late fifteenth century little German music survives. The professional, and predominantly aristocratic, singers of romantic love, the Minnesänger, were the German counterparts to the French Troubadours, and particularly flourished from c. 1150 to c. 1300. One of the most famous was Heinrich of Meissen (d. 1318). The nickname by which he was invariably known, 'Frauenlob', is a statement in one word of the basic sentiment of the Minnesänger. Another memorable name is Walther von der Vogelweide (d. 1230?). His tune printed as HAM 20b—'Nu al'erst lebe ich'—is interesting both as another echo of 'Victimae paschali' and as an example of the predominant shape of Minnesänger song, the 'bar' form, consisting of a repeated opening phrase (Stollen) and an afterpiece (Abgesang) which, as in this case, often includes some reprise of Stollen-material. An earlier song, 'Swa eyn vriund' by Spervogel (HAM 20a), emphatically repeats the phrase ccGGEGFE which works its way through the German consciousness and reappears in a hymn-book of 1539 as the second phrase of the famous Christmas tune 'Vom Himmel hoch' which is sometimes attributed to Luther himself. Note the unambiguous tonal shape of the phrase—C major, twelfth century or not—achieved by the no-nonsense jumps of a fourth from C to G and a third from G to E, and also the sturdiness of the accentuation following that of the words.

A Tyrolean, Oswald von Wolkenstein (1377–1445), is the first song-writer of whom a considerable corpus survives. His songs, whether in single line or in counterpoint, have an appealing vivacity of expression both in their texts, which range over most human emotions, and in their music, with its 'popular' rhythms and frequent unambiguous cadences. The whole collection, coupled with the lively stance of the one-eyed portraits on the title-pages, gives the strongest impression of *joie de vivre*. The successors of the Minnesänger were the Meistersinger and their heyday was the fifteenth and sixteenth centuries. They were middleclass craftsmen with an elaborate grading from apprenticeship to master. Hans Sachs (1494–1576) was the most famous of them, and the bar-form was the usual shape of their tunes. By far the most agreeable exposition of their principles and practice is that supplied (including a near-bar-form Preislied) by Wagner in his opera *Die Meistersinger von Nürnberg*.

In the fifteenth century there is one field in which Germany can claim an exclusive corner, that of organ music, the herald of centuries of supremacy. The Tablature of Adam Ileborgh of Stendal (1448) and the Buxheim Organ Book of c. 1470 contain preludes (Praeambula) which though rudimentary establish an instrumental style which has nothing to do with contemporary vocal models and which indeed is uniquely characteristic of the organ, even occasionally specifying pedals (HAM 84). It is a sobering thought that organ pedals hardly existed in England three centuries later. Two famous figures were the blind Munich court-organist Conrad Paumann (1410–1473), who wrote notable elaborations on song-tunes (HAM 81), and Arnolt Schlick (before 1460–after 1521), also blind, whose most famous piece is the appropriately euphonious 'Maria zart' (HAM 101).

One can gain an impression of the richness of German musical life towards the end of the fifteenth century from the *Glogauer Liederbuch* (c. 1480). When one considers the chance preservation of a manuscript of 294 items, including a large Latin repertoire, some German songs both sacred and secular, and a large pot-pourri of instrumental pieces, all for the use of a comparatively remote and modest town in Silesia, one suddenly realizes that the comparative lack of other historical sources can be seriously mis-leading. Notable among the German items is a three-part setting of 'Christ ist erstanden' whose close imitations make the wide-ranging Alleluias into a veritable peal of eager bells. Following the trend of the beginning of the century the pieces are mainly in three parts, but there is a beautiful love-song à 4, 'Ich bin erfreut', whose final cadence has an expansive flowering which we shall meet again. Amongst the instrumental pieces 'Die Katzenpfote' stands out with its very lively fast syncopations.

As we enter the sixteenth century we are suddenly confronted with German masters sprung fully armed from nowhere, so to speak, who have mastered the current international language of imitative counterpoint in four or more parts. Heinrich Finck (1444/5-1527) was the director of music of the court of Duke Ulrich at Württemberg 1510-13. His 'Missa in Summis' (CW 21) though sometimes stiff melodically shows an early grasp of the imitative technique of which Josquin des Prés was the universal master. Obviously Duke Ulrich's establishment had the resources to perform in six parts (seven in the Credo). A remarkable hymn-setting is a pentecostal one (CW 32) in which three intricate instrumental parts surround a dexterous combination for voices of the two plainsong tunes 'Veni sancte spiritus' and 'Veni creator spiritus'. Some of his later hymns, posthumously included in the hymn-book (1542) of Luther's friend Rhau (CW 9), show an imitation in advance (Vorimitation) of each successive line of the tune, prefiguring a favourite technique in keyboard preludes on chorales (*vide infra*).

Thomas Stoltzer (dates uncertain) shows an interesting transi-tion from the somewhat out-of-date style of his Easter Mass (c. 1520) (CW 74) in which the four voices tend to jostle each other in the style of the previous century, to the magnificent writing of his one firmly dated work (1526), the 37th Psalm, set to Luther's recent translation: 'Erzürne dich nicht' (CW 6). This is an outstanding example of technique which has achieved complete freedom from the time-honoured props of plainsong whether plain or ornamented. Each phrase springs solely from the accentuation and expression of the words, without prefabrication, and the six voices (seven in the last part) are used with a wonderful sense of 'choral orchestration' with duets and trios, now high, now low, alternating with clear counterpoint and monumental chord-effects.

Although a Netherlander by birth, Heinrich Isaac (c. 1450–1517) has a place here for his considerable output of German song, and for his influence on German musicians, especially his pupil Senfl (*vide infra*), during his period as a court musician of Maximilian I, chiefly at Innsbruck. The tune 'Innsbruck, ich muß dich lassen', later taken into sacred use for the hymn 'O Welt, ich muss dich lassen' (the subject of two organ chorale-preludes by Brahms), was set twice by Isaac, once for four voices in a chordal style which prefigures the Lutheran Chorale, but with a beautiful elaboration (a flowering, as it were) of the final cadence; the other setting is originally instrumental but with counterpoint overflowing the cadences, and with a canon in the two inside voices. It is this version which appears as the second 'Christe eleison' in his famous 'Missa Carminum' in which different songs are used as a basis of each movement (CW 7). Isaac's most impressive achievement is the great body of liturgical music called the *Choralis Constantinus*—choral music of Konstanz, which included a complete setting of the Proper of the Mass for the whole church year. A late motet, 'Regina caeli laetare' (CW 100) is a model of the unity amid variety caused by subtle cross-references of snatches of themes and rhythms, even from widely separated parts of the piece; this technique is particularly notable in the 'alleluias' which suffuse it.

Ludwig Senfl (c. 1486–1542/3), Swiss-born, succeeded his teacher Isaac as Maximilian I's chief musician, and at the death of Maximilian moved to the court of William IV of Bavaria at Munich. The range of his art was almost as wide as that of his cosmopolitan teacher's, and critics have seen in his work as a whole a more consistent smoothness of expression. Certainly in his Marian-motet 'Ave rosa sine spinis' (CW 62) the four outer voices weave round the middle one (which carries in slow notes a melody 'Comme femme' used by the great Josquin) an euphonious and exquisitely balanced web of sound which hints at Palestrina, though the repeated emphatic rhythms of the closing pages are foreign to the latter's style. Many of Senfl's German secular songs achieved publication in his lifetime. The song was usually given to a tenor voice and its accompaniment to two instrumental parts above and one below. These are far from being unco-ordinated props. With true German workmanship they are made into relevant and interesting companions and the whole into a satisfying contrapuntal experience. Senfl carried this penchant for melodic combination further in 'Doppel-lieder', in which he would combine with a contrapuntal accompaniment two different songs. He was a friend of Luther and in 1530, when Luther was facing the anguish of being an outlaw, consoled him by dedicating and sending to him a motet which is a fine example of his expressive style: 'Non moriar sed vivam.' Luther responded with the gift of a bookcase.

In view of the ferocities in other fields it is perhaps surprising that the Lutherans, for a generation at least, were quite un-political in their view of Catholic music. They regarded the music of Josquin as a joint heritage. It was patently the best musical style and therefore the motet (and the use of Latin) had an honoured place in their church music right down to Bach's day. In the well-found musical centres the movements of the Lutheran mass (Kyrie and Credo—of which Bach's in B minor is a piecemeal extension) were not in German. This recognition of the power of music and the insistence on harnessing it to God's service stemmed from Luther himself and from his musical lieu-tenant Johann Walther (1496–1570). But from these two spring the characteristic new feature of the Protestant service which was to have an immeasurable influence for two centuries, the verna-cular congregational hymn called the chorale. The tunes when not newly composed were adapted from sources ranging from plainsong to the highly secular. The tune which permeates Bach's 'St Matthew' Passion—'O Haupt voll Blut und Wunden'—is per-haps the most striking of the latter transformations.

Towards the end of the century the Netherlands influence began to be replaced by that of Venice where an illustrious suc-cession of musicians at St Mark's had evolved a technique of antiphonal choirs, usually two of four voices each, but on grand occasions employing even more choirs, both vocal and instrumental. Hans Leo Hassler (1564–1612) would in any case figure here as the outstanding German master of the period in mass, motet and secular song (especially his collection, the fountainhead of many such in the seventeenth century, called *Lustgarten neuer teutsher Gesäng*). His short visit to the Gabrielis at Venice brought forth not only Italian madrigals but a rich succession of polychoral pieces in up to twelve parts. The intoxication of the new splendours quickly spread through Germany. Michael Praetorius (1571–1621) copiously supplied the Lutherans with spiritual concertos for voices and instruments, of which that on the chorale 'Wie schön leuchtet der Morgenstern' is a fine and accessible example (Eulenberg miniature score and H.M.S.). Praetorius wrote detailed suggestions for the distribution of the supporting or substituting instruments in Part III of his *Syntagma Musicum*, a work of encyclopaedic detail on all matters musical which pioneered the steadfast musical scholarship with which German musicologists have enriched the world ever since.

But a more important Italian export in the early seventeenth century was the conception of the expressive and declamatory solo line with a subsidiary, but often expressive, harmony replacing the more 'communal' contrapuntal texture. The basic reason, clearly observable in Monteverdi's madrigals, was the incessant urge of humanism towards an emotional self-expression which was more direct and personal. The conflicts and resolutions (even if minor ones) which are the essence of counterpoint, were seen as distractions. The impatient young men bursting with something to say wanted to sweep away an apparatus which was all the more resented because it had reached its peak as a language. Ironically the so-called Baroque style which they initiated, expressive melody against harmony, coupled with an idiomatic use of instrumental colour, was itself criticized and adjured in the mid-eighteenth century, for the same reasons, by the young men who thought of Bach, if at all, as a contrapuntal fogey.

By far the greatest German composer of the seventeenth century was Heinrich Schütz, often Latinized as 'Sagittarius' (1585–1672). He was a pupil in Venice of Giovanni Gabrieli from 1609 to 1612, and overwhelming though the experience was he had the native force of genius to weld the new style to the craftsmanship of the old. Even the volume of Italian madrigals, published whilst he was still in Venice, shows him speaking a language, not a dialect. His many subsequent masterpieces have as their main trait a passionate and precise gift of instant characterization, whether of an emotion or a scene. This was the most prized quality in Baroque music—the 'Affekt' being one of the most-used nouns in musical writings of the entire period. Schütz's characterization could use the whole repertoire of realism—runs, chromatics, breath-catching sobs—with a sophisticated sense of balance which saved it from naivety. It extended to instrumentation as well. Like his teacher, Schütz can be reckoned one of the earliest orchestrators in that he wrote independent instrumental parts and often specified with precision which instruments were to play them. Anyone who has heard the four trombones in the bass solo 'Fili mi, Absalon' or the trumpets for Herod and the recorders for the shepherds in the Christmas Oratorio will not forget their instantaneous effect. Rhythm and harmony play their semi-realistic parts on occasion, as when Schütz himself calls attention to a rocking figure in the bass with 'the cradle of the Infant Jesus is now and then introduced'. Superbly equipped for opera-writing as Schütz must have been, it is sad that nothing survives of the music for five stage works he is known to have written. The most tantalizing loss is the opera *Dafne*, written in 1627 and thus the first German opera. The libretto is a translation of that by Rinuccini set by Peri in 1597 when opera was born in Italy. Other narrative pieces by Schütz were the *Resurrection Story* and the *Seven last words from the Cross*, of which the last three 'words' could be an epitome of this aspect of Schütz's art: the one striking chromaticism of 'I thirst', the breathless but triumphant cry of 'It is finished' and the inevitable but poised descent of 'Father, into Thy hands'. All these works have independent accompaniment. A less ostensibly dramatic but deeply satisfying infusion of new feeling into older choral techniques is found in the set of motets called *Geistliche Chormusik*, in whose preface Schütz tartly urges young composers to 'crack the hard nut of counter-point', and the final archaisms in a long lifetime often harrowed by war were the three settings of the Passion story which eschew both orchestral accompaniment and interpolated arias and revert to a quasi-plainsong recitation of the narrative, with choruses whose terseness increases their expressive power.

Johann Hermann Schein (1586–1630) avowedly followed the new style in his collection of motets called *Israels Brünlein*, which he described as being in 'a specially attractive Italian-Madrigal style'. The selection of five in CW 12 show his lively spirit, and even more spectacular is 'Die mit Tränen säen' in CW 14.

Organ composition developed with astonishing speed, notable figures being Samuel Scheidt (1587–1654), whose collection of variations and liturgical pieces called *Tablatura Nova* (1624) so delighted Brahms when it was published as the first of the famous series of *Denkmäler deutscher Tonkunst*; Johann Jakob Froberger (1616–1667), whose ricercars and fantasias are interesting for their frequent use of a single subject in various forms, and who is also the first German master of the harpsichord suite; Johann Pachelbel (1653–1706), whose preludes and variations on chorales are perhaps the most consistently enjoyable of all; and Georg Muffat (c. 1645–1704), whose organ toccatas are outstanding for their lively and idiomatic invention, and whose orchestral dance music with detailed direction for its performance 'in Lully's manner' make him the protagonist in German of the French style which Bach was to emulate.

Organ music and concerted vocal/instrumental music on a high plane were what drew the young Bach to Lübeck in 1705 to hear Dietrich Buxtehude (1637–1707). The best of his organ music shows unmistakable traits contributing to Bach's style—rhetorical fantasy, pedal solos, massive suspensions exploiting a wind-supply beyond the reach of human lungs. With Buxtehude a solid fugue is always likely to dash off into a striking whimsicality, and one feels that this quasi-extempore aspect brings one near to a Portuguese etymology claimed for the word 'Baroque': a mis-shapen pearl (HAM 234). Of the concerted works on a large scale one of the finest is 'Gott hilf mir' (part of Psalm 49) in which the realistic flounderings of the soloist are halted by the rock-like assurance of the choir. The work includes a typical Lutheran movement, a chorus over which the tune of a chorale sets its evocative and clinching seal, the noblest example of which is the first chorus of Bach's '*St Matthew*' *Passion*. Of the many cantatas for two voices one of the most moving is 'Ich suchte des Nachts' where the soul seeking the Heavenly Lover encounters the watchmen in the night and the violins suddenly give way to two unison oboes who softly and slowly play a patrolling-call, a wonderful evocation of one of the duties of municipal windplayers. Though rarely making, by Italian standards, severe technical

demands, the chamber music of Buxtehude is of solid workmanship with a great and unpredictable variety of movements in each
work.

The violin in Italy first imitated, then transcended the expressive vocal technique of the Baroque style, but as usual in Germany
the gestation period is long, and then suddenly as with Bach's
chamber music, an effortless mastery appears almost without ancestors. But passing mention should be made of Heinrich Franz
Biber (1644–1704), whose violin sonatas call for a high degree of
virtuosity and whose Passacaglia for unaccompanied violin must
have inspired the violin chaconne of Bach.

J. S. Bach (1685–1750) is the supreme example of the German
capacity to absorb heterogeneous materials and transmute them
into a new creation, 'new' not in the fashionable sense (Bach can
hardly ever have been fashionable) but renovated by a hitherto
inconceivable combination of expressive and intellectual power.
Circumstances, and perhaps personal preference, meant that he
never essayed an opera, though the sense of dramatic timing and
characterization displayed in the 'St Matthew' Passion makes one
sanguine of his chances, but in all the other genres of music of his
day he achieved an indisputable pre-eminence. The three main
centres of his activity were Weimar (1708–1717), Cöthen (1717–
1723) and Leipzig (1723–1750). At Weimar, where inter alia he
was court organist (his last official organistship, incidentally), he
wrote most of the organ works and a large number of church cantatas. Most of the chamber music and non-church keyboard
music, for example the suites, book I of the '48' and the concertos,
date from Cöthen, whose court being Calvinist had no church
music of any elaboration, as Bach well knew when he insisted on
going there. He was indeed in detention for some time at Weimar
for 'too stubbornly demanding his dismissal'. Recent chronological research, by transferring much 'Leipzig' church music to
the Weimar period, has somewhat altered the picture of Bach as
a dedicated church musician. He made his presence felt at Leipzig
almost immediately with the first performance of the 'St John'
Passion, the dramatic power of whose crowd choruses together
with the spectacular treatment of such things as Peter's weeping
(specially imported from St Matthew's narrative) must have
made the stolid Leipzigers sit up. The 'St Matthew' Passion also
belongs to Leipzig as do such parts of the B minor Mass which are

not reworkings of earlier material. So do the final stupendous demonstrations not only of fugal ingenuity but of rhetorical power, the *Musical Offering* and the *Art of Fugue*. But the general impression of Leipzig is of an initial sublime outburst, followed by increasing disillusion as the old warm sense of the Church's musical mission was chilled by the cool intellectual breezes from France. To a disciple of Voltaire or Rousseau, St Thomas's, Leipzig must have seemed an archaic irrelevance.

In musical terms the cry 'Back to Nature' meant not only a drastic simplification of texture so that melodies could be untrammelled in echoing every nuance of 'Empfindsamkeit', but also a curbing of the former pretensions of music so that it could become, in the words of even so eminent an enthusiast as Dr Burney, 'an innocent luxury'. This new 'galant' style coincided with the rise of the orchestra from the bondage of accompaniment to a self-sufficient, and indeed overwhelmingly popular, artistic medium, playing symphonies. The two main orchestral schools were Vienna, where the works of Georg Wagenseil (1715–1777) and Georg Monn (1717–1750) (see HAM 295) nurtured the young Haydn, and the famous 'army of generals' at Karl Theodore's court at Mannheim, led by Johann Stamitz (1717–1757) (see HAM 294) and Franz Xaver Richter (1709–1789), an orchestra whose electrifying attack and highly disciplined dynamics made an indelible impression on Mozart.

A bridge between old and new was J. S. Bach's second son, Karl Philipp Emanuel (1714–1788), who retained the family's integrity of workmanship, and by his success in inventing melodies capable of expressing quicksilver changes of emotion, as well as forms to give them coherence, earned the grateful respect of Haydn and Mozart. Indeed some of his keyboard work and some later symphonies prefigure Beethoven. The music of Bach's youngest son Johann Christian (1735–1782) shows the galant style in a charming and uncomplicated light (see piano sonata op. XVII, No. 4 in HAM 303). Mozart obviously never forgot his first encounters with J. C. Bach's music in London.

The opera composer Christoph Willibald Gluck (1714–1787) entered upon an unpromising scene. Opera in Germany had briefly flourished at the beginning of the century in two centres for both of which George Philipp Telemann (1681–1767) had written: Leipzig and Hamburg, where Handel had served an apprenticeship before disappearing from German history. But thereafter Italian opera was universal, a formalized insipid affair, quite barren of the frenzied emotions which brought it to birth around 1600. Writing operas in Vienna (in Italian of course) Gluck suddenly broke with the old stereotypes and for most of *Orfeo* (1762) and for all of *Alceste* (1767) and *Paride ed Elena* (1770) sustained a new relationship between music and drama, particularly shown in continuity of action and the avoidance of a barren alternation between action-bearing recitative and plateau-like arias in a comtemplative void. The 'reform' operas were not really successful, and he left to crown his work in France, but his work had direct repercussions on both Mozart and Wagner.

The work of Franz Joseph Haydn (1732–1809) contains in one long lifetime the transition from a variety of uncertain styles to the fully fledged classical style, at least in instrumental music. He brought the symphony from the world of opera overture and street serenade to be the supreme vehicle of orchestral eloquence, drama, pathos and wit which we find in the final twelve 'London' symphonies. He to all intents and purposes invented the classical string quartet, though here the process was quicker, because well before the half-way mark in their prolific catalogue—in op. 33 if not indeed in op. 20—we are enumerating different masterpieces rather than tracing a gradual development, let alone an 'improvement'. Nevertheless the last complete quartet, op. 77, No. 2, and especially its andante, has some claim to be Haydn's most sublime work. In the fields of opera and concerto Haydn was less at home, but his two late choral works, *The Creation* and *The Seasons*, are nature-poems which have a felicitous simplicity which is out of reach of the unsophisticated. The 'Representation of Chaos' which opens the Creation, is an orchestral piece containing passages of *Tristanesque* audacity.

Haydn was the son of a wheelwright. His country origins inflect his melodic idiom and he made his lonely way to mastery and originality chiefly at the Versailles-like palace of Esterhazy. Wolfgang Amadeus Mozart (1756–1791) was the son of a professional musician, Leopold (1719–1787), whose treatise on violin playing had won him some European esteem. By the time he was a young man Mozart had already appeared as a prodigy in the courts of Europe and with his phenomenal gifts had devoured the experiences which London, Mannheim, Paris and

Italy had to offer, and had taken what opportunities he could to show that he could play the local cognoscenti at their own game. It is not difficult to imagine the despair of a man with God-like gifts welling up in him, who had seen and tasted the heady wine of the resources of Europe, and who knew that all were seemingly out of reach in his home town, down-at-heel, Philistine Salzburg. If some of Haydn's melody is tinged with earthiness and rhythmic irregularity, Mozart's language is that of Italian opera, its frequent feminine cadences being a direct reflection of the preponderance of feminine cadences in the Italian language. Compare for instance the enchanting serenade in *Così fan tutte* ('Secondate, aurette amiche') with the strikingly similar andante from the serenade for wind octet K.388, or compare Cherubino's first song in *Figaro* with the identical rhythm of the first subject of Symphony No. 40 in G minor. The last is an example of the almost unbearable poignancy of an 'entertainment' idiom being suffused with 'Sturm und Drang' emotion—music weeping through its smiles. When every genre has its masterpieces an arbitrary list of personal favourites is as undesirable as it is difficult. The piano concertos, mostly written for his own concert use in Vienna, show a unique mastery of the formal problems of the medium. With virtually no precedents to guide him Mozart evolves enchanting patterns, different in detail each time, whereby a cornucopia of themes can be used in profusion and shared between the forces. Another great achievement is the build-up into long stretches of coherent, action-matching music of the operatic finales. Of the operas, *Idomeneo* (1781) and *La Clemenza di Tito* (1791) spring from the tradition of opera seria, whilst the more naturalistic opera buffa is represented by *Figaro* (1786), *Don Giovanni* (1787), which owes to Gluck's *Alceste* the example of a genuinely preparatory overture and the use of sepulchral trombones, and *Così fan tutte* (1790), perhaps the most perfect expression of the style. The German-language Singspiel—musical play with spoken dialogue —is represented by *Die Entführung* (1782) and *Die Zauberflöte* (1791). In this as in other late works, e.g. the finale of Symphony No. 41 and the Fantasia for clockwork organ, Köchel No. 608, Mozart shows a contrapuntal mastery fertilized by a personal rediscovery of Bach.

Mozart and Haydn both broke with patronage and took to free-lancing towards the end of their careers, Mozart in direst poverty, Haydn amidst universal acclaim. Ludvig van Beethoven (1770–1827) left Bonn for Vienna in 1792 and thereafter was no man's servant. The force of his genius overcame all obstacles, even the catastrophe of deafness to which he responded with the *Eroica* Symphony, of which the hero is not Napoleon but Beethoven himself, as he defies Fate by a majestic assertion of man's creative will in a work which in the scope of its emotions, the vehemence with which they are expressed, and in sheer length of its span exceeds all predecessors. At one intellectual leap the nineteenth century is upon us, and music, though no longer ostensibly God's handmaid, speaks to mankind at large with compulsive power. Beethoven makes this point when he takes his leave of the symphony in the last movement of No. 9 by setting with men's voices and the majesty of trombones Schiller's phrase 'Seid umschlungen, Millionen' ('ye millions, I embrace ye'). Beethoven introduced himself to Vienna as a virtuoso pianist, and his thirty-two piano sonatas and the five piano concertos bring to the repertoire an intensity of emotional expression and a quasi-orchestral fullness which was beyond the range both of the instruments and the manners of the eighteenth century. The virtuosity of technique required for the *Appassionata* op. 57 or the *Hammerklavier* op. 106 is an integral part of their effect. The decisive leap forward at the beginning of Beethoven's middle period, marked in the symphonies by No. 3, comes in the piano sonatas at op. 31. The opus numbers after 100 mark his 'third period', in which the music, though still capable of elemental outbursts, also reaches hitherto unexplored other-worldly heights of fantasy and intimacy coupled with a daring plasticity of form. It is here, after the sublimities of the 9th Symphony and the *Missa Solemnis*, that the string quartet comes to its peak as the vehicle of Beethoven's last thoughts.

It seems hardly possible that Beethoven and Franz Peter Schubert (1797–1828) should both have lived in Vienna for thirty years without meeting until Beethoven was on his death-bed. But such was the modesty of Schubert that he could not bring himself to confront such a colossus. With so little opportunity of hearing Schubert's purely instrumental music in his lifetime—none of his symphonies, for instance, had public performances—it is not surprising that the public of his day did not realize that even here Schubert held a candle—a quite unusual candle—to Beethoven. But from the start they recognized Schubert's mastery of the German art-song, for a partnership of voice and piano, called a Lied, of which Schubert for all practical purposes is both the creator and perfector. He was born at the historical moment which allowed his fluency and youthful ardour both in joy and sorrow to be applied without self-consciousness to the new lyrical nature-poetry which sprang up in all its simplicity and dewy freshness before the hotter breath of later Romanticism had spoilt or any rate altered it.

The once-and-for-all settings of Goethe's 'Gretchen am Spinnrade' (at the age of seventeen!) and 'Heidenröslein', and of Heine's 'Doppelgänger', possibly the most frightening song ever written, are in themselves enough to guarantee immortality. When one adds the hundreds, literally, of other songs, and the symphonies and chamber music, one can only be amazed that such creativity could be vouchsafed to one man. The intense lyrical feeling is also evident in the instrumental music, and results in a formal layout both of paragraphs and of keys which is different from Beethoven's (the question of inferiority does not arise). Schubert is a master of harmony, and his modulations, whether on a small or large scale, are a perennial delight. Hear for instance the middle of 'Der Hirt auf dem Felsen' for voice, clarinet and piano, or the last section of the andante of the 'Unfinished' Symphony. Schubert is not by any means exclusively lyrical; he can compare with Beethoven in grandeur (the last movement of Symphony No. 9 in C) and in succinct and enigmatic drama (the first movement of the C minor piano sonata).

The traits of the music of the Romantic period are so various that it is difficult to assign them a common attribute. Perhaps the dominant urge was to escape from the all-too-commonplace here and now. Hence the nostalgia for the distant past, the escape from things seen to things imagined (fairies, ghosts, devils), the escape from old forms of rhetoric to the cult of the exquisite miniature, but paradoxically the urge in some composers towards the very large gesture. Robert Schumann (1810–1856) was a composer of the new breed. He was born in a literary milieu, was as articulate in words as he was in music, and founded the *Neue Zeitschrift für Musik* in 1834, in order to enlarge his verbal assaults on the sluggish, second-hand attitudes of the Philistines. His most characteristic music was in the shorter forms of piano pieces and songs. It is difficult to overestimate the freshness of the piano writing in vivid character pieces amongst his early work. He had no real models. The short piano pieces of Beethoven, typically called *Bagatelles*, are indeed chips from the workshop compared with such pieces from the Fantasiestücke (typical name) as 'Des Abends', 'Warum?' and 'In der Nacht'. Schumann's aphoristic miniatures make their point, as do Heine's lyrics, by the studied punctuality of their symmetrical rhythmic schemes. This symmetry which is the essence of a piano piece like 'Träumerei', is a source of weakness in larger forms, in which his most successful essay is the piano concerto. Heine only swam into Schubert's ken in time to evoke a few masterly songs, but with Schumann he inspires a cycle of songs, *Dichterliebe*, which for compressed emotional power and striking utterance can stand with Schubert's best.

Felix Mendelssohn (1809–1847) had inborn gifts hardly inferior to Mozart's. At sixteen he had written his astonishing octet for strings with its fairy-like third movement, and at seventeen he made an incontestable claim on fairyland with his *Overture to the Midsummer Night's Dream*. In this, as in his other concert-overtures (a new genre) and in the symphonies he acquiesced in the externals of classical forms and filled them with beautiful orchestration and, especially in the *Italian* symphony, picturesque ideas brilliantly civilized. Posterity owes him a further debt for his public performance, a hundred years after the first, of Bach's '*St Matthew*' *Passion*, thereby stimulating the movement towards the great complete edition of the Bach Gesellschaft.

In the history of Romantic opera the first name is indisputably Carl Maria von Weber (1786–1826). In the ninth bar of the overture to *Der Freischütz* (1821) the horns evoke the German forest. From that epoch-making moment things Italian began to recede. Drinking songs, hunting songs, sweetness and light, darkness and devilry; naïve sentiments perhaps but all clothed in the brilliant orchestration which was Berlioz's envy—all these caught the German consciousness in a grip which has never relaxed and which smoothed the way for Wagner, who is indeed prefigured in Weber's *Euryanthe* (1823), an opera written in continuous well-integrated music, but hampered by an unwieldy libretto.

With Richard Wagner (1813–1883) Romantic opera reaches its culmination. The increasing tendency to interpenetrate musical ideas with literary and picturesque ones, the basis of 'programme music', was only at its lowest level an exercise in musical imitation; the underlying reason was the feeling that all arts should flow into one another, subservient not to each other but to a greater whole; in Wagner's case that total dramatic idea which he called a Gesamtkunstwerk. He complained in *Opera and Drama* (1851) that in opera 'a means of expression (music) had been made the object'—and the object of opera was drama in the total sense (shades of Gluck appear). If there was one man with the intellect, genius, and indomitable self-assurance to achieve the Gesamtkunstwerk it was Wagner. It is staggering to imagine the qualities of a man who could embark on libretto, scenario, and music of what was to become the mighty tetralogy of *The Ring* without in the least knowing if and where it would ever be performed, turning aside *en route* to toss off *Tristan and Isolde*. Thanks to Ludwig II of Bavaria he did succeed, and the specially built opera house at Bayreuth, opened in 1876, became as it were a Baptist temple in which the faithful were initiated into the Gesamtkunstwerk by total immersion. Wagner's champion in his years of struggle was the Hungarian virtuoso pianist and composer Ferenc Liszt (1811–1886), from whose symphonic poems, and *Faust* symphony in particular, he drew encouragement in his plastic use of themes. Wagner's Leitmotive—guiding themes—were not subjects in the classical sense of actors in a symphonic drama, but audible companions of the emotional situation. They could herald people, in a visiting-card sense, but their purpose was usually more subtle, to show what was in a character's mind or to impress on the audience the purport of some stage action. This symphonic flux of Leitmotive assisted Wagner's other ideal of 'Endless melody', whereby whole acts of the drama flowed incessantly without the traditional breaks (again Gluck writ large) and this in turn meant a constant modulation. The flux of chromatic harmony in *Tristan* is sometimes so deliberately ambiguous that theorists have seen in it the beginnings of 'modern' harmony (or non-harmony). Be that as it may, there are few symphonic satisfactions as great as the immense recapitulation, forming the 'Liebestod' at the end of *Tristan*, of some of the love-music of Act II, a perfect example of the congruence of symphony and drama.

In an opposite camp, though not of his own seeking, was

Johannes Brahms (1833–1897). It was as if the prevalent nostalgia of late Romanticism had produced a man born after his time. He brought back to luxurious life the classical instrumental forms, the warmth of his harmonies being tempered by the severe integrity of his workmanship. The new wine in old bottles is most potent in the two piano concertos and in the finale of the fourth symphony. His chamber music, admired by Schoenberg, rescued a genre which had markedly declined since Schubert, and the tenderly yearning slow movement of the clarinet quintet strikes many listeners as the quintessence of Romanticism.

Anton Bruckner (1824–1896) was the odd-man-out *par excellence*. He was a devout Catholic of child-like faith amongst composers who were articulate and sophisticated agnostics. The large-scale symphony, when at length he trusted himself to compose one, was a form which had given way to the symphonic poem, with none of Brahms' yet written. Bruckner's symphonies with their expansive lyricism sometimes redolent of Schubert but using far greater formal freedoms, have at last escaped the deadly charge of being unlike Brahms', and the seventh is particularly prized for the airy bucolics of its first movement and the magnificent adagio in which a quintet of tubas assist in homage to Wagner.

In contrast Gustav Mahler (1860–1911) was a great conductor who had at his baton's end the finest players in Vienna (which perhaps at that time meant the finest in Europe). He was also the master, as a composer, of the large orchestra which was his almost inevitable requirement, since he claimed for the symphony that 'it must embrace everything'. This view sometimes leads to whole processions of complexes of themes as in Symphony No. 3, or the assembling of the huge vocal and orchestral apparatus of Symphony No. 8. But the largest forces are often handled with filigree finesse. A *fin-de-siècle* nostalgia for irrevocable springtime and childhood is a recurring motif, as in *Lieder eines fahrenden Gesellen* and the end of the fourth symphony. So is the funeral march, perhaps a strong premonition of the death of pre-war Vienna. Certainly the sense of farewell is overpoweringly moving in the final adagio of the last completed symphony (No. 9) and explicit in the final song, 'Abschied', of the great song-cycle *Das Lied von der Erde*.

The history of the Lied concludes with the works of Hugo Wolf

(1860–1903), who in intervals of health produced outpourings of tremendous variety and vividness with an especial bent for the dramatic and sardonic, and of Richard Strauss (1864–1949), whose early songs such as 'Ständchen' and 'Morgen' are clearly already immortal. But young Strauss also burst upon the world with orchestral tone-poems of incomparable *élan*, notably *Don Juan* (1888), *Till Eulenspiegel* (1895) and *Don Quixote* (1897), in all of which the programmatic elements were held in the tightest formal control. In opera his *Salome* (1905) with a dissonant orchestra adds a still-powerful *frisson* to Oscar Wilde's play, and *Elektra* (1909) continued the same vein of realistic psychological exploration. In *Der Rosenkavalier* (1911) the delights of legato singing and the Viennese waltz reasserted themselves. It is a matter of unresolved debate whether with the possible exception of *Ariadne auf Naxos* the rest of Strauss' output has anything significant to add.

As ever, the end of a period of increasingly elaborate technique found its eager young men impatient with the apparatus and longing for more direct expression. To Arnold Schoenberg (1874–1951) the harmonic system of key-relationship seemed to have been worked to death, and at a time when his painter friend Kandinsky (from much the same artistic compulsion) discarded the representational element from his art, Schoenberg discarded the use of key. In this 'atonal' period the melodrama *Pierrot Lunaire* (1912) is the principal work. But he soon realized that composition on any extended scale required not negative but positive principles of construction. After long gestation he arrived at the method of composition, now usually known as serialism, whereby for the duration of a piece the twelve different chromatic notes were heard in a basic recurrent order (Grundgestalt) or by way of variety in 'crab', i.e. running $12 \rightarrow 1$ instead of $1 \rightarrow 12$, or in the inversions of these forms. His first composition to make thorough-going use of this method, in which indeed it is clearly audible, is the *Waltz for Piano*, op. 23, No. 5. Although Schoenberg's theories have exerted an enormous influence on twentieth century music his compositions as such have had tardy acknowledgment, but one may safely reckon the *Orchestral Variations* op. 31, the violin concerto op. 36 and the fourth string quartet op. 37 as secure in esteem.

Of more immediate appeal was the work of Alban Berg (1885–

1935), whose attitude to serialism was less rigorously anti-tonal, and in whose music a latent Romanticism was clearly audible. His violin concerto with its final quotation from a Bach Chorale has been long accepted as serialism-without-tears, whilst his first serial piece, *Lyric Suite for String Quartet* (1925), and his dramatic masterpiece, the opera *Wozzeck* (1920) based on Büchner's play, are universally admired.

Anton von Webern (1883–1945) in his atonal period had already produced some of the most ravishing and exciting instrumental sounds of this century in the five pieces op. 10 (1913). When he embraced serialism the sparse textures and tiny allocations to each instrument disconcerted listeners used to more pneumatic sounds, but it is this very clarity and the rigorous order of his terse works which has made them a bible to composers and a pleasure to sympathetic listeners, particularly the Concerto op. 24 and the Variations for piano op. 27.

A critical estimate of Paul Hindemith (1895–1963) is now uncertain. His neo-Baroque craftsmanship and his extraordinary capacity to write sympathetically for any instrument led him to the conception of Gebrauchsmusik (workaday music) whereby he attempted to bridge the gulf between 'producers and consumers of music' by offering acceptable but not heaven-storming pieces more or less on demand. Little of this music had lasting success, but it seems unlikely that such noble works as the opera *Mathis der Maler* (1938) and the symphony based on it will long remain unheard, and repertoire-starved organists are grateful for the three sonatas.

The expulsion of leading musicians by the Nazis and the banning of much seminal new music as 'decadent' dealt modern German music a blow from which it has only recently recovered. As this chapter is history, not prophecy, and is already too long, it must suffice to leave the reader with two names: Karlheinz Stockhausen (born 1928), a leading exponent of electronic music and an exciting post-Webernian experimenter in sound combinations in groups of players, e.g. *Gruppen*, Cologne, 1958; and Hans Werner Henze (born 1926), by comparison Romantic and eclectic, but one of the few living Germans to sustain with highly individual ideas a large output in genres including symphony and opera, notably *Boulevard Solitude* and *The Bassarids*.

INDEX

Apart from a few exceptions only the main authors are listed here.

429